BOOKS BY PATRICIA BOSWORTH

Anything Your Little Heart Desires
Diane Arbus: A Biography
Montgomery Clift: A Biography

My father, Bartley C. Crum, right after Truman appointed him to the Anglo-American Committee of Inquiry into Palestine, circa December 1945.

ANYTHING YOUR LITTLE HEART DESIRES

An American Family Story

PATRICIA BOSWORTH

SIMON & SCHUSTER

SIMON & SCHUSTER
Rockefeller Center
1230 Avenue of the Americas
New York, NY 10020

Copyright © 1997 by Patricia Bosworth
All rights reserved,
including the right of reproduction
in whole or in part in any form.
SIMON & SCHUSTER and colophon are
registered trademarks of Simon & Schuster Inc.
Designed by Edith Fowler
Manufactured in the United States of America

10 9 8 7 6 5 4 3 2 1

Library of Congress Cataloging-in-Publication Data
Bosworth, Patricia.
  Anything your little heart desires :
an American family story /Patricia Bosworth.
     p.   cm.
  Includes bibliographical references.
  1. Crum, Bartley Cavanaugh, 1900–1959.
2. Lawyers—California—Biography.
3. Diplomats—United States—Biography.
I. Title.
KF373.C74B67   1997
340'.092—dc21
[B]   97-2198   CIP
ISBN 0-684-80809-9

ACKNOWLEDGMENTS

THIS book began as a memoir about my father, but I knew almost immediately that I had to go beyond my own recollections. I couldn't just rely on what he'd told me about himself or what I'd witnessed as a young girl.

I wanted to tell the story of his public life, but at the same time I wanted to give equal weight to the private story of what had happened to our family. The choices my father made, the political positions he took irrevocably affected my mother, my brother, and me. And of course I wanted to juxtapose everything against the historical events he was part of, whether it was the opening of the Golden Gate Bridge or the death of Liberalism. Maybe then I could finally begin to understand him and in the process I could arrive at a version of my own past and feel it was true.

This book could not have been done alone. My deepest thanks to all those who gave so willingly of their time and energy to this project.

I owe a special debt of gratitude to my cousins, James Wiard Sr. and James Wiard Jr. They helped me piece together my father's Sacramento childhood and his college years at Berkeley; Jim Jr.'s many letters to me over this decade have been a huge comfort and support. My thanks too to other cousins: to Bartley Cavanaugh Crum Jr. and Maggie Cavanaugh.

I'm deeply appreciative as well to Minna Logan, Helen McWilliamson, the late Herb Caen, Ellen St. Sure, Barbara Sutro Ziegler, Jane Neylan Childs, Harry Bridges, my dear nurse Nell

Brown, my godmother Lib Logan, Mary Kohler, Steve Fisher, Peter and Edla Cusick, and William Wallace. These people were all close to my parents in various ways. They clarified much.

I will be forever grateful to Arthur Mejia for his memories of my brother at Deerfield. Thanks as well to some of my brother's other friends: Bill Chamberlin, Steve Rubin, and Michael Rumney.

Special thanks must be given to the late Ruth Bishop. She made me aware of the invaluable contributions my father made in both Willkie presidential campaigns.

Journalists Ruth Gruber and Gerold Frank both recalled for my benefit the months they spent reporting on my father's role in the Anglo-American Committee of Inquiry into Palestine.

I was lucky enough to have spent an afternoon interviewing former Committee member the Honorable Richard Crossman M.P. between sessions at Parliament in London during the summer of 1966. I interviewed him about Zionism and partition.

And thanks as well to Raphael Silver, Adele Silver, and the late Yehuda Hellman and Aviva Hellman, and Abraham Feinberg.

I will always remember the many conversations I had with the late great critic Diana Trilling. Her knowledge of the Cold War period and McCarthyism challenged and informed me.

And Blair Clark generously made available to me his report on why *PM*, aka the *New York Star*, failed.

I am grateful as well to Myra Appleton, who first encouraged me to explore the father/daughter relationship in *Lear's* when she was editor of that magazine.

And to Victor Navasky, who urged me to write about my father and his times. The assignments he gave me while he was editor of *The Nation* helped me move ahead with my book.

My deepest appreciation goes to Linda Amster, who helped me for close to ten years with research. She was always available to supply a fact or offer an informed dissent. I can't forget her enthusiastic support.

Thanks as well to my assistants Liddy Detar and Catherine Park, superbly organized and forever patient, and to Annie Ngara, my current assistant—they all helped me pull together the vast trove of materials I'd assembled.

Scholars of the Hollywood hearings such as Griffin Fariello and Stefan Kanfer gave of their expertise. Others whom I want to acknowledge for their astute suggestions include: Steven M. L. Aronson, Michael Anderson, Carol Rossen, Linda Gottlieb, Lucy Rosenthal, Carol Hill, and Ralph Blum.

I feel privileged to have been able to draw from my mother's journals, letters, and notes as well as my father's diaries, notebooks, and unfinished autobiography, as well as his book, *Behind the Silken Curtain.*

I am indebted as well to the following archives, collections, and organizations for use of their materials: the State Historical Society of Wisconsin; New York Public Library for the Performing Arts at Lincoln Center; the oral history department at Columbia University; the Harry S. Truman Library in Independence, Missouri; the Franklin D. Roosevelt Library at Hyde Park; the Meiklejohn Civil Liberties Institute at the University of California at Berkeley; the Bancroft Library at the University of California at Berkeley; the Willkie archive collection at the Lilly Library at the University of Indiana in Bloomington, Indiana; the Rabbi Hillel Silver archive at Temple Tifereth Israel in Cleveland, Ohio; and the Middle East Library in St. Anthony's College, Oxford, England.

To my agent, Owen Laster, who has been there for me since the beginning of this project, thank you. And thank you everyone at Simon & Schuster: Gypsy da Silva, Randee Marullo, Carole Bowie, Rebecca Head, and Chuck Adams—you all kept me going with your unfailing good humor and grace.

And last but not least—my deepest heartfelt gratitude to my editor Michael Korda, who had faith in my book and never lost his enthusiasm during its ten years of gestation. He gave my story distinct shape and form.

For Tom Palumbo

Only part of us is sane; only part of us loves pleasure and the longer day of happiness, wants to live to our nineties and die in peace, in a house that we built, that shall shelter those who come after us. The other half of us is nearly mad. It prefers the disagreeable to the agreeable, loves pain and its darker night despair, and wants to die in a catastrophe that will set life back to its beginnings and leave nothing of our house save its blackened foundations . . .

—REBECCA WEST

PROLOGUE

HE night before my father committed suicide, my mother gave a dinner party. Of course the dinner party wasn't mentioned in subsequent accounts of his death. A *New York Times* headline dated December 11, 1959, read

BARTLEY C. CRUM,
LAWYER, 59, DIES

Acted in Cases Involving
Civil Rights—Won Million
in Rita Hayworth Divorce

The obit went on to say he'd bought the New York tabloid *PM* from Marshall Field and was a liberal Republican who'd been a Wendell Willkie campaign aide.

The fact that he'd killed himself by swallowing an entire bottle of Seconal washed down with whiskey wasn't mentioned either, but then we'd kept it a deep dark secret; not even our relatives knew the truth.

Actually, Mama had called some mysterious person at United Press International to hush it up—the same mysterious person my father had telephoned years before when a frat buddy of his had walked into the East River and the family wanted it kept quiet.

My father could do that sort of thing. He knew a lot of people. Earl Warren, Robert Kennedy, Cardinal Spellman, Henry Luce. On the walls of his New York law office there were photographs of himself laughing it up with President Truman and two Secret Service agents in a Chinese restaurant. And on his desk he kept color snapshots of himself with Chaim Weizmann and Golda Meir.

His association with Israeli leaders was referred to in only one eulogy, which appeared in the *American Zionist* and called him "a fighter for justice—a man who spent his prime years fighting for a homeland in Palestine for uprooted European Jews."

During the winter of 1946, President Truman had appointed him to the Anglo-American Committee of Inquiry into Palestine. The committee's task was to discover if it was feasible to allow one hundred thousand Holocaust survivors into the Holy Land. Great Britain's foreign minister Ernest Bevin promised he'd follow the committee's recommendations in spite of an immigration restriction to the contrary.

My father toured filthy, crowded internment camps all over Eastern Europe, interviewing scores of DPs frantic to get to Palestine. He tried to give them reassurances that they would, but he knew that the State Department wanted to protect American oil interests in the Mideast so they secretly supported the Arab campaign to keep the Jews out. And Great Britain secretly supported the Arabs, too.

Later Daddy helped persuade the committee to agree to a policy (supported by Truman) that would issue one hundred thousand immediate-entry certificates to Palestine for the Jewish refugees, and once back in the United States, when the committee's recommendations were ignored and Bevin went back on his promise, my father ended any chance of a government career for himself by publicly pointing to what he considered the double-dealing of our State Department and the British foreign office.

He wrote a book about his experiences on the Committee; it was called *Behind the Silken Curtain* and it was a near best-seller. He would often tell me that his work with the committee was the most rewarding thing he'd ever done.

For a long time he approached life with supreme self-confidence and an attitude of entitlement. He glided through experiences seemingly undaunted by disappointments or fears, or even doubts.

He juggled corporate accounts like Crown Zellerbach paper

along with pro bono cases: Chinese immigrants, unwed mothers, teachers unjustly fired for refusing to sign loyalty oaths.

Then, at the start of the Cold War in 1947—when fear of Communism let loose a wave of political oppression in this country that seems almost incomprehensible today—my father became one of six lawyers defending the Hollywood Ten, that group of screenwriters and directors accused of larding their films with anti-American propaganda. They had refused to cooperate with the House Un-American Activities Committee and testify as to their political beliefs.

My father spoke out frequently against the blacklist and against the FBI, which was fueling the anti-Communist obsession by identifying alleged "subversives" through wiretapping, informers, and guilt by association. He kept pointing out that all this Red-baiting was inconsistent with American ideals.

His critics labeled him a show-off and a self-promoter for getting his name in the papers so much. Mama used to call him "my high-wire artist." She respected his crusading, but she wished he would stay home. Which he did on occasion, especially when we were having a party. My parents were party people. They loved the ritual of collecting groups of friends and acquaintances and mixing them—priests with labor leaders; fashion designers with journalists; landscape architects with politicians and spies. They moved in and out of our homes, first in California, and then in New York.

Mama produced the parties, while Daddy virtually consumed them. The older I got, the more I wondered, where did this wild assortment of people fit in—into the larger scheme of things that made up my parents' lives?

The guest list rarely included any of Daddy's relatives from Sacramento or college buddies or even the radical lawyers he drank with—and some of these people were actually closer to him than the so-called "rich and famous" he courted.

I can still see him standing in the center of our living room in San Francisco, a slight, natty figure in a pin-striped suit, greeting an unending stream of people. There was a dash about him, a lean elegance. He had large, dreamy brown eyes and slick black hair cut short on his neck. His rosy cheeks accentuated the delicate incisiveness of his profile.

Men invariably surrounded him when he spoke. It was almost a sexual thing, my mother said, because he exuded a real power in his prime. He had an access to power—to the White House, to media—albeit a limited access to power, but power nonetheless. He was like an actor. He had the capacity to become every role he played—lawyer, radio talk-show host, author, crusader, friend of the controversial and the famous.

During some of these parties, I would be at the entranceway —watching, watching. I must have been about eight or nine years old when I was allowed to do that. And my father would catch sight of me and call out, "Hey, baby! Give your old man a kiss!"

I would move hesitantly through the crowd in my black velvet dress, black velvet bows in my hair—so proud to be drawn into his enchanted circle.

"Have you met my daughter?" he would ask whomever might be standing next to him—it could be the playwright William Saroyan, wild-haired and wild-eyed; or the brooding, somber novelist John Steinbeck.

Then his arm would creep around my shoulders and he would continue, "This is my daughter, Patricia . . ."

And to each man I'd curtsy as I'd been taught, and then my father would demand, "Isn't she beautiful, you guys?"

I believed I was the cherished one, the favorite.

In another corner of the living room, Mama would be watching, too. Mama—tiny, blond, sparkling with imitation jewels. Later I would skip over to her and whisper, "I'm going to marry Daddy when I grow up."

And Mama would laugh very gaily and say, "Oh, no, you're not!"

Eventually, I stopped insisting I would marry Daddy, but for years I thought I wanted to be like him. I remember that as I was climbing the stairs to my parents' brownstone for the dinner party on that last night before he committed suicide, I still imagined I could be at least as glamorous as he was. At twenty-five, I'd already been married and divorced and was earning my living as an actress. I had just finished making *The Nun's Story* with Audrey Hepburn.

I found my father in his usual place, standing in the center of the living room. He was talking with New York Senator Jacob

Javits and his wife, Marian, while fashion designer Pauline Trigère —hoarse-voiced and wearing blue-tinted glasses—hovered nearby. Mama had invited them over for cocktails before the actual dinner. She'd wanted a few extra friends around to toast Daddy's fifty-ninth birthday, which had occurred two weeks before, on November 28.

Daddy didn't look fifty-nine. Oh, he had a slight paunch, but his grin was still boyish. I watched him light Pauline's cigarette and then rush over to freshen her drink. He was famous for his manners. During the blacklist, whenever he obtained a clearance for a client, he'd write thank-you notes to everyone who had given evidence pro or con.

He usually made an effort to be nice. I never heard him pass judgment on anybody. "Nobody is worthless, my darling," he'd say to me, "but nobody is that terrific either."

I wondered what he thought of the people who had arrived just after I did: Al Steele, the chairman of Pepsi-Cola, and his wife, movie star Joan Crawford, followed by Maître Suzanne Blum, a coarse-skinned dumpy woman who was one of the most powerful lawyers in France, representing the Duke and Duchess of Windsor and Rita Hayworth's European interests. My father used to confer with her about Rita whenever he was in Paris.

He introduced the Steeles to Blum; I think he was hoping the three of them would hit it off. They didn't seem to.

I remember that he started to cough. He did smoke four packs of Pall Mall cigarettes a day, so he invariably coughed a lot. But when he saw me, he stopped. "Hey, baby!" he called out. "Give your old man a kiss!"

As I moved toward him, I could hear our Chinese cook, Toy, talking to himself and sharpening knives in the kitchen at the far end of the room; the guests pretended to ignore the noise.

Toy had been our cook on and off since we lived in Berkeley during the 1940s; back then he'd just prepare delicious meals and appeared quite serene. But lately, whenever Daddy invited a prospective client to the brownstone, Toy would begin talking to himself and sharpening knives.

On that last night, the knives were clanging so loudly that Daddy had to run into the kitchen; soon the clanging and clashing stopped. Toy spoke only broken English, but somehow he and my father were always able to communicate; they often had long incomprehensible talks together.

Toy adored my father. Daddy had gotten Mrs. Toy out of Shanghai years ago, and Toy felt indebted; he worked for my parents a couple of times a week; the other nights he cooked for some millionaire on Sutton Place.

I don't remember much more about that evening except the friends invited for cocktails drifted off and the dinner party proceeded. It was typical of most of the dinner parties my parents had given over the years—filled with a mixture of trendy guests and close friends. The parties fitted perfectly into the highly pressured worlds in which they both lived.

Neither of them liked to be by themselves for too long, so they arranged their lives so that they wouldn't be. The result was, as far as I was concerned, an increasing inability to relax. I had wanted to talk to Daddy alone that night about my engagement to a man Mama violently disliked, but I didn't have the chance.

More friends dropped by for brandy and coffee after dinner. The last guest—one of Daddy's oldest buddies from San Francisco, Peter Cusick (a former CIA agent)—left around 1:00 A.M., calling out to my father that he'd see him at the Council on Foreign Relations the following afternoon.

All of that was forgotten the next morning when Mama summoned me back to the duplex. I lived not too far away in a studio apartment off First Avenue on 66th Street, so I arrived in time to see Daddy being carried out the door in a body bag.

Then came the phone calls. I answered most of them. Some of them were guests from last night's dinner party who wanted to say what a great time they'd had, and "wasn't Bart in fine spirits?"

There would be a pause and I'd have to answer, "My father is dead."

I WAS told by one of Daddy's law partners that I chose the coffin at Campbell's; I have no recollection of that, but I do remember wiping makeup off my father's cheeks so he wouldn't resemble a transvestite when friends came to pay their respects.

Mama and I attended the funeral mass and managed to get through a lunch afterward at the Harvard Club; after that was over we had to wait huddled on the street for a long time to get a cab. It was freezing cold.

We returned to the brownstone in the late afternoon, exhausted. Toy greeted us. He always arrived like clockwork to prepare dinner; there he was, standing in the center of the living room, his arms full of groceries.

Mama took one look and whispered to me, "*You* tell him. I can't." Then she bolted upstairs.

Toy gazed after her in bewilderment. "Where Mr. Crum?" Daddy was often home from the office by this time, and, drink in hand, he would greet Toy effusively and then often follow him into the kitchen to observe how he prepared our next "feast."

"My father is dead." How else could I say it? "My father is dead."

With that Toy threw the bags of food into the air and they fell on the rug, splitting apart. The ducks rolled out—absurdly pink and naked (roast duck was Daddy's favorite)—and there were the ingredients for a lemon pie, which Daddy would have prepared himself. He loved to bake.

And then Toy began wailing like a banshee. He fell onto the rug and began writhing back and forth, clutching his stomach and screaming as if he were in terrible physical pain.

I stood there wishing I could join him on the floor and writhe back and forth myself, experiencing the spasms of emotion I knew were inside me but that I could not release.

Minutes went by, and then Toy stopped wailing and grew very still. Without a word he rose, picked up the food—including the lemons, which had rolled past the umbrella stand—and disappeared into the kitchen.

I went over and sat down on the big white couch facing the fireplace. Surrounding me were familiar objects that had accompanied us on our many moves—from Berkeley to San Francisco to various apartments and brownstones all over New York.

There was my grandfather Bosworth's Chinese screen, several old clocks ticking wildly, the strange pale-green marble bust of my mother done during the 1920s. There were piles of newspapers and magazines on a side table, and walls of books. And there was the Italian Renaissance desk, a present from my father to Mama on their tenth wedding anniversary; its glistening tawny wood was polished to a fine sheen. On it was a jade inkwell and a small blackened china figurine of a horse, the only remnant from a fire that had engulfed our house in Berkeley long ago. The horse had been a gift from my grandfather Bosworth to Mama; she'd placed it on a shelf in the nursery directly above my brother's bassinet, but the flames hadn't touched the china figurine, though it was so badly stained with smoke that the stains could never be removed.

Whenever I saw that tiny blackened china horse, I was reminded of how Daddy had saved my brother's life in the fire—my brother, Bartley C. Crum Jr., was three and a half weeks old; I was two and a half.

PART
ONE

CHAPTER

1

I REMEMBER watching my father's pale naked form disappear up into the crackling flames that had suddenly destroyed the nursery on the third floor of our house in Berkeley. I remember hearing his frantic cries of "The baby! The baby!" grow fainter and fainter while my mother and I stood as still as statues in the garden outside.

It was a clear, cold California night. Full moon. The hills looked black above our house. The trees seemed even blacker. Acrid smoke billowed toward us, mingling with the pungent scent of the eucalyptus groves rustling nearby. Presently, the smoke covered the moon.

Mama and I waited for what seemed like hours, gripping each other's hands until, just as the wailing fire engine arrived on the steep drive below, my father emerged panting from the house. His entire body was covered with soot, and he couldn't stop hopping up and down because the soles of his bare feet were badly burned, but he was smiling a goofy, triumphant smile because my brother —my three-and-a-half-week-old brother, Bartley Crum Jr.—was safe and miraculously sleeping in the crook of his arm.

Still standing next to me, Mama made little mewing sounds in her throat; then she tore off her blue satin robe and ran to my father and tried to wrap it around him. I ran after her, and for one brief second we huddled close together—a family unit—one of the few times I ever remember us being literally close. Mama kept dropping the robe because Daddy was jumping up and down with the pain, but she kept trying to cover his nakedness and he wouldn't let her. "I'm okay, Cutsie," he murmured, using the nickname he often used for her (her real name was Anna Gertrude), "I'm okay." His eyes glittered out of soot-blackened rims, but they were staring not at her but into the distance.

His expression seemed haunted, almost crazy, as if he'd witnessed a holocaust and survived it—indeed he would later tell us that the experience of running across the glowing coals of the nursery floor to the baby's bassinet and feeling the fire racing after him was "like running away from death."

He didn't even seem to notice that our garden was filling with neighbors from adjoining houses on the hills. Firemen appeared dragging rubber hoses through the ivy beds so that they could shoot geysers of water directly into the windows of the blazing nursery.

It was a wonder there was so much movement in the night, so much purpose. Flames streaked through the dark cool air, sparks fell and then melted away on the ivy beds. My cheeks felt burning hot.

An ambulance arrived. White-coated medics bearing a stretcher pushed through the crowd. One of them tried to take my brother out of my father's arms, but he refused to give him up. "I'll take Bart to the hospital, thank you very much."

And with that, he literally danced across the grass—he was in such agony—and Mama ran after him holding up her blue satin robe like a shield.

The fire roared orange in front of me, jiggling powerful heat. I stood transfixed by the blaze, trembling with excitement, and after a moment someone knelt at my feet and a kindly face pressed close to mine. It was our nurse, Nell Brown, who had incredibly plump freckled arms and a warm stomach I loved to cuddle on.

She hugged me so close I could taste her tears. "Don't you ever forget this night, little doll. Your papa is an awful brave man."

THE fire in the nursery became family lore along with the time Mama saved *my* life at Lake Tahoe, where we were vacationing. I'd been crawling around our cabin, nosing into wastebaskets and nooks and crannies, and she noticed something bluish around my mouth; she stuck her finger down my throat, and once I'd vomited she rushed me to the Reno hospital, where my stomach was pumped out and the doctors announced, "Your daughter swallowed enough rat poison to kill eleven men!"

Between them my parents had saved both our lives—my brother's and mine—and then almost immediately shifted their attention back to what they were really interested in, themselves and each other. I don't mean they didn't love us—I think they loved us very much—but they approached parenthood as they approached every other experience, with the intention of doing the best job in the shortest possible time. They wanted to fit parent-hood into the wider scheme of things.

While Daddy's feet healed at Peralta Hospital in Oakland, he kept notes of every new word I ever uttered when I visited him, but he also saw clients and used the time to begin writing a long, distinguished essay on "Mr. Justice Edmonds and some recent trends in the law of civil liberties," which was eventually pub-lished in a California law journal.

As for Mama (also known as Cutsie Bosworth—former crime reporter for the *San Francisco Call Bulletin*), she kept on strug-gling to finish a novel she'd been trying to complete since her honeymoon. But she also organized her schedule so she would be home in time to help our nurse, Nell, feed and diaper my baby brother, Bart, and to play a bit with me.

Sometimes they went away without us on weekends, and when they came back Mama would show us snapshots Uncle Carl had taken of Daddy riding horseback in Grass Valley or Daddy kissing her passionately on top of a sun-baked hill. I'd never seen them kiss that passionately in real life.

These snapshots were glued into a leather album along with pictures of a lavish costume ball in Piedmont—Daddy dressed as a swarthy Rudolph Valentino, Mama posed as a sexy Sadie Thomp-son in *Rain*.

I used to pore over that album when I was a little girl, study-ing my parents' expressions—radiant, self-confident. Their smiles were dazzling, but finally impenetrable. I could never figure out what was going on in their heads.

In my memory we seemed to exist always in a state of con-stant drama, of perpetual excitement. And no matter what the crisis, Daddy always made it more than bearable.

Once he insisted we hide out in our garage during an earthquake. I remember my brother and I huddling in the backseat of our roadster convertible while our parents sat in front. We were surrounded by pitch darkness and an eerie, greasy smell. Far away, we could hear a rumble and growl from deep within the earth. Pure waves of energy moved under our feet, and Daddy explained to us that San Francisco was on the tip of a peninsula squeezed between two of the most active earthquake faults in the world; to the west of the city, the San Andreas fault, which dived into the Pacific; to the east, the Hayward fault, which happened to form smack at the base of the Berkeley hills—less than a mile from our home.

"We are living very precariously, my darlings," he announced. "We will always live precariously if we stay here, but I think it's much too beautiful to leave."

OUT of the blue he would sometimes say, "Develop your five senses."

"Is there a sixth sense, Daddy?"

"Sure, there is," he'd answer. "There's panic."

I thought he was joking until after I grew up and realized he must mean the terrible sense you have inside yourself when you've taken on too much and you feel irresponsible—to your talent, or to your family, and certainly to yourself—and it's too late to do anything about it.

Daddy must have experienced a lot of panic in his life. Of course, everybody experiences panic. But Daddy considered himself first and foremost an Irishman and a Catholic, meaning that beyond his ebullience and charm he was a master of concealment.

"What will you *do?* What will you *do?*" Mama would cry when some problem arose—another money crisis; another murky political harassment—and Daddy would either remain silent or answer, "Never explain—never complain." This was a maddening little ditty he had picked up from his mother, Mo Cavanaugh, the most self-protective and hidden of women.

I was never sure whether I should value my father's elusiveness or beware of it. Actually, his talent for concealing was a trait he undoubtedly inherited from his maternal grandparents, Bartholomew Cavanaugh and Kate McTernan, a wily couple with "a lot of moxie" (as Daddy used to say) who'd escaped the potato famine in County Sligo by immigrating to Boston in the 1850s. Then, like thousands of other Irish immigrants, they had journeyed to California during the gold rush.

For a while, legend had it, Bart Cavanaugh panned for gold in places named Piety Gulch and Puke Ravine before moving with Kate to San Francisco when that city was the gaudiest and most violent place in the nation. ("Five thousand unsolved murders in one year," a newspaper account said.)

In San Francisco the Cavanaughs raised eight kids (Mo Cavanaugh among them), and Bart Cavanaugh saw to it that his family became the prime unit for emotion and survival as he slaved away as a boiler maker. For a time, he worked at the United States Mint. Every so often he'd sneak off to a bar and get roaring drunk; he usually carried his shillelagh with him.

By the late 1860s, he and Kate moved everybody to Sacramento, where he became county sheriff. They built a two-story frame house at First and I streets opposite the state capitol. Sisters and brothers took turns bathing in the kitchen on Saturday nights behind a screen. There was an outhouse in the yard.

Not long after the move to Sacramento, Bartholomew fell ill with tuberculosis, so Kate took over the family finances. For extra money she rented out the ground floor of their house as a bond office; later it was transformed into a bar (this was before Prohibition), and finally into a coffee-grinding establishment.

Just before World War I the eldest Cavanaugh son—my great-uncle "Black Bart" Cavanaugh (who was already a successful bookie at the age of twenty-one)—turned the basement of the house on I Street into a betting parlor, complete with steam bath. The place soon became a very popular private "club" for most of the police in Sacramento as well as some of the local politicos. Supposedly the ballots of several elections were counted there.

As the years went by my great-uncle forged many friendships and loyalties with his cronies and obtained patronage jobs for various relatives, including a job for his favorite sister, Mo, a slender girl with soft dark hair and thin lips. She became the first female stenographer in the state of California. Mo kept the job until 1896, when she married James Henry Crum, a burly bronco buster.

For a wedding present the couple was given a pretty little ranch on the banks of the Feather River, where Mo had a Chinese cook and raised peacocks. Their first child, a daughter named Estelle, was born in 1895; five years later, a son (my father) was born. It all seemed perfect and harmonious until James Henry ruined everything by gambling the ranch away in a drunken poker game, and he and Mo were forced to move to Sacramento and live with the Cavanaughs at the tumbledown house at First and I.

Mo never reconciled herself to living in reduced circumstances. She was so angry about losing the ranch that she had her sister Kate sneak down to St. Mary's Cathedral and ask the priest to baptize her baby boy "Bartley Cavanaugh" instead of "James Henry," as had originally been planned. And my father grew up in that house on First and I, until he left for college in 1918. He was raised by his mother, Mo, and her spinster sisters Maggie and Kate, who shared a bedroom off one of the parlors.

James Henry lived there, too, a silent, often drunken, presence. At some point, he managed to get a job as a telegrapher for the Southern Pacific Railroad, and he would amble down to the train station early in the morning and come back after dark; the Cavanaugh sisters would serve him supper, but there were few words exchanged. He lived in a state of perpetual disgrace for thirty years; he was never forgiven for gambling the ranch away (his own father refused to speak to him on his deathbed).

Nobody ever said anything out loud, but James Henry was thought to be a failure. Daddy once told me that he loved him, but that they were never close.

UNTIL recently, I knew nothing about any of Daddy's relatives. The collective memory of the family was avoided because my mother, who had very grand pretensions about *her* beginnings, thought Daddy's family was "shanty Irish" and beneath her. As a result, we never spent a single holiday with either the Cavanaughs or the Crums.

In fact, my brother and I traveled to Sacramento only once; I believe it was in the late 1930s and this was because my grandfather was recovering from some sort of stroke and Daddy wanted us to meet him.

I remember us all standing in a big backyard, the grass

tickling our legs. We sipped iced tea from heavy green glass tumblers while Mo, slightly disheveled in a baggy print dress, hung on Daddy's arm. I remember staring at my grandfather's beautiful snow-white hair and wondering why his ruddy face was all twisted. He didn't say a word, he just held my hand.

It was so hot in the backyard I could hardly breathe. And there was a brownish haze around the Tehachapi Mountains and the Sierra Nevada range; we could see the mountains from the yard. When we left a short time later, Daddy hugged his father very tight and then told us we would be taking a walk before we returned to the hotel.

Mama had stayed behind in our suite; she'd been felled by a migraine and we'd left her lying on top of the bed with a wet sheet over her nude body and her eyes covered with cotton pads soaked in witch hazel.

My brother and I moved with my father through the silent shady streets. Although it was late afternoon, the parks and sidewalks were empty because of the terrible glare of the sun. Eventually we approached the American River, where "gold had been discovered," Daddy told us, and where he'd swum naked as a kid. He said Mo had caught him swimming there once, when he was supposed to be taking a piano lesson; she'd plunged into the river up to her hips and dragged him onto the bluffs and then twisted his ears—"like she wanted to twist them off."

"Oh, Jesus, she hurt me, my darlings," he told us, laughing. "But I never cried out."

IT'S perhaps an apocryphal story that Daddy had nursed at Mo's breast until he was four years old, but it was common lore among our family. "It was the beginning of all his troubles," Mama said.

"I never heard of such a notion," my cousin Jim Wiard (Daddy's nephew) wrote me. But, he added, "Mo did dote on Bart." And sometimes his older sister, Estelle, nicknamed "Sally," was ignored. "Mo loved Bart to distraction. She was determined he would be special. She fed him stories about Andrew Carnegie and Thomas Edison, poor boys who came from nothing and achieved greatness. She paid for extra piano lessons and he was tutored in Latin and German. Didn't Bart use his German when he attended the Nuremberg trials?"

Meanwhile, his aunt Katie was teaching him about his soul and how it was a violent battleground for good and evil. "Your entire life is about saving your soul," she would say. "Your entire life is about redemption."

And he attended daily Mass with her and he read the Gospels; he was an altar boy; he appeared very devout. "Bart has the gift of faith," Aunt Katie would say.

For a while he toyed with the idea of becoming a priest, but in the end, the law won out; it was more flexible and more logical than the Church; it was about moral and emotional transactions.

As a teenager, my father took all sorts of odd jobs to earn extra money for college. He delivered mail in a horse-drawn cart; he tutored friends in English grammar and Latin.

At eighteen, summering at Inverness with his family, he courted a girl named Billie. She had red hair and freckles and she was older than he was—by some four or five years.

Women loved him. He was a tease; he was funny, he was touching. "He had a smile that made you smile right back," an old friend, Helen McWilliamson, said. "And he was always giving you compliments. 'You look wonderful,' he'd say. 'You look marvelous!' But with such intensity you couldn't quite believe it. Later you would think, 'Did I really look that good?' "

As a young man, he positively radiated good nature (as later on he would negatively radiate stress). "He was the first person to buy you an ice cream cone; he always remembered birthdays and anniversaries; he loved giving presents; he'd go out of his way to do something for you—run an errand—arrange for tickets to a concert. But he'd make rash promises too; once he told me, 'I'm going to take you up in a private airplane,' " Jim Wiard remembers, "but he never did."

He charmed everybody but his own mother. "You can't pull the wool over my eyes," Mo would say when she caught him in a fib or an exaggeration. She was terrified he'd grow up to be like her brother Black Bart, a charmer if there ever was one, but master of the "Irish switch"—he could shake hands with a friend while soft-soaping an enemy with the other.

Daddy had plenty of opportunity to observe his uncle weaving his magic spell; as a teenager, he would hang out in Black Bart's betting parlor with his first cousin, also named Bart Cavanaugh, who later went on to become a powerful city manager of Sacramento during the 1940s and was one of Earl Warren's principal confidants. Together the two boys would observe their uncle playing cards or taking bets or schmoozing with his cronies about California's future.

Much of the talk centered around the Southern Pacific Railroad. California then was virtually dominated by the railroad, and corruption prevailed. The Southern Pacific controlled the legislature and newspapers and individual senators—that is, until Hiram Johnson became governor in 1910; he was such a tough, honest governor, he put a stop to it. It was an incredible story, since his father, Grover Johnson, was the chief lobbyist for the railroad. That struggle—between public and vested interests; between a lone crusader, Hiram Johnson, and a corporation; not to mention the battle between father and son—these were dramas the two Barts could and did recite by rote. I have often thought that hearing these stories in that smoky, cramped betting parlor might have fueled my father's fascination with politics and supported his deep feelings for the mysteries of power. ("In politics you can have what you have in religion," he wrote Mama from the Willkie presidential campaign train in 1940. "You can have a sense of incarnation. All the guys I'm working with—along with Wendell—Cabot Lodge, Russell Davenport and Paul Smith—we're all searching for a meaning in life.")

Just before he left for Berkeley and college in 1918, my father and his cousin took a trip together to Reno and the ghost towns nearby, and they weekended at Lake Tahoe, which was still surrounded by falling-down mining camps.

How Daddy loved the land his relatives had helped discover. As soon as he could afford a car, he crisscrossed the state, taking trips to places as diverse as Death Valley and Sugar Bowl, long before it became a ski resort. He explored Big Sur; he drove to Hollywood when it was still mostly orange groves; and he kept returning to San Francisco.

He could get wildly drunk if he wanted to; San Francisco had more speakeasies than any other city in the country—little bars along Union Square and in the Tenderloin, near California and

Hyde streets. He could stagger drunk into the wide-open gambling that went on in the alleys of Chinatown, or he could visit a bawdy house and then careen down to the waterfront on a cable car.

Mostly he wandered the hills, ending up more often than not in Pacific Heights. Sometimes he'd stand outside the Spreckels Mansion perched on Octavia and Washington streets, a big white elephant of a building with ornate columns and verandas overlooking the bay. Daddy told me he had fantasized about living near that house—and one day we did.

CHAPTER

2

THE University of California opened up new worlds for my father. His letters to Mo were filled with enthusiastic descriptions of Berkeley's winding streets and breathtaking vistas. And he wrote as well about his favorite teacher and first mentor, Max Radin, an elegant, mustachioed attorney originally from Kempers, Poland, who taught constitutional law and wrote mystery novels on the side.

After the rituals of hazing, Daddy became a member of the Kappa Alpha fraternity in 1919, and later of Phi Delta Pi. He joined the Army Reserves and went on maneuvers. (I have a nutty, blurred photograph of him being thrown into the air from a blanket by his buddies.) By his junior year, he was one of the most popular bachelors on campus. The *San Francisco Examiner* took a picture of him escorting silent-movie star Clara Bow to a prom.

He wasn't a leader—he was too unconventional—but he had ideas about everything and he was good at executing them. He was a catalyst. A classmate, Portia Hume, told me he had a "bravado —a kind of cocky assurance." He and Portia took public speaking together in Doc Smithson's class. "Bart loved making entrances and he loved to rage." Once he regaled his classmates to helpless laughter with a speech about how the shimmy had recently been condemned by the Catholic Archdiocese of Ohio.

To help pay his tuition he started teaching English at the extension division of the university, and he taught international law there as well from 1922 to 1926. In the summers he worked as a cub reporter for the *Sacramento Bee* and served as a stringer for United Press. He ended up working at the morgue of the *Oakland Tribune*, which "Silk Hat" Joe Knowland owned.

After he graduated from Bolt Hall and began practicing law in San Francisco he continued to live in Berkeley.

ONCE a month, Mo would come down from Sacramento on the train and clean the apartment my father had rented, two cramped dark rooms high in the hills on Panoramic Way. She would dust and sweep, and then she would search the place for liquor. It was the beginning of Prohibition, and deaths from consumption of undiluted alcohol were frequent, but chances are Mo was more worried about how problem drinking ran in our family.

Daddy would come home from work and see what his mother was doing, and he would chase her around the living room, but not before she managed to hurl the latest bottle of bathtub gin into the fireplace. Then she methodically began to clean up the mess.

"I'm just going to go out and get more, Mother," Daddy would say.

"Not while I'm here you won't," she'd cry and throw herself dramatically against the door. And Daddy would laugh and laugh. "You remind me of Mary Pickford as Little Nell."

He would keep on teasing and cajoling her until she began to melt by the door, and finally he would lead her to a falling-down couch and regale her with his latest adventure: he had flown in a private plane over the Santa Cruz mountains; he'd gone on to play golf at Pebble Beach.

Mo never met any of his friends; she didn't think he saw many girls. He kept saying he wasn't going to get married for a long time. Too much else to consider, he said, too much to do. The temptations of the flesh would just have to wait.

That is, until he met Anna Gertrude Bosworth, the archetypical flapper. Tiny blond Cutsie, as everybody called her, who had large inquiring eyes and a naughty laugh and wore simple flowing Castle frocks and buckled shoes.

She and Daddy were never formally introduced. They simply knew each other by reputation. He knew she'd been kicked out of her sorority, Phi Beta, for "acting wild." She knew he was working as a lawyer for William Randolph Hearst.

One Saturday afternoon Mama saw Daddy striding down Channing Way in Berkeley. "He was wearing a Varsity sweater and baggy pants; his black hair was slicked wetly back and his eyes were twinkling. He was the handsomest thing I'd ever seen!"

He paused and grinned. "So you're the infamous Cutsie Bosworth," he had murmured, and she could feel her cheeks reddening. "I've always wanted to take you dancing."

She told me later she had thought to herself, Oh, my God, stop it. I've been longing to dance with you forever and forever.

For a while, they met secretly for talks and "boodling" in the shadows of the Greek Theater, since Mama was engaged to marry "Shake" Baldwin.

"No girl in her right mind would marry a guy named Shake," my father had teased.

He sent her bunches of flowers and a jade inkwell and a delicate lace hanky, and he would phone her every day. Finally she broke her engagement to Shake and they started spending a great deal of time together, "dating in earnest."

After I grew up, Mama would confide that she had never been attracted to a "good man" before she met my father. "I had always been drawn to world-weary, cold-hearted men—to bastards," she told me. "Never to anyone decent."

"Bart Crum is an innocent," she wrote in her journal. "I am falling in love with his gentleness. What a strange sweet nature he has."

If she felt that he seemed too eager to please, that he wanted everybody to love him, that he insisted on seeing both sides to a question, of being, above all, "fair," she didn't say.

Mostly, in the journals she left me, Mama characterized my father by his actions.

"Bart tells me he has no interest in *accumulating* money, but he does want to *earn* a lot, because he says in America it's a badge of accomplishment. However, he wants to *spend* it immediately. He is as extravagant as I am. He bought me a pearl ring from Gump's. I forced him to return it because I knew he couldn't afford it."

He was already starting to take on clients who couldn't pay their bills. "I told him to start charging or you'll die broke," Mama wrote. "We got into an argument—he says he'll always take on people who are helpless, people who need to be defended because they cannot do it for themselves." Then she added, "I wish I liked more people. Bart seems to like everybody." Then: "Bart is too trusting."

EVENTUALLY, she brought my father home to her family for Sunday lunch. Home was a squat one-story shingled house set amid a riotously lush garden at 17 Bonita Avenue in Piedmont.

Before the meal, they toured the library; the room was crowded with maps of California, books on wildlife, gun racks, stuffed deer heads, saddles, and a pair of antique Chinese screens.

Everything belonged to my grandfather, Charles Bosworth, a tall, stern rancher born in Grass Valley, who now sold life insurance in his office on Market Street.

His favorite possessions were the Chinese screens—beautiful black lacquered things, festooned with gold-leaf dragons and birds. When we were little, my brother and I would play hide-and-seek behind them.

The screens had been given to Granddad by his late beloved wife, Anna Hoffman. He used to refer to her in the present tense, although she'd been dead twenty-three years and he had gone on to marry Julie, his former secretary, in 1914. She bore him a son, Lansing Bosworth, handsome as a movie star but retarded. He resided in a state institution in Napa County.

There were no photographs of Lansing or Julie anywhere in the library, only pictures of his first wife, my late grandmother, Anna Hoffman. In one picture she appears tall and dignified, masses of dark hair swept up from her neck; she is holding Mama, who is still a baby, and they are standing outside the Bosworth home in San Rafael, where she died in 1905 of tuberculosis. An ardent Christian Scientist, she'd refused to see a doctor.

After her mother's death, Mama became, at the age of six, "the little lady of Daddy's house"—first in San Rafael, then in Piedmont. "Before I was ten, I was helping plan the meals with our Chinese cook."

And she polished her father's boots until she could see her own reflection in them. "He taught me to be neat as a pin, and to never shed a tear. So I never cried. Even when I was in great emotional pain."

She missed her mother; missed her tenderness and her approval. "The loss of a mother is the greatest female tragedy," she told me. But she didn't tell her father that. She never told him anything unpleasant; certainly not about how her brother Carl held her underwater whenever they went swimming, to the point where she felt sure she would drown, and how he made fun of her boyfriends, made fun of her ambitions.

By the time she was seventeen, she suffered from excruciating migraine headaches and had the beginning of an ulcer. Her father was never satisfied with her. When she was third in her class at school, he told her she should have been first.

In between classes and appointments with various doctors, her father taught her to box (later he would teach me, too), and he insisted Mama ride, although she was terrified of horses. And as if that weren't enough, there were frequent campouts on weekends, too, days and nights of rigorous climbing—along with a string of pack mules—through the John Muir Trail at the edge of Yosemite Valley.

I have a photograph of Mama taken right after she and her father scaled the heights of Mount Whitney (14,494 feet), the tallest peak in the Sierra Nevada range. Her face is a study in anguish (with a suggestion as well of a self locked off), possibly because she was sharing a tent with her new stepmother.

"Julie took Dad away from me. I never forgave her." Mama told me this over and over when I was little, how she resented Julie and was jealous of her.

Still our grandparents were both very much around our house while we were growing up. In fact, when our nurse Nell took her day off, Julie would often drive over from Piedmont and cart us to the indoor ice rink in Oakland, where we'd careen around on rented skates. My brother and I loved her.

Julie was a loyal, devoted soul; if she knew Mama hated her, she never let on. I can still hear her exclaiming, "Ye Gods!" I can still see her tall, gaunt presence (she was well over six feet) roaming about our garden in Berkeley brandishing a trowel. Her great genius was as a gardener; she could make anything grow. Daddy often said, "I swear Julie talks to plants." Even Mama had to admit Julie knew what she was doing when it came to soil and drainage, but other than that Mama maintained, "Julie can never do anything right."

Her disdain went back to the first lunch Julie prepared for Daddy in 1925. The chicken was overcooked, the gravy too watery, the broccoli mushy. Mama refused to eat the meal and ran to her room. Julie left the table crying.

Meanwhile, Daddy and Granddad tried to have a conversation, but they were having a difficult time since Granddad didn't approve of the Catholic Church, and to make matters worse, he was a fervent isolationist; they were not in tune politically either.

So they stuck to one topic: boxing. That's all they talked about in those first months, and then Mama would interject with some nugget like, "Have you heard Jack Dempsey's nose has been bobbed so he can get into the movies?" and they'd start laughing.

While they were courting, my parents laughed a lot. "Cutsie was madly in love with Bart Crum," said Lib Logan, Mama's best friend and my godmother. "She wanted to marry him, she was determined to marry him, and the more he resisted, the more she had to have him."

He kept telling her he was ambivalent about marriage. Oh, he cared about her, yes. "You are full of brains and energy, and if anyone understands this boy . . . you do," he wrote her once. But he was too restless to be tied down so soon.

Midway through their courtship he started to break dates, making excuses about being too busy. Once she invited him to accompany her to Carmel for the weekend where she was to participate in a golf tournament. He said he'd already made plans to visit his mother. Mama got suspicious, so she insisted on driving him to the train. As it pulled away she hopped back into her car and sped to the next station in time to see him jump into an open roadster with some of his old frat buddies.

She was so furious, she stopped speaking to him and ran off to live in Europe, first in Madrid and then in Paris, where she rented a room from a French family, took classes at the Sorbonne, and mastered the art of fine cooking at the Cordon Bleu. When she returned to Piedmont in the spring of 1928 she refused to come to the phone when he called.

In the meantime, she began dating all sorts of men—divorced men, older men, and rich men—and she took a job at the *San Francisco Call Bulletin* covering disasters.

During the course of covering a murder, Daddy offered to

drive her up to the scene of the crime, a ghost town in Sonoma County, and their romance started all over again. A few weeks later, they got officially engaged.

"I feel everything and anything is possible with Bart and me," Mama wrote in her journal on the eve of her wedding. "EVERYTHING AND ANYTHING. I am absolutely ecstatic."

MY parents were married on the evening of October 11, 1929, at the Claremont Country Club, in front of two hundred guests. Mama commanded that there be no electric lights, only flickering candles. She planned each detail, right down to the gold cloths on the round tables and the lush garlands of fruit and flowers, which seemed to encircle the entire dance floor.

Mama even created her wedding dress of rich ivory satin—it was designed like a medieval bridal robe, so there was no decoration save an extra-long tulle veil—and she wore slippers encrusted with rhinestones (I used to clump around in them up and down the nursery).

My parents honeymooned in Honolulu. The Neylan firm had business there, something to do with Dole pineapple, and Daddy was handling it, so the trip could be written off as a business expense.

On October 29, the day of the great Wall Street stock market crash, he and my mother were on the island of Hawaii watching the Kilauea volcano erupt, so they didn't learn until the next day that 16.4 million shares had changed hands. When they did, they fed on the news—the papers described factories and steel mines closing, men jumping off skyscrapers to their deaths, and banks failing. President Hoover's campaign slogan, "Prosperity is just around the corner—a chicken in every pot," sounded pretty ironic when they saw the breadlines in San Francisco.

They returned home to discover that Mama's entire inheritance from her late mother had been lost in the crash. Granddad had insisted on investing all of it just before they left on their honeymoon. "I no longer had a penny to call my own," Mama said.

CHAPTER

3

OTHERWISE, the Depression didn't affect my parents too much. Luckily Daddy had a job and he was glad to have one. Many young lawyers were driving buses. He and Mama had one asset: just before they got married, they had bought a spacious shingled house at 62 Panoramic Way, right near Daddy's bachelor apartment. It overlooked San Francisco Bay and the Berkeley campus.

They moved in as soon as they got back from their honeymoon and started fixing the place up—putting in rose trees in the front garden and vegetables in the back. They tried to be frugal. Mama would buy three pounds of hamburger for a quarter at the A & P and bake a meat loaf with onions and bacon on top, and Daddy said he never peeled a potato without planting the skin.

In the early days of their marriage, they did everything together. After work they took an upholstery class in Oakland, or they would bring home stacks of books from the public library and read them aloud to each other. Charles Dickens and George Bernard Shaw. Shaw was Daddy's favorite writer because he was a playwright, an essayist, and he was Irish. Words were his weapon and his shield.

As the Depression worsened and more banks and factories closed, and the homeless rioted in the streets of Washington, Daddy painted their living room dark green to soothe Mama's headaches, and he built shelves and a funny-shaped desk for his study and put a bust of Nefertiti, queen of Egypt, on his windowsill.

They completed the last room of the house on the eve of Roosevelt's election. Together they hung reproductions of some of the world's greatest art treasures on the stairwell leading up to the third floor of what would be our nursery. Botticellis and Rembrandts were mixed in with Lautrec posters and Van Gogh's terrifying *Field of Crows*. Mama wanted us to develop a "visual imagination," so she would move the prints around: Rousseau's vivid green jungle went back and forth from sun porch to hall. But one poster remained in the same place: *Las Meninas* by Velázquez. The Baby Infanta and the Palace Dwarf. Those images never budged from above my bed.

In every one of our homes, and we lived in many, Daddy would always set aside some quiet corner with a prie-dieu where we could say our rosaries or offer up a prayer. In Berkeley in the main hall there was a small statue of Our Lady with a votive candle burning. When we moved to San Francisco in 1942, Daddy hung a little painting of St. Francis of Assisi (who was my brother's favorite saint) out on the terrace. It got all warped from the fog.

During World War II, my parents purchased a genuine altar made of smooth white wood from an antiques shop near Santa Cruz. The statue atop the altar proper was reminiscent of one of those fifteenth-century Fra Angelico portraits of the assumption of Mary Mother of God into heaven. The Madonna seemed almost life-size; she stood proud and tall, with a halo attached to her head and three plump cherubs at the hem of her flowing robes. Mass could have been said on that altar. The tabernacle was there with its chalice—ready to be filled with the Blood of Christ.

This altar stood on the porch of our country house at Aptos, by the sea, and when we moved to New York in 1948, Daddy had it shipped to our new weekend place in Garrison, on the Hudson. "We loved that altar," Mama said.

Usually Daddy's need for religious objects around the house conflicted with Mama's sense of decor, which ran to leopard-print upholstery and polished Louis Quinze antiques. Another object she responded to was a heavy old crucifix Daddy kept in his study. It had belonged to his grandmother McTernan and had been blessed by the pope; she'd carried it with her when she journeyed from Rome to Boston to California at the start of the gold rush in 1849.

The Christ figure seems terribly twisted in agony on the cross; a crown of thorns is jammed onto his skull. Whenever I glance at Him (I have the crucifix by my desk), it reminds me of the times Daddy and I recited the Stations of the Cross together, and it's the only Catholic ritual he ever taught me, so I never forgot it any more than I forgot the first times he took me to Mass in San Francisco at Mission Dolores, which Father Junípero Serra founded five days before the Declaration of Independence was signed; Daddy liked going to Mass there every day, if he could.

He even tried to go on those mornings when he had had to work "like an animal" in John Francis Neylan's office the night before. Sometimes he would stay up until dawn finishing a brief, and he wouldn't even take the ferry back to Berkeley; he'd fall asleep at his desk.

Neylan was a tough Catholic conservative. Thought to be one of the most influential men in California, he was a special kind of mentor for my impressionable, idealistic father.

Although he was a law school graduate, Neylan started out as a reporter for the *San Francisco Call Bulletin*. He was covering local graft prosecutions and caught the eye of its chief prosecutor, Hiram Johnson. When Johnson became governor of California in 1910, he appointed the twenty-four-year-old Neylan as chief financial officer of the state.

In 1918, Neylan opened a law practice, and William Randolph Hearst retained him as an attorney that same year. The following year, he assumed the role of publisher at the *Call*. Slowly, he took over as Hearst's general counsel and began to bring financial order out of the chaos that plagued the publishing tycoon's empire.

Hearst could not stop spending money. His buying consumed him, even during the Depression. A typical purchase—an entire Spanish abbey, which he had knocked down and shipped back to New York, where it disappeared into one of his already bulging warehouses.

His movie companies and publishing ventures brought him tens of millions of dollars, but it was never enough. Neylan had to keep juggling Hearst's vast mortgages—up to fifty million dollars a year in outgoing payments.

Daddy quickly became invaluable to Neylan in helping him unknot Hearst's tangled affairs. He worked very hard. He was always there when Neylan needed him, and he watched and learned while Neylan hired and fired Hearst personnel, negotiated newspaper contracts, and oversaw Hearst's five other papers on the West Coast, all while remaining publisher of the *Call*.

Soon Neylan was depending on my father more and more. He had a talent for mediating, for strategy, and he was always trusted by both sides of a case.

Soon Neylan and Daddy were trying cases together. He would even stand in for Neylan at San Simeon, Hearst's vast retreat near Big Sur, and he would occasionally stay on for one of Marion Davies's luncheons or parties.

He met Charlie Chaplin at San Simeon, as well as Charles Lindbergh and Winston Churchill. Once or twice Daddy even exchanged a few words with Hearst himself, whom he described as a "prehistoric shade of gray."

Eventually, Neylan began treating my father like the son he'd never had, his daughter, Jane Neylan, said. And they were related in a way. Neylan's wife was my father's second cousin.

Daddy would have supper frequently with Neylan in his suite at the Palace Hotel, and he and Mama spent many weekends at Neylan's estate in Woodside, a lavish place with a swimming pool and tennis courts. When we were small, my brother and I went there, too. Neylan was my godfather.

AT the time two of Daddy's closest friends were Peter Cusick, who went on to work for the OSS, and reporter Paul Smith, who would soon become, at the age of twenty-six, the wunderkind editor of the *San Francisco Chronicle*. Smith also had grandiose dreams of running for president of the United States. If he won, he promised he would appoint Daddy as his secretary of state.

The three friends would meet practically every evening for drinks, and back in 1934 they were beginning to speculate about what was going on down at the waterfront. There were rumors of an impending strike inspired by Communists. Paul was trying to get an interview with a ragged little Australian named Harry Bridges, who was threatening to lead the strike. Paul said Bridges hung out at an Irish bar on Jones Street and all he talked about was how there had to be a strike because the longshoremen had been exploited enough.

One evening my father and Peter Cusick wandered down to the docks. They wanted to see what Harry Bridges was so angry about.

"We ended up at the Embarcadero," Peter told me years later. "The Embarcadero was nicknamed the 'slave market' because hundreds and hundreds of men just milled around, hungry and despairing, waiting to be chosen for work. This was called the 'shape-up' system of hiring. It was corrupt, it encouraged violence, and it encouraged extortion. And it had been going on for years."

The Depression aggravated the problem, and the shipowners didn't help. They flooded the piers with cheap labor as well as with drifters who would work for free, and meanwhile the longshoremen, led by Harry Bridges, started to organize and protest for better wages and better working conditions, starting off with a real union hiring hall.

When the shipowners turned down the longshoremen's list of demands, the longshoremen struck on May 9 with a coast-to-coast walkout. Within days other maritime unions joined in. There were outbursts of violence as employers hired large numbers of strike-breakers to load cargo behind a shield of police.

By July 5, on a day that became known as Bloody Sunday, the Embarcadero became a "vast tangle of fighting men" as two thousand National Guard troops stormed the picket lines with sawed-off shotguns and vomit gas and six thousand strikers retaliated.

My parents watched the "battle of Rincon Hill," as it was called, from a friend's apartment in the marina.

"Barricades were erected," Mama wrote in her journal. "We heard rifles firing and then we saw mounted police advancing towards the hill. Paul Smith was with us and he had binoculars. 'Hey look, Bart!' he shouted. 'What the hell is that?' Somebody had rigged a huge slingshot composed of inner tubing and was using it to lob cobblestones into the lines of police. And then the police opened up with tear-gas grenades.

"We watched men overturning police cars and other men yelling 'Kill them! Kill them!' " Mama wrote, "and the police fired back with rifles and two men were killed and a couple of hundred strikers wounded."

The following morning there was a dramatic parade to protest the death of the two pickets.

Tens of thousands of workers moved in solemn procession up Market Street led by Harry Bridges. Behind him came the caskets on flatbed trucks. Thousands more, including my parents, lined the sidewalks and watched.

"Everything was halted," Mama wrote in her journal. "No streetcars, no traffic. Bart didn't even light a cigarette. We just held our breath. We knew it was a gigantic protest for justice. . . . Underneath San Francisco was in turmoil. We knew a general strike would be called. We'd heard 150,000 workers would join it."

On July 14, 114 unions went into session, and all voted to join the strike.

At this point Hearst ordered Neylan to organize a special committee made up of top Bay Area newspaper publishers. The committee would shape all future strike stories and "monitor" the news in such a way that the public would turn against the strikers. Hearst believed Harry Bridges was part of a "vast Communist conspiracy" aimed at blocking transportation up and down the Pacific coast.

My father assisted Neylan at that meeting and others, held in the Palace Hotel. He recalled that nobody asked if there was proof of a Communist plot or if Bridges was a member of the Party.

In subsequent days 130,000 more workers left their jobs all over northern California, and they remained off work for three and a half days. Meanwhile, the *Examiner* and the *Chronicle* ran hysterical features screaming, "Blood in the streets—city at war! San Francisco near starvation!" (In truth, Bridges made sure food trucks could move up and down the hills freely. He had told his men the strike would be lost if the city wasn't fed.) But Neylan's fiercely orchestrated newspaper campaign ignored that detail and threatened to drown the general strike in a sea of hostile false propaganda.

When the press tried to justify a series of terrorist raids in

East Bay union halls, Mama jumped into her car and drove around to see what was actually happening. She reported back to Daddy that the men and women who were arrested or beaten up were simply workers on relief. She found the Workers Center in Oakland "blood spattered from wall to wall."

"The whole thing is unconstitutional—reminds me of the Palmer Raids," my father scrawled in a notebook.

Every so often Paul Smith would appear at our house on Panoramic Way and have loud arguments with my parents. He couldn't get his interview with Harry Bridges published in the *Chronicle,* and he blamed Neylan and thought Daddy should quit his firm immediately. And Daddy would explain very quietly that even if he wanted to he couldn't—he had a family to support, and besides, he didn't believe in the general strike; it was tantamount to a revolution, it had resulted in mob violence, and he was dead set against that form of rebellion.

After weeks of chaos and terrorism all over the Bay Area, with produce rotting and stinking up Fisherman's Wharf, Neylan called another meeting with the publishers' committee and dock-worker employers and advised them that both sides must go into arbitration. This is ridiculous, he said in effect. You have to consider the workers' rights—the employers' grievances.

Neylan's intervention was one of many steps by many men, including Bridges, Roger Lapham, and the head of the Teamsters Union, who banded together to settle the strike.

All my father did was "act like a fly on the wall at Neylan's meetings," he told me. "I answered the phone. I served iced water to guys like Joe Knowland of the *Oakland Trib.*" Years later he told Joe Barnes he would never forget the game playing, or the manipulations by the press, or the way Harry Bridges masterfully consolidated union power.

In the end, Bridges got what he wanted: better pay, better working conditions, and a joint hiring hall with dispatchers elected by the men themselves.

His leadership in the strike "literally galvanized labor in America." It made him both hated and feared, especially in San Francisco.

When Daddy was chief counsel for Safeway stores, he finally

met Harry Bridges face-to-face in 1935. They confronted each other during strike negotiations between longshoremen and warehouse men.

"It was prickly because Harry was aware of my association with Hearst, so he was as cold as ice. Talked very fast. Boom! Boom! He knew exactly what he wanted—wouldn't budge, but then he warmed up when he found out that I'd rejected so-called 'damaging evidence' against him that he was Communist. Informers swore up and down he was a 'Red.' We studied the evidence and found it completely false," Daddy wrote.

Then they started running into each other at Paul Smith's dinner parties on Telegraph Hill after Paul became editor of the *Chronicle*.

"I got to know Harry very well," my father wrote in his report to the Justice Department in 1953 when his own loyalties were being questioned.

As for Harry, he told me, near the end of his life, "Yeah, your father and I were friends once. He used to stick his neck out for me all the time. For no reason he'd defend Harry Bridges. He was a goddamn puzzle, your father. He took the most idiotic risks for me. He was so reckless, and to what end? What did he get out of it? He damn near destroyed his career for me. Why? Do you know?"

I can still see Harry—arms like a spider—pacing around our living room in San Francisco wearing a threadbare coat. The strenuous pulling of the longshoreman's hook had left one hand resembling a claw. He smoked more cigarettes than Daddy. He was always irascible. Lean face. Hawk eyes. My brother and I used to giggle about his big nose.

When I was little, my parents must have talked a lot about Harry because I seem to have bits of his history imprinted in my brain. How Harry was shipwrecked twice and saved himself by floating ashore on his mandolin; how he was persecuted for his militant unionism; how for thirty years the United States government tried to deport him on charges that he was an alien and a Communist because his policies and politics often ran parallel to the "Party line."

There were four deportation trials. Two hearings before the

United States Supreme Court. There was even a motion made in 1939 introduced in the House of Representatives to impeach Frances Perkins, secretary of labor, for her failure to deport him.

Mama covered the trials and tried to write about the experience. "Ever sell that story, Cutsie?" Harry would tease.

My brother and I would often watch our parents and Harry Bridges go off to Trader Vic's for dinner. Trader Vic's was in Oakland; it featured Polynesian food and fake rain on the roof.

Once I asked my father what made Harry such an effective leader. "Because he doesn't care whether he's liked or not," he replied.

I always thought that what happened to Harry Bridges—his persecution by the United States government; the gross violation of his civil rights—radicalized my father. But what happened to Harry had nothing to do with the choices Daddy made or the mistakes he made either.

At the core of Daddy's being was his Catholicism, his search for redemption as he struggled to find a deeper, more dedicated purpose to his life.

For a while he volunteered for court-appointed cases in San Francisco, representing Chinese aliens and impoverished murderers. For a while he helped John Steinbeck and his wife raise money for migrant worker families—there were thousands of them all over northern California living in poverty and filth.

He was trying to be a good father, too. Mama was sick a lot when we were small, so it was Daddy who would often take us on outings. On a raw day in May 1937, he brought us to the opening of the Golden Gate Bridge. I'll never forget how in one great leap the orange span of bridge and its web of cables was outlined against the dark cliffs of Marin County.

Two hundred thousand people were attempting to walk back and forth across the bridge. We were buffeted by such gusts of wind, it was impossible; we only reached halfway. Daddy kept shouting at the top of his lungs, trying to point out Land's End, but we could barely see the battered stretch of rocks and cliffs on the south side of the Gate through the fog. The winds grew fiercer and fiercer. The bridge began swaying back and forth, and my brother began crying.

Usually when we returned home from outings such as this,

Daddy would hustle us upstairs to the nursery, but sometimes Mama would be "all right again," and we'd find her splashing around in a bubble bath. Behind her stretched a wall of glittering glass bricks.

As soon as he saw her, Daddy would take off his jacket and kneel down beside her and begin caressing her bare tanned back with a big, soapy sponge. The bathroom would grow steamier and more perfumed as my brother and I stood by the door watching while Daddy's shirt and tie got soaking wet and Mama seemed increasingly excited, and then she would start giggling and calling him "my lord and master" and he would address her as "my Venus on the half shell."

AFTER Daddy was appointed counsel for Safeway stores, he started to be away from home a lot, traveling around the state as he got more involved in labor law; meeting with the Teamsters and fruit farmers and milk drivers all at once, helping regulate prices and production.

Once, he helped settle a milk strike in Alameda; afterward he spoke to a couple of young strikers who were terrified that the police would beat them up for picketing. Daddy explained that they had a perfect right to assemble and speak freely; the Constitution protected them.

Daddy used to credit some of his interest in First Amendment issues to Alexander Meiklejohn, the controversial educator who recently had lost his job at the University of Wisconsin, where he had been conducting an academic commune (twenty students and six professors living together and studying the Age of Pericles for a year).

Alex lived above us on La Loma Avenue in Berkeley with his wife, Helen, and he used to drop by our house for coffee in the morning. I'd peek out of the nursery window and see him talking with Daddy in the garden. He had a high-pitched voice, which seemed totally at odds with his weighty concerns.

He and my father would study the philosophy behind the First Amendment and how it connected with the National Labor Relations Act protecting free speech, and the paradoxical concept of "freedom," which Alex didn't think people should have unless they were taught how to use it.

In January 1934, Alex opened the free experimental San Francisco School for Social Studies; it operated on a vacant floor of H. Liebes department store near Union Square. Daddy had already raised money for it and convinced men like Robert Sproul, then president of the University of California, to sit on its board.

The school was attempting to teach adults how to govern themselves; it catered to "the worker." Half the student body of three hundred were members of either the Ladies Garment Workers or the Bakery Drivers Union; the other half were college dropouts or rich Bay Area socialites, such as the willowy Barbara Sutro.

Alex used to say that you have to understand the law before you can understand or change society and that social change can come about only through education.

He was using Plato's *Republic* and the United States Constitution as a basis for discussion in his classes, as well as readings from Supreme Court decisions that another teacher, Myer Cohen, had translated into "accessible language." Occasionally my father would sit in on a class.

Everybody wanted to discuss what was going on in California because by 1935 the New Deal was already floundering. Some of the programs weren't working; some of the laws Roosevelt had instigated were being declared unconstitutional. Welfare payments were swollen, migrants were unable to get work picking fruit in the valleys; there was a terrible drought followed by monsoon rains. The dock strike had led to more labor violence throughout the Bay Area; unrest was blamed on the Communists.

Much of the school supported Upton Sinclair's End Poverty in California program. Novelist Sinclair, a Socialist turned Democrat, was running for governor of California, and Daddy was attracted to him because he had this crazy idea about land colonies (land farmed communally), and he was for the single tax (which would hurt the rich and help the poor). Daddy had to keep quiet, however, because Hearst was already mounting a blitzkrieg media campaign against Sinclair. Neylan received daily bulletins from the "Chief," even on the day that Hearst had lunch with Hitler.

So the students at Meiklejohn's school were frankly uneasy about my father. After all, he was a "Hearst lieutenant" and not to be trusted, especially since he sat on the school board.

Myer Cohen said that Alex wasn't threatened by my father's political ambiguities. "Bart Crum is here to learn like the rest of us," he told his students flatly. "He's all right—he's all right," and that was that.

In the end, Daddy worked after hours for Earl Warren's re-election as district attorney of Alameda County, and he drove all over the East Bay organizing volunteers for Warren. During the campaign he met almost everybody who would become politically powerful in California during the next decade: Edmund Brown, Clem Whittaker (probably the first "political consultant"), and, last but not least, Artie Samish, a fat man with a beguiling grin who was Sacramento's chief lobbyist and, according to his biographer Bob Thomas, "the secret boss of California."

Samish could push laws through or stop them cold. He kept a dossier on every assemblyman, congressman, mayor, and district attorney in the state, and he didn't hesitate to use the dossiers at election time. His clients ran the gamut from racetracks, labor, and trucking to cigarettes, but his principal lobby was the liquor industry. He was paid huge fees to protect the interests of those involved. In return he was given the use of forty thousand bars and liquor stores to promote political candidates.

His motto was "Select and elect": select politicians who would be friendly to his clients, and he would get them elected.

Samish took a particular liking to my father; they would hang out together at his San Francisco office in the Kohl Building, talking politics. (Ultimately, Daddy would become his lawyer when Samish was charged with evading $71,000 in income taxes. He got him off.) With Samish's help, Daddy raised $35,000 for Warren's campaign; that was big money in those days. By the time Warren won the election, my father was hooked on politics. He thought he had made a difference; he enjoyed being part of a team, and there was a sense of excitement and expectation about the politics of California.

Working in Neylan's office was starting to bore him in spite of the fact that through 1937 Neylan was literally saving the Hearst empire from total bankruptcy by all sorts of wheeler-dealer moves. My father was more interested in what was going on in the newly formed National Lawyers Guild, an association of progressive lawyers that was supporting the New Deal and fighting the more conservative American Bar Association, which was hostile to the welfare philosophy of the Roosevelt administration.

Daddy was invited to join the guild in late 1937 along with Abe Fortas, Thurgood Marshall, and Arthur Goldberg, and he immediately began working on guild committees to help extend New Deal welfare measures.

In Spain, General Franco's brutal insurrection against the liberal (and legally elected) government was to provide a focus for most progressive elements in America, both Communist and liberal. When Hitler and Mussolini supported Franco's efforts and America remained neutral on the subject, my father joined the American Committee to Save Refugees.

Through that committee, Daddy met John Dos Passos, who came to San Francisco to solicit funds for a documentary called *The Spanish Earth*, which Ernest Hemingway and Lillian Hellman were backing. Daddy helped them raise money. In the process he met Dorothy Parker, who had just been to Madrid, where she had seen churches burned and priests murdered. She and my father became friends as well as key figures in the Joint Anti-Fascist Refugee Committee in 1939, which helped exiled remnants of the defeated Loyalist forces; later the FBI would target JAFRC as a "dangerous Commie front."

Back in 1938, Daddy would speak at almost any antifascist fund-raiser in the Bay Area. He made speeches in Los Angeles, too. Sometimes he would take Mama, and afterward they might drop by Stanley Rose's bookshop off Hollywood Boulevard, a popular writers' hangout. Aldous Huxley was a regular, and so were Christopher Isherwood, Broadway playwright Robert Sherwood, S. J. Perelman, and novelist Nathanael West.

Mama met William Faulkner at the bookshop; he was getting loaded in the back room. She told him about her almost finished novel, based on a murder committed in a California ghost town. She was calling it *Strumpet Wind*. Faulkner said he liked the title and agreed to read the galleys, but then somebody interrupted them and asked if they would sign a petition and Mama said no and Faulkner wandered off; he never did read her book.

Mama never lent her name to anything. By 1938, Daddy was on the letterheads for Youth of Democracy, Citizens for Harry

Bridges, Oakland Rally for Free Spain, as well as the Scottsboro Boys Fund. The Scottsboro Boys were nine black youths framed for rape in 1931, tried quickly, and sentenced to death. For the next seven years, Communists worked feverishly on the case; it became—along with the Spanish Civil War—the cause célèbre among left-wing liberals.

John Neylan often accused my father of being "politically naïve"—particularly when it came to the Scottsboro case—and of being used by the Communists as an "unsuspecting liberal."

Daddy would always answer very politely that he didn't feel "used," that he knew Communists were involved; in fact, they were involved in most of the causes he felt passionate about. Unlike other political groups, Communists didn't just talk, they acted, organizing demonstrations for the unemployed and leading strikes for the California farm workers.

He had already worked on committees with guild lawyers who were members of the Party, but it didn't matter to him since together they were opposing Hitler's expansionism and trying to create a broad antifascist coalition.

Besides, nobody ever said they were members of the Party. There was this secrecy thing which Mama and he both thought was ridiculous since you could tell if somebody was a Communist just by listening to what he had to say.

In the meantime, my parents would throw dinner parties and mix Communists and liberals and even anti-Communists and nobody ever noticed. This was in 1938, just before the Hitler-Stalin Pact. The young activist lawyer Carey McWilliams, almost finished with his book on migrant workers, might drop by along with Roosevelt Democrats Melvyn Douglas and his wife, Helen Gahagan, and the journalist Edgar Snow, just back from China. Over coffee, Alex Meiklejohn (who was a Socialist) might wax eloquent on poet García Lorca's murder, and the guests would fall silent because what he was saying sounded like a sinister movie plot.

Afterward, there would be dancing in the garden and music would float up to the nursery and my brother and I would run to the window and peer down.

The patio was shadowy. Daddy had hung Chinese lanterns in the trees and they rocked back and forth, blinking like giant fireflies. So many couples jostling together near the rose beds. Our parents stood out, Daddy in a dark suit, Mama quite often in a flowing white gown and imitation emeralds. She and my father were such graceful, supple people and they really enjoyed dancing together. Every time I watched them, I believed they must be madly in love, as they bent and swayed, moving across the bricks. Occasionally they would trip on the bricks and then burst into laughter. They thought they were indestructible then, and so smart and beautiful and well connected that nothing could ever touch them.

In April, Mama's first novel, *Strumpet Wind,* was published by Covici Friede; it was the story of a mail-order bride who poisons her husband so she can run off with her sexy Mexican lover. It received good reviews, and Neylan got it serialized in the *Call Bulletin,* and it was briefly on the local best-seller lists along with *Snow White and the Seven Dwarfs* and Mann's *Magic Mountain.*

There was a great deal of publicity in the *Chronicle* and the *Examiner* about Gertrude Bosworth Crum (Mrs. Bartley Crum)— the dynamic little hostess/housewife/mother who also wrote. And Bette Davis telephoned Mama personally; she was considering optioning the novel, and Mama was elated because she said people often mistook *her* for Davis. She had the same big protruding eyes and haughty mouth, not to mention the same caustic manner.

As for my father, he had just been made a member of the exclusive Bohemian Club, and *Time* magazine had singled him out as being of great importance in the law firm of John Francis Neylan.

Neylan didn't like my father attracting so much attention; every time he spoke at a rally or won a case, there would be some kind of interview or pithy quote from him. "A good lawyer doesn't promote himself," Neylan said.

Still, he continued to throw plum cases my father's way. Throughout much of 1938, they worked together defending the powerful banker Herb Fleishhacker, who was alleged to have made a $348,000 profit out of loans from his Anglo Bank to a Portland shipyard deal for steel during World War I. At the same time, he was being accused of buying 150 acres of oil-rich land in Lost

Hills, California, from the Lazard family (of Lazard Frères and Co., now the most powerful mortgage house in Europe) in 1915 and paying them $33,000 when the land was actually worth $300,000. My father charged Lazard with malice and fraud for bringing the case to court eighteen years after the land's purchase.

The cases dragged on for months and threatened to expose Fleishhacker's alleged corruption, but he didn't seem worried. Instead, he finished building a zoo in Golden Gate Park and the largest indoor salt-water swimming pool in the world; he named both after himself. Fleishhacker was hugely rich (his bank was loaning great sums of money to Hearst); he owned sugar plantations, hydroelectric plants, hotels.

Daddy used to visit his office and find him playing dice with Artie Samish; what he couldn't forget, Daddy said, was that Herb's dice were made of solid gold.

He loved reminiscing about Herb. Herb worked sixteen hours a day; he could relax only by playing practical jokes. Years later, Daddy could always get a dinner party roaring with laughter by imitating Fleishhacker passing around exploding cigarettes to assorted financiers and then watching them light up and go crazy when the cigarettes went off in their faces.

What my father didn't mention was that he and Neylan lost the Fleishhacker cases, and the judge ruled that Herb must pay penalties to the tune of $651,579.61.

Nor was it ever mentioned that afterward, Neylan angrily accused him of withholding a crucial piece of evidence in the Lazard case, and although he immediately produced his own memo on the subject, which proved he had withheld nothing, Daddy was so angry at being accused of doing something he hadn't done, he resigned. This happened in May 1938, while Mama was promoting *Strumpet Wind* around the Bay Area.

There were various versions of what happened next. Jane Neylan says her father returned home looking stricken and announced that "Bart Crum would be happier at another firm—that he was more interested in politics than the law—he could take as long as he liked to clear out, but he had to go."

If my father was upset about the break, you couldn't tell by the enigmatic letter he wrote to John Neylan on May 13, 1938.

Dear Chief,

I've resolved a lot of things in my mind and distilled they come to about this:

(1) I'm going (to practice law) absolutely alone; not even an office boy. That means I'll do everything from running my own errands to filing papers, research and consultation with clients (if any). It also means that my overhead will be at a minimum until I'm damned certain I can afford more; and even then not until I physically can't do it all myself—the theory being that contraction is more difficult than expansion.

(2) I've shopped around for an office with a small room for a stenographer. The best I've found is in the Hunger Dulin Building adjoining Web Clarke's office. It's good because I'd have the use of his library. The rental would run to $110 for both rooms. This seems high, but landlords don't seem to know a recession is on.

I think you know what a wrench it is going to be not to be with you. Fourteen years ago this month, I appeared in your office . . . you had agreed to see me and Mrs. Neylan had put in a good word. I had a feeling even before I saw you that I would be with you a long time. It has been a great experience for me. Will you, as a favor, knock my plan to pieces if it doesn't seem sound? There is a great deal I don't know. I only know I want to start out on the right basis.

Regards—Bart

For the rest of her life, Mama would maintain that leaving Neylan's firm—resigning, being asked to leave, whatever it was— was the turning point in my father's career, that he was "never the same" after that.

Neylan had been his mentor, she said, a "powerful father figure." He kept searching for father figures, and he never found one again like John Neylan—a man who was protective, stern but caring, and who also pushed a great many clients his way.

But the letter my father wrote Neylan expressed none of those sentiments. Because he never discussed what he *felt*. He saw great virtue in leaving personal things unsaid.

CHAPTER

4

A s soon as he started practicing law on his own, we saw increasingly little of our father. He would leave the house very early and come back late from San Francisco, typically accompanied by some exotic friend, such as the FBI agent Melvin Purvis, currently the most famous man in America because he'd recently shot the notorious gangster John Dillinger to death, and before that he'd gunned down "Baby Face" Nelson and "Pretty Boy" Floyd.

In person, Purvis was mild mannered and tiny as a jockey. He might appear in the nursery bearing gifts like Junior G-Men badges for us. (He headed the "Melvin Purvis Junior G-Men Corps" part of a promotional campaign for "children who eat Post Toasties," sponsored by General Foods.) We'd pin the badges on our pajamas while Mama would be protesting that it was too late, we were supposed to be in bed. And then Daddy would tell her to calm down; he wanted Purvis to enjoy the view.

The view was spectacular. After the fire, the nursery had been remodeled and now there was a huge window carved out of the front room so we could look directly at San Francisco Bay.

At dusk the city's hills would be rimmed with gold; then, as the sun set, they would slowly disappear into the darkness—the shoreline seemed to vanish entirely—and then, as soon as the moon came up, San Francisco would burst forth again, all twinkle and glitter.

So we were quite content to remain up in the nursery, my brother and I playing with our toys and gazing out at the view.

Downstairs was the grown-up world—quite awesome to us—governed to some extent by Mama's temper tantrums. They were subject of much theorizing during our childhood because we never quite knew *why* she was so angry so often. It usually had something to do with her not being able to get what she wanted.

She already had a mink stole and a sable coat, but she wanted a leopard coat. She wouldn't stop complaining until Daddy presented her with one, and when he did, she paraded around the nursery in it, causing our nurse, Nell, to say very quietly, "You have too much, Mrs. Crum. You've been given too much."

Mama didn't argue with Nell, even though Nell was only twenty-one and we were her first charges. She had emigrated from Canada with her parents, who lived in Alameda. Nell was jolly and dignified and totally devoted to us. She couldn't have children. "You're my kiddies," she'd say.

We spent most of our time with Nell. We ate our meals with Nell in the nursery, played Sorry! with Nell when it rained, and took walks with Nell up in the hills behind the university and back on dusty roads where there were still goat farms tucked away behind tangles of poplar and madrona trees.

I remember we watched a baby goat being born. There was a great deal of blood and I felt nauseated and turned away. But my brother kept on looking.

Bart Junior was small and delicate with tawny skin and huge, questioning gray eyes. Shy in the complicated way exceedingly intelligent people are shy, he was also as quiet as a shadow. He seemed to prefer being alone, curled up with a book (he began reading very early) or with his telescope (he was fascinated by the stars). Later the piano became his main interest. Eventually, he would barricade himself within his eccentric mind while I lived out every reckless desire.

I always felt life's intensity in his presence. As a little boy he telegraphed enormous hurt.

Sometimes when we were alone in the nursery, I would throw a rubber ball at Bart, but he'd refuse to catch it, letting it bounce off him; then he would toddle away.

He didn't speak to anyone but me until he was six years old. He could have spoken; he just didn't want to. So between ourselves, we created a language of our own—a kind of pig Latin no one but us could understand. And we spoke it in front of our parents, which used to exasperate them because they didn't want to be left out of anything.

When Bart was four, Mama enrolled him in Erik Erikson's special nursery school at the California Institute of Child Welfare at Berkeley. Erikson, a Freudian who introduced the phrase "identity crisis" into the language and went on to become one of the most influential psychoanalysts in America, had just established a center on campus where so-called normal children could be studied long-term in experimental play situations.

Attending Erikson's school didn't open my brother up; he remained silent and wary.

Then, in the spring of 1939, Nell left us temporarily to have an operation. She was replaced by a beautiful young Eurasian girl named Jewel. Jewel had olive skin and a ripe body bulging and spilling out of her clothes.

Often in the evenings she would take off her shoes and run barefoot around the nursery, and we'd follow her. Sometimes she would let us play with her toes. "This little piggy went to the market. This little piggy stayed home. . . ." Then she would roughhouse with Bart on her bed—she'd pretend to wrestle with him, and he'd struggle in her arms.

Our parents would visit the nursery before we went to sleep. They were usually on their way to somewhere, Daddy in a tux, Mama rustling in taffeta or silk and smelling of delicious perfume.

I remember on one particular night Daddy handed me his top hat to play with. I began collapsing it over and over again like a silken pancake while Mama fussed over my brother, Bart, until Jewel playfully grabbed him away from her and began rolling around with him on the bed. It was almost as if she were showing off.

Mama watched for about a second before pulling my brother roughly back into her arms. He started to whimper; Jewel looked confused. Daddy reached out his hand, urging calm. "Cutes," he began, "let's talk about this."

Mama snapped, "There is nothing to talk about!" and she mentioned the words "abnormal behavior." Then she yanked open the closet, stuffed Jewel's meager belongings into a bag, and ordered her to get out, and before we knew it, the nurse was being hustled down the stairs. We didn't even have a chance to kiss her good-bye. It happened so fast I was still holding on to Daddy's top hat. He ran back to retrieve it and then he was gone.

Bart was desolate after Jewel left. The only person who seemed to cheer him up was Mel Purvis. By that time he'd left the FBI and he was practicing law in San Francisco. He would visit us on weekends, sleeping on our living-room couch while his new apartment in the city was being painted. He took Bart on piggyback rides in our garden and tickled him until he almost laughed.

One night Mel read us a chapter from his autobiography, *American Agent.* When he reached the section on capturing Dillinger outside the Biograph Theatre in Chicago, he admitted being very nervous, and he didn't *really* tell us how Dillinger was killed. When we asked him, he said vaguely that there were a lot of agents milling around there that day, and besides, there is no great honor in killing a man.

I always wondered if Bart remembered the detail I did—that in order to outwit the law, Dillinger dipped his fingers in acid so no one could trace his prints.

I kept wondering, but not for very long; mostly I lived in a dream world, gliding around the nursery on my stomach. I used a rug as a toboggan and I'd skim past my toys, my mind an utter blank.

Meanwhile, Bart retreated deeper into himself.

And then, two months after she had left, Jewel sent him a postcard announcing that she was married, and pregnant, and that she missed him very much.

Not long after he received her card Bart started having trouble going to the bathroom. He began retaining his bowel movements, first for a few days, then for a week, and Mama got worried and she would sit with him as he perched on his potty scowling and silent, and then another nurse was hired, a Miss Brot. Tall and horsey, she determined to take charge. She gave Bart an enema and he promptly retained that, too.

Doctors were called in, specialists; our pediatrician prescribed castor oil, then hot water and lemon juice. Daddy phoned Mo; she came down on the train from Sacramento and stayed in the nursery all afternoon. She decided there was some deep conflict inside my brother that he could not verbalize.

That's when Daddy invited Erik Erikson over for lunch.

Before he arrived we were told that he was a very important person and that he had worked with Margaret Mead at Harvard, so we must be especially polite. Erikson wanted to see Bart with our entire family; we were all going to have lunch with him.

It was the first time we had ever had a meal with grown-ups, and we became tense with excitement. I dressed in my frilliest party frock, Bart in a navy blue sailor suit. We sat together by the door in the front hall, waiting and waiting.

Erikson, a genial, stocky man with thick wavy hair, came bounding in with Daddy. He moved straight to my brother and stuck out his hand.

"Hello there, sir!" he cried. I could see Bart abandoning himself to the joy of allowing his pudgy little fist to be enveloped by Erikson's big, strong fingers. During lunch my parents carried on a stream of conversation with Erikson, who soon engaged my brother, encouraging him to speak about whatever was on his mind.

I don't remember how he accomplished this, but in no time at all this hitherto mute little boy began to speak—quite loudly and in a clear, precise voice.

"Aren't dreams wonderful?" he demanded in artificial grand tones, rather like Mama—it was something Mama might have said to him.

What followed was a description of a series of terrifying nightmares he'd had: of stinging bees, and of a longing for an elephant to live in our house. He was afraid of the stinging bees —they wanted to eat the sugar in his stomach—and he was worried that the elephant might burst if it came inside.

Later he brought Dr. Erikson to our nursery and showed him some of his favorite books, among them the one with the picture he liked best—a drawing of a gingerbread man floating in open water toward the mouth of a wolf.

"The wolf is going to eat the gingerbread man, but it won't hurt the gingerbread man because," my brother said loudly, "he's not alive, and the food can't feel it when you eat it."

Erikson later wrote of these revelations that he "thoroughly agreed with him," reflecting that "the boy's playful sayings converged with the idea that whatever he accumulated in his stomach was still alive and in danger of bursting."

Erikson asked Bart to show him the pictures he liked best in other books. Bart immediately brought him *The Little Engine That Could,* and he turned to the picture of "a smoke puffing train going into a tunnel while on the next page it came out of the tunnel not smoking."

"You see," Bart said, "the train went into the tunnel and in the dark tunnel it went dead."

Erikson was now sure my brother had a fantasy that he was filled with something very precious and very alive; if he kept it in, it would burst, but if he released it then it might come out hurt or dead. In other words, he was pregnant.

My little brother thought he was having a baby.

At the end of their talk, Erikson encouraged him to draw his favorite animal—an elephant. And then he asked where he thought elephant babies came from.

My brother replied "tensely" that he didn't know. So Erikson rapidly sketched the drawing of a lady elephant and diagrammed her anatomy, making it very clear that there were two exits, one for bowels and one for babies.

Some children do not know this, he said. They think bowel movements and babies come out of the same opening—in animals and in women. Before he could continue, Bart very excitedly told him that while Mama was pregnant with him she'd had to wear a belt to keep him from falling out of her when she sat on the toilet. He had proved too big for her opening, so he'd been born by cesarean section.

Erikson went on to explain that while it was not possible for him to have babies, it was important for him to understand the reason for his fantasy.

He would come back tomorrow for another conversation.

As soon as Erikson left, my brother ran to the bathroom and had, according to Mama, a "superhuman bowel movement."

WHAT had caused my brother this emotional conflict? To retain both the content of his bowels and to have a pregnancy fantasy?

Erikson told my parents that after imagining Jewel pregnant, Bart had tried to hold on to her by *becoming* her. Once he thought he had a baby in him, he remembered what Mama had said—the dangers about birth and pregnancy—and he could not let go for fear of "killing the baby" inside him.

Years afterward I finally asked my brother why he had talked so volubly to Erikson when he was usually so silent with all of us.

"That guy asked me interesting questions. Nobody else did."

During the next weeks Dr. Erikson returned to our house several times to counsel both my brother and our parents. He explained that by letting Jewel go, they had inhibited Bart's natural male sexual responses and he had become enraged.

My parents accepted that, Mama in particular; both she and my father treated my brother very gently and with great compassion. Even so, he suffered a relapse and developed an enlarged colon.

By then Brot had been fired and Nell, recovered from her operation, was called back into service. When Bart was rushed to Peralta Hospital in Oakland, Nell went with him, and she moved a cot into his room and never left his side.

My parents visited every day. I wasn't allowed to, which upset me so much I'd retreat into our garden and have lengthy conversations with imaginary companions until the sun went down. Then our new cook, Toy, just arrived from China, would take me into the kitchen and teach me how to eat fried rice with chopsticks. He spoke no English yet so we just stared at each other. He was very thin and wore black silk pajamas.

Finally Mama and Daddy would return from the hospital and make a great fuss over me, kissing and hugging me and assuring me that my brother would be all right, and then they would disappear and go on with their lives.

I'm sure they cared about what was happening to Bart; they just couldn't show it. They held back. They held back out of a curious sense of reticence. And it wasn't as if they didn't love him; they loved him terribly. They loved us both terribly, even passionately, and of course we loved them, but family intimacy had to be avoided.

Their way of showing affection was through worrying. They were terrific worriers. They worried about our "happiness"; they worried about our "health"; they worried about our "successes" in school and in friendships; they worried about whether or not we were "polite" enough or "considerate" enough of other people.

Their concern made us anxious.

Eventually, Bart and I picked up their habit of worrying.

And I developed another habit. Whenever a crisis arose, I could feel an invisible wall slide down in front of me, pressing against my stomach muscles, digging a frown between my brows.

"You were born frowning," Mama said.

CHAPTER

5

AFTER Bart's "troubles," he and my father would go on long walks together around Berkeley, ending up at the Greek Theater near the stadium, or they'd drive to Oakland and stop at Lake Merritt to feed the swans. "But we never said a word to each other," Daddy told me years later. "Not one word." They were both such private souls—father and son—they found it almost impossible to connect.

Daddy possessed that charming façade he had built up to mask his proud reserve; Bart had nothing to hide behind except his remoteness. "Sometimes he reminds me of a little old man," Mama said.

I accepted my brother for the silent gentle presence he was; I kept assuring myself he was fine. I didn't question his sadness either.

For a while in the evenings when he was home, Daddy would climb the stairs to the nursery and read to us from some of his favorite books—*Alice's Adventures in Wonderland* and *Grimms' Fairy Tales*.

One story captured my brother's fancy. It was the tale of mythical Icarus, who didn't know his own limits; who flew so close to the sun that the heat melted the wax that bound his wings and he plunged to his death into the sea.

Icarus, who soared beyond safety—my brother loved that scary image. When we were alone together in the nursery, he would stretch out his little arms and flap them and then run around and around the nursery until he got dizzy, and sometimes he fell down. In early 1940, I think it was, he began building a huge pair of paper wings. "To fly away on," he would murmur. "To fly out the window and into the clouds."

My parents didn't discourage my brother in his fantasy. Since the "bathroom incident," as it was referred to, they were often almost self-consciously indulgent toward him. He said they were "insincere."

"I am not wanted," he informed me. "I am an unwanted child."

I know this wasn't true. Mama had confided in me that she had planned on four children, and that she was devastated when after Bart was born her doctor told her that it would be too dangerous for her to have more babies.

She said she had longed for a "big warm family" to make up for her own "dismal" little one ("no mother—a hypocritical father and brother who never stopped belittling me").

She used to tell me she was jealous of my closeness with Bart; it was something she had never experienced with her own brother Carl, a gruff, handsome former rancher who now sold real estate in Watsonville. He and his wife, Libby, who chain-smoked Camels, would drive to Berkeley at least once a month and have boisterous Sunday lunches with my parents. I never saw any friction between Mama and her brother then.

Carl and Libby invariably brought their daughter along. Elena, my cousin—blond, freckled, pudgy—was exactly my age, and while we were growing up we were as close as sisters.

While the adults were laughing and talking and drinking great quantities of wine in the dining room, Elena would join my brother and me in the nursery and we would play together very contentedly all afternoon.

Sometimes near dusk both sets of parents would visit us. Often tipsy, they would weave into the nursery and watch as Elena and I tried to help Bart construct his paper wings. They would talk about us as if we weren't there.

"How cunning!" Aunt Libby would chortle, and Mama would agree, "Yes, they *are* adorable."

We felt embarrassed.

Mama made me promise I would come to her immediately if

I thought "the wings business" was getting out of hand. So far it hadn't; I secretly hoped my brother would never finish building those wings—I had a funny premonition that he *would* fly too close to the sun.

I used to watch him, seated on the floor of the nursery with his rolls of white shelving paper, measuring tape, nails, pieces of silk and bits of wood and string and pots of glue. He had to be working from some scheme (although he had no diagram, no blueprint) because miraculously the wings took shape. "What will you do once you finish?" I'd ask.

"Fly to China," he would answer. "Fly to Timbuktu."

Nell was worried, too; she and I watched as the wings spread out like some gigantic monstrous butterfly, half covering the nursery floor.

After they were all assembled, Bart tried to attach one wing to his shoulder and arm with Nell and I helping him, but the wing was so cumbersome, he toppled to the floor and lay there very quietly, staring up at the ceiling.

He realized at once that they were too big, so in the next hour he tore them up and started all over again, very systematically. He was so small and silent and slight, it took him close to five months to rebuild the wings to proper size.

By then it was July 1940, and my father was about to write speeches for Wendell Willkie's presidential campaign. That's all we heard that summer: Wendell Willkie! Wendell Willkie! Wendell Willkie! Willkie, a big shambling lawyer from Indiana who had no political organization and had never run for office, had just been nominated by the Republican Party in one of the greatest upsets in political history.

At the convention in Philadelphia, Willkie had defeated Harold Stassen, Thomas Dewey, and Robert Taft on the sixth ballot, and without even a floor manager to help. "Just the force of his galvanizing personality," my father recalled. "Wendell came across to the public like a bolt of lightning."

It's hard to explain the Willkie miracle except in terms of a vacuum of leadership and the urgency of the time. "He was an old-fashioned, hell-raising, hard-wrangling liberal," Marcia Davenport said. He possessed intellect, warmth, and humor, and was overflowing with ideas. "And he could charm the birds off a tree."

Clearly the time was ripe for a new voice, one that sounded fresh and honest, and Willkie's peculiar talent combined idealism with realism. He had gone from practicing law to becoming president of a billion-dollar utility corporation—Commonwealth Southern; he differed fiercely with the New Deal's handling of the Tennessee Valley Authority; among his advocates he was known as a "super-salesman for business in its fight against government interference."

As a presidential candidate, he would fight the New Deal for pitting class against class, but he would also fight the Republican Party for its isolationism. A lot was happening in the world; a week after the Hitler-Stalin nonaggression pact was signed, the Nazis invaded Poland; England and France declared war on Germany; then the Soviets invaded Poland. Willkie began warning that Hitler intended to take over all of Europe. It was a time of confusion and dismay, with Roosevelt insisting on remaining neutral.

Years afterward, Gardner Cowles would say, "Adolf Hitler nominated Willkie. With the fall of France and the Low Countries, American public opinion shifted overnight—and that was responsible for Willkie's nomination . . ." The convention had gathered at "one of the most stupefying moments in the history of Western civilization," Henry Luce said.

In the midst of this, Daddy was asked by editor Ralph Ingersoll to join a group of Willkie aides. Ingersoll had suggested Daddy because Daddy knew everybody in California politics from Earl Warren to Artie Samish, lobbyist supreme. Daddy would be invaluable since Willkie's supporters were largely from the East—Henry Cabot Lodge; the Cowles brothers, who ran *Look* magazine; *Fortune* editor Russell Davenport, who had promoted Willkie to dazzling effect in the media. It was Davenport's idea to portray Willkie as a real life version of *Mr. Smith Goes to Washington*—the angry liberal fighting the corrupt politicians of both parties.

He and my father, along with economist Elliott Bell and congressman Charlie Halleck from Indiana, would become personal advisers to Willkie, joined of course by a few hard-eyed professionals. They would write speeches, they would plan campaign strategy; for a brief period they existed in a state of "happy chaos."

"Bart says he *must* work for Willkie," Mama wrote in her journal in late June 1940.

> He promises to be back in San Francisco every fortnight to see me and the children. He is terribly excited about serving this visionary. I told him I was worried about his need to serve someone instead of making money! And his need to have another "hero" in his life (John Neylan and Harry Bridges being the other ones).
>
> And then I said "and perhaps in the process you'll become a hero yourself?" He roared with laughter when I characterized his ambitions as heroic. "Tell that to my father confessor."
>
> The only thing I know about Willkie is that, although he is very much married, he is also Irita Van Doren's lover. Bart professes to know nothing about this aspect of Willkie's life . . . but what I wanted to make clear, and we stayed up 'til 4 A.M. arguing about it; if he leaves San Francisco for most of the summer what will happen to his clients? And how will he pay our bills?
>
> To which he replied with typical blarney, "Oh Cutsie, I'll take care of my clients and I always pay our bills eventually."

Mama didn't add that they were mostly her bills. She was becoming an obsessive shopper; there was too much of everything in our Berkeley house (and in all our subsequent homes). The kitchen was overstocked to bursting; the bathroom cabinets bulged with creams, perfumed bath oils, imported soaps, stacks of soft monogrammed towels. "What is this, a department store?" my father would explode from time to time.

For some reason, however, he didn't curb Mama's extravagance; he never questioned the contents of her vast closets—they took up an entire wall of her bedroom. I was still small enough to hide there, and it became a favorite pastime of mine to creep inside and fall against a mink coat or wrap myself in the folds of her sable cape. Then I would breathe in the perfumed darkness . . . oh, those afternoons long ago, when I'd rub my cheek against the velvet nub of some new evening gown or scratch my nail across a taffeta bow.

In contrast, Daddy's possessions were meager—a few thread-bare suits, ties, and tux; one slightly battered homburg—yet to me he always appeared supremely elegant.

He seemed to take pride in rejecting "worldly goods" for himself, but he appreciated beauty as much as Mama and he loved buying lovely things for her, like the exquisite old chess table that moved with us from house to house, the gorgeously patterned Persian rug, the silver candelabra, the inlaid trays. He draped a diamond bracelet across the keys of a baby grand piano for her fortieth birthday. She returned the bracelet the following day "because you know damn well we can't afford it," but she kept the piano.

Throughout their marriage he would shower her with imprac-tical gifts, the exception being the summer of 1940, when all he sent her were a few postcards from places like Amarillo, Texas. He was completely caught up in the exuberance and the confusion of the campaign.

"The Willkies in a daze," he scribbled in a note datelined Broadmore Hotel, Colorado Springs, Colorado.

> They plan to stay here five weeks to rest up for the rest of the campaign—Luce thinks too long. Mailbags piled up in their hotel suite. Only one secretary; they need at least three; Paul Smith had been called in to pull things together . . . Everybody complaining about lack of organization . . . Unan-swered open telegrams . . . Answered phones . . . Oren Root says Willkie tackles problems like a trial lawyer, approaching a jury in a circular manner. Goes around and around an issue, trying one thing and then another until he discovers what works. . . . Willkie tells me that when he was nominated at the Convention, all that disorganization of his was to his advantage. "Nobody could accuse me of making any deals," he says. He is contemptuous of professional politicians. Al-most nobody else says what he thinks but Willkie does time and again. He speaks very frankly with the press. It doesn't occur to him that speaking out may hurt his chances at getting elected. He has yet to delegate authority. Russ Davenport thought he was going to be the final arbiter in the campaign, but now he and Charlie Halleck will split the honor. As for my role, I'm expected to be called on to perform a certain

number of functions . . . I'll do what I have to with, I hope,
good grace.

Daddy's role in the campaign was later described by Max
Rabb as "West Coast strategist and networker." Rabb, then a college student, later a millionaire owner of supermarkets, was a gofer
for Willkie. He remembers "Bart Crum as a charmer. . . . What a
comer he was. He created his job really, and in the process per-
fected his own formula for political organization . . . he knew all
the power brokers in California so he networked there . . . he introduced Willkie to men like financier Charlie Blyth and Roger
Lapham (who went on to be mayor of San Francisco)."

Eventually, my father enlisted dozens of young liberal Republicans all over the Bay Area as Willkie volunteers. He got Mama
to mobilize the women voters in Oakland and Piedmont (with
my brother and me handing out Willkie buttons). He organized
telephone canvassing in places like Walnut Creek. And he fired up
the press—feeding intriguing items to publisher Clarence Lindner of the *Examiner* and Herb Caen, who now had a column in the
San Francisco Chronicle.

"Bart Crum helped mobilize the West Coast—we mobilized
the East," said Oren Root, who'd had the brainstorm of creating
hundreds of Willkie for President clubs early in 1940. These clubs
contributed to the groundswell of support that nearly got Willkie
elected.

In July Daddy flew to Los Angeles and, along with movie
producer Walter Wanger, organized a ticker-tape parade complete
with klieg lights cutting through the night sky and seventy thousand people shouting "We want Willkie!"

By August the Germans were blitzing London, while in retaliation the RAF was bombing hundreds of German cities and towns.
Daddy helped Henry Luce write one of Willkie's best speeches on
foreign policy, which the candidate wanted to deliver to a huge
crowd in San Francisco.

Meanwhile, up in the nursery in Berkeley, my brother and I
were being tutored in French by a squat mademoiselle whom we
came to hate for her grand manner. I directed so many spiteful
taunts at her that she finally spluttered, *"Merde alors,"* and upped
and quit. We were also taking piano lessons from Miss Roa, whom

Daddy nicknamed "the stork," gleefully comparing her legs to toothpicks. She came by the house on Wednesday afternoons and had us play scales on the grand piano in the living room.

Bart learned to read music very quickly and was soon playing quite well—little Grieg pieces, some Schubert, some Mozart. He loved music. He also loved to listen to it on our Victrola, and would sometimes pretend to conduct the Beethoven symphonies we heard rolling from the disks. By the time he reached his teens he was a good musician. (I, unfortunately, mastered only one piece —"Für Elise.")

When we weren't being tutored in music or French, Mama was "polishing" us. "Your mother treats you both like inanimate objects, not human beings," a classmate of mine once commented after spending the weekend at our house.

First she would wash our hair with Conti's Castile soap until it was "squeaky clean"; then she would clip our toenails and file our fingernails and swab out our ears with Q-Tips until we begged her to stop. (Later a doctor told her she mustn't clean our ears so much, because she'd removed all that was good along with all that was bad.) And then she would rub a greasy unguent on our eyelashes, "so they'll grow longer and thicker," and then we would lie naked under a sun lamp. This was in the days before anyone knew that too much sun on the skin can cause cancer.

Mama would lie under the sun lamp, too—oiled and glistening. She had a round, firm little body, muscled from playing tennis and golf, and there was not one blemish on her skin—no freckles, as there were on mine.

She would remain under the lamp each day until she had turned a lovely shade of "café au lait." Her tawny complexion, along with her upswept honey-blond hair and bright red lipstick (she carried lipstick and a compact from one room to the other), gave her an exotic appearance.

She looked particularly glamorous the day she left us to join Daddy on the Willkie campaign. She was wearing a form-fitting purple wool suit decorated with a sunburst diamond clip; a purple hat shaped like a pancake was tilted over one eye. Doused with Joy perfume, she radiated sexual energy. Bart couldn't take his eyes off her. After she left the nursery he murmured in our secret language, "Mama is beautiful."

■

MY parents arrived in Elwood, Indiana, in time to see Willkie moving down the street in an open convertible as thousands cheered and swarmed all over the car—reaching out to touch him, to shake his hand. Two hundred fifty bands played, hundreds of American flags flapped and waved in the sweltering heat. It was supposedly the biggest political rally in history.

"Total carnival atmosphere," Mama noted in her journal.

> Townsfolk hawking wares: Willkie mugs, Willkie ties, Willkie pillowcases. . . . It was so hot (over 102 degrees in shade). I look a wreck. My silk dress from Magnin's plastered to my girdle. I feel sticky and old suddenly. I have turned forty, but Bart still addresses me as his child bride. If only he would call me his woman just once. . . . I didn't want to make an appearance today, but Bart insisted. . . . Willkie almost fainted from the heat, from the excitement and pressures . . . he misplaced his speech! Lost it . . . didn't know where in the dickens it was . . . turned out he'd left it in another town and a police motorcade had to zoom off and retrieve it.
>
> Before he spoke he removed a wad of chewing gum from his mouth. Disgusting! But the crowds loved it. Two hundred thousand people stood under the glare, with the sun beating down on them unmercifully. Willkie challenged FDR to debate him on key issues such as the war in Europe and the economy. He ended with what would be his campaign slogan "only the strong can be free—the productive can be strong." The speech fell flat. Too much expectation beforehand . . . Charlie Halleck agreed with me. He does feel that Willkie is such a curiosity to most people they'll want to see him even if they're unconvinced he can be president. The theory is that if he can be seen and heard by enough Americans he can get elected . . .

"Wendell has terrific crowd appeal," my father maintained to us. "He is absolutely magnetic."

It was different when you heard him on the radio. My brother and I used to sit in the living room listening to Willkie, his raucous voice an audible expression of the urgency and passion he was pouring into his crusade. Willkie himself called it a crusade, and as the contradictions of his position multiplied, his passionate intensity grew.

"Willkie is the underdog. Everybody is in awe of his stamina," Daddy would tell us. "Willkie sounds like a sideshow barker," our grandmother Julie declared. She was taking care of us while our parents campaigned, and she was secretly for Roosevelt. We weren't aware, of course, that FDR never mentioned Willkie's name in public during the campaign and refused to debate him on any issue.

And speaking of Roosevelt, my brother and I fell in love with his mellifluous, soothing tones. He was a masterful speaker, never talking down to his audience; empathizing, never patronizing.

How we loved to listen to our radio, with its messages and fantasy. There were, of course, no images to go along with the voices, so our big wooden console held a special power: it brought us not only Hitler's screams of rage but Jack Benny and Fred Allen cracking jokes, not to mention the suitcases and boxes that tumbled weekly out of Fibber McGee and Molly's closet.

Sometime that summer we listened to Daddy on radio, too; whenever he came back to California he would give a rousing speech for Willkie on station KYA in San Francisco (it was a station he later bought). He would speak dramatically about the enlightened leadership that Willkie was going to give the nation after he was elected; Daddy's voice always sounded boyish and eager; he spoke rapidly, with a harsh western twang, words tumbling over themselves.

MAMA joined the Willkie Special in October, as the campaign entered its final phase. The dark green twelve-car train would meander around the country over rusty freight spurs that had never before carried passenger cars; through the Midwest and mountain states, to the West Coast and back again. It would travel nineteen thousand miles in fifty-one days. It was estimated that Willkie averaged between twelve and fifteen speeches a day. Then there were the scheduled stops that called for a motorcade or a major address—all this in an attempt to convince a public weary and wary of politics that he was the right man to lead them.

Mama's original plan had been to write an article about the

train for the *San Francisco Examiner,* but to her journal she confided, "I don't know whether I can now. Because I cannot tell the truth about what is going on." (Ultimately she did publish a rather insightful piece that Willkie praised.)

The train is in a shambles. Complete confusion. Schedule foul-ups. No coordination. Everybody short-tempered and exhausted. Marcia Davenport, the novelist, says it's the amateurs vs. the professionals. There are vicious struggles between the Old Guard (Joe Martin) who secretly thinks of Willkie as an interloper and an outsider and really wants to destroy him! Most of Willkie's aides have never been in a political campaign before and they act it. Apparently, Russell is the worst offender. He's disorganized and arrogant. But since he is responsible for Willkie being nominated, Willkie is utterly loyal to him . . . besides, Willkie still tries to do everything he can himself; he hates to be beholden to anybody.

We are all jammed into the "squirrel cage"—that's where the reporters are—some fifty odd—and the dictating machines—and the typists. There are also two detectives as well as a doctor, Harold Grey Barnard, who is supposedly here to soothe Willkie's throat. He has given so many speeches in the past three months he can barely croak. He is a non-stop talker; talk, talk, talking all the time. He refuses to use the P.A. system that has been put on the train; it is madness here.

Bart is in his element. Drinking and carrying on with the boys. He writes and rewrites speeches along with Cabot Lodge. Bart is considered the American history expert. He can reel off quotes from Abe Lincoln or Bob La Follette . . . he will rewrite drafts and drafts (always in longhand on the yellow legal pads he loves) and then Ray Morley and Russell rewrite them . . . totally. Willkie often doesn't get a speech until minutes before he's supposed to give it. Often as not he throws the speech away and ad libs and often contradicts the position he's taken earlier. Still he attracts audiences. Thirty thousand in Tulsa apparently and fifteen thousand in Albuquerque and so on. . . . Jim Hagerty's assessment: Willkie scatters his fire—gives too much away. Bart's impression of

Wendell: The Old Guard pros are not allowing him to be his own man—allowing him to swing along in that irresistible free wheeling style that originally won him the nomination. Marcia says Willkie's style often threatens Republicans and panics Democrats. I think he's divine—especially to women. Something about that huge energy of his . . . something about his ideas; his convictions. He shouts himself hoarse about the events in Europe and Roosevelt's silence: he says FDR simply won't discuss the issues that are troubling people; Hitler for one.

A dialogue with the candidate as he moves from car to car . . .

"Cutsie . . . Cutsie? What kinda name is that?"

"It's my nickname, Mr. Willkie."

"You don't look like a Cutsie to me." (Voice hoarse with fatigue—eyes stare me down. I find my neck, my face burning . . . my heart pounds. Does he hear???)

"Do I look like a Gertrude?" I stammer to the man who may be the next president of the United States. "It is my given name."

"You look like a Maura," he answers . . . "you look like a Maura . . ." And with that he is gone, surrounded by aides. Speaking of aides, only Charlie Halleck and Russell have direct access to "the Boss" as he's called. Everybody else gripes about this but Bart doesn't seem to mind.

Indeed, after the election my father wrote Willkie, "One of the things I resented about the train was the apparent belief by a lot of the guys that they always gave you a treat when you saw their bright shining faces. It was my conviction that you could get along very nicely without staring down my Irish mug . . . and I would be called upon when needed."

He was increasingly called upon to arrange meetings with Willkie and various disparate voting groups. He loved setting things up, putting people together, and then fading into the background ("Bart had a lot of ideas, but he lacked the skill at infighting necessary to translate a lot of his ideas into action," Peter Cusick remembered).

Still he was often successful in his attempts to build ties with a bloc of voters alienated from the political system (the liberal

Republicans, the anti-Roosevelt extremists, the fringe groups, the independents who hadn't voted since 1933).

"Bart could speak with all these types and get some of them excited about Willkie," Cusick went on.

He believed Willkie was enough of an original to appeal to all these eccentric minorities. And not only that, my father believed—with Willkie—that the independent voter was one whose political function had been atrophied by the same pressure that made him an independent.

Once he got Harry Bridges together with Willkie for a meeting at the Palace Hotel in San Francisco.

"He is not my boy," Bridges told my father afterward, but the volatile labor leader also refused to endorse Roosevelt. "He has betrayed the rank and file," he growled. So he wouldn't support either candidate.

NOT long after that, Willkie made an unscheduled stop at our house in Berkeley. It was dusk, and our Chinese cook, Toy, kept the press outside in the garden while Willkie met with Alex Meiklejohn in our living room to discuss some pressing civil rights legislation. I remember how physically huge Willkie seemed— gigantic, rumpled, stained. His brown suit was wrinkled; his thick black hair lay long and curling on his neck. Nobody bothered to turn on any lights; only one lamp burned by the window, so that Willkie's shadow loomed across one wall as he spoke to Meiklejohn. His shadow moved with him as he reached for the telephone to receive a call from his mistress, Irita Van Doren, in New York.

Meanwhile, my father and other Willkie aides milled about, talking softly and urgently among themselves. I was relegated to passing salted almonds on a silver tray while Mama mixed drinks.

Midway through the excitement, Daddy had to be called away to the nursery. My brother had, after many months, finished the construction of those paper wings. He was threatening to jump out the window with them and fly away.

I remember Daddy running up the stairs (did he ever walk?), and then he knelt down beside Bart, who was on the floor struggling to attach one wing to his little arm.

Daddy praised the construction of the wings and how beautiful they were and how Leonardo da Vinci couldn't have done any better. And then he added—very quietly and intensely—that while the idea Bart had to fly into the clouds was wondrous and courageous, he really shouldn't do it right now because it was pitch dark out, not even a moon, and Bart wasn't a bat, so perhaps he should wait—wait until daybreak at least. When it was light, they could talk again.

The next morning came and Daddy returned to the nursery as he promised. He had brought along an engineer he knew, who explained—as an expert—just why it wouldn't be possible for him to fly properly with those wings, that it wasn't safe. Bart had supreme common sense; he was as logical as he was fanciful. When it was explained to him in a sensible manner how it would not be technically feasible for him to stay aloft in the air on those wings, he abandoned the idea at once.

All he said afterward was, "I wish you'd explained this to me in the first place. I wasted so much time."

WHEN he got back on board the Willkie train, Daddy took to phoning Bart whenever he could. But first he would ask for me. Our conversation was always the same and it made me feel uncomfortable.

"Hello, my darling!" he'd exclaim. "You're looking very beautiful."

I'd counter with, "Oh, Daddy, you can't see me. How can you say that?"

And he would laugh. "Oh, I *know* you're beautiful, sweetheart."

Then he'd ask me to "please put that son of mine on the phone," and I would hand my brother the receiver and he would listen very solemnly while Daddy spoke to him.

Their conversations were brief:

"Yes," Bart Junior would say. "Yes, Daddy. Okay. Okay. Yes. Okay." And then he'd hang up the receiver and go trotting back to the nursery.

I would run after him. "What did he say? What did he say?" I always wanted to know.

"He told me to take care of Mama until he gets back. I said I would, but frankly it's much too big a responsibility."

OF course, my brother and I had no idea of the strain Daddy was under. In city after city he watched Willkie facing open hostility whenever he spoke; particularly in blue-collar areas, he was pelted with eggs, tomatoes, a cantaloupe, once even a bedspread. The *Times* kept a scoreboard of hits and misses.

By October, France had fallen and the Battle of Britain raged; fear of war became a major concern of most voters. Both candidates were buffeted back and forth by the tide of events. Each man felt obliged to alter earlier positions as public opinion shifted wildly over the volatile situation in Europe.

Joe Martin, chairman of the Republican Party, kept badgering Willkie to stop his "bi-partisan nonsense" and attack Roosevelt as a "war monger." And Willkie, desperate to win, altered and revised what he had been saying all these months; he started sacrificing his identity and sense of purpose, to the point where many of his strongest supporters, such as newspaper columnists Walter Lippmann and Dorothy Thompson, moved away from him.

He began making statements he would later regret, culminating in the following incident, which Paul Smith and my father witnessed together. Willkie was being pressured by Colonel Robert McCormick, the powerful publisher of the *Chicago Tribune*, to end his speeches with the phrase "If you elect me President, I will not send your boys to war." McCormick had boarded the train somewhere in the Midwest and remained closeted with Willkie for hours in his private compartment, drumming the phrase into his head. Willkie was tired and depressed. Finally, he called Daddy and Paul in to ask their opinion. Should he make this kind of statement or shouldn't he?

They both advised against it, saying that he would go against everything he had stood for in the campaign. Willkie agreed, but McCormick kept at him relentlessly until he got off at the next whistle stop.

Willkie drooped with fatigue; he had given six speeches already that day. "He was punch-drunk from exhaustion," Daddy recalled; he remembered watching him stagger to the platform at the back of the train to say a few words to the small crowd who awaited him.

Daddy told me that he and Paul Smith half-listened to the speech from the squirrel cage. The PA system was on and they could hear Willkie, with his Indiana twang, delivering the usual comments about the desirability of peace in the world, and then suddenly the phrase "If you elect me President, I promise I will not send your sons to war" rang out.

As soon as the speech was over and the train had lurched to a start, Paul ran into Willkie's compartment in time to see his butler serving him a drink. Willkie sat slumped in a chair, dazed with fatigue.

"What made you decide to say it?" he cried.

"Say what?" Willkie mumbled.

"You used McCormick's slogan."

Willkie seemed stunned; his eyes filled with tears. "Oh, no. I couldn't have. If I did—couldn't I retract it?"

My father, meanwhile, was checking with all the reporters to see what they were doing, and they were all typing away madly. He and Paul realized they couldn't convince the press that the Republican candidate for president was overtired and had said something unintentionally. Of course it was picked up by the press all across the country. Later Roosevelt used the phrase in *his* speeches. "We are both such goddamn hypocrites," Willkie said bitterly. "Now I know he's gonna win."

The final tally on election day: 27,247,160 votes for Roosevelt; 22,360,000 for Willkie.

Ultimately, Willkie would be thought of as a "me too" candidate, as someone who did not want to get rid of the New Deal as much as finely tune it. (The two candidates were actually too much alike philosophically, FDR speechwriter Robert Sherwood told my father years later.)

Times reporter Turner Catledge had another opinion. "Willkie spread himself too thin," he wrote. "He attempted to answer too many questions—passed up too many opportunities—the very nature of his campaign complicated rather than simplified the campaign itself."

Daddy returned home gray-faced. He had lost ten pounds, and he was coughing more; his cigarette intake had increased. He told us he was determined to help Willkie win in 1944, and he assumed a key role in attempting to rebuild a campaign infrastructure—he hung on the phone, he wrote letters, and he kept in constant touch with "the Boss."

He insisted that Willkie had inspired thousands of independents with new political faith and zeal. He received over one hundred thousand letters of support after his defeat, he said.

Mama disagreed. "Willkie is a lost cause, Bart," she kept saying. "I want you to stay home now with your family."

She said this so often he got exasperated. "Oh, Cutsie, please," he murmured. "Please, please *shut up.*"

On November 28, 1940, Willkie wrote a letter to Daddy, which he kept framed on his desk for the rest of his life:

> My Dear Bart,
>
> It is impossible in a letter to express my gratitude for the sacrifice you made in your own practice to accompany us on our campaign. Believe me, I am deeply grateful. I can truthfully say that one of the highlights of the campaign was the pleasure of knowing you and working with you and I sincerely hope that I may have that pleasure again.
>
> I wish you could convey my regards to Mrs. Crum and thank her for the very fine article she wrote about our train. It was a very constructive and entertaining piece.
>
> Best of luck to you in your practice. It ought to be a gratification to you to know how much you contributed to the spreading of a doctrine which as we know must prevail.
>
> Yours gratefully and sincerely,
> WENDELL WILLKIE

In the months that followed, Daddy began practicing law again and he flung himself back into state politics; things were in utter confusion since the Hitler-Stalin Pact—even on the lowest level of local government the fragile coalition of leftists and liberals had been destroyed by the conflicts that the pact had generated. There was a genuine reactionary movement in California; Harry Bridges kept being threatened with deportation. The Smith Act was passed in late spring of 1940, calling for the fingerprinting and registering of all aliens. There were accusations that the State Relief Board was riddled with Communists.

In the fall of 1940, Congressman Jack Tenney sponsored a bill to banish the Communist Party from the California ballot.

My father felt the bill was unconstitutional and he stormed around the state speaking out against it, but it was passed by both House and Senate and wasn't declared unconstitutional until two years later.

However, after that, Tenney and my father were mortal enemies, and remained politically opposed, particularly when it came to First Amendment issues.

At home, of course, none of this was ever mentioned. Daddy seemed more concerned with buying a house in the country so he and Mama would have a proper garden and we could all be together on weekends. He began taking us on long drives over the Santa Cruz mountains and down into Carmel and Pebble Beach. Or we would go to Marin County, piling into our roadster with the top down, and Bart and I would sit in the backseat and there'd be a picnic basket next to us filled with little jelly sandwiches and cold roast chicken and sweet pickles and deviled eggs wrapped in wax paper and thermoses of cold V-8 juice. Sometimes we would cross the Golden Gate Bridge in sunshine and emerge in fog.

There were many lonely, unpaved dusty roads leading into the parched Napa hills, thick with deep green oak and conifer. We would chug along, stirring up big clouds of soft brown dust. Above us the arched blue sky seemed timeless with promises.

Eventually, we might stop and tour a dilapidated old ranch house, deep in a forest of redwood and madrona. We saw several old Victorian houses, shuttered and cobwebby. Mama said no to everything. Another time we stopped at a place called Calistoga. We visited a prune ranch and a vineyard and a horse farm. We drove through pastures smelling strongly of cow dung. We passed cornfields and apricot orchards, and a modern house made entirely of glass perched on a cliff overlooking the sea.

One Sunday we were invited to lunch with a millionaire Daddy had gone to college with: a tanned, balding man with a cruel face. He owned a thousand acres in Grass Valley. We were introduced outside his stables. He started flirting with Mama almost immediately, but Daddy seemed to pay no attention.

After touring the property, which included a vast hothouse

filled with rare plants, we changed into bathing suits and gathered around his pool. The pool was round and set in the middle of a beautifully manicured lawn; the grass felt soft and wet against my bare feet.

The water in the pool was a lovely shade of pale green. It lapped against the sides of the pool as Mama drifted from one end to the other on a rubber pillow. She was wearing a tight halter and shorts; I could see the outline of her buttocks. She lay on her stomach, dragging her hand lazily through the water; the water rippled and sparkled in the sun.

Daddy sat on the side of the pool watching her. It was the first time I'd ever seen him in bathing trunks. He appeared pale and soft; his shoulders were white, but with a sprinkling of freckles, like mine. His neck, though, was sunburned. Mama's skin was much prettier, I decided. Glossy brown.

For a while I stood in the shallow end of the pool; then I dived in. I had been taught to swim when I was two, and I felt totally at home in the water; I loved paddling back and forth, back and forth, my feet kicking, my arms flailing. The sun dappled the water with golden squares. For one minute I gazed up at the sky and was blinded and felt afraid.

Around two we left the pool and were taken up to a brick patio off the house where a buffet was set up on a big glass-topped wrought iron table. There were fresh fruits—apples, pears, and grapes piled in an epergne; big cheeses melting on a silver platter; loaves of sourdough French bread; and a fish salad, heaped in a bowl. Mama was oooing and ahhing, when suddenly Daddy asked sharply, "Where's your brother?"

Before I could answer, he had turned and run down to the pool and jumped in with an enormous splash.

We followed in time to see him hoisting Bart out of the water and giving him artificial respiration while Mama screamed and cried. I did nothing except stare at my brother's inert body; he looked so tiny, so forlorn.

(Daddy told me later that he had found my brother lying very peacefully at the bottom in the shallow part with his eyes shut tight. "Oh Jesus, Jesus, Jesus, have mercy," Daddy said.)

Miraculously, Bart survived the incident as he had survived

the fire in the nursery. He didn't even have to go to the hospital, although a doctor came and examined him carefully. He vomited up a lot of water and then he fell asleep.

On the way back to Berkeley, we stopped at a small Catholic church to say a prayer of thanks. I went in with Daddy, but Mama stayed in the car with Bart on her lap.

Sunlight illuminated the rainbow-colored stained-glass windows, which depicted the Stations of the Cross. In the darkness near the altar, a dozen tiny candles flickered and sputtered. Daddy dipped his fingers in the holy water font and crossed himself, and then he genuflected and knelt down in a pew and began sobbing into his hands.

PART
TWO

CHAPTER

6

WE didn't buy a house in the country for a while. Instead, in December 1941, Daddy abruptly sold our Berkeley home and moved us to San Francisco to a rented duplex apartment at 763 Bay Street, overlooking Fisherman's Wharf. He said we would be saving money by renting.

How we saved money I never knew, since we still seemed to live extravagantly: private schools, trips to Lake Tahoe and Hollywood; and then there was Mama's wardrobe, which seemed more lavish than ever.

But for about a year we did exist without our cook, Toy, and our place was smaller. Bart and I briefly shared a room. Then Mama moved my brother to the maid's cubicle off the kitchen. We were too old to share a space, she said (he was seven and I was nine); we needed privacy.

As for Mama, she took the master bedroom with its panoramic view of Golden Gate Bridge, and Daddy slept on the living room couch. He had his favorite possessions nearby on the coffee table —the fierce old crucifix and a copy of Samuel Butler's *The Way of All Flesh.*

But when I saw him sprawled there, it seemed as if he were a visitor in his own home.

He and Mama had had separate bedrooms in Berkeley, ever since Bart was born. We were told it was because Mama had been so ill, with her ulcer and her migraines, that she had to be alone.

Now Daddy explained that he slept on the couch instead of

with Mama upstairs because he kept her awake with his terrible snoring. He did snore horribly—snuffling, groaning, almost choking. But I think the reason actually might have been because he often downed one or two drinks before he turned off the lamp, and Mama didn't approve.

I was too young to think there was anything wrong about his dependence on liquor. I used to tiptoe over to him to kiss him good night, and he would be propped up on the pillows with a glass of whiskey nearby, and a cigarette smoking in an ashtray. It seemed so warm and cozy there—only one lamp on, the rest of the room in darkness. He would be reading, and he'd grin and pat the couch, meaning I should lie down next to him for a few minutes, and we would hug each other and he'd tell me I was his "masterpiece."

Sometimes the radio would be playing next to the couch—staticky music "because we're high on a hill," he'd say—but we did hear the first news of the bombing of Pearl Harbor on that radio. It was after breakfast actually, a terrified announcer blurting out an early bulletin from the Hawaiian island: "We have suddenly and deliberately been attacked by the Japanese navy and air force . . ."

Daddy called out to Bart and Mama and we ended up listening to the radio most of the day—listening to scary reports of how 363 Japanese war planes had pulverized the American military base at Pearl Harbor within three hours of unremitting attack; 8 United States battleships sunk, including the *Arizona*; 2,400 servicemen and civilians killed; and 2,000 wounded.

War was declared on Japan the following day by President Roosevelt. And Congress voted to declare war on Japan's axis partners Italy and Germany.

Daddy planned to enlist. Peter Cusick was already in the OSS and Paul Smith quit the *Chronicle* and joined the marines. I don't know what happened—why my father ended up staying in San Francisco—something about his poor eyesight, or his age. He was forty-two. But he was very disappointed. He really wanted to serve his country.

Within weeks the excitement and terror subsided and we all went on with our lives. On Sundays, after High Mass, Daddy would take us down to the Embarcadero so we could wave at the troop ships as they moved through the fog and under the Golden Gate.

Then we'd walk home. Mama would be waiting for us, still in her pink quilted satin robe, and Daddy would make dollar-size pancakes for us.

Of course the war never touched us except in the form of rationing, which we hated because it meant we often couldn't get luxury items (butter, steaks) unless Daddy obtained them on the black market, which he sometimes did.

There was only one minor family crisis. My grades were so bad that when I switched schools from Anna Head's in Berkeley to Miss Burke's in San Francisco, I was told I would have to repeat the fifth grade.

In contrast, my brother—a straight A student—was jumped ahead a grade as soon as he began attending Town School.

By this time, I had convinced myself I must be stupid. I suppose it dated back to hearing someone tell my parents, "Patti is the pretty one—Bart is the smartie pants." When I repeated this to my brother, he retorted, "You're not stupid, you're just lazy," which was probably closer to the truth.

Whatever the case, Mama and Daddy were both very disappointed in me and they showed it; I'd been accustomed to their total indulgence, so I hid in my closet, gorging on candy, which I did whenever I was upset about something—feeling very disgraced.

Without asking, Bart came to my rescue. From then on he served as my tutor. He would appear in my room after school and stand over me as I did my homework, encouraging me to keep at it when I complained an assignment was too hard. He helped me fathom the mysteries of Latin grammar, he showed me (once or twice) that arithmetic could be fun.

I had little interest in school until I got an A in composition class and discovered I like to write. My brother was as pleased and as proud as Daddy. "See?" he teased me. "You're not as stupid as you thought."

DADDY gave a great many speeches during 1942, a few at the Glide Church in the Mission District. He was one of the first people to describe the Nazi atrocities in the concentration camps and to tell the public that they were being "too apathetic," and that something should be done.

He also helped organize rallies like the one called "Tribute to Russia Day," held at the Civic Auditorium to honor the Russian war effort.

And he spoke on radio, too, debating local labor leaders, questioning them as to how to maintain worker morale in defense plants. He would always praise Harry Bridges as the union leader who in return for agreeing to a no-strike pledge during the war asked that there be no union busting.

Whenever he could, he would publicly defend Harry, who after four years of convoluted court proceedings was still fighting deportation. "Harry is the most hounded, searched, spied on, wire-tapped guy in America," Daddy said. "I don't get it."

And then he would tell us about running into his old boss John Neylan in the bar of the Bohemian Club, and Neylan would accuse him of being "loony" on the subject of Bridges: "When are you gonna wise up, Bart?" he'd ask.

He would laugh in retelling the story: "Can you imagine what would have happened to me if I was still practicing law in his office?"

After leaving Neylan, Daddy had been offered a number of partnerships, but he had turned them down in favor of "practicing solo." From 1941 through 1948 he shared office space with attorney Phil Ehrlich in the Russ Building. Ehrlich was a sober, hardworking, skillful attorney. They made a good team.

David Silver, another lawyer in the firm, recalls how my father took exceptional care of his clients: "He understood all the issues involved in every case—he was extremely intelligent—but he didn't enjoy the tedious aspects of the law so he didn't bother with them—Phil did."

Even so, Daddy enticed some very big clients into the firm—people like Nate Cummings, who during the war was amassing millions in a vast frozen-foods company, Sara Lee, which became part of General Foods. He met my father at the University of Chicago when Daddy was participating in a series of lectures with Alex Meiklejohn on how America had to redefine itself during the world crisis. Cummings was so impressed with Daddy's charm and reasonableness that he decided to let him handle some of his business. Later he offered him stock in his company instead of a fee, but Daddy refused. He could have become a millionaire, Cummings said.

He never understood my father's attitude about money. Daddy loved *having* it, loved *spending* it, but he had no idea how to *handle* it. Cummings would tell him that it's no crime to be rich; you can have ideals, but you can have investments, too.

To my knowledge, Daddy never kept a savings account (Mama didn't open one until the 1960s). He paid most of our bills in cash and spent money as fast as he earned it. "I'm always behind the eight ball," he would joke.

During the war more wealthy clients came his way, like Dextra McGonogle (whose father had built the Santa Anita Racetrack), but Daddy always seemed to be scrambling—handling divorce cases along with corporate accounts; negotiating for unions; writing up reports. He estimated once that he did 60 percent of his legal work "for free"; he had only a secretary to help him.

But nothing was ever denied us. We were both tutored in French; Bart had music classes; I attended special art school. We took weekend trips constantly to Pebble Beach, Carmel, Lake Tahoe. And an unending stream of possessions kept arriving at the apartment for Mama—antiques, china, silver—and there were masseuses, health-food experts, holistic doctors, to help her cope with her delicate stomach and her migraines.

Our cook, Toy, had returned, so there were many dinner parties.

Once I asked her why she hadn't ever cut back. "I wanted to," she insisted. "I was worried about money all the time. I knew we were living beyond our means, but I was too ignorant to do anything about it. We had no savings, no insurance, no investments. And we could have had all that. Your father never thought in terms of security for his family. But with his clients, he was fantastic. He was always thinking in terms of security for *them!*"

BY mid-1942, Daddy was spending half his time practicing law and half his time was devoted to politics. He campaigned for Earl Warren when he ran for governor of California, and he helped run Robert Kenny's successful campaign for state attorney general.

Although he respected Warren ("He's a master of nonpartisan politics," he'd say), he was closer philosophically to Kenny, who had a feisty commitment to civil liberties. The brash, engaging Kenny was then one of the most powerful Democrats in the state (and the unofficial leader of the left-wing Democrats). The youngest man ever to be appointed to a judgeship, as state senator of California he had blazed liberal legislative trails; he was now Democratic attorney general in the Republican governorship of Earl Warren. He had also been a banker, lawyer, businessman, and lobbyist before that, as well as a founder of the National Lawyers Guild, the national association of left liberal lawyers formed in 1936 when the nine old men of the Supreme Court were blocking all of FDR's progressive legislation. *Liberal* was a term that guild members, Communist and non-Communist alike, used to describe the sensibility of the guild—and each other—in the 1930s and early 1940s.

In 1942 my father served as president of the San Francisco chapter of the guild, and he and Kenny were extremely active in the group, which kept defending New Deal legislation (social security, health insurance, extension of civil rights and liberties).

They mobilized guild members to support FDR's pledge to Russia to open a second front against the Nazis in Europe; they also tried to persuade Wendell Willkie to become president of the guild (they envisioned it as a coalition of forces—progressive Democrats and Willkie Republicans), but Willkie refused. Even then the guild was too controversial for him; he thought he would jeopardize his presidential chances with the right-wingers in the Republican Party.

Daddy and Kenny used to have long martini lunches with journalist John Gunther when he was in San Francisco during 1943 researching California for his book *Inside U.S.A.*

After one of those lunches they all drove to Reno to go gambling—gambling was one of Kenny's passions; another passion was Benzedrine. "He gobbled bennies like peanuts," Mama said. She thought Kenny got Daddy hooked on Benzedrine.

Be that as it may, Daddy was a supreme networker for Kenny and Gunther. He introduced Gunther to Harry Bridges and Artie Samish, the powerful lobbyist whose political connections stretched from coast to coast.

Gunther gave my father credit for helping him research San Francisco personalities in *Inside U.S.A.*, and Daddy was inspired by their discussions to write a romantic essay about California ("California is unpredictable—wonderful—tragic—state of the future—gateway to the Orient"). He hoped *Fortune* would publish the piece; it didn't.

Even so, he sent the essay to Willkie as "food for thought."

He was always sending stuff to Willkie—speeches he had made about him, newspaper clips, cartoons, reminders that a lot of people hoped he would run for president again.

By late 1942, Willkie began planning his political comeback. He knew it would be difficult. At the last Republican National Committee meeting in December, Harrison Spangler, the committee's new chair, made it clear that he thought it would be unfortunate if Willkie were renominated.

However, whenever he spoke in public, Willkie continued to draw bigger crowds than any other leader in or out of power. He would attack Republican congressmen for conservatism at home and isolationism abroad, even though he knew it would hurt his presidential chances with party regulars. It didn't matter to him; he described himself as an independent. He became more popular and more famous after his spectacular trip around China, Russia, and the Mideast in early 1943. His subsequent best-selling book on the trip, *One World,* made people think in terms of global unity for the first time.

But Willkie had no illusions about where he stood. The public loved him, but the professional pols disliked him heartily. He didn't care. So he set about pulling together his own machine made up of loyal followers like my father and Russell Davenport; like Gardner Cowles, his brother John, and Ralph Cake, the Harvard-educated lawyer from Oregon; and like Sam Pryor, head of the Republican National Committee in Connecticut. His candidacy was still undeclared, but they began to meet secretly in his law office on Wall Street to discuss strategy.

Ruth Bishop, a Willkie aide who went on to work at the United Nations, recalled that whenever Bart Crum was there, he would emphasize the importance of winning the California primary. He believed that if Willkie won those fifty electoral votes, it would be tantamount to winning the nomination.

My father was sure Willkie could do it if he had a strong enough organization to back him. He had all sorts of ideas as to how such an organization should work, but, unfortunately, most of his ideas were never realized—certainly not his concept of a national network. One of his ideas, however, did come to pass: Daddy kept promoting the idea of "image politics," a new concept for 1943, pushing the candidate's persona as much, if not more than, the issues. He thought Willkie should hire Clem Whittaker and his wife, Leone Baxter, who, along with Murray Chotiner, were becoming the shrewdest political PR people in California ("They can twitch the uninformed electorate by their nerve ends," Teddy White later wrote).

"Clem will try to charge you a thousand bucks a month," my father wrote to Willkie. "I'll get him to charge you five hundred." And he did.

BY January 1943, the Willkie forces gathered momentum and Daddy agreed to run Willkie's northern California primary campaign. (In those days, because of the size and diversity of the state, not to mention the crude means of communication, it was necessary to have two distinct campaigns—one in San Francisco and one in Los Angeles.)

Willkie had hoped to put my father on salary as a full-time political strategist, but funds were not available, so Daddy worked part-time. He had already rented a small office next to his own in the Russ Building and staffed it with a couple of volunteers. It was understood that his travel and meals would be paid for, as well as the operational costs of running the office—all of it to come out of a small fund raised by Willkie loyalists.

For the next nine months, Daddy traveled around the state talking with precinct leaders, local congressmen, mayors, newspaper editors. He spent a lot of time coordinating efforts in Los Angeles with Walter Wanger and Darryl Zanuck, who were big Willkie supporters.

My father seemed to have no interest in power for himself. All he cared about was getting Willkie's ideas across to the voter and the local politician. He'd make speeches around the Bay Area, talking about "Willkie as the conscience of the Republican party

... Willkie is the guy who can choke out isolationism ... Willkie's stamina and faith and even recklessness are jolting state leaders into making fresh appraisals of the American scene."

At the same time he wrote almost daily reports to Willkie: "Fresno looks good for you ... so does San Jose ... Earl Warren showing contempt for state chairman Tickle."

There are also asides on the growth of labor as a political force, particularly in the Central Valley (California's growing agricultural empire), and he wrote of the conflicts within the Cameron/Knowland/Chandler axis (these were three powerful newspaper publishers: George Cameron of the *San Francisco Chronicle*, Harry Chandler of the *Los Angeles Times*, and Joe Knowland of the *Oakland Tribune*). "The Republican Party is virtually run by this trio," Daddy wrote. "You must seduce 'em in order to win."

In March he warned Willkie that he had learned through an excellent source that "The Republican State Committee game is to have their delegation pledged to Earl Warren as favorite son and stacked against you."

From then on he kept urging Willkie to meet privately with Warren to make sure he would not run as a "native son," but Willkie didn't meet with him until it was too late.

Late that spring my father had dinner with Warren in the governor's mansion and wrote Willkie: "Earl insists he has not made up his mind ... he says nothing will be done until he's had the opportunity to talk to you."

There were rumors that the California delegation would betray Willkie; so Daddy tried persuading state senator Bill Knowland (who went on to serve in the United States Senate from 1945 until 1958) to side openly with Willkie then and there, but Knowland did not, and Charlie Blythe, Willkie's principal fund-raiser, quit, although he maintained to my father that he'd always stick by him.

There were other problems, too. John Hamilton, former national chair of the Republican Party, was urging the organization of "favorite sons" delegates in twenty states to block Willkie's efforts in the primaries, and other (more conservative) candidates were emerging to compete against Willkie, such as General Douglas MacArthur, Tom Dewey, and Harold Stassen.

From the moment he endorsed Lend-Lease and became FDR's "ambassador" to London, Willkie's leadership within the Republican Party was strongly disputed.

After a meeting with Willkie's makeshift staff in New York, Daddy wrote to my mother: "Nobody is setting things up properly around the country for Wendell. . . . No real effort is being made to fight the strategy of guys like Stassen. . . . There is no strong support from any party leaders. . . . Even so, Wendell seems blithely confident of his messianic powers, but I am frankly depressed."

Mama was depressed, too. She suffered from Daddy's long absences from home. She felt torn—her sense of neglect and self-pity mixed with respect, almost reverence, for his political idealism and his need to accomplish great things.

Daddy always asked Mama to come back east with him and she generally refused. "I don't want to play second fiddle to Wendell," she'd tease. But her real excuse, she said, was she wanted to stay with us. She was a devoted and involved mother, alternately spoiling us and trying to discipline us; she seemed to have little interest in what my father was doing in politics. "I'm apolitical," she would say.

Nor did she ever become particularly friendly with the wives of the men my father worked with in the Willkie campaigns, like Russell Davenport's wife, the novelist Marcia; she would speak enviously about Marcia's "independence, her wit."

Mama's friends were "girls" she had gone to college with, like wealthy Piedmont socialite Lib Logan, or Judge Mary Kohler, a sturdy, purposeful, deeply religious little woman who had prematurely white hair and a blinding smile that never let up. Mary was around the family a lot; she served as confidante to both my parents. Indeed, one weekend she could be off on a religious retreat with my father (they had been law students together), and the next week she might be found in our living room urging Mama to go to an analyst when she began suffering from insomnia and getting writer's block.

Although Daddy did everything to encourage her to continue her novel writing, Mama was finding it more difficult because her books kept being rejected by publishers.

She completed one more novel in 1943, *First Lover, Last Love.*

The plot revolves around a married woman, small and blond like Mama, who leaves her stuffy professor husband after falling madly in love with a dashing radical lawyer, who seems to resemble Daddy.

After *First Lover, Last Love* was turned down by several publishers, Mama took to her bed with a severe migraine. As soon as he came back from New York, Daddy ministered to her with soothing words and chicken broth. He literally spoon-fed her until she felt better—and they went off by themselves for a long weekend, "down the peninsula." When they returned, Mama was beaming. Daddy announced he had bought us a house in the country—an old Spanish ranch located ten miles out of Santa Cruz in a hamlet called Aptos.

He explained he had been able to afford the property (it cost around seven thousand dollars in 1942) because he'd just received a retainer from a wealthy new client.

The ranch itself was a two-storied white-shingled affair set at the bottom of an incline and surrounded by untamed gardens. Beyond the gardens were rough, unplowed fields, which dipped at one point down to a stream. The stream fed directly into Monterey Bay and the Pacific Ocean, which was less than two miles away and half hidden by orchards. The fourteen-acre property ended at a redwood forest, which today is a national park.

For the next six years we spent every weekend at Aptos and all our summers and most of our holidays as well, and Aptos, rather than San Francisco, became the backdrop of some of my most vivid and disturbing memories.

CHAPTER

7

ALTHOUGH Daddy professed great love for our new country place, he was rarely there, particularly that first summer —the summer of 1943—because he was in Washington working as special counsel for Roosevelt's Committee on Fair Employment Practices.

As a result, Mama's anger increased. It boxed her in; it wouldn't let her relax. She would occasionally have screaming fits if we did something to displease her, and it could be something as silly as my getting a pimple.

Her behavior became impossible; whenever she flew into a rage, my brother and I would try to stay out of her way. She was never physical with us, but her anger was so violent it terrified us and we didn't understand it. We didn't understand that the rage came out of enormous frustration and loneliness and pain.

Once, in the middle of a tirade, I asked her quaveringly, "Aren't you happy, Mama?"

And she answered, "No, as a matter of fact, I'm not, but, then, only idiots are happy. Someday you'll understand."

I never thought I would, but I do now.

IN May 1943 she wrote in her journal:

I see myself as I am, a spoiled, vain, dissatisfied woman. My nature has grown too soft from too much good fortune—too much privilege, the monotony of my marriage (or lack of marriage) has lulled me into apathy. I long for a calamity of some kind to shock me out of my rut. . . .

The only thing I really want to do is write—and I can't. I'm blocked. Am I a failure? I have been depressed. Unable to sleep. I refuse to take pills. I am seeing a psychiatrist. Recommended to me by Mary Kohler. A Dr. Bernard. Sad, wrinkled face. Very Jewish. He tells me I must write. "It will be your salvation," he says. From what? I say. He doesn't answer. Just stares at me with pouchy sad eyes that seem to say I have seen it all and nothing shocks me. Will I ever tell him my innermost thoughts about Bart? Am I doomed to say out loud what I want—what I need? Will I always conceal myself and my frustrations about—is it—12 years of marriage. I doubt I'll tell him. So we have many uncomfortable silences together.

THROUGHOUT May 1943 Mama continued to write copiously in her journal—noting that her insomnia and depressions were growing worse—until she impulsively hired a mysterious drifter to work in our gardens.

It all began one morning—one early dawn, actually. Mama had been unable to sleep so she wandered out onto the sundeck of our house at Aptos and surveyed the land spread out before her.

This was the view she and my father liked best, because you could see almost all of the fourteen and a half acres of our property from that deck: the west field planted now with scratchy golden grass and feathery loquats, and, directly below, weedy beds crowded with rhododendron bushes and tubs of tomato plants.

Both my parents were passionate gardeners, and someday they planned to build a brick-walled rose garden in those weedy beds. Then, they said, the garden would be ablaze with sweet-smelling, velvety Étoile de Holland roses.

That morning, Mama stood on the sundeck watching the fog roll in from the Pacific Ocean and she saw a mysterious figure emerging from the redwoods at the edge of our property.

The man was dark and he appeared very tall—almost gigantic, in fact—and from that distance he seemed faintly menacing.

He had a bundle on his back. For a moment he stood tense and poised, looking from the left to the right, almost as if he were afraid he was being hunted. Then he plunged into the tall grasses of the west field, moving like an animal. Suddenly he stared right up at the sundeck; Mama was sure he had seen her, so she dropped to her knees behind a deck chair (she was nude under her nightgown).

The drifter then appeared to start forward, to come closer so he could actually confront her, but suddenly he wheeled and marched to the far end of the field where there was a steep, overgrown trail that pitched under oak and sycamores and then disappeared down to a winding stream that fed into a bay called Rio Del Mar, near Monterey. We could always hear the pounding of the waves from our windows, even if the shutters were closed and bolted.

Later that morning Mama described the drifter excitedly as she fixed us waffles and sausages in the kitchen. "His hair is glossy black like a jungle cat's, he has tanned skin—maybe he's a Gypsy!"

The drifter's presence excited her as nothing else had since we moved to Aptos for the entire summer, possibly because Daddy had been away in Washington for weeks and Mama was extremely restless.

In the days that followed, the drifter appeared on our property again and again, sometimes at the top of the hill, sometimes in the field; he always seemed to be studying our property, evaluating it, scrutinizing it, and then he would disappear.

Then my brother and I saw him sauntering through Aptos, the tiny hamlet less than a mile from our house. (Today, Aptos is the heart of computer country, but forty years ago it was a one-gas-station village where Mama did her shopping at a rundown A & P after getting her mail from the little post office. Every so often a train chugged through Main Street to its destination, Watsonville, artichoke capital of America.)

Subsequently, we heard that the local police had forbidden the drifter to cook his supper over a campfire he had built under the railway trestle, where he slept every night, wrapped in newspapers. Apparently the police were worried; there had been no rain in California in months and everybody was afraid of fires.

Then Fred Tillman, our neighbor across the stream, who owned a dairy farm, announced that the drifter had knocked on his door and asked if he needed a gardener. "I can do anything," he had bragged. "I'm a magician with plants."

Tillman was put off by the man's ragged appearance, but he was so courtly and soft-spoken—"he's obviously very well educated"—that he allowed him to weed his garden, and eventually the drifter gardened for other neighbors in the area.

Since it was wartime and there was little help available anywhere, the drifter was soon in much demand, but even after she heard he was doing odd jobs for many of her friends, Mama made no effort to contact him, and she tried to do the gardening on our property herself (with our inadequate help). We would water and weed and rake together, but we barely made a dent; the property was just too huge.

Mama would never call out to the drifter, although he continued to appear on our land, usually surveying it from the top of the hill. He and Mama would scrutinize each other from a distance. "There he is again!" she would cry when she saw him. "There he is, God damn it!"

However, it was as if she sensed that very soon he would finally saunter down the hill, past the poplar trees and cypress, and come down the garden path to offer his services to us.

MAMA and I were sitting on our sun-drenched brick patio at the front of the house, painting our toenails "fire engine red," when the drifter appeared out of nowhere.

"I need work," he told us.

We started because although his voice was soft and cultivated, his looming presence cast a shadow over the bricks.

"I need work," he repeated.

"I'm sure you do. Mister . . . ?"

"My name is Happy," the drifter said. He moved closer to us and Mama put on a cardigan sweater. She was wearing a halter and very short shorts. "Happy what?" she asked.

"Happy Kanta," he answered.

"An odd name," Mama countered; she was trying not to stare at his tattooed arms.

"Your land is beautiful," he murmured. "But I could make it more beautiful."

"A modest statement." Mama went back to painting her toenails. Glossy-red drops of polish fell on the bricks, where they glittered like jewels. She wiped them up with a piece of Kleenex and then dipped the brush back into the little bottle.

The drifter watched her. He had a tense face—a ravaged, dissolute poetic face. For some reason an image flashed in my mind: ex-convict! His eyes were sneaky, foxy, the eyes of a con artist.

Mama kept painting her toenails, very carefully, very deliberately. She obviously didn't want to look at him.

"I could have you arrested for trespassing," she told him finally.

He shrugged. "I fell in love with your property the moment I saw it. I kept coming back to see if it was real."

Mama smiled slightly, still gazing at her feet. "It *is* beautiful, we know that. My husband and I bought this place less than six months ago and we have some very grand plans for it. We're going to plant an apple orchard."

"On the sloping hill near the cypress?" Happy interrupted.

Mama glanced at him. He'd guessed right.

"And you could dam up your stream and make a very deep swimming pool," he went on dreamily. "And plant forsythia bushes along with purple and white irises."

"Yes, well, we haven't been able to do anything we've wanted," Mama exclaimed, her tone impatient. "Everyone's off to the wars—the only help we've had are either drunks or lazy adolescents." She paused. "Why aren't you in the army?"

"I'm an epileptic."

"Oh."

"I felt I should tell you that before I began working here."

"*Have* I hired you?"

He shrugged again and lit a cigarette. He had powerful hands, filthy hands, dark with the soil of many gardens, I suspected.

"I've worked in nurseries and estates all over the country," he went on softly, intensely. "I know everything there is to know about flowers and plants and trees, haven't your friends told you?"

"They may exaggerate. Where were you last employed before you came to California?"

"I worked for the parks system in Boston."

"I presume you have references?"

"I lost them, but maybe you could phone."

Mama suddenly stood up and told the drifter coolly, "Perhaps we can discuss this further," and she touched my arm, which meant I was to follow them, which I did, down the wide path that encircled our house.

From that path other paths fanned out which crisscrossed our gardens; directly ahead of us was a clump of tall redwood trees, near the brick patio where we had been sitting.

So I followed them down and around those paths.

Ahead of me, our dogs—Mama's poodle, Bonbon, and our cocker spaniel, Frisky—ambled and sniffed at the drifter's work-boots. We were surrounded by warm sun and masses of green— the gray green of our olive trees, the yellow green of the mulberry, the pale green of the rustling poplars (my favorite tree).

Far away I thought I could hear my brother, Bart, practicing on the piano in the living room, playing a Mozart sonata he loved. Something in the back of my mind told me, "You will never be part of anything so beautiful again."

Mama and the drifter must have walked for close to an hour, around and around our place. "It's a pretty conventional garden," I heard him say.

"That's what makes it so restful, but it does need tending." She paused by a bed of ivy near the front of the house. "I want this bordered in Shasta daisies, white Shasta daisies."

"If you want that, you shall have that," the drifter murmured.

Reaching the front of the gate, they strolled out into the graveled open area reserved for parking cars. The sky seemed to meet the earth around them. Up the hill by the highway the great cypress trees rose into the heavens, guarding our property; they resembled cut-out black paper trees leaning against a pale-blue horizon.

"I would make a checkerboard garden for you—roses mixed with lavender and pansies and sweet William."

I listened, hypnotized, as this strange, rather sinister man rambled on about his dreams for Aptos Ranchos. "I would incorporate the front garden with the back—blend it—and there could be a cutting garden with dozens of glads and sweet peas—there could be tubs of rhododendron—we could decorate one path with plum trees and there could be a long bed of strawberries somewhere. I like strawberry plants, don't you?"

The drifter was hired the following day, without those references from Boston. They couldn't be obtained, but Mama did check with her neighbors and they all praised the drifter's politeness and his astonishing "green thumb." Then she phoned Daddy in Washington and told him she had found a gardener who promised to turn Aptos Ranchos into a "veritable Eden."

THE transformation started at once.

Happy Kanta weeded, he pruned, he trimmed hedges, he stapled vines. He replaced our worn grass paths with hard-packed dirt paths, which were then watered and raked.

I associate the sound of whirring sprinklers with Happy because he watered constantly. There was always the smell of damp earth everywhere, and whenever I biked around the garden paths, I could see the sparkle of a million drops of water on the ivy beds and big white Shasta daisy bushes.

We used to watch him, my brother and I, because he didn't waste a single motion as he trained roses around the fruit trees or intertwined wisteria and clematis. He could stand patiently over a delicate new begonia plant, watering it for minutes at a time, holding the nozzle very carefully so only the roots would be soaked. Then he might press the soil tenderly with his fingertips; his expression was one of melancholy ecstasy.

His first big project for us was the victory garden at the back of the house, facing the kitchen. He planted corn, carrots, tomatoes, potatoes, onions, and garlic—staples for soups and stews.

In the weeks that followed, Mama wrote Daddy of the garden's progress and of Happy:

> What makes him so odd is his unflappable *poise* in spite of the fact that he calls himself a bum. He tells me he has ridden the rails all over the United States. "I am always escaping, Mrs. C.," he tells me. "If I had a car, I'd feel like a real American."
>
> He knows everything there is to know about flowers and plants and trees—he knows how the Babylonians planned

their hanging gardens; how during the Renaissance the Italians turned gardening into a fine art. . . .

His ideas for our property are wildly imaginative. For example—he envisions white beehives dotted amidst a huge white garden with at least thirty varieties of white flowers!

Mama was concerned for us because Happy was an epileptic. She explained the condition, told us we must never be alone with him.

In those days epilepsy was a taboo subject; if someone in a family suffered from it, it was kept a secret or else talked about in hushed tones.

Naturally, the drifter's epilepsy made him all the more intriguing to us. We waited impatiently for him to have a seizure, but in the year and a half he was with us, we never witnessed him experiencing an attack.

Later, when we got to know him better, the drifter confided that he would always experience an "aura" that would warn him of an impending attack. "If you should see me starting to shake, just keep calm," he instructed us. "Whatever you do, don't hold me down. But it is not true that during a seizure I'm going to swallow my tongue!"

Since the drifter's arrival, Mama's rages had almost completely subsided. In the mornings she would work beside him in the gardens, raking weeds into piles, then tossing them into a large cardboard box.

She was writing, too, on a card table set up on her sundeck. She would sit at her typewriter most afternoons, pecking away; she'd be wearing a halter and very short shorts. Her shoulders glistened with baby oil and iodine, a mixture that supposedly gave her a darker tan.

She had started keeping notes on the drifter. "He is thirty-eight years old (he says)," Mama wrote.

Born in Boston, mother abused him—he ended up in foster homes—used to break into places "for fun." Seems completely rootless, won't explain how he was educated—says he'd tended bar, taught rug weaving to survive. He will not tell me how he learned about gardens. He says after being a bum for about ten years he suddenly felt sick of it—he was broke and he was filthy—so he hit upon the idea of being certified as insane, mainly so he could sleep in a clean bed. For several months he was locked up in a nut house, but he grew to hate the experience—"like being buried alive" he said. So one night, very late, he escaped from the institution by climbing out a window and shimmying to the ground on a pair of knotted sheets!

He appears to have sought out elements in life that are beyond reason—that go beyond the rational . . . he appears to want primal experiences which are meaningful and cruel. So do I. So do I.

And on another page of her journal:

I asked him if he'd ever settle down in one place and he replied "Nope" because then he'd feel trapped.

He has already threatened to leave us. "I may stay a year. I may stay only another month." He says he doesn't know. But in the meantime, he promises to do a great deal of work on our property. However he must do it according to *his* plans. He has already made notes and diagrams for the various gardens. . . .

"I can't help it," he confided—his voice alternately mocking and then earnest. "I think of these gardens as *mine*. I dreamt of gardens like this when I was in the madhouse—a field surrounded by cypress. Wild gardens with a stream running through it . . . I am very possessive about this land. Is that okay?"

Every day we walk together around the property and I see the progress he has made—and it is glorious.

Later when I'm alone a thought comes to me—that the dream gardens he'll create for us are ones he's fantasized about for years, the white gardens and the rose gardens—and in creating them he may be forced to come to terms about a lot of things about himself. Maybe he has to garden to save himself! Perhaps I'm romanticizing him, perhaps not. I started off viewing him clinically, but I fear my interest in Happy Kanta is far more than clinical.

Every afternoon we walk somewhere on the property and he describes the plans he has for our land—such grandiose dreams—for a white garden and a rose garden.

Sometimes I imagine I am falling under his spell. Am I attracted to his unconventionality? He never wears a watch. Has no concept of time. I am so rigid, so organized right down to the minute, I can't imagine being any other way and yet his eccentricities are seductive . . . or is it the gardens he's creating for me? So warm and hidden and maternal . . . I feel I am being *loved* in my gardens. Is that the irresistible pull?

In her notes she says she thinks his drinking is controllable because he told her he would never drink on the job.

But we saw him drinking during the day, when he was taking a break down in our meadow near our stream. He was with two other vagrants. We assumed they were vagrants because their clothes were as tattered and filthy as his; they were passing a bottle of wine back and forth and whispering conspiratorially.

We imagined they must be plotting some hideous crime; we had no proof of this and nothing happened then; it's just that the drifter looked so dark and unaccountable, lounging in our meadow and passing that wine bottle back and forth to his vagrant buddies.

THE drifter made my brother and me uneasy because Mama was spending more and more time with him. As the gardens flourished, their relationship seemed to deepen. We began to monitor their comings and goings—constantly, warily.

If we ran from window to window on the second floor of the house, we could observe them as they strolled around the property. We could spy on them as they paused at the new rose garden Happy was planting under the sundeck, or the lath house he was building directly opposite the back porch.

As a couple they radiated an aura of sensuality. Happy— big-shouldered, with muscley brown arms straining under a sweaty pullover; Mama—tiny, slender, gazing up at him. When she was in the sun she almost always wore a brilliantly patterned silk scarf about her head.

It was my first experience as a voyeur and it was disquieting. I learned something about that peculiar frisson of being an observer—how people appear more interesting when they don't know you're watching them.

Sometimes Bart and I would run outside and confront them

on the path as they stood close together, deep in conversation. Whenever they saw us they would jump apart and Mama would hug us to her bosom, crying out, "You must hear Happy's plans, children!" but we didn't want to; we'd wriggle out of her embrace and dash off.

Sometimes we'd bike all the way to Santa Cruz and wander around the boardwalk; sometimes we'd swim for hours at Aptos beach, jumping recklessly into the waves and letting the undertow pull us far out, and then we'd fight our way back through the roiling waters and collapse panting on the soft wet sand.

But often we'd spend entire days inside our hideout, a one-room shack we shared next to the abandoned guest cottage, which was about a quarter of a mile from the main house on our property.

We loved our hideout. In one corner of the room Bart "invented" potions with his chemistry set or studied bugs under his microscope.

On the other side of the room (separated by a screen) I'd set up a dressing table, covered with Mama's discarded cosmetics— half-used powders and lipsticks, mascara, and rouge. I'd sit in front of a big cracked mirror slathering myself with makeup in hopes of covering my freckles.

I wanted to be an actress. Daddy was encouraging me. He gave me books to read: biographies of actresses like Gertrude Lawrence, Sarah Bernhardt, Eleonora Duse, and Katharine Cornell. Recently he'd taken me to see my first play in San Francisco. Helen Hayes was playing Harriet Beecher Stowe, author of *Uncle Tom's Cabin*.

At the hideout, I'd pretend to be Helen as Harriet, walking around in a circle the way she did onstage. What a gritty, determined little woman she was! So full of zeal. And what a hold she had on her audience.

Later I would practice singing "La Vie en Rose" in the manner of Edith Piaf. Daddy insisted I sounded just like her; in fact, he would have me perform the song for dinner guests, and he'd lead in the applause, assuring me I was going to be a great star. "You can be anything you want to be," he'd say.

At the hideout, my brother would usually bring me back to reality by telling me quietly, but firmly, to "please shut up." He thought I was a lousy singer and he wished Daddy wouldn't tell me otherwise.

During those wartime years at Aptos, Bart seemed mostly all right. There were fewer depressions and he seemed less remote.

He was doing exceedingly well at the Town School. He'd made a close friend in Arthur Mejia, who appreciated his wry sense of humor, his taciturn ways. He was starting to have heroes, too: Beethoven and Albert Einstein—in these men he saw what human beings were capable of achieving. His strangeness was subdued.

With Daddy away so much, Granddad Bosworth became, just before he died in the summer of 1943, an authority figure for Bart. A tall, courtly man always dressed in a beautifully cut tweed suit, he was domineering, bombastic, so different from my gentle phantom father.

He would exit and enter rooms at Aptos at a stately, leisurely pace; he had the presence of an actor. (Indeed, his uncle was Hobart Bosworth, the silent-screen star of *The Sea Wolf*.)

While he was with us he gave Bart a .22-caliber rifle and showed him how to use it; he also taught him how to box. Once he took us into the woods behind our house and demonstrated how to build a campfire and use a compass.

The drifter continued that process of teaching us to explore nature. He would lead us on strenuous walks through the woods, no matter what the weather, taking us to places that we never knew existed, like the "ghost forest"—clouds of gray trees covering a cliff deep in the woods, like an "umbrella of spruce," packed so densely green it tugged at our lungs.

And as he walked, the drifter would pick flowers, and promptly name them. "Shooting stars, yellow violets, buttercups, red columbine, forget-me-nots, bluebells . . ." his soft, insinuating voice echoed through the redwood groves, which were *Sequoia gigantea,* alive before the Parthenon, "the oldest trees in the world," Happy said.

He saved his favorite place for last—a waterfall miles and miles from our house near a deserted mining camp. The water was so cold it felt like ice had melted in it.

I remember we urged the drifter to swim with us, but he

shook his head. "Can't swim," he mumbled, kneeling on the bank scowling, his shirt off, arms festooned with tattoos.

A month went by. We didn't know that Daddy had been so impressed with the drifter's plans for our gardens that he had hired him full-time. Starting in July, he would be our gardener/caretaker and would live in the abandoned guest cottage.

CHAPTER

8

Not long after he began working full-time for us, my brother and I saw the drifter on the beach, sharing cigarettes with a young boy he introduced as Slim. Slim was homeless and an orphan, he told us sadly. They had met when they were both riding the rails.

Once we came upon them lying behind a sand dune. Happy was caressing the boy's ear, much as he would an animal. The boy seemed completely detached. The gesture was languorous and sensual, and creepy, too, and we didn't know why.

In retrospect, it was peculiar that we never told our parents what we had seen; maybe it was because the drifter's strangeness was so new and so fascinating to us, we didn't want it or him to go away.

Happy didn't bring Slim onto our property—not at first, and in the beginning not while we were there. Daddy had told him he could have no "minors" working with him in the gardens. For a while Happy abided by that; he was very proper in his behavior around Mama and Daddy.

He was working very hard, planting and landscaping. He never seemed to stop, and when he wasn't working in the gardens, he was building something, like our balcony—it jutted out from a tree trunk at the far end of the main garden, and seemed to hang suspended over the tangled path that led to our stream far below.

■

EVENTUALLY, the drifter was allowed free access to our house, and
began wandering in and out—always with the excuse that he had
to carry in extra logs for the fireplaces or fresh flowers for the
mantels.

He might end up borrowing a book from our library, and
sometimes, if Daddy was there, he'd invite him to have a cocktail
and then he'd ply him with questions.

What did he think of Wendell Willkie?

"Dunno, Mr. C."

Was the drifter a Republican or a Democrat?

"I'm a nothing, Mr. C. Never voted in my life and don't think
I ever will."

He seemed uncomfortable talking about politics; less so when
he mentioned his life on the road.

He had been in a number of fights, some in a hobo jungle.
One fight was over a blanket—his blanket. Two other bums fought
him for it with knives and a razor blade. "I got cut up pretty
bloody," he told us.

"Was anyone killed?" my brother wanted to know.

Happy didn't answer.

He and Mama behaved very formally with one another, at
least when my brother and I were with them. He would address
her rather mockingly as "Mrs. C.," and she would order him about:
"Do this! Do that!" And he'd warn her, "Don't snap the whip too
hard . . ." There was an increasing tension between them, which I
couldn't understand.

I remember once watching them run through the rain together. I was standing on the back porch. Mama had driven back
from the grocery store; the drifter was helping her take packages
out of our station wagon. Suddenly a storm broke—thunder, lightning, and a rushing downpour of rain.

They were caught in it as they stumbled up the path, side by
side, very close. Happy was juggling the packages and she was
laughing. I had a funny feeling that the rain was exciting her
terribly.

They reached the kitchen, panting and drenched to the skin.
I could see Mama's nipples sticking up through the wetness of her
blouse. The material seemed glued to her flesh.

I could have left them alone together in the kitchen, but I

didn't. I insisted, over Mama's protests, that I would help put everything away, and I did, very slowly and methodically. As usual she had bought too much—too many cans of chicken soup and bags of rice and beans and coffee and sugar. The drifter watched us, leaning against the sink, smoking a cigarette. His black hair was plastered against his head from the rain.

Finally, Mama announced that she had to get out of her clothes and into a hot shower or she would catch her death of cold.

The drifter bowed and left.

As soon as he was gone she started stripping in front of me, in a fury—tearing off her denim skirt and blouse, kicking off her sandals; she unhooked her bra, she pulled down her panties—until she was completely and definitely nude.

Her small breasts heaved.

She stood glaring at me for about a second; then she stepped out of her panties, left her wet clothes in a heap on the floor, and ran upstairs to her bedroom, looking as if she were about to burst into tears.

She looked as if she were about to burst into tears a lot that summer.

Her father, my granddad Bosworth, had died, and she had attended the funeral and accompanied the coffin to the graveyard with her brother Carl, but she hadn't allowed us to go.

Daddy was in Washington so she'd been alone with her grief, but she would not give in to it. She wouldn't cry. She loved her father more than anybody, she always told me, but she would never cry for him because he wouldn't have wanted her to. "Dad taught me it was weak to show emotion," she said.

In July 1943, she wrote in her journal: "The only consolation I have right now since Dad's death is the glory of my gardens and the companionship of my children. But overall, my dissatisfaction remains vast—with myself and my life with Bart."

Meanwhile, Daddy kept receding from us, my ghostly phantom father, appearing at Aptos in the dead of night after we were all in bed, staying forty-eight hours, sometimes less, then vanishing into a taxi.

It was difficult to keep up with his schedule; it was always changing. Two days in Washington with Wendell Willkie on the Schneidermann case, a week in New York. He almost commuted from San Francisco to Los Angeles, where he had a small office. He was working on cases in Beverly Hills and on Willkie's campaign.

Travel, with its illusion of perpetual mobility, was now an ingrained habit with him. It was a way of life. So Mama and my brother and I had to endure endless weeks of waiting, of expectations dashed—he was coming; he was not coming—for the weekend.

How often we had driven with Mama to the little train station in Watsonville to pick him up from either San Francisco or Los Angeles and he wouldn't be there. He always had an excuse. He would call saying he had missed a connection; some meeting had come up; so-and-so had appeared in his office.

Usually there were guests waiting back at Aptos—a dinner party about to begin. His voice over the phone was invariably exuberant, oblivious to the fact that he had ruined plans. He was away for most birthdays and many holidays, and Mama would rail at him: "How could you? Don't you want to see the people who care about you? Don't you want to see your children grow?"

And he would be effusively apologetic, and when he finally did return, he would show up bearing expensive, impractical gifts.

But he had to keep moving. Looking back, I realize it was a way of avoiding all sorts of responsibilities—including creditors.

It must have been absolutely grueling for him. Wartime travel was a nightmare: trains were packed with soldiers, and transcontinental air travel was still a novelty. By plane it took fourteen hours to reach New York from San Francisco.

We didn't particularly care that he used to go drinking with FDR's speechwriter, Pulitzer Prize–winning playwright Robert Sherwood, or that he was getting to know Harry Hopkins, FDR's sickly Machiavellian aide who lived in the White House and was distrusted by many because he had so much influence on the president.

My father was especially pleased that he'd had dinner with Willkie and William Schneidermann, not too long after Willkie defended him in a landmark case in front of the Supreme Court. Daddy had done preliminary work on the case in late 1942, meeting with Schneidermann several times in San Francisco.

William Schneidermann was secretary of the Communist

Party in California. He'd had his citizenship revoked on the grounds that when he applied for naturalization, his membership in the Party hadn't been revealed. Willkie's defense: Congress had never made being a member of the CP a bar to natural citizenship; he added that American Communists had the right to advocate changes in the Constitution by the peaceful process of amendment.

The Supreme Court was bitterly divided about this case and fought for months over Schneidermann's fate, but in the end they decided in his favor in June 1943.

The decision affected many thousands of people. It was later used to stop deportation proceedings against Harry Bridges. ("Wendell Willkie is the only man in America who's proven he'd rather be right than be president," Bridges joked.)

Willkie wrote to my father about how glad he was to have defended Schneidermann. "It was the thing to do," he wrote. "Of all times civil liberties should be defended now."

Daddy talked a lot to us about that, but also about how proud he was to be counsel to Roosevelt's Commission on Fair Employment Practices (the long-overdue hearings into racial discrimination on the Southern Pacific Railroad). In the summer of 1943 he met for hours with A. Philip Randolph, head of the Pullman Car Porters, and Walter White of the NAACP, hammering out new antidiscrimination policies that would hold throughout the war, but unfortunately not after.

My father was much praised for his work on the commission: "Bart Crum was the driving force here," a congressman wrote. "He focused public opinion on the unfair working conditions that until now have been unknown to the mass of Americans."

But compliments gave Daddy little pleasure. "I am itching to do more," he wrote to Willkie, and he confided his dream of joining the OSS: "My friend, Peter Cusick, is in London working for Wild Bill (Donovan) and loving it."

Willkie wrote back urging him not to do it—he was needed more here—and then he added that if he had a few more men like my father, his campaign would be "in the bag."

Whenever Daddy left us again for Washington, Mama would explain that it was because he was invaluable to Wendell Willkie. How, we didn't know. Daddy was untouchable, unknowable.

After I grew up, I discovered that aside from his work on the presidential primaries, Daddy also served as liaison for Willkie, passing messages to him from Roosevelt via presidential aide David K. Niles.

Niles, round-faced and inscrutable, was a mysterious figure around Washington. Totally unknown to the public, he was extremely influential with Roosevelt and later with Truman, but he always kept to himself, never speaking to the press. He held on to his privacy; he believed it was essential for a presidential aide.

When my father knew Niles, he was a part of Roosevelt's "shadow cabinet" (which included Supreme Court justice Felix Frankfurter and speechwriter/lawyer Sam Rosenman, another FDR intimate; these men devoted themselves to Roosevelt, and stayed out of the public eye).

Niles had gotten his start in politics in 1924 working for maverick senator Robert La Follette. Then, in 1928, he organized the support of independent voters for Al Smith when Smith challenged Herbert Hoover.

Niles's skill with minorities impressed Harry Hopkins, already an influential confidant of FDR; he enlisted Niles to rally the support of blacks and Orientals in Roosevelt's presidential bid in 1932.

After Roosevelt won the election, Niles became an important part of his inner staff; by Pearl Harbor he was indispensable—always behind the scenes, working night and day along with other aides, all of whom had a passion for anonymity. They labored together near the executive suite in a line of little offices called "Death Row."

"That's because when you worked for Roosevelt, you worked till you dropped," Daddy told me.

I have a vague memory of Daddy meeting Niles during the first Willkie campaign, around 1940. Daddy was trying to get our cook Toy's family out of China, and Niles pulled some strings and got them out. Daddy was grateful; the two men struck up a friendship.

And Niles was impressed with the job my father was doing, organizing the independent vote for Willkie—they both shared a passion for politics.

By early 1941, Daddy was asked to pass messages to Willkie

from Roosevelt through David Niles. "I was designated to make certain communications to the White House," he wrote.

The first message, right after the 1940 election, asked whether Willkie would be interested in going on a goodwill mission to London for FDR regarding Lend-Lease. Willkie did go and bore a handwritten note from the president to Winston Churchill.

There were many other messages after that. They were usually delivered by phone or in person. Occasionally, Daddy would meet Niles in his office. Niles rarely wrote letters—in the many cartons of records left by him, the vast bulk of messages are those written *to* him. He preferred to make his contacts in person so there would be no written record.

My father passed some of these messages from Roosevelt to Willkie and some from Willkie to Roosevelt, all via David Niles. (Daddy wasn't the only messenger; there were many others, including Sam Rosenman.)

Like Niles, Daddy kept no written records of the messages either. And he never discussed them, although once he did divulge the contents of one message, but long after the fact.

In 1952, my father dropped Willkie biographer Joe Barnes a note about a last message—in 1944, "when Niles approached me in New York to ask whether Wendell would want to be FDR's personal representative in Europe over everyone including Eisenhower, and could Wendell come to Hyde Park to discuss the matter?"

PETER CUSICK had a theory as to why Daddy agreed to play this role of messenger. "Bart enjoyed being privy to top secret stuff before anyone else. It was exciting and he could keep confidences and he seemed to have no hidden agenda, which is why Niles trusted him."

Niles phoned my father often in those years, mostly at Aptos. I even picked up the phone a couple of times and said a few words to him. He was always very friendly; he seemed to know a lot about me—maybe Daddy had told him I wanted to be an actress. I remember him asking me about that, but I had no idea he was such a formidable power broker, wheeling and dealing with Democratic leaders and opinion molders.

"Dave was the only guy I've ever known who used his power creatively," my father told me near the end of his life. "Dave taught me that power doesn't have to be all pejorative."

MY father sought out Niles's advice when Willkie was debating whether to run for the presidency in 1944. In a letter written in April 1943, Daddy told Willkie of his confidential meeting with Niles "concerning you and the Presidency. Dave says your enemies are roughly the same enemies as the President, but in many instances their hostility is [greater] because you are the potential, you are the threat that must be eliminated . . . both you and the President derive support from the masses, but the President has the advantage because he can keep the machine boys in line . . . oh, and Joe Martin is no friend of yours . . . none of these things are particularly new, but I set them down for what they are worth. . . . Dave also implied that the war won't be concluded by 1944, so the President will be 'compelled' to run, if he can get the nomination . . . the Republicans want the weakest opponent, a man who represents the reactionary, no recognition of our (new) global position, an escapist's view of the 1940s, a return to the theory that all men should be free to starve."

DADDY wrote a great many letters to Willkie in 1943, sometimes two or three a day. He wrote very few letters to Mama then, and most of these letters have been lost. I have never found any from her either, although I'm sure they corresponded, since he was away so much.

As I recall, she was spending more and more time with the drifter in the newly built lath house, a damp, silent, fragrant place. Together they planted begonias and fuchsias in redwood bowls.

She began depending on him for advice: "Happy, should I paint the dining room pale blue?" I heard her ask him. "Should I hang the mirrored prints in the hall, Happy?"

I remember him lingering in the kitchen, watching her cook. I came upon them just after she had baked her wonderful "white cake," which my brother and I especially liked because of its rich bittersweet chocolate frosting.

She had already finished frosting the cake when I walked in, and she was holding the spatula for Happy to lick.

He made little grunting noises of pleasure as his tongue flapped up and down the chocolaty surface of the spatula.

"Chocolate will be my downfall," Mama was telling him breathlessly.

MEANWHILE, their game playing intensified. From Mama's journal, July 20, 1943: "The tenure of our relationship is changing. I invite his gaze . . . I tempt him."

July 26: "When I work with him in the lath house I breathe in his sweat and I want to sink my teeth into his glossy brown back like a vampire!"

July 29: "I dream of running off with the drifter and becoming a vagabond."

August 8: "We keep measuring each other. Taunting. Testing. I won't allow him to touch me and that arouses me. My body feels alive again. I am starting to dress in what I think may please him. In my yellow dress with the bare midriff. He whispers he wants to kiss my bellybutton and my heart beats so rapidly it scares me. But I am wary of him, too. I will try not to make him angry. I have no actual proof of this, but I suspect he is hopelessly unbalanced."

And then Happy did the strangest thing. He took us—Mama, Bart, and me—on a long walk in the woods, and proceeded to get us lost. We didn't return home until the moon came up and we were all tired and hungry and scared. Mama was furious; her legs and arms had been badly stung by nettles.

Daddy was waiting for us; he was upset, too. Happy said nothing—no apologies; he just melted away.

We sat in the kitchen, going over what had happened.

"But Happy was just pretending to be lost!" my brother cried.

And Mama agreed.

"Jesus God, that would never have occurred to me," my father said.

"Well, it occurred to *me*," Mama said irritably. "I was just too terrified to say anything." And then she added, "I think we should fire the bastard for being so irresponsible. He was playing with us. And I'm sure he's laughing his head off now in the Aptos bar-and-grill."

I couldn't believe she was calmly arguing to fire the drifter when she was secretly so passionate about him.

In the end Daddy convinced Mama Happy should stay. He was doing such a sensational job with the gardens, he said, and besides he'd paid him two months salary in advance. Admittedly, he was strange . . . but . . . The subject of Slim came up. They both agreed the boy shouldn't be allowed on the property. Daddy promised he'd talk to Happy about that before he left.

As soon as the discussion was over, my brother and I raced upstairs so we could talk between ourselves.

I was positive Mama was having a "thing" with the drifter, so I couldn't understand why she wanted him fired. Bart was equally positive Mama was *not* interested in him. "She's intrigued," he said. "But that's all. Mother has too much taste," he said.

I wasn't so sure. I was starting to be disappointed in her, and in most adults. Except for Daddy, most adults were hypocritical and two-faced, saying one thing when they meant another.

And I was no better. In school, I'd be nice to some girl I actually despised because I wanted to learn her secrets; I would entice her into confiding in me so she'd tell me her problems, then I'd try to solve them (like Daddy did).

I was starting to hang on the phone with some of my classmates, collecting their confidences, their secrets. It gave me a false sense of power.

My brother used to scold me. "Stop sticking your nose into other people's business," he'd say. "It'll get you in trouble; and stop talking out of both sides of your mouth."

I remember once trying to make him feel better when I saw he had a depression coming on. I showered him with extravagant compliments about his brilliance in math, expecting that might raise his spirits.

"Oh, shut up," he begged me. His face drew taut and pale.

"Everything will be all right," I assured him. (It was a phrase Daddy used constantly.)

"Everything is *not* going to be all right," Bart told me. "Your lying doesn't make it any better."

To make up for getting us lost in the woods, Happy tried to be ingratiating. He fixed us a rope swing near the myrtle bed on the hill above our hideout; we were able to fly through the air on that swing and then drop down into the thick green myrtle—it was so dense it pillowed our falls.

Meanwhile, Mama and Happy resumed their game playing, or whatever it was.

I never knew what went on between them—a flirtation or an actual affair—because she was never specific in her journal, but she did keep a lot of notes.

August 21: "He wants me to visit him at the guest house at night. That I will not do."

August 30: "He has finally caught me, held me, humiliated me, brutalized me and I loved it and I hate myself for loving it. My response astounds me. I no longer feel so helpless. Do I confess this to Dr. B.? I think not. I still have the romantic vision of sex as the great reconciler, the great comforter. I still dream of someone who will rouse me as if from the dead. Is being controlled by a male the all-pervasive experience in a woman's life?"

Near the end of the summer, I saw them kissing in the pantry. They had no idea I was lurking in the shadows, but I was, and I held my breath as Happy muttered something I thought must be obscene and his hand gripped her rump and she actually shuddered.

Then he glided away and out into the garden, leaving her panting against the sink, her face radiant, flushed, yielding. I had never seen her so beautiful—so totally self-consciously pleased.

I told no one what I had seen, not even my brother. I kept Mama's secret, choking on it. I could not believe she could prefer this shaggy, tattooed stranger to my wonderful, gentle father. Still I said nothing.

Was it because I didn't want to split loyalties? Or cause trouble? Certainly I wanted to keep peace in our uneasy household, but every time I saw Mama kiss Daddy in the same yielding, radiant way she had kissed Happy, and Daddy would act surprised and laugh, I felt sick.

I hated Mama for what she'd done, but I began copying Daddy's manner with her—a manner both indulgent and teasingly affectionate. I sensed he knew something funny was going on, but he didn't seem to care—he didn't seem to care whether she was unfaithful or not, so why should I? But I did anyway.

CHAPTER 9

IN October, Daddy phoned to invite us to join him and the Willkie entourage in Los Angeles for the weekend. There were plans, he said, to go over the *One World* script Lamar Trotti had written, but this was also a political trip because Willkie had been campaigning all over California, pushing his liberal philosophy.

He had virtually announced his candidacy in *Look* magazine on October 5 with an article entitled "How the Republican Party Can Win in 1944."

Still, Mama had to be persuaded to join Willkie. She didn't want to miss a weekend at Aptos, she said, because she had to oversee Happy's work in the gardens. Otherwise he might get "out of control" again.

My brother and I made such a fuss she finally agreed to go.

It was a relief to be a complete family again. I remember hugging Daddy frantically the minute I jumped off the train. I clung to him until he started laughing, saying, "What's this all about?"

I didn't know how to explain.

We stayed at the Garden of Allah, off Sunset Boulevard. That big Spanish-styled main hotel with its twenty-five bungalows surrounding a lotus-shaped swimming pool was a Hollywood legend.

"All sorts of interesting people are here," Daddy told us as he drove us there from the station. It was true: humorist Robert Benchley; *New Yorker* writer S. J. Perelman; actor Melvyn Douglas;

movie star Joan Bennett (she and Mama tried on each other's hats)
—they all moved in and out of our bungalow that weekend. I know
because they all signed my autograph book. Daddy had met most
of them through various Popular Front causes he had been involved with in Hollywood, especially the Hemingway documentary
on the Civil War, which he'd helped raise money for with novelist
John Dos Passos.

What a time it was for my brother and me, so much crammed
into a couple of days. It was our introduction to the highly pressured, glamorous world Daddy had created for himself away from
us, his juggling of politics and law.

I remember an October 1943 calendar he propped up on the
dresser. It had lists of trials and pretrial hearings, court appearances for both Los Angeles and San Francisco, written briefs to be
delivered, client meetings in places like the Bel Air Hotel—all
sandwiched in between a Willkie rally and a party at Eddie G.
Robinson's—and something was penciled in about the Spanish
War refugees with Dorothy Parker's name attached to it.

I remember the phones never stopped ringing. I remember
Attorney General Robert Kenny barging in at some point, and I
realized as he poured himself a drink that he had a withered arm.
Kenny used to kid Daddy a lot about doing "too goddamn much—
you'll kill yourself."

As the years went on, more and more people criticized him
for doing too much, for rushing into court and improvising; he had
too many clients. He had a good memory, but he wasn't always
well prepared.

How he managed to take us on a tour of MGM Studios in
between everything he had to do for Willkie and his clients that
weekend at the Garden of Allah I'll never know, but he did. And
we had chocolate malts at Schwab's Drugstore, too. (While we
were there he identified the young Ava Gardner padding past us,
barefoot. She was on her way to the magazine rack.)

He took us to some of his favorite haunts as well.

We ate dinner at Chasen's—"the best steak and garlic toast
you'll ever taste." And we went to the Players, which film director
Preston Sturges had built with his first movie money. Daddy told
us it was Sturges's "plaything," a restaurant bar and meeting place
for writers and actors. Humphrey Bogart and his then wife, Mayo

Methot, drank in the bar there every night. I remember climbing up to the little screening room on the top floor of the Players. It had originally been a private dining room where Howard Hughes secretly took his favorite girls. "Hughes wrote notes to himself on the tablecloth," Daddy said.

The only bad experience we had was going to Ciro's to see Sophie Tucker, "the last of the red-hot Mamas," perform. Tucker was a fat dyed-blond grandmother type (at least seventy-five, Daddy surmised). Dressed in white sequins and mink, she sang lustily, boisterously, songs like "The Darktown Strutters' Ball" and her theme song, "Some of These Days."

Between numbers she would talk about her career, which had begun in vaudeville and climaxed at the Ziegfeld Follies. She had gotten her start as a "yeller" for Decca Records. The audience gave her a standing ovation.

Daddy was acting as her lawyer for something, so we went backstage after the show. I couldn't get over how old and dumpy Tucker looked in her dressing gown surrounded by baskets of dying flowers. But her energy was huge. She was still "on" from the performance, and for a while she kept up a stream of patter, most of which I'm sure she had said hundreds of times before.

Daddy being Daddy told her she looked beautiful. But Tucker would have none of it. "Come off it, Bart. I'm older'n hell."

We all stared at her. An uncomfortable silence followed, and then—why, I don't know—Daddy asked me to sing. I was unprepared. As for Tucker, she did a mock double take—I could almost hear her saying, "What do I need *this* for? I just wanna soak my feet!" But she growled, "Why not?" and beckoned me forward. So I opened my mouth and tried, amid the blazing lights and the smell of cold cream and B.O., to sing "La Vie en Rose."

I could see myself reflected in her dressing-room mirror—a freckle-faced, straggly-haired girl of eleven with a terrified expression. Midway through my rendition of "La Vie en Rose," Tucker bellowed, "I can't hear ya, kid, and you're standing right in front of me!" I burst into tears.

Daddy yelped with embarrassed laughter, and Mama hustled me and my brother out into the night, leaving my father behind to deal with his volatile client alone.

AT breakfast the next morning my parents had a discussion about whether or not I should have sung for Sophie Tucker. In the end, it was decided it hadn't been a good idea. Daddy apologized for putting me through such an ordeal.

The following year he sent me to a coach, who tried to help me get rid of my stage fright. The only thing she was able to teach me was how to throw my voice. Years later, Daddy would brag that his daughter could call a cab better than any man.

But on that morning in Hollywood, so long ago, I wondered what Mama thought. She mainly listened when he spoke. She had been jubilant all that weekend and very affectionate with us and with Daddy. How could she be so two-faced, I wondered, when I'd seen her so recently passionately kiss another man?

I couldn't understand her abrupt changes of mood, or Daddy's changes of mood either. His affability seemed forced. I was sure he was under pressure because he kept coughing convulsively; he did that whenever he worried.

And he worried because he kept receiving phone calls from sources in Sacramento who said that Governor Warren wasn't going to admit he wanted to run for president, nor would he admit he wasn't going to give Willkie those crucial fifty electoral votes.

At a big fund-raising party for Willkie at Pickfair, Mary Pickford's estate, I watched my father with the candidate. Actually I saw the candidate close-up, lumbering out of a guest bathroom, buttoning his fly while Daddy guarded the door.

As soon as Willkie emerged, he was literally descended upon by a horde of noisy admirers.

Almost immediately, he took on the blind gaze of the super-celebrity.

Daddy tried to attract his attention. "Hey, Wendell—you remember my daughter . . . Patricia?" But Willkie stared right through me. No eye contact.

Experiencing public life meant maintaining an exquisite distance.

But it was weird because I felt I *knew* Willkie, or thought I did until that moment, since Daddy talked about him endlessly, and I'd heard him on the radio, seen him in newsreels, and we had photographs of him all over the house. I guess I'd internalized Willkie, but that of course didn't mean he saw *me*.

Ordinary people saw you. However, ordinary people didn't run for president of the United States.

After the fund-raising party, we drove up the Pacific Coast Highway and headed home.

A poll of GOP leaders taken that month in San Francisco showed Willkie leading both rival candidates, Warren and Dewey, by a comfortable margin.

There seemed, in fact, to be enthusiasm for Willkie's brand of liberalism all over the Bay Area. My father had done a great job rallying support from powerful men like George Cameron, publisher of the *San Francisco Chronicle*.

There was an impromptu gathering in our living room, with the usual assortment of lawyers, journalists, and San Francisco opinion makers munching Mama's hot hors d'oeuvres and arguing about Willkie's eccentric appeal.

Before he left California, Daddy convinced Willkie to appear in Magnin's department store window to sell war bonds and "shake the flesh."

"It did a lot of good and sold some bonds," Daddy noted in a telegram to Attorney General Robert Kenny some weeks later.

Willkie wrote Daddy subsequently, "Thank you for all your help. I have never known a fellow as loyal and generous as you."

But in spite of Daddy's efforts, there was already a "Stop Willkie" movement in twenty states that was increasing in scope. The Old Guard Republicans were furious at Willkie and his "progressive ideas." He was a "political turncoat," some of his critics said, for supporting FDR's aims so totally in the war.

Big Republican bosses like Herb Brownell had already tried to convince Warren to run in the primary and thus deny the state's fifty delegates to Willkie.

At the end of October, Willkie finally visited Warren in Sacramento. The governor admitted that, yes, he was running in the primary, but not as a candidate, he assured Willkie—just to hold the fifty delegates together at the convention, he said.

My father subsequently advised Willkie that he needn't be forced out of the primary even if Warren decided to run. But Willkie wouldn't listen; he refused to deal with this particular issue until it was too late—he was more concerned and angered with the attacks from right-wing Republicans such as Edgar M.

ABOVE LEFT: My father, Bartley Cavanaugh Crum, with his mother, "Mo," in Sacramento in 1901

ABOVE RIGHT: My father as a teenager

BELOW: My mother, Anna Gertrude "Cutsie" Bosworth, with her mother, Anna, and brother, Carl

Daddy *(right)* as a law student at the University of California at Berkeley

Cutsie shortly after her marriage, getting her usual suntan

Patricia, Bart Crum, and his father, James Henry Crum

Cutsie, kneeling in front of step-mother, Julie, and father, Charles Bosworth, after they climbed Mt. Whitney

Cutsie, Bart, and Patricia at Lake Tahoe

Father and daughter in Berkeley

Patti in her little black velvet dress

Bart Junior, age four, when he was attending Erik Erikson's school

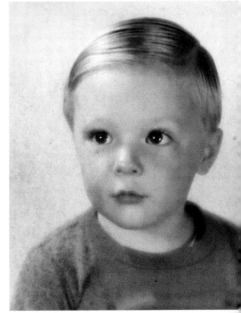

Mother and daughter in identical
Lantz dresses at Aptos

Working for Willkie in 1940

Aptos Ranchos, California, circa 1944

The Crum family in the garden at Aptos; the only picture of us all together

Happy, Bart, and Patti in the woods

Happy's beautiful rose garden

Harry Truman and Bart Crum during the 1944 presidential campaign

Harry Bridges and Bart Crum *(right)* in San Francisco, 1945

OPPOSITE:
Left to right, Hollywood producer Walter Wanger, Cutsie, actress Joan Bennett, and Bart Crum lunching in the Paramount commissary in 1942

Bartley Crum and his most famous client movie star, Rita Hayworth, in Reno, Nevada, after she signed a divorce complaint from husband, Prince Aly Khan

Bart Crum *(second from right, in profile)* at the founding of the United Nations in San Francisco with Earl Warren at far right

Bart Crum inciting the crowd at the American Zionist Emergency Council rally at Madison Square Garden, June 1946

My father with *New York Post* reporter Ruth Gruber outside Bergen-Belsen

The Anglo-American Committee of Inquiry into Palestine (Bart Crum center, in profile in back row)

The Committee during meetings in Jerusalem (Bart Crum standing) in 1946

The Hollywood 19 in Washington just before hearings began, October 1947. *Front row, left to right:* writers Lewis Milestone, Dalton Trumbo, and John Howard Lawson, and Bartley Crum. *Center row, left to right:* writer Gordon Kahn; directors Irving Pichel, Eddie Dmytryk, and Robert Rossen. *Top row, left to right:* Waldo Salt, Richard Collins, Howard Koch, Albert Maltz, Herbert Biberman, Lester Cole, Ring Lardner Jr., and attorney Martin Popper

Left to right: Adrian Scott, Bartley Crum, and Eddie Dmytryk when they thought everything was going to be all right

AP Wide World Photos

UPI/Corbis-Bettmann

Dalton Trumbo leaves stand after shouting "This is the beginning of an American concentration camp!" Bart Crum *(left)* and Robert Kenny are behind him.

The day they bought the newspaper *PM* from Marshall Field. Bart Crum *(left)* and editor Joseph Barnes are telling reporters they now own the left-wing tabloid (May 1948)

Last summer at Aptos; Bart Crum with daughter and son

TOP: "The wild party" at Poletti's villa on Lake Geneva (Patti in front row, *third from left,* in her mother's lace dress)

CENTER: Brother and sister after being sent home from school in disgrace

BOTTOM: Bartley Crum visiting with his mother, Mo, in Sacramento, 1954

AP Wide World Photos

Bart Crum testifying in front of the Senate Rackets Committee, July 1959 (Godfrey Schmidt is sitting behind him)

Patricia Bosworth backstage in *Mary, Mary,* about to finally go on as "Mary" in 1963

Gertrude Bosworth Crum just after her cookbook, *A World of Menus and Recipes,* was published in 1978 and named one of the best cookbooks of the year

Queeny (who'd joined the Stop Willkie movement), the hugely wealthy head of Monsanto Chemical Corporation.

Queeny, who hailed from Missouri, had supported Willkie to the tune of $96,000 in 1940; now he was harshly critical of Willkie's freewheeling liberalism—particularly when it came to defending Communists.

Eventually, the two men traded insults at a luncheon in St. Louis for big industrialists. And Willkie ended up shouting, "I don't know whether you're going to support me or not, but I don't give a damn. You're a bunch of political liabilities anyway." Following this confrontation, Willkie's popularity soared.

Both Gardner Cowles and my father urged Willkie to show more restraint; he couldn't afford more enemies in the GOP, they said. By this time Willkie was fighting mad. He wanted to cut loose from all party moorings.

Mid-fall, Willkie's candidacy was opposed by the party machine in New York, Pennsylvania, Ohio, and even in his home state, Indiana. "It got so bad we started thinking about forming a third party," Ruth Bishop recalled. "We explored the possibility, but the legal and technical hassles made it impossible to do in less than a year."

Daddy was in on some of those third party discussions in New York, and he continued to work for Willkie on the phone and through the mail whenever he returned to San Francisco.

His files thickened with letters and telegrams to precinct leaders, congressmen, financiers around the state—eloquent, persuasive letters attempting to get support for Willkie's candidacy. But in spite of his efforts, the California primary campaign collapsed. Too many powers in the Republican Party were dead set against it.

"Willkie forgot—ignored—a very important rule in politics," Daddy said later. "Loyalty to party. The crazy thing was a lot of Republicans secretly agreed with his philosophy but rejected his leadership because he was so far out!"

BY mid-January, Willkie decided to file in the New Hampshire and Wisconsin primaries and he asked Daddy to go to Madison to organize the campaign there. But since there weren't adequate funds to pay him, Daddy had to say no.

Gardner Cowles was the only friend who traveled with him in those last exhausting weeks.

For thirteen days Willkie campaigned across the snowy Wisconsin countryside. At one point he had to slog two hundred miles through a blizzard. He kept talking and talking and talking. He talked about taxes; he talked about the potential for a United Nations; he talked about the future of America after the war.

"The Boss gave forty speeches in thirteen days," Daddy wrote Mama from Washington, D.C., where he was trying a case. "His throat is giving him a helluva lot of trouble."

In the final week of the campaign Willkie attracted a crowd of five thousand in Sheboygan. Afterward someone said, "If this is any indication you should win big."

"Yeah." Willkie grinned. "If they vote for me."

When the Wisconsin primary was held on April 4, 1944, none of Willkie's loyal band of followers thought he would be defeated so utterly. He received not one electoral vote.

"I find it hard to believe," Daddy wrote in a notebook. "Of the four candidates who filed in Wisconsin, Wendell was the only one to campaign and he failed completely. As for his rivals, Stassen was on a boat somewhere in the Pacific, MacArthur was in Australia, and yet Wendell thought he could win and that the people would listen to him. I think his ideas about the future and postwar America were bigger than politics, bigger than the Republican Party and that is precisely why he lost."

BY this time, spring 1944, we were back in school in San Francisco, but Mama continued driving us to the country every weekend and Daddy started joining us again there as often as he could.

He and Mama would invariably help the drifter weed and water in the gardens or plant bulbs in the lath house; they would have discussions as to whether or not Happy should order a certain kind of shrub because it attracts butterflies.

Occasionally, they would even follow the drifter out to the north field, where he was preparing the earth for the apple orchard. Sometimes they would dig right by his side for hours, and we'd bring them iced Coca-Colas.

They would be talking so intensely that Daddy often insisted the drifter join us for supper so they could continue their conversations. On those evenings, Mama might prepare wondrous dishes for us such as ratatouille (a garlicky vegetable stew made from fresh eggplant and tomatoes from the victory garden), or cheese ramekins filled with heavy cream, and as she served us she might flirt with the drifter. When he didn't respond, she would bait him so cruelly he'd slink off, a glowering look on his face.

Daddy would chuckle with embarrassment whenever Mama flirted. In retrospect, I wonder if he was aware of her obsession with the drifter or if he ignored it as he subsequently ignored the other men who appeared to mean something to her at various times in their marriage. He never seemed the slightest bit jealous, which I think maddened Mama in the beginning. Looking back on it, it was almost as if he welcomed the drifter into our home because then he would no longer have to be so sexually responsible.

We hated sharing our meals with the drifter while Mama poured him goblets of wine from the crystal decanter and occasionally placed her hand on his shoulder in a disturbingly familiar way. Once I remember he sat in Daddy's chair at the head of the table. We showed our disapproval by refusing to eat the delicious food Mama placed in front of us. And afterward, Bart hung my big rag doll, Mary Ann, from the rafters of the second-floor ceiling.

"Happy in effigy," he told me grimly. Mama made him cut down the doll immediately.

CHAPTER

10

DADDY was in Los Angeles when we arrived at Aptos one rainy evening to discover Happy was gone. We assumed he was doing one of his "disappearing acts," as Mama called them. And then the sheriff of Santa Cruz phoned to say that Happy had been arrested for being "wild drunk on the boardwalk." He'd been with a boy named Slim; they tried to rent a motel room, but he hadn't had any money. He'd started acting crazy—foaming at the mouth, twitching.

Soon other facts emerged. Earlier in 1943, Happy had been arrested in Chicago for draft dodging; he had jumped bail and fled Illinois, hitchhiking across the country until he landed in the woods behind our property.

He had other entries on his police record: arrested for drunken driving; shoplifting (twice); suspected of robbing a liquor store. He had several aliases—Harry Kanter, Henry Kabot; his real name was Harold Kantawiscz. During 1940, he had been incarcerated in a mental institution in Rhode Island, where his epilepsy had been misdiagnosed as an extreme form of schizophrenia.

Mama passed this information on to Daddy, and then told us she hoped Happy would rot in jail. But the following morning she drove in to Santa Cruz to see him.

We never knew what had passed between them. Within two hours she was back home, her face clenched. All she would say was that he was very sorry for all the trouble he had caused. He would be sent back momentarily to Chicago to stand trial for draft dodging. She thought it was for the best, she told us—at least he would be gone from our lives.

"He was disruptive, wasn't he, children?" she asked. "Now we'll have a little peace around here."

I think she meant *she'd* have a little peace.

BUT Daddy decided to take on Happy's case. It wasn't the first time he had decided to save someone disreputable. Part of his law practice was devoted to defending impoverished thieves and murderers pro bono. He always insisted "everyone has worth." For years he had been driving out to San Quentin prison one day a week to teach illiterates how to read and write.

So Mama couldn't convince him it might be more sensible to leave Happy Kanta in jail. It seemed to make no difference that he might be unstable or even dangerous. Because Daddy was maintaining—improbably—that the drifter's talents for gardening outweighed his murky criminal past. "He's a rebel—he's a free spirit," he told us. "I'd like to give the guy another chance," he said.

To which Mama scoffed, "You don't have to save *everybody.*" One of the longest running arguments of their marriage was her insistence that my father's need to save people fed his ego. I can still hear her saying, "What are you trying to do? Become a saint?"

Daddy always ignored that question. He disliked introspection. I can't recall that he ever engaged in any kind of serious self-examination. He certainly never explained *why* he did anything. Least of all why he seemed to enjoy "saving souls."

They fought about Happy Kanta's fate for days. I think she hoped to be rid of him so she wouldn't be tempted anymore, but eventually, in between everything else he was doing, my father flew out to Chicago and met with the drifter and then managed to convince both the Illinois draft board and the courts that Happy Kanta was incapable of serving in the United States Army because of his epilepsy, therefore he wasn't guilty of anything.

The judge agreed to release him if my father would hire him back as our gardener, which he did, and Happy returned to us sometime in mid-May of 1944.

On May 19, Mama scribbled in her journal:

H.K. back. I am desolate . . . but I will hide my feelings behind my "sunny smile." Happy ignored me; I ignored him. I hate the sight of him—tattooed, unshaven. He clumped into our living room, a bundle on his back and thanked Bart for getting him out of jail . . . as well he should. Then my darling husband offered him a drink and asked him to stay for dinner! He refused both, thank God, and wandered off into the night.

I did *not* want to show my uneasiness, certainly not in front of the children—I waited until they'd gone up to bed and then I told Bart in no uncertain terms that I thought we were making a huge mistake taking him back. I have huge trepidations. Inside myself I was asking (can I stay away from him? I am still attracted to the bastard!). But out loud to Bart I said, "We still know so little about him and what we do know is not good." And then I added that I had never wanted him back (which is the truth) and why hadn't he listened to me? "Doesn't my opinion mean anything to you?" I asked. "Why don't you ever listen to me? *Why is that?* And why don't you pay more attention to me and the children?"

Awful memories came back to me in a flood. The experiences I've had at being abandoned . . . I remembered the night young Bart was born and Big Bart was out giving a speech somewhere in Oakland. I remembered some of the other times—there have been so many. Birthdays. Holidays. Even Dad's funeral—when he left me alone. My beautiful home is sad compensation. I am so completely alone and miserable . . . The children are restless, questioning. I won't talk against their father to them so they love him unconditionally.

I wanted to scream "I almost gave myself up to our gardener for God's sake and you never noticed." But I didn't say that; instead I asked him again, "Why don't you pay more attention to us?" He gave me an odd look. A cold look, which shook me terribly. "Well?" I demanded. "I'm not going to dignify that question with an answer, Cutsie," he said, and he went back to his reading.

MEANWHILE, Happy was still creating brilliant gardens for us—a carpet of daffodils at the front of the house; a new wood garden of foxgloves and violets; the apple orchard on the hill—but he was overcome by uncontrollable fits of restlessness. He would disappear for days at a time.

We'd invariably find him holed up at the ramshackle Aptos bar-and-grill, a dank unpleasant place smelling of beer and mildew. Mama would order Bart and me to scurry in there and bring him back. He might be at a table playing cards with a noisy group of men from the local garage. He kept his table laughing, but they all looked vaguely uneasy, as if they would prefer to be somewhere else.

Once we saw him swallow some brandy and take four Benzedrine tablets. Another time he carried a live baby mouse, wriggling, out of the toilet, and swung it around by its tail. "Lookee what I found!" he crowed. "I ate a mouse like this—roasted it when I was starving and it tasted like shrimp!"

We could never persuade him to leave with us, but after we had confronted him he'd usually come home a few hours later. Outside in our station wagon Mama was waiting and we'd describe what we'd seen to her. She would just shrug.

She wrote in her journal: "He knows it is OVER between us. At first he thought I was teasing him. But I'm not. He is very surprised. He didn't expect me to behave this way. It is hell for me, but now it is strictly business. He doesn't like it at all. Maybe that's why he keeps disappearing. He is angry. But he'll come back. He'll come back to the gardens because he has to finish them."

Indeed the results of his labors were extraordinary. His careful seasonal planting had worked: iris and white lavender blooming in April; delphinium and carnations in May; and by June his "pièce de résistance" (as Daddy called it), the rose garden, burst into flower in the stone-bordered beds directly under Mama's sundeck.

I've never forgotten that garden; I used to walk around it in wonderment, breathing in the sweet fragrance of those roses. All sorts of roses, dozens of roses: yellow tea roses, pink damask roses, and deep red Étoile de Holland roses; they were opening their soft velvety petals to the sun and they bombarded our senses with perfume and color, such glorious rich colors.

I remember my brother and I clipped great bunches of roses and the thorns scratched our fingers and drew blood, but we kept on clipping them anyway. Mama took a snapshot of us holding a basket of roses just before we carried them into the house.

Friends of my parents would drive down from San Francisco just to see the gardens and my brother and I would trail behind them, hearing their comments and their gasps. It was unearthly almost and there was such a profusion of flowering everywhere and the bees buzzed and the birds twittered.

"It *is* perfection!" Mama would cry out.

At some point Daddy would call out, "Happy! Happy! He's the creator of this splendor," and the drifter would emerge from the shadows. Sullen, uncommunicative. He would be in his filthy workclothes, his swarthy face glistening with sweat, and everyone would congratulate him on his "exquisite" work. He would say nothing.

On these occasions Mama tried to avoid him. She would grab me or my brother and hide behind us. She never took off her dark glasses during those weeks. I remember Bart telling her, "You look funny."

When the tour of the gardens was over, a noisy luncheon usually followed on the porch, with Mama describing how she prepared her famous cold lamb marinade.

I was more interested in watching Edla Cusick. She was Broadway costume designer Ailine Bernstein's daughter and I thought she was the most elegant woman I'd ever seen. She had jet-black hair cut as short as a man's and she wore a monocle in one eye—I wanted to ask her how she kept it from popping into her plate. Next to her actress Ina Claire was talking baby talk to the journalist John Gunther while landscape architect Tommy Church tried to serve them both salad from a huge green china bowl.

By then the invasion of Normandy was on and it was the prime topic of conversation. Against incredible odds of weather and German resistance, 154,000 men had landed in the first twenty-four hours of Operation OVERLORD, and they were being supported by something like 5,000 ships and 11,000 planes. The bloodiest and costliest fighting of the entire war ensued. We followed the battle on the radio and in the newsreels that June, watching Allied bombing fleets keep up relentless raids on German industrial sites and railways.

In mid-June, finally, Happy finished plowing the field for the apple orchard and began planting the trees. When he wasn't around, my brother and I used to ride our bikes through the furrows in the earth, and we'd topple off continuously into the deep rich dirt.

Often we would pedal to the top of the hill so we could gaze down at the riotous colors of our gardens, and occasionally we'd see Mama working side by side with the drifter. But it was obvious they weren't communicating. They were in fact barely speaking to each other. Either my brother or I had to tell Happy what Mama wanted him to do.

The drifter now served as our handyman, repairing faucets in the kitchen and building shelves near the pantry. I remember the time our toilet overflowed in the downstairs bathroom late one afternoon and I had to ask him to fix it.

I ran all over the gardens trying to find him, but he seemed to have vanished; then I realized he was probably taking a break. I found him bare-chested and barefoot, lounging in a deck chair on the little patio off the guest cottage where he was living. He was drinking from a bottle of whiskey. Music streamed from a portable radio.

He scowled when he saw me, obviously annoyed at the intrusion.

"Mama says the toilet's overflowed and you must come up and fix it immediately—please?"

" 'Mama says the toilet's overflowed and you must come up and fix it immediately—please?' " he mimicked tipsily, then he gave me a lewd look. "What do I get for it?"

"I beg your pardon?"

Rising unsteadily to his feet he held out his arms.

I backed away.

"Dance with me," he pleaded thickly. "Les' jes' give it a whirl."

In the background the music throbbed and pulsed.

"Mama says . . ." I began, and then I darted out of the patio.

"Yeah, yeah, I know, your toilet's overflowing," he called after me. Then he added, "I wonder if her shit is any different than mine," and he grabbed a tool box and staggered behind me to the house.

Within an hour he had repaired the toilet, but then we heard the sound of a shower beating down in the bathroom, raining on the thick plastic shower curtain.

"What on earth?" Mama came running out of the kitchen. She tried the bathroom door; it was locked, so she began rattling the knob. Still there was no answer.

Eventually the water stopped running, and a few moments later the drifter emerged, looking scrubbed and clean. He was still barefoot and bare-chested, his trousers rolled up to expose tanned muscular knees, and he had wrapped a thick peach-colored towel around his head, giving him an exotic appearance; he looked a little like an Arab potentate.

"I was drunk and now I'm sober," he informed us, padding very grandly into the living room, where he began pulling volumes off the shelves; they fell to the floor with a crash. Soon there were dozens of books surrounding him as he stood swaying near the fireplace. He appeared almost in a trance.

"Do you know what the doctor told me in the loony bin?" he asked us. "That my only importance to people is my nuisance value. The only way I can be noticed is by causing anxiety."

We stared at him. Then he grabbed a book from the floor, opened it, and began to read from Byron's *Cain.*

> *"Cain! What hast thou done?*
> *The voice of thy slain brother's blood cries out,*
> *Even from the ground, unto the Lord!—* . . .
> *Henceforth . . . a fugitive shalt thou*
> *Be from this day, and vagabond on earth!"*

The drifter shouted this last sentence in a deep, awful voice, and then he turned to us. "The first man on earth to go crazy was Cain. Did you know that, Mrs. C.?" and he snapped the book shut and dropped it onto the floor.

The noise made him start, and he gazed at us beseechingly. "Forgive me, ladies, I forgot where I was for a moment." Then he sank to his knees and began to sob. "I killed a child once," he confided.

"How?" Mama breathed.

"By running him over. Outside Boston. I was seventeen. I'd

been drinking. Cars weaving between trees. Two cars in front of me. This little tyke came darting out into the street. I didn't see him. Don't know where in hell he came from. It was over in a second. I gunned my car and drove off very fast. Was never caught."

And then he was babbling about the waitress in the Aptos bar—she'd been fired. He was hoping he could help her find work soon because she had two babies. "She wants me all the time," he said, but he found her repellent. "All she asks for is to be eaten. . . . All she asks . . ."

Mama sat up on the couch. "Go to your room, Patti!" she said to me.

I wouldn't budge.

Happy sat back on his haunches. "Don't you have anything to say, Mrs. C.? A word of sympathy? Or a taunt? You used to taunt me. You used to show me a little contempt. How do you feel about me, Mrs. C.? With your bare feet all manicured. You look at me with those great sad pop eyes of yours, and you make me feel like a fuckin' fool."

"There is a better way to describe you, Happy Kanta," Mama told him sternly.

"Sure there is, Mrs. C., and you know it." Rising from his knees he started to walk unsteadily toward her. "I'm crazy, Mrs. C."

Mama grabbed for the object closest to her, a huge velvet pillow, and she tried to shield herself with it.

The drifter began to laugh, a maniacal horse cackle. His dark eyes looked haunted; his mouth was drawn back, showing discolored teeth.

"Don't worry, Mrs. C., I won't lay a hand on you. I am too soused." Suddenly he looked old and tired as he turned and walked unsteadily out of the room.

Mama watched him go; she was trembling. But in a second she seemed to recover herself.

"Happy!" she cried out. "That's one of my best monogrammed towels you have on your head!"

He whirled on her in a rage. "You want it? You take it!" he spat, and flung the towel at her.

Mama caught it. As soon as he was out of sight she clasped

the towel to her breast and buried her face in the material, which now stank of whiskey.

AND still, incredibly, she and Daddy kept him on.

We had an account at the local hardware store and nursery, and one morning without asking permission, Happy proceeded to order some heavy power tools, including a tractor, and he also ordered one thousand strawberry plants and artichoke plants. They were deposited on our drive, all these plants. They surrounded our station wagon, blocking every inch of the road, stretching almost to the cypress at the edge of our property. It was unbelievable.

Mama came marching out of the house. She refused to sign the sales slips and sent everything back immediately. When Happy discovered this an hour later—he had been down near the stream—he and Mama had a violent argument. That was when she told him he was finished and to pack up his things and get off the property within twenty-four hours.

I AWOKE the following morning smelling smoke. I could hear my brother calling to me hysterically, so I ran out of my bedroom and onto Mama's sundeck, which was just off the upstairs hall.

Bart was already there, jumping up and down in his blue-and-white-striped pajamas and yelling, "Fire! Fire!"

Flames like orange tidal waves were moving across the north field, eating up the apple orchard in what seemed like a matter of seconds.

Then the lath house exploded to the right of us—below and beyond the vegetable garden. It was as if a bomb had burst inside it. We heard wood crackling merrily and then we heard Mama screaming, "Children! Get out of the house at once!" We looked down and saw her in her robe and slippers running crazily up and down the garden path.

We raced down the stairs and out into the smoky dawn.

Sirens began to wail across the hills and from beyond the woods. It was as if there were about to be a terrible air attack—in fact, the same sirens were used when there was a warning (always false) that the Japanese were about to bomb us.

The wailing increased as fire engines from most of the little towns around Santa Cruz came bumping down our drive.

I recognized the Aptos butcher and the postman and a few local boys clinging to the town's one fire engine. They were shouting almost gleefully as they pulled out hoses and trained great geysers of water on the shooting flames.

We just stood there, clinging to each other, feeling the intense heat, breathing in smoke. Our eyes streamed with tears. I kept praying I'd wake up and it would all be a bad dream.

It took two hours to get the blaze under control. At some point the fire chief and the police told us that the drifter had probably started the fire. More specifically, he had set many little fires, and these had been designed to destroy everything he had created for us, the most beautiful portions of our gardens: the lath house with its delicate plants; the new apple orchard.

He'd dug trenches around the orchard and the lath house and stuffed them with gasoline-soaked papers. He probably had done this in the dead of night, possibly with the help of Slim and his vagrant buddies.

"Not a trace of any of 'em," the police said. The fruit-stand owner on the highway had seen Happy and Slim board a Greyhound bus shortly before 6:00 A.M.

For some reason, Happy hadn't tried to burn down the house with us in it. He didn't burn down the guest cottage or the hideout either. Nor did he burn the rose garden; he just trampled it with his boots—and he had uprooted most of the bushes. The rose garden looked so awful—mutilated—torn apart as if by some monster. It was beyond repair.

"He ruined everything that meant something to me—ruined, ruined," Mama sobbed. I had never seen her cry before.

"The guy was crazy, Mrs. Crum," one of the policemen said.

She was crying uncontrollably. "My husband and I felt sorry for him."

"Not worth it, Mrs. Crum—this was a real bad man. You're lucky to be alive."

"CLOSE call with disaster and now Happy Kanta is gone," Mama confided to her journal.

> This is the second time we've had a fire in our home. The first was in Berkeley when my darling baby son and my husband

almost died. Now a fire in the gardens. The place smells of smoke, trees and flowers are blackened and dead. I telephoned Bart in New York. He seemed enormously sanguine about the whole thing. All he cared about was us, he said. "You and the children are safe," he said, "gardens can be planted again, you are indispensable." I asked him, "When are you coming home?" and he assured me, "As soon as I can get a plane ticket."

Now I am finally alone in my bedroom where I have only the most disturbing thoughts for company. When I stop to think about it I am no better than our drifter, a.k.a. bum, wanderer, pathological liar, bisexual, maybe thief. . . . This past year I used him, first as a sort of specimen I wanted to examine (like a blob of blood under a tiny square of glass), then as someone who would titillate and arouse me. At the start I marveled at him because he seemed to be creating a personality *just for me*—devil, fallen angel, flesh and blood human. He was tattooed, he was dirty; I used to see his genitals bulging inside those filthy trousers. . . .

We ended up playing fantastic sexual games with each other while my beautiful house and gardens provided the setting, my children, my husband the supporting players in this silly melodrama.

On the whole, an utterly distasteful business because I was never sincere. I was always toying, manipulating, but then so was he. . . . I hated being part of Happy's act, along with the boy Slim and the waitress. . . .

But, oh God, he whiled away so many hours for me. Hours that should have been wholesomely lonely. Instead I permitted them to be sordid and yes, exciting (for me). I don't think I ever felt quite the delicious shame of his young boys; was it only two or three weeks ago when I caught him with Slim in the guest house?

But I never took him seriously, any more than I would have some wild animal at the zoo. . . . What happened between us happened because I had so much leisure . . . so much free time. And he did once hold me in his thrall. . . . Those hands, up between my legs, inside my womb, fingering me, I throbbed afterwards, got cramps, thought I was about to menstruate.

How could I have been so foolish? So reckless? So irresponsible? (But wasn't Bart equally irresponsible hiring him back?) I saw the way Happy gazed longingly at my son and my beautiful little daughter.

I have never been attracted to good men, with one exception, my husband. Most of the men I loved used me and I used them. I have always been drawn to cruel types (that detective in San Francisco who practically raped me). Of all the men I have loved, if I loved him at all, he was the most evil (or were my feelings based on lust and fantasy?).

The drifter did what he did out of spite. He destroyed our gardens out of spite. He seduced Slim out of spite, partially out of spite, because I refused to go to bed with him. Spite is what drove him to lie, to turn against us because we were basically positive.

The thing is he knows exactly what he's doing, he is doomed to know what he's moving towards (but doesn't everyone?). Every time he deliberately made an immoral choice he was aware of it.

I am not sure now he was an epileptic, I am not sure he was crazy although he acted crazy sometimes. I do know he is a pathological liar; he once told me he'd murdered a man in Utah—was that the bum who tried to steal his blanket? He once told me he had a brother. He once told me he had a wife and child in Boston.

What did he really want from us, for himself? Certainly for a time he wanted solace, a place to rest. . . .

When we were alone together he didn't seem all bad. But he was bad for me in that he awakened in me a deep sensuality I never realized I possessed. He brought out good qualities in me too, my tenderness and generosity. (I find I am swallowing my tenderness, my generosity of spirit often now because I am so deeply angry at Bart.)

Happy was sensitive to my every dream for our gardens. That made me love him for a moment. Even as he tried to hurt and control me.

We were never really intimate. As I am with Bart. Odd, there is an intimacy one shares with one's mate that transcends sex and desire, domestic comfort, feeling at ease, knowing what the other person is thinking. But I don't know very often what Bart is thinking; he keeps his thoughts to himself. . . .

I enjoyed feeling superior to the drifter. I acted superior around him. (I have never felt superior to Bart.)

But Happy Kanta created my gardens, the gardens that are now gone, the rose gardens, the white gardens, the orchard. Now much of everything he created he destroyed. . . . My gardens. I think they possessed a luminous mystical quality that compensated for Bart's absences from me. . . .

Perhaps this is as it should be, the destruction is a penance. I didn't deserve such beauty. Oh God, I must have been lonely and stupid to have been taken in by Happy on so many levels!! And to have been so shaken by the experience.

I will never forget him.

I used to scold him for planting so extravagantly. I finally forbade him to buy so much. Is that why he set the fires? Or was it because I no longer could allow him to touch me, get close to me?

I think I fascinated him as much as he fascinated me.

THE following morning, Bart and I sneaked down to the guest cottage, as if to make sure Happy was gone. His bedding was piled in the middle of the mattress, with other soiled laundry wrapped inside a plump bundle of sheets (later Mama burned everything).

Several books from our library were lined on the floor and a few were on the bedside table.

There were flowers in two vases and succulents in pots and in glasses. The key to the door was placed on a completely cleared desk.

Inside I found a note copied in Happy's girlish hand.

It read:

> To whom shall I hire
> myself out? What beast
> must be adored? What
> holy image must be attacked?
> What hearts shall I break? What
> lie must I maintain? In what
> blood must I walk?
> —RIMBAUD, "Season in Hell"

CHAPTER

11

EVENTUALLY the gardens in Aptos were repaired, although the process took months. Mama asked our friend Tommy Church, the great landscape architect, to drive down from San Francisco and redesign the property so the remains of Happy's extravagant signature would be obliterated forever. New gardens emerged on a far simpler scale. Then locals were hired to weed and water and maintain the land, and another caretaker, Carl Mueller, a funny old German with a dirty mustache, was hired, and he moved into the guest house to oversee everything.

After that, Aptos Ranchos took on another kind of significance for my parents. When they were there together they lavished passionate, intense attention on the house, the kind of attention they no longer could seem to give to each other—or to my brother and me.

A routine was established. Every weekend they were together in the country they would spend cleaning (although everything was immaculate to begin with).

I can still see them moving through the various rooms—sweeping, dusting, vacuuming, polishing. The rooms were painted in shades of pastel, pearl gray, salmon pink, and they all opened into one another. The windows were shuttered so that light filtered in, making patterns of gold on the candy-striped banquettes in the dining room and across the black lacquered floors.

The cleaning would continue into the early evening. When it was over, if there was time they might check on the progress of the gardener; otherwise they would collapse on the patio. Lying in deck chairs, they would begin to drink cocktails.

Meanwhile, my brother and I would be delegated to the kitchen to polish the silver, an unending collection of teapots, sugar bowls, engraved pitchers, and ornate candelabra, as well as dozens of pieces of flat silver, the "coin silver" from Gump's that my parents had received as a wedding present. We were told to "buff" the Venetian glass goblets until they sparkled. Mama's idea, along with exposing us to "great art," was to make us aware that we were lucky enough to be living among beautiful things. Our delicate antique eighteenth-century chairs, the Italian Renaissance desk, the gold-framed prints of English country estates, were all meant to give us a sense of order and security.

Then, why did I feel so anxious whenever some expensive new possession turned up? Because I knew Daddy often didn't have the money to pay for it.

There were piles of unpaid bills on the little ship's desk in the hall that Daddy swept into his briefcase every so often and carried away with him. Mama never bothered to open them.

Once I shopped at a delicacy shop in San Francisco; it was a place my father loved. I told the owner I was "Bart Crum's daughter." He beamed. "What a wonderful person he is! He always makes me feel good when he comes in here. We have such interesting conversations. He buys the place up, charges hundreds of dollars of stuff." Then his voice trailed off. "There is one big bill withstanding."

As time went on there were more instances of unpaid bills: irate creditors phoned the house; we received dunning letters, which Mama threw away.

Daddy did his utmost to shelter us from any unpleasantness. But most of the creditors weren't as nice as that delicacy-shop owner.

THERE were a lot of unpaid bills that summer, the summer of 1944, when Daddy went campaigning for Roosevelt. Tom Dewey had been nominated for president in June on the Republican ticket, and Daddy and Russell Davenport felt the Dewey platform was "so mealy-mouthed" that they threatened to bolt the party.

There were no references to Willkie's ideas for a United Nations, they said; there was no strong civil rights policy either.

So Daddy and Davenport, along with Joe Ball, formed the Independent Republicans for Roosevelt (Roosevelt having won the nomination for a fourth term as president), and Daddy began campaigning around the country; once or twice he appeared with Harry Truman, FDR's then unknown vice-presidential candidate.

Nobody knew why FDR had picked this plainspoken former haberdasher from Independence, Missouri. Granted, at the last minute FDR had decided that Henry Wallace was too unpopular with party leaders to be retained as vice president, and too ineffectual. "Henry was a true eccentric," Daddy used to say. "He'd play tennis for hours, walk around the White House in his bare feet; some people think he's a mystic." He was a great farmer who did wondrous experiments with corn (he had been secretary of agriculture before his four-year tenure as vice president).

Still, there were rumors that FDR had asked Willkie to be his vice presidential running mate before he asked Truman. And that at another moment he had urged Willkie to at least support him rather than Dewey.

That alone signaled to my father and Russell the intensity of the liberal/conservative split in the Democratic Party. They both sensed it would be inevitable for a splinter party to form by 1948.

WHENEVER he was home, I would listen and watch as Daddy hung on the phone with David Niles or Ruth Bishop, one of Willkie's aides, or Drew Pearson, the Washington newspaper columnist whose column, "Daily Washington Merry-Go-Round," Daddy occasionally wrote when Pearson was on vacation.

Pearson once told my father that Willkie should have run for vice president with Roosevelt and he wrote Willkie to that effect, "because if we had a non-partisan Democratic Republican ticket, the liberal forces would be insured one hundred percent. It would make way for party regrouping." Meanwhile, Willkie was formulating his own ideas. In the spring he had met with David Dubinsky, president of ILGWU, about plans to create a national third party —not for 1944, but for what was sure to be a postwar-year election in 1948. Dubinsky suggested he should establish a power base first and offered him the Liberal Party nomination for mayor of New York in 1945. Willkie was enthusiastic, sensing that if he could be elected mayor of New York, it could be tantamount to launching a third party.

"As we drank coffee and brandy at the end of the long evening," Dubinsky reminisced, "we were all inspired by the belief that we made an historic decision—one which would surprise not only the city but the country as well."

Next Willkie discussed his plans with Pennsylvania's ex-governor Pinchot, who had been an organizer for the Bull Moose Progressive Party in 1914. Pinchot encouraged him to attempt this "new setup in American politics, to merge forces with FDR, take the liberals out of both parties and form a new truly liberal party, leaving the conservatives to fend for themselves." As it stood now, the reactionaries in both parties had nothing in common with the liberalism of the administration.

When FDR heard about Willkie's plan, he was delighted. He had been talking about a realignment of parties since 1938, but Willkie was the first Republican leader he thought qualified to join him in such a momentous project.

(FDR and Willkie developed a curious relationship; they met only twice, but they kept in touch by letter and countless messages. They liked each other but were always wary of each other. "The President had to have total control and he did that by telling everybody different things until the last minute—a cat and mouse game," Daddy said. "Wendell liked to have control too but he was straight about it.")

The president wanted to meet with Willkie immediately about forming a new Liberal Party, but Willkie said no, not during the campaign, so instead, after a secret lunch at the St. Regis with Sam Rosenman, with Willkie spelling out his ideas all over again and Rosenman filling him in on Roosevelt's, a series of oblique messages were passed back and forth by letter and phone throughout the summer, sometimes by Rosenman, sometimes by my father, who was also negotiating a proposal (via Dave Niles) that Willkie go to Europe as FDR's official representative as soon as the war was over.

Willkie wouldn't give an answer to that proposal or to the

suggestion that he be Roosevelt's representative at the United Nations. He said he would decide about one or both after he had dinner with my father in California in September.

In the meantime, in late July, Daddy continued to go off around the country making speeches for FDR. Sometimes he would make an appearance with Orson Welles, who was campaigning flamboyantly for Roosevelt on his own.

When he was in New York, my father might attend meetings of the Independent Citizens Committee of the Arts Sciences and Professions, an eclectic group made up of Communists, fellow travelers, Democrats, and Republicans. Its rallying point was loyalty to FDR and making sure he was reelected.

ICASP was the brainchild of Broadway press agent Hannah Dorner and the bearded, rotund sculptor Jo Davidson (whose bust of President Roosevelt still graces every dime). Davidson often conducted meetings in his cluttered studio on West Fortieth Street; he acted as a kind of talent agent, providing the likes of Helen Keller, stripper Gypsy Rose Lee, and philosopher John Dewey to appear at rallies. (Later the FBI would label Davidson a subversive for his activities in the 1944 election.)

Daddy was active with ICASP, especially on radio. He'd orchestrate conversations with Frank Sinatra and Humphrey Bogart in broadcasts that went from coast to coast. Once Henry Wallace joined him; he was gallantly campaigning for FDR even though he'd been kicked off the ticket.

At some point during his trips east, Daddy would visit Willkie. "Wendell's idea of a good time was sitting around with a group of us, Ruth Bishop, Gardner Cowles and me," Daddy wrote. "We'd eat steak and potatoes and apple pie with cheese—Wendell's favorite meal—he'd listen to us sound off about everything under the sun and then *he'd* start. Once he recited Hamlet's big speeches for us; he'd memorized the play as a kid. Another time he reminisced about how much he loved teaching American history to high school students back in Indiana. The last time I saw Wendell he was thinking about buying the *Chicago Daily News*. His office down on Wall Street was crowded with friends. He did not say he would vote for Roosevelt but he was impatiently waiting out the election."

Daddy never mentioned how awful Willkie looked. Terribly

overweight, he never exercised and he smoked four packs of cigarettes a day. He and my father used to tease each other about which of them smoked more.

In late August, during a trip to Indiana, Willkie suffered a heart attack on the train. He refused to go to the hospital. Days later, when he reached New York's Penn Station, he was so weak he could hardly walk. Rushed by ambulance to Lenox Hill Hospital, he suffered another coronary. He didn't want the public to know, so the hospital announced he was suffering from a stomach disorder. But his trusted associates knew. Ruth Bishop kept Daddy informed. "Willkie just didn't take care of himself," she recalled to me decades later. "Even in the hospital, after the heart attacks, he kept smoking."

ON October 8, 1944, Wendell Willkie died. Daddy received the news at Aptos.

I was running down the stairs when the phone rang and I heard him cry out softly, "Oh, dear, no!"

I stopped. His voice sounded so anguished and despairing.

"What's the matter, Daddy?"

He was standing dressed in his faded overalls by the little ship's desk in the hall where the telephone was. He held his hand over the receiver. "Wendell's gone . . . he had thirteen heart attacks." He turned away to end the conversation. "Sure. Yeah. Okay . . . absolutely." Then he hung up and immediately lit a cigarette with the crack of a kitchen match.

"I'm sorry, Daddy."

"So am I." His back was to me but I could hear him inhale and then suck deep on the Pall Mall.

Then, without turning, he murmured, "Come on down and give your old man a kiss." And he reached out his arm but still didn't face me.

I ran down and hugged him close. Then I stood on tiptoe and pressed my lips to his cheek.

His stubble of beard scratched my mouth.

HE didn't attend Willkie's funeral in New York, but Ruth Bishop reported various details—how a crowd of 3,500 massed outside the Fifth Avenue Presbyterian Church and listened to the ceremonies over loudspeakers. There were many eulogies. Someone mentioned that Willkie had never sacrificed his principles to satisfy his ambitions.

Daddy attended the memorial services in Oakland. I accompanied him and stood in the back of the hall watching as he spoke to a large, racially mixed group at the American Institute of Fraternal Citizens on Telegraph Avenue.

He quoted Marquis Childs's column in the *St. Louis Post-Dispatch,* something about Willkie being "a Gulliver among Lilliputian politicians." Willkie put himself at the service of democracy, Daddy said, and then he started talking about his dream "to find a way of coalescing the liberal forces of American life, American political life." He stressed the need for that, the hunger for that, among radicals, among independents, and among those who do not feel welcome in the Democratic or Republican parties. And he would pick up on that theme in the final weeks of campaigning for Roosevelt as he shuttled back and forth across the country, appearing at rallies and dinners. Now and then there were notes in the press that "San Francisco attorney Bartley Crum is being considered for an important government job." There were rumors that he might be offered a federal judgeship when the campaign was over, that he might run for Congress or even for governor.

"But on whose ticket?" someone asked.

Daddy denied that he wanted to run for anything. "I just want to practice law." That was his pat answer. Mama would urge him to commit himself once and for all. He'd answer, "But I can't afford to." And she'd counter with, "It's what you want to do, be in politics, face it."

She was trying (as she put in her journal)

to work harder on MY MARRIAGE. To be more of a political wife. To get involved in some of the causes Bart is committed to: the Spanish Refugees, Roosevelt's re-election. I am attempting to educate myself, but it doesn't come easy because I am simply not that interested. Bart has always asked my advice (although he has rarely followed it). I tell him to slow down, to weigh things more carefully. I tell him he often goes off half-cocked. For the first time, I'm accompanying him to functions at the Russian Embassy, to a few speeches. It is usually a bore. I also outline and clip articles I think he should read. . . . I've started to criticize his speaking style; sometimes he is awfully hammy. He doesn't like criticism and he'll pout like a little boy when I tell him. He's still away too much.

I find this hellishly difficult. The other day I asked Bill Knowland's wife Helen how she coped, and she said, "You have to develop separate interests, otherwise you go mad!"

IN the months that followed Willkie's death, Daddy started to drink more. He was back and forth, traveling from San Francisco to Los Angeles and sometimes Washington, trying to concentrate on practicing law, but that's when I noticed it—the drinking. He would down one or two cocktails, one after the other, as soon as he walked into our apartment on Bay Street.

He got a touch more argumentative after the bottle of "good red wine" he would consume at dinner. Mama usually would sip one goblet.

Afterward, I'd pour him his nightcap of brandy, then he would have a couple of whiskeys before I helped make up the couch for him in the living room.

He'd always insist that drinking didn't affect him, that he "could hold his liquor as well as any man," and indeed he never ever seemed drunk or even tipsy, and his speech never slurred. However, once in the middle of supper he told us he had to lie down on the sofa, and then he proceeded to pass out and Mama couldn't rouse him. She didn't seem particularly concerned (maybe it had happened before, we just had never witnessed it). She said nothing, just pressed her lips together, and eventually she covered him with a blanket, assured us he would sleep it off, and went up to bed on the second floor.

My brother and I thought he looked terrible. Skin pale as a corpse. So we decided to stay with him for a while.

After what seemed like a long time, Bart tiptoed over to my father's silent form and tentatively laid his cheek on his breast.

"I can hear his heart pumping; I guess he's okay," my brother said. However, we remained with him for a few more minutes before creeping off to bed.

The following day when we ran down to the kitchen before going off to school, Daddy was already up, drinking a cup of coffee and reading the *Chronicle*. He seemed in good spirits.

"Did Mama banish me from her bedroom?" he asked genially. We knew he rarely visited Mama upstairs, but we didn't want to embarrass him so we said nothing.

"No, Daddy," we chorused. "You passed out."

"Did I? I have no memory of that."

"You had too much to drink," my brother told him.

Daddy stared at him very hard. "You're absolutely right, son," he said. "Absolutely, positively." And then he jumped up from the table and moved to the stove. "I'm going to make us all French toast!"

Which he did, with plenty of powdered sugar and melted butter, and then Mama appeared in one of her beautiful lacy, flowing robes and behaved as if nothing out of the ordinary had happened the night before.

Years later I came across Mama's copy of *The Lost Weekend* (Charles Jackson's classic novel about an alcoholic). On the frontispiece is the inscription, in her handwriting, "San Francisco, 1944"; she underlined key passages throughout the book and listed page numbers on the back jacket. Some of the descriptions seemed to fit Daddy's condition.

An example: "Why [are] drunks almost always persons of talent . . . gifted . . . lovable . . . why are so many brilliant men alcoholic?" (This last is underlined twice.) And finally: "He only wanted to be the Artist [and Mama added: *"the Lawyer, the Politician, the Crusader"*], with no thought to the meaning of the word, just as he wanted to be, or fancied himself to be, especially when drinking, an actor without ever thinking [what it meant] to go on a stage . . . or a pianist without taking music lessons or a husband and father without marrying."

Mama's underlinings in *The Lost Weekend* and later in books by Freud and Karen Horney helped me understand what private agonies she must have been going through.

At the time she never talked to me or my brother about

Daddy's heavy drinking, although much later she would refer to him as a "functioning alcoholic." But we ignored it—it was simply a given along with his alarming intake of cigarettes. And since he was usually so funny, so seemingly in control, in spite of his drinking, we didn't give it much thought.

PART
THREE

CHAPTER

12

IN November 1944, Roosevelt won a fourth term as president, but the effort of the years in office was taking its toll. He was exhausted. His hand shook whenever he lit a cigarette. He had lost twenty pounds. He used his wheelchair more often in public, sinking down into it after he made a speech to Congress.

"Everybody's concerned with FDR's health," Daddy said when he came back from one of his quick trips to the capital in December, just after the election.

He said Robert Sherwood had told him that the president's neck looked old and wrinkled, that his shirt hung on him, that he complained he had no appetite, that when he did eat, he couldn't taste his food.

Still, he was planning to meet with Churchill and Stalin at Yalta, a resort on the Black Sea. They would discuss plans for a final defeat of the Axis and hoped to start organizing the postwar world.

"A pretty hefty order," Daddy said.

He added that Stalin was forcing FDR to come to him. "It is outrageous since the president is so frail, but Stalin refuses to travel." He went on to say that FDR's staff had put a special agent near the president on the Casablanca flight, an agent who was also an expert swimmer. "It's his job to keep the president afloat if the plane crashes in the ocean," Daddy told us.

LESS than three months later, on April 15, 1945, Roosevelt died in Warm Springs, Georgia. I remember hearing the news in school during study hall. One of the teachers announced his death and for several minutes there was a stunned silence, followed by murmurings and a few sobs.

For twelve years Roosevelt's presence had dominated America. I had never known another president. None of my classmates had. Even if you hated him, no one could deny the enormous hold he had on our imaginations.

I REMEMBER that Daddy stayed up very late in the days right after Roosevelt's death. He was on the phone a lot to Dave Niles (who had agreed to stay on as a Truman aide, along with Sam Rosenman, FDR's principal speechwriter, who also had agreed to help the new president).

According to Daddy, Truman was completely unprepared to take over as commander in chief. "He'd never been in the map room, he'd only met with Roosevelt a couple of times."

He seemed so provincial after Roosevelt's elegant dynamism. It was predicted that Truman would end the power of the New Deal intellectuals like Henry Morgenthau and Frances Perkins and instead surround himself with mediocre party hacks from Missouri.

Daddy would wonder about Truman's leadership qualities— his commitment, if any, to progressivism, particularly when staunch Democrats were starting to feel stranded because of, Daddy would say, a lack of apparent White House support. In California, favoritism was being shown to men like archconservative millionaire Ed Pauley instead of professional liberals like Robert Kenny.

"I have kept my confidence in Truman's integrity of purpose," Daddy wrote to former FDR aide Sam Rosenman, "but the resignation of so many New Dealers makes for the dissolution of the coalition of progressive forces in government."

A WEEK after FDR's death, the United Nations opened in San Francisco. Mama drove Bart and me down to the Civic Center to witness the occasion. There was such a jam-up of cars, we had to park some distance from the center, and we pushed our way through the crowds. I remember Mama was wearing her favorite bottle-green wool suit and tiny, very expensive Lilly Daché hat with a green feather plume that covered half her cheek.

The streets and buildings downtown were festooned with flags, and thousands jammed the sidewalks to cheer as the delegates made their way into the gilt and plush of the Opera House. Some were in burnooses and colorful turbans. When the entire delegation from Saudi Arabia swept in majestically in their flowing robes, Mama joked, "They're here under the guidance of Standard Oil of California."

Daddy met us at the entrance. We had special box-seat tickets because he was one of a hundred lawyers who had been chosen to help draw up the UN charter; he was representing the Lawyers Guild (as its national vice president). He and other members of the guild were pushing for mutual accommodations between the United States and the Soviet Union.

And they didn't stop pushing even after a volatile meeting with Averell Harriman at the Fairmont Hotel, in which Harriman outlined his concerns about the "menace of Soviet expansionism," their true objectives in Eastern Europe. He predicted trouble with the Soviets after the war. They wouldn't keep their promises. To believe otherwise was unrealistic and dangerous. He felt it was crucial to let the Russians know we were going to maintain a strong military establishment.

My father dismissed Harriman's suggestions. He was excited that day; his eyelids blinked nervously. He told my brother and me we were witnessing a historic occasion, the establishing of an organization that would forever maintain the peace.

WE took our seats at 4:30, as Secretary of State Edward Stettinius, an improbably handsome man with silver hair and thick black eyebrows, gaveled the audience to order.

"My God, he's divine," Mama whispered.

Then, from the loudspeaker, came the voice of President Harry Truman, over long-distance hookup. His voice sounded very flat and midwestern as he drawled out words to the effect that the UN was a symbol of America's idealism.

I was supposed to write a report on the United Nations for my school newspaper, so I tried to take notes. I still have a smudged list on lined paper pasted into an old scrapbook, with some of the world figures Daddy pointed out: "John Foster Dulles, Anthony Eden, Jan Masaryk of Czechoslovakia, Cordell Hull . . ."; and

Daddy obtained a glossy UPI photograph of himself sporting his special United Nations button and posing with Chinese diplomat Wellington Koo.

The United Nations sessions lasted two months, and during that time Daddy and other guild members spent hours urging the Truman administration to support international efforts at cooperation, particularly with respect to atomic energy, reconstruction of war-torn Europe, the war-crime trials in Nuremberg, and unrestricted access of Jews to Palestine.

At the close of the sessions a crowd pressed into our apartment for a party. Harry Bridges was invited, along with a skinny Adlai Stevenson and Alger Hiss (then unknown); sculptor Jo Davidson; Hollywood producer Walter Wanger and his wife, movie star Joan Bennett; dancer Katherine Dunham; I. F. Stone; Dalton Trumbo; opera singer Lily Pons; Robert Kenny; Herb Caen; and Paul Robeson.

Before the guests arrived, Daddy had given us a rundown on Robeson: that he was the son of an ex-slave, that he had been a football star at Rutgers, and that he was a great interpreter of Negro spirituals. (His rendition of "Ol' Man River" remains a landmark in the movie version of *Show Boat*.) He was also a fine actor who ranged from playing a title role in Eugene O'Neill's *The Emperor Jones* to his recent triumph as Othello on Broadway.

But Daddy was most impressed with his record on civil rights, his fierce championing of racial equality. He devoted much of his time and energies to the National Negro Congress and the left-wing unions of the CIO. Lately he had been fighting to desegregate major-league baseball teams.

Now Robeson was at the United Nations as president of the Council on African Affairs. He was already concerned that the UN would totally ignore the colonialism issue; he was worried, too, that black Africans would continue to be exploited and that they might not get the right to vote. He argued for a militant black movement decades before it became a reality.

None of this information prepared me for the grandeur of his presence. He seemed huge in our living room, absolutely enormous; he dwarfed everybody else, and he was so magnetic and gracious to me, holding my small hand in his warm gigantic one —I felt I could tell him anything and he would listen.

Near the end of the party, in the midst of a discussion, Robeson suddenly pulled me onto his lap. The entire room fell silent as
he crooned me a lullaby. "Hush li'l baby, don' you cry . . ." His
gorgeous bass baritone vibrated in my ear, my heart beat very, very
fast . . .

"You'll never forget this night," Daddy told me.

LESS than three months later the atomic bomb was dropped on
Nagasaki and Hiroshima and the war ended abruptly. I recall, as
in a dream, the noise in San Francisco on V-J Day, horns and
sirens wailing, buzzing. My brother and I seemed to be part of a
violent surge of excitement in the city; we wandered up and down
the hills with our parents, watching cars being smashed up on
Fillmore Street, soldiers and sailors careening around Fisherman's
Wharf.

We must have walked for hours around North Beach, ending
up in Chinatown for supper. I got sick to my stomach and so did
Bart. "Too many fried dumplings," Daddy teased.

NOT long after V-J Day we moved to a big, rambling three-story
house at 2626 Green Street, between Divisadero and Broderick.
The house, full of light and views, was only a block away from the
Presidio, but those buildings were half hidden by rustling eucalyptus and pepper trees.

As soon as we moved in Mama started redecorating on a
massive scale, and she had Tommy Church redesign the back
garden. From my window I could look down on a green-gray maze
of ivy shrubbery and potted plants divided by a graveled walk. I
could see the crumbling orange Palace of Fine Arts from my window, too, as well as an aquamarine stretch of San Francisco Bay.
How I loved my room, spacious enough for my *Nancy Drew* mysteries, my collection of storybook dolls, my stacks of movie magazines.

My brother had his own room, too, down the hall; he played
music constantly.

Our parents had the top floor to themselves.

Daddy had bought the house from Louise Bransten, a client
who was becoming a close friend. Louise—slender, tense, and
very blond—was around a lot, at every one of Mama's dinner

parties. At one point it was rumored that she and my father were lovers.

Louise was an heiress. Daddy subsequently sold the dried-fruit business she'd inherited to Consolidated Foods for $18 million.

She was said to be one of the leading left-wingers in the Bay Area. Her ex-husband, Richard Bransten, had founded *New Masses*. While she was still at Vassar she had led striking dock-workers up Market Street in a dramatic march; she later built a house for Communist Party leader Bill Schneidermann "because she felt sorry for him." Recently, at my father's urging, she had given ten thousand dollars to the Spanish Refugee Appeal.

Mama told me Louise often went dancing with Harry Bridges and was "very close" to Paul Robeson. I had seen them at our house once or twice, walking by themselves around and around our garden. "They were," according to Robeson biographer Martin Duberman, "devoted friends and sometime lovers."

As long as she lived in the Green Street house, Louise Bransten's phones were tapped by the FBI, presumably because she was seeing so much of Robeson, who was being closely surveilled by the FBI; he was revealed by J. Edgar Hoover as a "Soviet apologist."

The phones remained tapped while we lived there, but we didn't know it, although we suspected it finally. Nor did we know that Daddy was being surveilled by the FBI as well.

Actually, his surveillance had begun in 1942, not long after he became president of the San Francisco chapter of the Lawyers Guild. By 1944, his opposition to the Bureau's penchant for wire-tapping and political deportations had brought him to the attention of Hoover. He did not know Hoover was watching him, nor was he aware that dozens of FBI agents and informants were mingling in the crowds at Madison Square Garden the night he chaired a big rally for the Joint Anti-Fascist Refugee Committee in September 1945. He was too busy raising money to help two hundred thousand Spanish refugees exiled in France.

The rally was also being scrutinized by HUAC (the House Un-American Activities Committee), a witch-hunting organization targeted at the American left; its tactics were always questionable

—smears, lies, name-calling. HUAC was convinced that JAFRC was a Communist front.

Midway through the rally Daddy announced a transatlantic phone call from British Labourite Harold Laski, who proceeded to assail Vatican politicking with Franco. His remarks were not only broadcast in the Garden but also heard on the radio and out in the streets.

Afterward Catholic organizations protested Laski's remarks by sending postcards to HUAC demanding an investigation of JAFRC and charging that it engaged in political activities on behalf of the Communist Party.

Thousands of leaflets were passed out around New York in which actor Frank Fay called Daddy a Catholic traitor for introducing Laski to the Garden audience. According to Fay, being anti-Franco was a symptom of anti-Americanism. Soon after, Congress voted to make HUAC a standing committee.

Subsequently, my father and other members of JAFRC, like Dorothy Parker and Dashiell Hammett, were cited for contempt by HUAC because they refused to submit lists of their contributors and supporters.

Daddy paid no attention to these attacks. He had been involved for close to ten years in various so-called Popular Front organizations devoted to combating fascism, so he was used to being called names.

By late 1945, Daddy had a paradoxical image in San Francisco; he was a Republican corporation lawyer with a reputation for espousing radical causes. "A notable independent progressive," historian Alonzo Hamby wrote in his book *Beyond the New Deal.*

"Bart Crum was one of the most visible personalities in the Bay Area right after the War," columnist Herb Caen recalls.

> He was a real mover and shaker in those days, into everything —the local elections, Chinatown politics, you name it. He was also part of The Cabinet, a special table at the Palm Court of the Palace Hotel. The Cabinet had been going strong for eight, ten years and it met every day five days a week and Bart was a regular, along with a shifting cast of characters:

Mayor Lapham; Louis Lurie, the real estate tycoon; Harry Bridges; Senator Bill Knowland—when he was in town; attorney Bill Wallace—urbane, mocking, perpetually raised eyebrow. Paul Smith, editor of the *Chronicle,* back from the wars, might be there too, bragging about his exploits on Guadalcanal and Iwo Jima; Pierre Monteux, conductor of the San Francisco Symphony . . . these were just some for the regulars, no women allowed. . . . What did they talk about? Mostly politics. It was *the* place to be invited for lunch. . . .

Bart Crum had a troubled air about him. He was always looking over his shoulder. I could never figure him out. Nobody could. What kind of lawyer was he? Did he care about money or didn't he? We all knew he helped a lot of people, but nobody could ever get a bead on him . . . or what exactly he wanted.

Mary Kohler thought he had created an image of himself as the glamorous crusader, which he tried to live up to but couldn't quite. He also had to make a living, and that was even harder because he was much more interested in politics and hanging around Sacramento than he was in collecting fees. A few of his clients were dissatisfied. Even Dextra McGonogle, who paid him a large retainer to help her handle her fortune, would get annoyed at him when he was slow in answering phone calls. To keep her happy, he often had to take her dancing when she would fly up to San Francisco.

Then Daddy would drop by Mary Kohler's and complain that Mama was spending too much money, and then Mama would phone Mary later and let loose with a litany of complaints about my father's extravagance.

She was especially angry when he spent a big hunk of money buying new church bells for St. Joseph's in Soquel, where we attended Mass on weekends. "We needed that money for household bills, for the mortgage," she cried.

He was impulsive; he was driven—and restless, too. He would disappear from home from time to time, telling us only that he was going up to the Bohemian Club for a couple of days. Otherwise, he'd say he was off to a "religious retreat." But often, he was actually seeing his mother. He would sneak up to Sacramento, but he didn't tell Mama since she and the Crums and

Cavanaughs still didn't get along. (Mo had never once been invited to Aptos.)

Anyhow, my cousin Jim would "pick Bart up at the airport and then we'd go to some Chink place for chow mein and over to Mo's. Bart would sit around schmoozing with his mother and sister Sally for hours, telling them everything that was going on in his showy life. Once he confided that he had a Jewish mistress back in San Francisco, but we thought he was joking. He seemed to know everybody; he'd talk about visiting Mary Pickford in Hollywood—we'd laugh a lot. I don't remember exactly what he said that made us laugh, but he always made us feel good."

A *TIME* magazine memo written by San Francisco correspondent Fritz Goodwin on December 1, 1945, stated:

> On his forty-fifth birthday, celebrated this week, jaunty convivial Bartley Crum is still trim, boyish, slick-haired, handsome in a casual elegant sort of way that women appreciate.
>
> Crum never hesitates to mount the speaker's platform for anything he believes in and this has taken some doing in view of the fact that he earns his living as counsel for clients like Owl Drug, United Drug and Borden's Milk; but he'll talk about and publicly espouse racial equality, anti-discrimination, fair employment practice legislation, anti-Franco agitation, the Russian War Relief . . . to date Crum has successfully and stalwartly carried water on both shoulders without spilling any client or compromising his liberal principles. He is Vice President of the National Lawyers Guild, national Vice Chair of the Political Action Committee, the California Chair of the United China War Relief . . .

Goodwin summed up my father like this:

> Working both sides of the political and ideological street, Bartley Crum has not gone very far in any one direction and gives the impression that he never will. About all he has achieved is a wide personal popularity among widely diverse groups of people, and the apparent satisfaction of his own conscience. He says he has no political ambitions whatsoever

and he has never shown any inclination to seek political office. At this point in his zigzag career Crum seems satisfied with his personal status: a financially successful lawyer, a sought after public speaker, and husband of novelist Gertrude Bosworth Crum (a.k.a. "Cutsie"), who wrote a thing called *Strumpet Wind.*

Goodwin ended with: "There is a frequently rumored possibility that Crum may succeed Harold Ickes as Secretary of the Interior in Truman's cabinet."

Indeed, a long feature in *The Christian Science Monitor* (also dated December 1, 1945) headlined COAST LAWYER MENTIONED TO FOLLOW ICKES. However, Daddy was quoted as saying he didn't want the job. "I think Abe Fortas is the best man for it," he said.

Years later, I discovered that months earlier, on August 10, 1945, J. Edgar Hoover, head of the FBI, had written a letter quashing all talk of Daddy as an Ickes replacement to General Harry Vaughan (Truman's top military aide). In the letter, Hoover attached a memo summarizing "information in the Bureau's files about Bartley Crum's background and activities—thought you'd be interested." (The information included the fact that the FBI had put Daddy under surveillance because of his involvement with the Russian War Relief and the Lawyers Guild.)

Other "information" included transcripts of taped phone conversations between Tommy Corcoran and Senator Bob La Follette, suggesting "Bart Crum as a replacement on the International Air Control Board and as Ickes replacement as well."

IF Daddy knew about Hoover's letter he didn't say. (I doubt he did.) There were rumors, too, that he might be appointed by President Truman as a member of a commission to investigate the plight of Jewish refugees. His name had been in the newspapers on a list along with Judge Learned Hand and Archibald MacLeish, and then it had been mysteriously removed, causing FDR speechwriter Sam Rosenman to write how sorry he was. "I think it was somebody in the State Department," he wrote Daddy in December 1945, and Daddy wrote back thanking him for his concern. "If you dish it out, you've got to expect a sock in the jaw now and then, don't you?"

He assumed the State Department didn't want him because he had been too outspoken against Franco. At one point Secretary of State James Byrnes tried to eliminate him from the list because of his "leftist leanings," but Dave Niles intervened and persuaded Byrnes to push the appointment through.

Almost everything that went into the Oval Office involving the Jews filtered through Niles; he was the American Zionists' liaison to the White House, and he was their spokesman as well. He kept urging the president to commit to the idea of establishing an independent Jewish state in Palestine.

ON January 1, 1946, Judge Joseph C. Hutcheson of Houston phoned Daddy to say very formally, "The President asked me to invite you to serve with me as one of the six Americans on the Anglo-American Committee of Inquiry into Palestine."

Daddy agreed immediately, although he had been about to fly to Madrid to start defending some Spanish underground leaders who were still in prison.

My brother and I heard a lot about "the committee" in the next two years. The Anglo-American Committee of Inquiry into Palestine, which ended up being one of the most futile missions in history. However, during the next months Daddy was, as always, the supreme optimist, at least until he began educating himself on the subject. He would tell us that the committee (made up of six Americans, six Brits) would bring fresh viewpoints to an old problem; they would decide, after traveling halfway around the world and listening to dozens of experts on the subject, whether it would be feasible to allow one hundred thousand homeless, stateless Jewish refugees to immigrate to Palestine and how it would affect the people already living there—such as the millions of Palestinian Arabs.

Critics said what was needed was not a committee but a *policy* to cope with the hitherto unsolvable problem. Everybody had a different answer as to what precisely could be done to relieve Jewish survivors of their misery. Four hundred thousand had either escaped the death camps or emerged from underground, but instead of being welcomed by the world, they were shunted off to displaced-persons centers. Thousands of them longed to escape to the Holy Land to start new lives, but the British severely restricted Jewish immigration to Palestine with its White Paper mandate.

The State Department went along with this; if immigration wasn't controlled, it could pose a real threat to our security. It was vital for the United States to maintain a pipeline to Mideast oil.

Only Truman believed that after so much suffering and persecution the Jews deserved a homeland of their own; his conscience was pricked by Dave Niles and Clark Clifford. He was also under tremendous pressure from Jewish groups whose support he badly needed if he wanted to stay in the White House. So he continued to stand up for the Anglo-American Committee. Most of his foreign advisers (Lovett, Forrestal, Henderson) kept warning him that supporting a Zionist cause would antagonize the Arabs and might drive them into the arms of the Soviets.

Afterward Daddy would remind us that Wendell Willkie had been one of the first Americans to come to the aid of Jewish refugees. In 1944 he and Vice President Henry Wallace organized the Committee Against Nazi Persecutions, and Daddy started to make speeches informing the public about what was going on in the death camps.

But he would tell us he had been totally ignorant about Palestine. He had only a vague idea that Great Britain had done something reprehensible in issuing a White Paper in 1939 which restricted immigration in Palestine; he had no definite knowledge as to the terms of the document. "I knew Palestine was the crossroad of the Mideast, but I didn't appreciate fully the extent of its strategic or economic importance when it came to developing the Middle Eastern oil reserves and I certainly didn't realize it would be the key to power in the Mideast. Nor did I realize that the complexities of the Palestine problem had to be understood in terms of the vast struggle for power between the western democracies and Russia."

It was obviously a volatile issue.

I remember visiting his office in the Russ Building just before he took a plane to New York, and the place was a beehive of activity. Phones never stopped ringing; telegrams, letters, books, pamphlets, were piling up in his waiting room. The British Information Agency was ready to help; Zionist organizations were knocking at the door; the United States Army, the American Red

Cross, the United Nations Relief and Rehabilitation Agency (UNRRA), and various Arab groups all wanted to talk to my father before he left.

He dropped everything when his mother, Mo, came down from Sacramento to see him off. They had lunch by themselves at the Palace Hotel, and then she insisted on accompanying him to the barber to see that he had his hair cut properly.

"I don't want you going to the White House looking like a shaggy dog."

He grinned back at her, his eyes twinkling with excitement.

He had never traveled outside the United States.

WE were starting to get used to being without him. He was beginning to exist as a fantasy figure, not flesh and blood. Maybe that's why Mama suggested that we help her document his travels while he was away.

My brother and I spent many evenings together in the living room, gluing maps of the Middle East and various partition plans into a big leather scrapbook, along with news clips and postcards and photographs; everything was very carefully glued on pale, thick pages. This was our effort to make Daddy's trip, so murky and unfathomable, come alive for us.

He wrote us letters, too, and some of them were glued into the scrapbook as well. But the contents of his diary on the committee as well as longer letters and notes were mailed directly to Mama. She kept everything very carefully in a file cabinet. Some of the material was later published in *The American Scholar* magazine. The bulk of it was used as the basis for his book about the committee entitled *Behind the Silken Curtain*, published by Simon and Schuster in 1947.

While he was still in the United States, he also phoned us. In Washington he would usually stay at the Mayflower Hotel and, unless he had dinner with a friend (Dave Niles or Sam Rosenman), he'd remain in his room to call us.

The night he arrived in the capital for the start of the Anglo-American Committee was no exception. When the phone rang, we knew who it was; we immediately got on extension phones and had a pretty lengthy conversation—Mama, my brother, and me.

I don't remember what we talked about. Usually it was rambling, inconsequential stuff, about the gardens at Aptos and how they were coming along, and how one of our dogs was sick, and about our classes at school. But that night, after the usual preliminary chitchat, Daddy told us he had neglected to stick a copy of Wendell Willkie's book *One World* into his suitcase and could Mama please find it "somewhere on my desk and mail it special delivery?"

Mama left the phone to locate the book on my father's desk. She returned moments later to say, "It isn't there."

Daddy insisted it was; if not, what about the other copies we had? Where were they? We did indeed own numerous copies of *One World*, paperback, hardcover, and even a special illustrated limited edition—a coffee table book that was numbered and signed by Willkie.

My brother and I were sent from the phones to find the books, and we searched everywhere—in the library, the living room, Daddy's study again, Mama's room, our rooms (since Willkie had sent us copies, too). We couldn't find any of them.

When we got back on the phones and told Daddy, his voice rose in sudden anger. "Jesus Christ, I don't ask you to do much, all I ask you to do is find a goddamn book."

And Mama didn't help. "For Lord's sake, Bart, you can buy another one in Washington tomorrow."

"That isn't the point," my father shouted. "Wendell inscribed the book to me. I want it. I need it. I plan to take it with me to London."

I can't re-create the rest of the dialogue. Neither my brother nor I could get a word in edgewise, so we ended up listening to our parents—who rarely raised their voices—scream at each other. I felt my stomach muscles tighten, I began to grip the receiver so hard my fingers ached, and then Daddy hung up without saying good-bye and Mama ran into her bedroom and locked the door.

Later on I believe we found the various copies of *One World* stuck somewhere amid our thousands of books. Mama even found the copy he wanted (inscribed by Willkie: "to a fellow idealist and conspirator"), and she sent it off to him special delivery. He carried it with him all over Europe and the Mideast.

That tattered copy of *One World* was obviously a good-luck charm, a talisman, like the crucifix he needed to have near him wherever he was, and which he never forgot. I used to ask him when he called long-distance—from Cairo, from Paris—"Do you have Grandma's [Kate McTernan's] cross, Daddy?" and he'd say, "You bet I do! I'd never forget that."

DADDY didn't stay angry long, no matter how emotional or intense the situation was. He would blow up and then he would calm down and go on with life. He didn't believe in holding grudges or in "stewing," as he put it.

So by the time he started keeping his diary of the committee —the following morning, that is—there was no mention of the lost book or that he even had spoken to us. He never wrote personally, so I didn't know what was going on deep in his heart.

He wrote in his diary in December 1945: "Up early. Drank coffee. Read newspapers. Drew Pearson phoned me as I was walking out the door. Anxious to hear how Truman really feels about Palestine. He reminded me that Jewish voters are a critical bloc for him in NY state (NY electoral vote thirty-five—biggest in presidential election). Wonders whether the President is being a political opportunist about the Jews or a genuinely good guy. Says Forrestal is bureaucratic voice of oil companies, says Loy Henderson sides with Forrestal; Dave Niles showed me the correspondence file from the State Department with Henderson's margin notes 'objecting' to my appointment on the Committee. I am too 'left wing' for him and he says the speeches I give are demagogic. Has he heard any of them?"

Later that day, another diary entry: "The American members of the Anglo-American Committee got together for the first time in an empty office in the State Department. Judge 'Texas Joe' Hutcheson presiding as chair.

"I had known the Judge, but only by reputation," my father wrote. "He had single-handedly broken the Ku Klux Klan in Houston when it was decidedly unpopular to do so. He is nearly seventy. Salty. An independent. Describes himself as an Old Testament Christian. He seems to be entering this investigation with a profound desire to find a just solution."

Other members of the committee were "mighty impressive," my father noted. They included Dr. James McDonald—enigmatic, silver-haired, pro-Zionist—who had been the League of Nations high commissioner for German refugees; Frank Buxton, Pulitzer Prize–winning veteran editor of *The Boston Herald;* Dr. Frank Aydelotte, an early Rhodes scholar and director of the Institute for Advanced Study at Princeton; and William Phillips, former ambassador to Italy.

It was Phillips, lean and distinguished, "the perfect diplomat," Daddy wrote, "who arranged our protocol in meeting the six British members of the Committee."

"We went in a body to meet them when they arrived in Washington by train from New York. Sir John Singleton, who, as Judge of King's Bench in London, will be Judge Hutcheson's opposite number (and rumored to be pro-Arab); Lord Robert Morrison, Labor peer; Richard H. S. Crossman, Labor MP; Major Reginald Manningham Buller, conservative member of Parliament; Wilfred Crick, advisor to the Midland Bank; and Sir Frederick Leggit, a labor conciliator who would later repeat the dictum, 'You can't force a solution in any dispute.' "

THE following day the committee held its first formal gathering as luncheon guests of Dean Acheson, acting secretary of state, at Blair House. Daddy wrote,

> I had been wondering ever since I left San Francisco what sort of reception I'd get from the State Department. But Dean Acheson greeted us all warmly. He acted as if he knew nothing about the earlier rejection of my name.
>
> After lunch the entire Committee made an official call on President Truman in the Oval Office. He told us that there had never been in the history of the White House such a tremendous volume of mail as that dealing with the DPs. He hoped we would be able to complete our investigation and present our recommendations in one hundred and twenty days.
>
> I wish I'd had the nerve to ask him if he was counting on the U.N. to solve the long-range problem of Palestine. . . .
>
> Before we left, one of my British colleagues asked him how it felt to be Leader of the Free World, to which Truman replied rather wanly, "I don't. I feel I am trying to carry on for somebody else."

CHAPTER

13

D
ECEMBER 1945:

Dearest Ones: The hearings are taking place in the old State Department building on the sixth floor. The press surrounds us. There are a great many photographers snapping pictures, journalists from around the world. Only a few members of the public. . . . We will be listening to Arab and Zionist witnesses. Rabbi Hillel Silver, probably the most outspoken Jewish activist in the country, is boycotting the proceedings because he believes our committee is merely a stalling device to placate British. . . . Random thoughts: Most Arab witnesses assert Palestinian Arabs do not want Jews in Palestine and resent them. . . . While Jewish witnesses counter that Palestinian Arabs accept Jews; as proof point that Arabs settle near Jewish towns! . . . Economist Robert Nathan who spent nearly a year in Palestine analyzing Palestine's industry, agriculture, trade, power costs, housing possibilities . . . said that Arabs' living conditions had been improved by presence of Jews in Palestine and would be additionally enhanced by further Jewish immigration. . . .

One subject that continues to plague us: are the Jews a people or a religion? Crossman and I were both startled when Lessing Rosenwald, president of the Anti-Zionist American Council for Judaism, maintained that Jewish nationalism may be a cause of anti-Semitism. . . . When he did that everybody at the hearings stiffened.

The Arabs keep stressing that since Palestine is inhabited by an Arab majority it must become an Arab state.

And I mustn't forget that many thousands of Jews have converted to passionate almost fanatical Zionism . . . and this paradox: most American Zionists don't want to give up their citizenship and move to Palestine.

From another letter in December: "It seems to me that the majority of our British colleagues are pro-Arab . . . some of our American colleagues as well . . . Aydelotte for example and Phillips. They actually don't seem to like Jews very much. . . ."

And a P.S.: "I happen to warm to Dick Crossman. Labor MP, graduate of Oxford. Editor of the *New Statesman* before going into politics. . . . He may be Prime Minister someday . . . he is absolutely brilliant and has a lot of confidence, but it is attractive confidence . . . not arrogant. . . . He argues constantly and thinks out loud, but then so do I."

My father also noted, "the hearings are something of an endurance contest. Not only do we listen to scores of witnesses all of whom have conflicting opinions—for up to eight solid hours a day we have been given mountains of material to study and to carry with us around the globe. I for one will not do that."

DADDY addressed one letter directly to my brother, Bart:

As for your hero, Albert Einstein, I had imagined him to be a smallish fellow, but when he arrived to testify, I saw a large man—over six feet with long flowing white hair almost to his shoulders and laughing eyes. Resembled a patriarch stepping out of some Old Testament tale.

The entire room broke into loud applause when he came in . . . ("I think they should wait until they hear what I say," I heard him mumble.)

He proceeded to be very critical of the British, comparing their involvement with Palestine to their involvement with India.

He ended up telling us our Committee was "nothing but a smoke screen" and a total waste of time. When I tried to argue with him he said the following in a benign tone of voice, "How do you know it is not?"

"I know from my own activities in the Committee," I said. Einstein implied that a *policy* had to be established regarding the DPs—not another investigation. "The Committee seems to be a smoke screen," he repeated gently.

I said I hoped he would judge us by our actions.

Dr. Einstein answered, "I would be glad to be wrong."

We were also sent the great scientist's autograph for my brother; that went into the scrapbook, too, along with a portrait of the entire committee standing on the steps of the Capitol (Daddy looking very pleased and proud, with the usual cigarette between his fingers).

IN subsequent days Loy Henderson, the round-faced head of the Near East Division of the State Department, briefed my father on "the dangers of Soviet expansionism and tried to explain that the State Department and the national security system placed little value on the moral claims of the Jews."

"As I listened to him," my father wrote later in his diary, "I couldn't help wondering if he knew I'd read his margin notes about me. And then I thought I don't much like professional diplomats."

He mentioned this feeling to Ladislas Farago, an expert on espionage, when they breakfasted together at the Mayflower Hotel just before he left for London.

Farago cautioned him to "try to please those who are in power and be careful. You're going to be spied on especially by the British and most certainly by the Russians."

Daddy laughed and shrugged. "Ladislas," he drawled, "I'm just gonna behave like I've always behaved . . ." Presumably he meant he would be honest and open. Years later Farago told me, "Your father's naïveté was staggering. But I think it was genuine, or rather his belief in America was genuine. He romanticized the country. He trusted the system then, he believed in the Constitution, he believed in our leadership." Farago was more cynical, having been a spy during the war. He knew about the State Department's double-dealing. He knew about the FBI and what they were up to; he suspected that my father was already on their shit list for being anti-Franco. Farago tried to tell him to be careful, but he didn't listen. "Bart said he couldn't be bothered."

■

FROM my father's diary on board the *Queen Elizabeth* on January 3, 1946: "The Committee's discussions grow more intense . . . our points of view differ radically, not just our approach to international problems and politics but the whole question of the press and press censorship and freedom of the press, and how much we should say to reporters during our journey. I feel we should speak openly and frankly with them and keep them informed; my British colleagues are completely against that."

And then he added, "The British are pretty negative about Zionism. They speak of the dangers of Jewish nationalism—that it is the other side of fascism. They say it could be Communism in disguise. I thought we were going to try and remain neutral. I feel very uncomfortable prejudging anything."

Then, mid-voyage, the entire committee was given top-secret State Department files to read dating back to 1920.

In every file, when promises were made to American Jewry regarding Palestine and immigration, messages would be sent immediately to the British foreign office and to Arab rulers reassuring them that no matter what public promises were made to the Jews, the situation would remain the same and nothing would be done.

My father was "absolutely staggered" by the content of those secret files, but when he expressed his feelings Richard Crossman laughed. "Doesn't it please you to know that both British and Americans are equally stupid?" he asked.

"No, it does not please me," Daddy wrote after describing a noisy conversation he'd had with Crossman and other members of the committee that accompanied a long night of drinking and arguing. "I suppose Dick would say that open covenants openly arrived at and world government under law are idealistic and not practical; but the results of the British and American policy in the Middle East are based on the cynical belief that we can be all things to all people. This alienates both Jews and Arabs and brings profound disillusionment to everybody else.

"The overall question is finally whether the western democracies have moral integrity; if we do we will win out; if we don't the Middle East will be the breeding ground for many wars."

CHAPTER

14

I N London, Daddy was spied on. "I am being tailed day and night," he wrote.

At the Hyde Park Hotel, where he was staying, he shared a room with a committee colleague, but found it "intolerable because I'm trying to keep a private diary and make a great many personal phone calls."

He finally asked for and got a single room, but not before a British member of the committee advised him to "choose his words more carefully over the phone." "This was a pleasant way of telling me my conversations had already been tapped," he wrote.

"Bart was the only member of the committee who had close ties to Washington and to presidential aide Dave Niles," reporter Gerold Frank recalls. Frank covered the committee story for UPI and remembers that my father would phone Washington practically every day between breaks in the hearings and from all sorts of places—a bar, a corner pay phone. He always managed to get through. Frank believed some of the other members were jealous of his entrée.

My father soon formed an alliance with Frank and *New York Post* reporter Ruth Gruber, who'd previously been Harold Ickes's aide in Alaska and then done extraordinary work with refugees in Italy. Daddy was particularly fond of the vivacious Gruber; they often had drinks or coffee together.

Gruber recalls: "Bart threw himself into the experience of being on the committee. He existed on nicotine and very little sleep. He seemed to have unending energy. He'd draft letters, summarize positions, see anybody who wanted to see him—Baron de Rothschild, Harold Laski, Chaim Weizmann; everybody felt comfortable with him."

He couldn't get over the British press. The Arabs' position was definitely favored; in Washington the Zionists had received most of the coverage.

The hearings were broken up by many opportunities to go behind the scenes. Daddy wrote us, "Yesterday, we were invited to a formal (but off the record) luncheon at the Dorchester given by Foreign Secretary Ernest Bevin . . . it was my first opportunity to see this guy in person. . . . He's a large, powerfully built man with heavy shell-rimmed spectacles and a way of holding his hands at his sides, fists clenched as though he was impatiently on the verge of getting something done that had to be done. He told us that the British government would accept our counsel—'We shall accept your recommendations,' he told us.

"Strange, because he had been so negative about Palestine in the past. That odious remark—when was it made? A warning to the survivors of the camps 'not to push to the head of the line.' " (Golda Meir said later, "But the Jews have always been at the head of the line to the gas chambers.")

Subsequently, my father discussed the morality of Britain's prime ministers with Jan Masaryk, foreign minister of Czechoslovakia. "Jan told me the following story," Daddy wrote us. " 'After Munich, Chamberlain came to see me in London. He told me about the Munich Pact and said, "I'm sorry but Czechoslovakia has ceased to exist. Why don't you take over Skoda Works? It would pay you one hundred thousand pounds a year, tax free.' " And Masaryk answered, 'My father raised me to be a diplomat. In school I studied music. Instead of being president to Skoda Works, I'd rather play piano in a brothel. I'd be far more comfortable and have great peace of soul.' "

There was one more crisis behind the scenes. Judge Hutcheson got so homesick he considered cutting the trip to Europe and the Mideast short so he could return to his beloved Texas. "We finally convinced the Judge to pull himself together," Daddy wrote. "What he wanted most of all it seems was a big glass of fresh American milk!"

He went on to say he had no time for sightseeing, although he did pass Buckingham Palace to watch the changing of the guard.

And one evening Dick Crossman and his wife took him to dinner to meet Connie Ernst, Morris Ernst's exotic, dark-haired daughter, who was sharing an apartment with Mary Hemingway in London. They were both working at the Office of War Information.

Connie remembers "a long boisterous evening with Bart Crum where a great deal of liquor was consumed. None of us felt any pain. Bart and Dick joked about how so far the hearings had turned up nothing that was even worthy of publication."

(Indeed, *Commentary* magazine later observed that the Anglo-American Committee hearings turned up little that couldn't be found in a public library.)

After London, the committee broke up and traveled to different parts of Europe to gather their impressions firsthand from the survivors. UNRRA had already polled 4,000 DPs: no one wanted to remain in Germany; 9 wanted to go to the United States; 2,619 wanted to go to Palestine.

My father and Sir Frederick toured DP camps all over the American Zone in Germany and Czechoslovakia. I kept track of them by tracing their itinerary on the world globe in our living room in San Francisco—Washington, London, Frankfurt, Munich, Nuremberg. I cut everything out of the newspapers that referred to the committee and Bart Crum, and I'd keep on pasting clips into the maroon leather scrapbook. Now I was the only one doing it— my brother and Mama didn't seem to care.

The clips got increasingly interesting just before Daddy and Sir Frederick reached Vienna. On the Czech border they were arrested as spies by the Russians and spent the night in jail.

Daddy managed to phone us when he was released. "A case of mistaken identity," he laughed. He'd been wearing a pair of long woolen underwear borrowed from his friend Peter Cusick (Peter was in the OSS in London), whose name was on the long johns. This silly little anecdote ended up in Drew Pearson's "Daily Washington Merry-Go-Round" and Herb Caen wrote a mention of it in the *San Francisco Chronicle*.

Otherwise Daddy's experiences viewing the DP camps were pretty grim.

"The occupation authorities are overwhelmed as Jewish refugees pour in from Poland, Czechoslovakia and Rumania," he wrote us. "Truman is insisting that the American zone be kept open so the stream of refugees never stops . . . DP housing facilities very bad. Make-shift. In garages, airplane hangars, some community centers . . . toilets backed up. Supplies almost non-existent at times and rations of food pitiful. Cheese and black bread served cafeteria style. Most DPs hollow eyed, dirty—some argumentative. The Nazi persecutions have increased their sense of homelessness and separateness . . . and now they have to endure the anti-Semitism of the guards—there are armed guards everywhere standing outside barbed wire fences . . .

"In Landsberg, over 6200 Jewish refugees are confined to an area which the Allies had rejected as unfit for German prisoners of war."

In each center Sir Frederick and my father met with survivors of Auschwitz and other death camps and listened to their horror stories. They described beatings, slave labor, they told of slow starvation. They'd watched relatives being used as guinea pigs and injected with lethal germs. Hundreds of unnecessary amputations had been performed; thousands of rapes. Children deported to the camps were usually the first victims of the gas chambers. One man told of burying his baby alive to save it from the Nazi butchers. (The infant was smuggled to Munich and is alive today.)

"We are questioning literally hundreds of people," Daddy wrote us. "We ask, 'Do you realize immigration to the Holy Land is no simple matter?' 'Yes, yes, yes,' they reply wearily, 'but it doesn't matter . . .' We are discovering that Zionism for the DP is the only way he wants to survive . . . to remain in Europe is to perish."

Whenever they left a camp Sir Frederick and Daddy were confronted by hundreds of DPs marching in silent demonstration, usually in the hideous striped uniforms they'd worn in Dachau or Buchenwald, and they held up banners proclaiming "Open the gates of Palestine!"

In Frankfurt Daddy was introduced to the only surviving Jewish rabbi in Germany—Rabbi Leopold Neuhaus. How had he escaped the gas chambers? The old man pulled a tattered letter from his coat pocket. It was signed "Von Hindenburg." During

World War I the rabbi had assisted some German soldiers in Prussia, and Von Hindenburg, then general of the German army, had written him a note of thanks. Showing that letter to the Nazis had saved the rabbi's life.

IN Stuttgart Daddy discovered there were only two hundred Jews left. Before Hitler four thousand Jews had lived and worked in Stuttgart.

Conversation in Munich with the minister of Jewish affairs— a Herr Auber, whose sole duty was to convince Jews to stay in Bavaria. "Hitler made a mistake," he told my father. "The Jews shouldn't have been killed—they were the great bankers, the great moneymen of Europe. It would be economically disastrous for all Jews to leave now. We must re-create a Jewish community so Germany can come back as a substantial world power."

"An unusual lesson in unusual economics," Daddy wrote us.

ITEM: "There are only a few Jewish children left alive in Europe. In a DP camp like Landsberg—with 5000 DPs—only 100 children."

NEXT stop, the war-crimes trial in the bombed-out city of Nuremberg. "Spent several hours with American investigators and a journalist from *Time*. What is emerging: the massacres in the death camps were deliberate . . . 34,000 gassed or burned daily at Auschwitz, in two shifts. . . . Survivors reciting their ordeals in the courtroom are periodically excused so they can recover their composure . . . but I'm told that boredom is creeping in; there is only so much horror one can absorb."

At one point my father asked to read the material on the Grand Mufti (the ex-mufti of Jerusalem—Haj Amin el Husseini, spokesman for the Palestine Arab party). "It was material that would incriminate him in the mass murder of the Jews; much documentation had been hidden in the Allied War Crimes Commission archive."

"I sat for an entire afternoon guarded by an American army officer while I leafed through thick piles of papers and notes," Daddy wrote us. "The record of the Mufti's intrigues was fantastic —Hitler was his friend so in 1941 he fled Egypt—took refuge in Germany and agitated openly for a 'Final Solution'; his radio broadcasts from Berlin were scathing anti-Semitic attacks. He encouraged the deportation of European Jews to Polish extermination camps; he personally sent 4000 Jewish children to the gas chambers at Auschwitz and he visited Auschwitz to make sure it happened. He was accompanied by Adolf Eichmann who was another close friend."

BEFORE leaving Nuremberg Daddy and Sir Frederick attended a private screening of unexpurgated films taken of the actual mass murders.

"I could not believe what I saw," Daddy wrote in his diary. "Hundreds on hundreds of corpses piled up like cordwood to be tossed into ovens. Until I saw these movies I'd only conceived of the brutality in my head. Men hung on meathooks until they died; Jewish children forced to run into the woods where they were shot like animals for sport. Piles of bodies pushed by bulldozers into big pits dug into the ground. The question about whether or not there should be a Zionist or Arab state fades into the background after witnessing such examples of human degradation."

Before the films were over my father ran out of the screening room to vomit in the snow.

The tour of the camps continued. And the questioning.

"One woman told us 'we know the massacre of the Jews didn't stop because of a change of heart. They stopped the killing because the war was over and they had no more power to kill us, but the hatred remains—the same murder is in their hearts.' "

"As for the German people—do they express guilt or shame? 'Very little,' we were told," Daddy wrote us. "The majority of Germans regret they lost the war and as for anti-Semitism—it is as strong as ever, particularly in Poland—three hundred Jews have been senselessly murdered since January and Polish Jews are fleeing Poland by the thousands—in terror for their lives."

"Sometimes when we finished our questioning we would find ourselves surrounded by inmates, pleading, tipping their hats, making little speeches about why they had to get to the Holy Land. Once a small wrinkled man planted himself in front of me, tears streaming down his cheeks. 'What have I done? Why am I here? When will you let me go?' "

This was the wish he kept hearing over and over, my father

wrote us—the dream, the longing, expressed in camp after camp
—"the goal of creating homes in Palestine; this was the explanation for the mass movement of the Jews across Europe. . . ."

In one poll my father was given DPs were asked to put down
a second choice if Palestine was unavailable, and hundreds wrote,
"Crematorium." In many camps Jewish women deliberately suffered abortions rather than bear a child on German soil.

In a last handwritten note to Mama, dated Prague, February
16, 1946, Daddy vowed "to reveal what I have seen and what I
have heard as soon as possible even tho [sic] I'm supposed to keep
my mouth shut."

The next thing we knew Daddy had called an impromptu
press conference as soon as he arrived in Vienna. Reporter Gerold
Frank and Ruth Gruber helped him to organize it.

Correspondents from Berlin, Paris, Prague, the United King-
dom, and America crowded into the office of the Displaced Persons
Bureau and "Bart Crum stood on a landing and described what he
and Sir Frederick had seen in the camps," Gruber recalled. "It
was quite electrifying. You've got to remember that nobody in the
world knew what was going on. Bart told it all—how the DPs were
penned up like animals in quasi-prisons instead of shelters, how
demoralized they were—half starved—still being persecuted . . .
most DPs had been assigned to camps in countries of their own
origins; this yoked Jews to their unrepentant tormentors—Poles,
Ukrainians. . . . Bart kept stressing this highly emotional and completely unfair billeting. . . . 'Unless these settlements are cleaned
out there will be mass suicides in the camps,' he said. 'The DPs
have lost everything—their families, their synagogues, their sense
of community; their last hope—their only hope—is to immigrate
to Palestine.' "

Nobody from the committee had spoken about any of this to
the press before, so the reporters practically stampeded to their
typewriters. The story landed on page one of *The New York Times*
and other papers around the world.

However, when the other members of the committee arrived
in Vienna and heard about the press conference, my father was
chastised and told that from then on only the co-chairs of the
committee could speak to reporters.

As if to prove their point, Sir John and Judge Hutcheson held

their own press conference the following day. At the conference
Sir John hit my father on the arm when he tried to answer a
question put to him by a man from Reuters.

"IT is obvious that the British are extremely annoyed by me,"
Daddy wrote in his diary. "But I do not regret what I've done.
Frank Buxton, the only real newspaperman on the Committee other
than Crossman, is quietly goading me on. 'This is no time for
discretion,' he whispered. I do not have a bad conscience for
having spoken out. I am not bound by secrecy. And we are talking
about human beings here, thousands of barbarously treated human
beings. I believe that since Sir Frederick and I had witnessed the
major part of the DP problem firsthand, the terrible conditions of
the camps, etc., it was up to us to inform the public; I still feel
that way."

He continued to make waves—talking to reporters when he
shouldn't, phoning Washington, educating himself on the subject
of illegal immigration, which was increasing all over Europe. He
knew David Ben-Gurion and Haganah had united in their efforts
to outmaneuver and resist British immigration policies, and he saw
some of the results when he visited the underground railway at
Villach—the tiny town in Austria near the borders of Yugoslavia
and Italy.

"Everything well coordinated," he noted, "aided by Americans, thwarted when possible by the British. There are trucks to
transport the refugees—plenty of forged passports—some Polish
Jews have walked on foot to get here and if they can sneak past
the British they'll catch the boats that are docked in the Adriatic
bound for Palestine."

In another letter to Mama he wondered "whether legislation
could be created to modify our immigration laws so death camp
survivors who have families in the U.S. could be united with
them."

WITHIN the week the committee had its first full meeting since
London; discussion immediately focused on the problem of illegal
immigration—should a special report be filed? It was quickly
decided not to since there was the equally pressing question of
whether to issue an interim report urging for the emptying of the

camps and the immediate admission of one hundred thousand Jews to Palestine. "So the DPs know we care about them and are trying to work out a solution as soon as possible," my father wrote.

The Americans were all for an interim report, but there were those British committee members who felt the Arabs would view the emptying of the camps as a political move. Instead, why couldn't the Americans follow British policy and close all borders immediately? That would take care of the overcrowding.

"But closing all borders would bottle up the avenues of escape for the Jews still in Poland," my father argued heatedly.

At this point Judge Hutcheson received word from Washington that President Truman preferred not to have an interim report. What political maneuverings were behind that decision my father didn't know. But, he wrote in his diary, he suspected the anti-Zionist, pro-Arab faction in the State Department. He got so angry he threatened to quit the committee.

The following morning Dave Niles sent him a confidential cable urging him to stay put, and of course he remained, but he felt "very disheartened." What really upset him was the unbridled anti-Semitism among the committee members. "Manningham Buller is anti-Semitic—so are Aydelotte and Phillips," he wrote in his notebook. "They don't even bother to hide it. So here we are 12 non Jews trying to solve the monumental problem of how to help thousands of Jewish survivors find a home. Dick Crossman said something very telling. He told me he thinks every non Jew has the virus of anti-Semitism in his veins. In times of moral stress his own moral resistance can break down and the virus can break out into the disease itself—so I suppose nobody on our Committee is immune."

On top of that he observed later in his book:

Anti-Semitism is particularly virulent in Vienna. Last evening Dick and I had drinks with a British officer in charge of DPs in the British zone. Here's a guy dealing with the problem of 4000 broken souls all living together crammed in little settlements established by the American Relief; they're all that's left of a Viennese Jewish community that once numbered over two hundred thousand!

"Too bad the war didn't last another three months," the

officer remarked. "They'd have all been done away with and we would have no problem."

Crossman and I stared at him and he stared back ice cold. "Yes, I'm anti-Semitic," he admitted. "I honestly hate the Jew bastards. I wish they'd all been burned to death."

I'm afraid I gasped at this and he turned his ruddy sweaty face on me. "Oh," he chided. "I imagine you have some of 'em as your clients, eh?" and he chuckled hugely.

"The Catholic Church is no better," my father went on. He'd met with various monsignors, including the head of Catholic charities, who told him, "We don't want to drive the Jews out of Vienna; that would be un-Christian." Then he added, "We don't hate the Jews, we just hate the Jewish spirit. The best solution to the Jewish problem would be to change the Jewish spirit to a Christian spirit." Daddy felt such shame at their so-called interpretation of Christianity, he excused himself and left the meeting.

In the next weeks a series of fat State Department envelopes stuffed with handwritten notes were mailed to San Francisco. Mama placed them carefully in the file cabinet along with everything else. Reading the notes fifty years later, I have the sense that my father was so caught up in the tragic complexity of the experience, he could barely jot everything down; some of his writing is illegible.

On a sheet of paper are virtual scrawls circa February 1946: "I have been advised that the Committee has two problems to think about: where the DPs are going to live and how Palestine will react if 100,000 Jews settle there." He added, "The DP dilemma is almost irrelevant to the conflict that's already going on between Palestinian Jews and Arabs." He ended that he had decided he couldn't begin to understand "the dimension of Zionism and the meaning of Zionism" until he reached Palestine.

He refers to Willkie in his notes—Willkie and his concept of justice. "Remember that any man who denies justice to someone he hates prepares the way for a denial of justice to someone he loves."

He refers to Willkie's book *One World*, too. Later he would give copies of it to some of the Arab intellectuals he met in Cairo and to a young Palestinian who served as his driver in Jerusalem.

CHAPTER
15

AROUND that time, late February 1946, Mama jotted in her journal: "Bart's hunger for justice, as he travels the globe, crusading for the Jews . . . his clinging to ideals is as powerful a drive as mine is for sex. I've decided that *his ideals* are his passion, exalting, libidinous, juicy . . . how odd and terribly sad we can't ever mesh the physical and the philosophical."

She made no mention of the problems my brother and I were having. Not long after Daddy went to Washington, Bart had been caught shoplifting at a Pacific Heights five-and-dime; I'd been briefly suspended from Miss Burke's for being "disruptive" in study hall.

We were both sent to Judge Mary Kohler's for "counseling," but she was late coming home from her job at children's court, so we had to wait a long time on her sun porch.

I remember watching the fog swirl and thicken above the sidewalk outside. The screens on the windows were rusty. In the distance fog horns hooted on San Francisco Bay. I felt momentarily depressed.

I kept wondering why Mary Kohler was so close to my parents, but, then, they had all gone to college together. She was tense and opinionated, something of a civic activist, something of a bohemian. She managed separate friendships with my parents—advising Mama to be less "sex obsessed"; talking law and Catholicism with my father.

When Mary arrived home from court, she guided me into her

office and wasted no time scolding me for making faces at my
study-hall teacher. (I'd been thrilled when the other students collapsed laughing.) "Why did you do that, Patti, dear?" she demanded, smiling the angry, radiant smile I've never forgotten—it
strained over big, white, perfect teeth.

"Why did you behave in such a manner?" she pursued
brightly. Her crisp voice had a slight edge.

"I was bored," I replied wearily. "Studying bores me."

"That won't get you very far. And making silly faces will get
you nowhere. You just did it to attract attention."

She said the same thing to my brother moments later about
his shoplifting. "You shoplift because it's daring! Shame!"

"No, you're wrong," he countered. "I stole those colored pencils because I wanted them. I'd already spent my paltry allow-
ance."

Mary then launched into a harangue about shoplifting: "It
was out-and-out thievery, what you did, but it's a temptation you
can't resist. Being privileged has made you soft. You think you can
get away with murder, but you can't. A poor little Negro boy would
be put in reform school," she threatened Bart. "As for you"—she
eyed me balefully—"idiots make faces—well-bred young ladies
do not!"

We expected her to say more, to dole out some punishment at
least, but then the phone rang and after answering it she hissed,
"Business call, have to take it." She was still smiling as she waved
us away.

And we raced down the steps of her house and over to Blum's
ice cream parlor on Polk Street, where we gorged on rich hot fudge
sundaes, and then we sneaked into another five-and-dime and I
shoplifted two lipsticks and Bart stole more colored pencils and
Mama never guessed.

Although she disagreed with Mary's assessment of us as
"psychologically hungry," Mama somehow believed that "Judge
Kohler" might be a healthy influence, so she spent almost every
weekend in the country with us until Daddy returned from the
Middle East.

We always dreaded her appearance because she was so con-
trolling, so moralistic. Her arrival meant a list of "must-do" activities: picnic on the beach, brisk walks through the woods, singing

at the piano, orchestrated conversation at the dinner table. Mama went along with everything; she seemed relieved that someone else was taking charge. But for all her anger and dictates, she usually left us alone, which we appreciated.

Mary often brought her three children along: Cathy, Richard, and Johnny, her eldest, a handsome, taciturn boy. I developed a violent crush on him, which Mary didn't approve of. When she found us necking behind a sand dune she pulled us apart. After that I wouldn't answer her when she addressed me, and my brother and I started communicating in our secret language until Mama threatened to tell Daddy, reminding us that "he'll be very disappointed in you."

"I'll be disappointed if you don't tell Daddy," Bart muttered.

Of course she forgot about our naughtiness when Daddy phoned from Egypt. His voice sounded far away, and as he traveled farther and farther away from us, we shoplifted more and more.

THERE were no more phone calls. My brother and I did receive a postcard addressed to "my kidlets" (his nickname for us) and datelined Cairo.

"I am here in the shadow of the Pyramids about to meet at Mena House in the same rooms where Churchill, Stalin and Chiang met Roosevelt." From then on we heard nothing directly from Daddy, but Mama continued to receive State Department envelopes filled with mementos: matchbook covers, hotel napkins, calling cards, and lists of people titled "People B.C. has spoken to so far."

She read one list to us out loud, hoping we could identify the names: "Ernest Bevin (British foreign secretary), Dmitry Manuilsky (Ukrainian foreign minister), George Backer . . . Dolly Schiff . . . Abe Feinberg (banker), Prince Faisal (second son of Ibn Saud), David Ben-Gurion, Golda Meir, Edward R. Murrow . . ."

Most of those people meant nothing to us, but it was our way of keeping Daddy's trip alive; still he remained so far away. I tried to imagine him bundled up in the oversized fur coat he kept referring to in his letters. He stopped wearing it once he reached Egypt. "It is hotter here than in the Sacramento Valley," he commented.

My brother started complaining that he couldn't remember

Daddy's face, so Mama found a dignified portrait he'd posed for when he was representing the Lawyers Guild at the United Nations.

I'd already pasted a collage on the back of my bathroom door—photographs taken when he was in Washington during the hearings on Fair Employment Practices and while he was a Willkie speechwriter. I cherished the images because in them he looked so confident—so happy.

The only visual reminder Mama kept of Daddy was a rather grim passport photo stuck in her dressing-table mirror. What dominated the room was a large, crude watercolor of her beloved poodle, Bonbon.

Bonbon was spoiled rotten; she even went to a special beauty parlor to be washed and clipped, then she'd return home with a pink ribbon on her topknot and she'd growl and snap at our dogs, two floppy, amiable black cocker spaniels, until they began growling and snapping back. They'd invariably get into a fight and my brother and I would have to separate them, and then Mama would banish the cockers to the basement, where they howled heartbrokenly. Bonbon, meanwhile, would be allowed to roam freely throughout the house.

It seemed that while Daddy was away Mama focused her energies on Bonbon and not on us. I can still see that poodle (oh, how I resented her!) in the front seat of our station wagon, craning her neck imperiously. She and Mama would drive all over San Francisco together, and for weeks that spring they both attended dog-training school and Mama kept a daily account of her achievements.

February 21, 1946: "Bonbon piddled on a newspaper in my bathroom when I gave the command."

There were few mentions of Daddy in this same journal, although he was writing to her almost every day.

From his diary, dated February 28, 1946:

> Cairo: a general strike to protest the presence of British troops; we are escorted into the city followed by armored cars and soldiers.
>
> The hearings: Arab leaders hopelessly divided by national rivalries. They are very, very wary about Jewish immi-

gration in the Arab world. According to one of my Washington sources, the State Department sent a secret memo to the Arabs assuring them the Committee's findings will not change the situation vis-à-vis the White Paper policy!

During the breaks the Arab potentates move about in full costume, long white robes, etc. They all wear polished English oxford shoes . . . resemble movie extras . . .

Nobody likes the idea of the Anglo-American Committee because the British are easier to handle *alone*. Even the Americans here are uneasy about our presence . . . they're afraid our conclusions will put a stop to the State Department's "double policy: one for the Arabs, one for the Jews" . . . the one FDR began during his double talk with Ibn Saud . . . almost nobody we speak to wants a Jewish state in Palestine . . . and the Arab leaders have no interest in the Jewish refugee . . . no interest, no sympathy, almost complete indifference . . . it seems beyond them.

On March 2 Daddy arrived in Jerusalem and described the city as "an armed camp. Barbed wire in coils on the street; soldiers man machine guns. Jittery atmosphere; lots of intrigue and surveillance."

A couple of days later he wrote to us, "I feel as if I'm smack in the center of some extraordinary political sociopsychological ferment. The Committee is maintaining offices near the Y (where the hearings will be held) but the bar of the King David Hotel has become our unofficial headquarters. Every special pleader in the Mideast is making an appearance. Jews, Arabs, Lebanese oil men from Texas, British spies, journalists from Moscow and the ubiquitous Arthur Lurie taking notes for Rabbi Silver who's back in Cleveland. It figures we have a Swiss bartender presiding over it all."

At the hearings Chaim Weizmann was the first witness. "Very impressive as he explained why he thought a Jewish home state could eliminate anti-Semitism. David Ben-Gurion next. When asked who is the head of Haganah he answered, 'I have no idea.' "

One morning as my father left the King David Hotel a man suddenly handed him some mimeographed statements addressed to "the Members of Anglo-American Committee of Inquiry" and signed "Head of Command, Jewish Resistance Movement."

The memo warned that virtually every Jew in Palestine belonged to the Movement and it would have to be destroyed before Haganah, the underground Jewish army, could be disarmed. The memo went on to say that they wouldn't interfere with the committee's work, but "if the solution of the Committee is anti-Zionist—resistance will increase."

"My British colleagues thought the document was infuriating," Daddy wrote, "even tho [sic] I pointed out that Haganah had been started in self defense—that it was a citizens army meant to protect and assure immigration . . . much discussion about whether or not Haganah should be disbanded and then Crossman pointed out that no government has ever been able to disband an underground resistance movement backed by the people."

Then an event occurred that dramatized his words. Four young Jews—members of the resistance movement—were killed in a clash with the British in Tel Aviv. More than 150,000 people attended their funeral.

"IT is pretty scary now," Daddy noted. "We go everywhere with bodyguards and an army jeep filled with armed guards behind our chauffeured cars." Still he managed to have dinner with Egon Egronsky, editor of the *Palestine Post*, who was giving fair coverage to all sides—Arab, Jew, and British—although he had to submit every story he ran to the censors. Daddy learned more about censorship when he and George Polk did a broadcast for CBS in which they discussed the committee's findings—the tape of their conversation was immediately destroyed by British censors. "Palestine is a police state," he wrote in his diary, "and I don't like it."

HE and the other Americans on the committee were getting tired of being shadowed by British Intelligence. "It has gotten worse since we arrived in Palestine. Tapped telephones, opened mail—they don't even bother to reseal it. Confidential replies from the White House are delivered to the British before they are delivered to us. We don't deal with the surveillance—we try to ignore it."

IN between the hearings Daddy traveled all over the Holy Land with a bodyguard and a translator. He visited kibbutzim and vineyards, he wandered around Palestinian villages; he spoke to as many different kinds of people as he could, from Jewish terrorists to Arab potentates. "I become more and more convinced that pressures are at work to keep Arab and Jew at each other's throats. It is to the British Foreign Office's interest to sow the seeds of Arab/Jewish hatred," he wrote in his notebook.

> I keep hearing how terrified Arab is of Jew and vice versa. But I hear nothing about what Jews really feel about the British. I know British prefer the Arab because most Arabs are illiterate and disorganized but the British loathe the Jews because Jewish leaders are so much smarter than they are and that intimidates them. . . .
>
> The British think they are playing it safe. They assume they will be able to control the Arabs indefinitely but that may not be the case. There is this paradox: most Arabs and Jews get along just fine. I see them riding on buses together —all over Jerusalem. I see them eating in cafes, having drinks at the King David Hotel. . . . But—and this is a big but—Arab and Jew are unable to sit down and publicly discuss their differences whenever the British are around. They can do so in private—and have with me—but not when the British are around, they clam up.

And then a scribbled note: "Among ourselves—McDonald, Crossman and I . . . we are beginning to talk about the possibility for partition. It could be a solution, with the Jewish agency as a provisional government."

Before he left Jerusalem in late March, Daddy met Chaim Weizmann several times at his home in the desert.

> He is a big man. High domed forehead, sunken eyes. He suffers from cataracts so he's almost blind. Dick and I took turns walking with him arm and arm very slowly around his garden (of which he is very proud).
>
> We spoke of the real problems. That there must be genuine communication between the two sides. What is it the Jews want? Unlimited immigrations—a Jewish state. And what do the Arabs want? Self government. Weizmann believes partition is the only solution. He said he'd discussed it with Churchill and Churchill supported it. I asked if he thought

there was another solution, another alternative. He said no. He is very wise and very gentle. I left at midnight to go to Mass in Jerusalem. Dick remained behind. Driving back, I couldn't help but think about what Weizmann has said to us.

That the issue facing the committee is finally not between right or wrong but between the greater or lesser injustice. Injustice he feels is inevitable . . . what he is saying is that the Committee must decide whether to be unjust to the Arabs or unjust to the Jews.

CHAPTER

16

ONCE in Lausanne the committee spent two weeks arguing and refining their positions. Bitterness and acrimony handicapped their discussions.

"We are starting to get on each other's nerves," Daddy wrote, and then he added, "It is finally pretty clear they [the British] dislike us almost as much as they dislike each other."

And it didn't help matters that British surveillance had intensified as a result of a leak to the press. "How it happened we'll never know," Daddy wrote. "But suddenly a Captain Ayers of the British Criminal Investigation Department of the Palestine Police who had been in charge of our security in Jerusalem appeared in Lausanne and took a room at our hotel—to reporters he explained he was 'on holiday,' to us he said he had come for our security. He asked permission to go through our rooms, look through our papers and destroy any documents we weren't going to use—when I made telephone calls I would find him on the end of my wire and when people tried to phone me the concierge (who I learned later had been paid off) would turn them over to the Captain. I started making my telephone calls elsewhere. Judge Hutcheson told me White House cables directed to him were first sent to the British counsel in Geneva—these included private messages from President Truman."

Meanwhile, letters, telegrams, and phone calls poured into my father's hotel room—"intercepted or not—they finally reached me"; by that time every Zionist in the world knew which side he was on.

"I am never left alone," Daddy said in another letter to us. "Tonight April 8, 1946, Arthur Lurie burst into my suite as I was taking a bath; sat down on the rim of the tub and demanded to know why everything was taking so long!"

The deliberations continued. At the end of the first week the meetings seemed hopelessly deadlocked.

"We are groping our way," Daddy noted in his diary.

Everyone agreed that the White Paper policy was a grave injustice and could not stand. My father, Crossman, and McDonald opted for partition, but the rest of the committee rejected the idea. (Later my father would write a special report to Truman explaining why he believed it was the only solution that would be accepted by Arab and Jew.)

One of the biggest sticking points: Sir John and Manningham Buller's insistence that the entry of one hundred thousand DPs be made conditional on the disbanding and condemning of Haganah, the illegal Jewish army. The committee members knew this was impossible; it had originated as a protest against Arab violence.

On April 16, 1946, Truman cabled Judge Hutcheson asking for a unanimous decision.

Unanimity was achieved only when it was agreed to include a recommendation to end terrorism on both sides, that Arabs and Jews cooperate with each other for economic development, and that compulsory education be introduced.

My father concluded afterward in his book that it was "the Judge and his leadership that kept us together. He would not permit our initial differences to result in the breakup of the Committee into British and American groups. If it hadn't been for him our final report wouldn't have been unanimous."

Afterward, there was a drunken dinner during which Sir John launched into a bitter attack against Judge Hutcheson. "What he said was what he really felt," Daddy wrote. "The recommendations of our Committee were in reality a defeat of his policies and he was mad as hell—he told me bluntly, 'we will certainly not implement any of this program—these are only recommendations.'"

The Anglo-American Committee's report was obviously the product of considerable compromise. There were no recommendations to create an independent Jewish state; there were vague assumptions that the Mandate for Palestine be retained by the British until it could be converted to UN trusteeship. But the report did address itself to the plight of the DPs; it recommended that the one hundred thousand Jews be let into Palestine immediately.

As soon as he returned to New York on April 28, my father and James McDonald met with Rabbi Hillel Silver to show him the report. (It is probable that either Arthur Lurie or Nahum Goldman convinced Silver to see my father and McDonald.) The magnetic, bombastic Silver (who had been against the committee since its inception) rejected their report on the grounds that it was "a complete repudiation of Zionist aims," and he said he intended to denounce it publicly.

But that would antagonize Truman about Zionism, my father maintained gently. Why not agree to compromise? For the next few hours he and McDonald hammered out another way of dealing with the issue—urge Truman to accept the recommendation about the hundred thousand Jews and postpone the decisions on the rest of the report.

Silver agreed and Daddy brought the same strategy to Truman the next day. The State Department was essentially negative, but Truman agreed and he allowed Silver and Emanuel Newman (another American Zionist leader) to draft a positive response about the report that could be released to the press.

My father helped them write it. He even added a small addendum of his own—a plea to protect the holy places in and about Jerusalem.

When the report was made public on April 30, Forrestal and Henderson were furious; Truman ignored their anger and pushed Ernest Bevin to lift the White Paper momentarily so that the DPs could leave their camps. But Bevin was furious, too. He denied he had ever promised to act on the committee's recommendations.

Daddy sent Dave Niles a long handwritten letter dated May 6, 1946, as he crossed the country by train to San Francisco. "President Truman should know Foreign Minister Bevin promised the entire Committee (at a private lunch in London) that the British government would accept the report and put it into effect immediately."

In subsequent weeks, the British Cabinet discussed the report at length and came to the conclusion that to agree to the committee's recommendation was to incite Arab wrath, imperil the British position in the Mideast, and allow Russia greater influence in the area.

Truman, meanwhile, publicly committed himself to the immediate admission of one hundred thousand Jews to the Holy Land.

CHAPTER

17

A FLURRY of excitement greeted my father when he arrived in San Francisco. Telegrams piled up on the hall table of our Green Street house; the phones never stopped ringing. He barely had time to embrace us before leaving to attend a reception in his honor at the Opera House, where he was to speak about his experiences on the committee.

We followed him there—my mother, my brother, and I—and then we sat in the audience and listened to him describe the tragic world of the camps. He finished by saying that the destiny of European displaced Jews was one of the terrible results of World War II and that the United States must support the idea of large-scale Jewish immigration to Palestine.

Afterward we pushed backstage, but we couldn't get close to him. He was surrounded by reporters and friends. We watched as he broke free and went off in a corner to confer with a group of rabbis.

It was like watching a stranger. We felt shy in his presence and totally separate from him. Mama whispered that he was doing something important historically and we must be patient. Patient for what?

That weekend Mo came down from Sacramento to welcome Daddy home; it was the only time she ever visited our Green Street house. We sat with her while Daddy gave us little bottles of holy water from Jerusalem, and then he tried to describe a few of the people he had met, such as Chaim Weizmann and Golda Meir.

Suddenly Mo grumbled, something like "those people will do you no good . . . you shouldn't be associating with them."

Daddy tried to laugh.

He would not admit that his own mother was anti-Semitic. "You can make an anti-Semitic remark and not be an anti-Semite," he told my brother and me.

I wonder if he really believed that.

AFTER the Opera House address he was deluged with requests to speak. His law associate, Philip Ehrlich (who hadn't wanted him to leave their practice to go on the committee), told him he must get back to practicing law.

But Daddy knew from private conversations that George Kenan considered the Palestine situation insoluble and that Clark Clifford didn't. He knew that if all else failed, President Truman would seek congressional approval for admitting the DPs into the United States. He wanted to play a role in the matter.

So he ignored Ehrlich's demands and went on accepting all speaking engagements. And he kept meeting behind the scenes with opposing opinion makers in the bewilderingly fragmented world of Jewish affairs.

"Zionist leaders like Rabbi Silver were arguing that to bring a hundred thousand DPs into America could weaken the purpose to establish a Jewish state in Palestine," the banker Abe Feinberg said. "Non-Zionists like Lessing Rosenwald disagreed. I called Bart Crum our Irish leprechaun. He worked very hard with Dave Niles to convince both sides that the first step was to start moving those refugees out of the camps."

"Obviously Bart has found another crusade," Mama noted in her journal. "Now he is going to save the Jews."

DADDY came and went from the Green Street house—one night he might be in Dallas describing immigration restriction, another night he might be in Los Angeles urging the Lawyers Guild to get involved in the controversy; he helped organize a Lawyers Committee for Justice in Palestine.

And in every speech he gave he condemned James Forrestal, secretary of defense, as being in cahoots with Standard Oil, implying that Forrestal was more concerned with the views of the

British Foreign Office than with White House directives—or his own president. Peter Cusick recalled phoning my father and telling him to "stop tangling with the heavyweights; Bart wouldn't listen. He'd been mentioned as a possibility for ambassador to Palestine, but after those speeches, no way—he was finished."

By August the flight of illegal Jews into Palestine was at its height. Daddy was still meeting behind the scenes with Dave Niles and Clark Clifford, trying to convince Truman that the only solution was partition.

The British, meanwhile, were stepping up their terrorism. I remember Daddy talking angrily about two refugee ships crowded with a thousand death camp survivors that reached Haifa only to be turned away with water hoses by the British and sent back to Germany.

In retaliation came the King David tragedy. An entire wing of the Jerusalem hotel—the nerve center of British authority—was blown up by Irgun agents (headed by Menachem Begin), and ninety-one people—Arabs, Jews, British—were killed.

Shortly after that, on August 22, 1946, my father gave a speech at the American Christian Palestine lunch. In his introduction he stressed that he was speaking in a purely personal capacity, but then, according to *PM*'s Alex Uhl: "Bart Crum tore into British and U.S. Officialdom and the handling of the Palestinian question in one of the strongest denunciations ever heard in Washington."

He charged that for years the State Department had been undermining official United States policy on Palestine and was now undermining President Truman's.

When asked to name the men in the State Department responsible for this he answered, "Loy Henderson," and suggested that his resignation be tendered immediately. Then he was asked how was it possible for middle-level diplomats to ignore a president's wishes. "I can only guess the President doesn't always know what is going on."

After the speech John Neylan phoned him to scold and *San Francisco Examiner* publisher Clarence Lindner actually exclaimed in a private note to *World-Telegram* publisher Herbert Bayard Swope, "I do wish Bart Crum would shut up!"

But Yehuda Hellman, who met Daddy in Egypt when he was a reporter for the *Palestine Post*, said,

What Bart Crum did was crucial. Truman hadn't been able to gain immigration concessions for the DPs. Bevin kept saying that even if some Jews were allowed into Palestine, most Jews would have to remain in Europe and Palestine could never be considered as a possible Jewish homeland. Bart focused world attention on what was going on behind the scenes in the State Department. He referred to the secret communications between Ibn Saud and Farouk of Egypt and the Husseinis of Jerusalem with the Middle East desk of the State Department. He brought all these secrets out in the open. The story had tremendous impact and the American public listened because Bart was a Gentile and Bart had been there. He had been in the Mideast, he had been in London—he had listened to the British tell him that the United States should play along with the Arabs. It was very theatrical and very dangerous because Bart spoke out at great risk to himself. He had nothing to gain and everything to lose.

Indeed, two weeks after he criticized the State Department, the *World-Telegram* ran the following story: "Bart Crum, who called for Loy Henderson's resignation, is a supporter of Communist controlled front organizations including the Lawyers Guild and the American Committee for Spanish Freedom as well as ICCAP, one of the most active mouthpieces of the Communist Party."

My father labeled the story as "the beginning of a red-smear campaign against me. Calling a man names is an easy way of avoiding the issues," he said. He laughed at reports that he was following the Communist Party line. "When I supported Willkie in 1940 I was called a patriotic American. When I supported Roosevelt in 1944 I was called a dirty New Dealer. When I supported Mayor Roger Lapham against the recall movement in San Francisco I was called an internationally known lawyer. Now, because I support European Jews' fight for life against British and American diplomatic strangling, I'm a Communist. Bah!"

Yehuda Hellman added, "In the minds of most Americans, the East European Jewish refugee was thought to be Communist —and many non-Jews believed this, and because Bart Crum was associated with not only Jews but Communists as a radical lawyer, it was a double bind for him, a no-win situation. But he didn't give it a thought in those days. He just barrelhoused ahead."

At the same time, he couldn't ignore the volatile state of American politics.

Domestic problems loomed. There were strikes everywhere: coal strikes, steel strikes, strikes on the railroads. The country was beginning to tear itself apart over its foreign policy, and ideological lines were being drawn between democracy and international Communism. Also, the ugly shadow of the atomic bomb cast a pall over everything—its forces of destruction were so huge it gave an existential character to the era.

After Congress turned reactionary in the November 1946 elections, Daddy worried that both parties were so ultraconservative he would have no candidate to vote for.

He made a couple of impassioned speeches to that effect; then, in December, he became one of the founders of the Progressive Citizens of America. Sculptor Jo Davidson and Frank Kingdon served as heads.

PCA envisioned organizing a nationwide network of politically activated communities with "housewives and factory workers and teachers" lobbying for the UN, pushing for rent control, fighting against antilabor legislation. The overall goal was to develop a third party that would support Henry Wallace's candidacy for president in 1948. It was an ambitious plan with the best of intentions. But there was a lot of infighting; PCA was always in some kind of chaos behind the scenes.

American attitudes were changing; the liberal line that a "friendlier" attitude would make the Russians cooperate more was thought to be preposterous by much of the public, and it was reflected in the dour articles John Foster Dulles published in *Life* warning that Communism was spreading.

Harold Ickes—briefly a power in PCA—didn't want a third party and wasn't sure Henry Wallace was the ideal presidential candidate because he was not a politician. Ickes predicted PCA would fail because it had no real grass-roots base, and because he thought its two hundred directors and thirty-man executive committee (made up of big names like Paul Robeson and Fredric March) was a sign of weakness rather than strength.

And then there was the question of whether or not to work with the Communists; that became the irreconcilable issue among all liberals.

Daddy maintained that Communists should not be excluded from PCA, and indeed they weren't. He went so far as to say he wasn't afraid of Communist infiltration; it could be handled.

But an important group of powerful liberals *were* afraid. Right after PCA was formed, anti-Communist liberals like Eleanor Roosevelt, Reinhold Niebuhr, and screenwriter Philip Dunne founded Americans for Democratic Action, and Communists were not welcome. As envisioned, ADA "would enable liberals to come to grips with the reality of Soviet power."

ADA members worried that American Communists were creating a new united front movement aimed at discrediting United States foreign policy. "We had to stop being naïve," Dunne told me years later. Dunne had worked with my father on Fight for Freedom during the war.

He thought Daddy was a "naïf." "He simply wouldn't admit that PCA was controlled by the CP."

In 1947 there was no real center for political operation in this country, so Communists had free rein to create all sorts of new fronts and diversions and illusions. It took my father at least another year to wake up to reality. By then the international tensions had grown worse and there was less common ground between liberals and Communists.

As a family we never questioned why Daddy was "sticking his neck out," as Mo put it. I imagined he believed, "If I don't do it—who will?"

To me he was a Don Quixote tilting at windmills—he was supremely heroic.

He thought he led a charmed life: he found it exhilarating to challenge the State Department; for a while he thought he could change the public's perception of America's role in the Middle East.

For a while he found it equally exhilarating to criticize the Truman Doctrine "as the end of an American policy based on the world."

The FBI stepped up its surveillance of him after he made that statement, but he didn't know that.

Throughout 1946 and into 1947, his name and face were in the newspapers almost every day, and at that point I imagined a romantic aura surrounding him—an almost mythic power.

BY November 19, 1946, the Anglo-American Committee's recommendations had not only been rejected by the British as a sellout to American oil interests, the Arabs had rejected it too and the Jews didn't much like it either, although it had remedied some of the injustices of the White Paper policy.

Daddy came home for a while; he stopped giving speeches. He was trying to finish his book, which he called *Behind the Silken Curtain.* He had been contracted by Simon and Schuster to write about the committee and what had gone on, and since the Mideast was never out of the headlines, he was being pressured to finish it fast.

Reporter Gerold Frank flew out from New York to help him shape and polish the manuscript. In the evenings they would sit in the living room and Mama would carry in trays of food and coffee and they would go over chapters with a red pencil. Occasionally, Daddy would read sections aloud to us.

He couldn't stomach the idea that so many lies were still being told, mostly in the name of oil interests and British imperialism, to perpetuate the historic antagonism that existed between Arab and Jew. "The Mideast is probably going to continue to be the most volatile place on the earth," he predicted. "But we [the Committee] have been played for suckers. The least I can do is tell what I know."

And he did.

THE following spring, political columnist Marquis Childs wrote this review of my father's book *Behind the Silken Curtain* for *The New York Times Book Review:*

"In the best and truest sense Bartley Crum is a man of good will. He challenges the realists and the cynics in the same way the late Wendell Willkie challenged them. In this there is the challenge of courage and honesty and yes, a kind of nobility, yet at the same time it is infinitely sad for it leaves us with yesterday's headlines describing the latest horror in Palestine and with the tragedy of the homeless Jews still barred from the land they were led to believe was theirs. The men of good will (like Bart Crum) have been defeated again by politicians who rely on power (politics)."

And in another review, in the *Herald Tribune* Harold Ickes wrote:

"The author is a San Francisco lawyer of distinction, a man well known for his independence of thought . . . he presents his facts with as much lack of passion as if he was leading an equity case in the courts, but it is only fair to warn the reader not to undertake this book unless he is willing to be swept along by simple and persuasive eloquence that is a natural consequence of marshaling of eye witness facts unaffectedly and cogently put . . . if the book contained nothing more than the chapter that deals with the secret file it would be well worth reading by every American who adheres to the policy of playing his cards face up on the table."

I pasted the review in the scrapbook when it originally came out.

I did not read it again until years later, when I found the Ickes review photocopied on the pages of one of my father's FBI files; it was Daddy's thickest file, 1947, when he was being surveilled on an almost daily basis, and I assume the FBI thought this particular review proved beyond a shadow of a doubt how subversive he was.

PART
FOUR

CHAPTER

18

W

E started to have trouble with our phones. There were a lot of them—several on each floor of the Green Street house—and sometimes they would all ring at once and sometimes they would all go dead.

On occasion a single phone would ring and I would answer it and nobody would be there. Instead there would be a humming. It would ring again and I'd pick up the receiver—"Hello? Hello?" Silence. The line would be dead.

My brother and I used to play a game: Who can get to the phone before it stops ringing? We would race around the house calling out, "I'll get it! I'll get it!" and we'd vault up and down the stairs to the various floors. Then we would grab the receiver and say breathlessly, "Hello? Hello?"

When they all rang at once we'd scream excitedly, and Mama used to get furious at us.

She was angry at the phones, too. Often she would be in the middle of a conversation with her friend Mary Kohler and the phone would begin to splutter.

And Daddy could never get through to Washington without something weird happening, like static on the line, or voices in other languages, fading, drifting off.

We kept complaining to the phone company; the repairmen would come to the house and would supposedly fix the faulty wiring or whatever it was. But then the phones would go bad again.

Daddy told us he had checked with the State Department and

with Dave Niles, who supposedly had checked with somebody high up at the FBI; he'd been assured our phones were not tapped.

Then one morning at breakfast Daddy announced to us that he thought he was being followed regularly by a "suspicious looking guy who hops onto the Hyde Street cable car and rides with me all the way to Market Street. He looks like an FBI agent so he obviously is an FBI agent."

But he told us he would treat the surveillance as Harry Bridges had—in other words, in a spirit of fun. (Once, back in 1943, after being tailed relentlessly by agents while he was in New York for a union conference, Bridges spied on *them,* tailed *them,* then described the entire proceedings to St. Claire McKellway, who wrote about it in a hilarious feature in *The New Yorker. The Daily Worker* picked up the story. The FBI did look pretty foolish.)

And Daddy's surveillance seemed pretty foolish, too.

(Notes from another one of his FBI files, dated April 1947: "special agents observed Bartley Crum at the St. Regis Hotel . . . he had lunch in the Oak Room . . . then went to Brentano's where he bought two copies of his book *Behind the Silken Curtain* . . . he walked to the Chanin Building on 42nd Street and Lexington Avenue where he went to the 29th floor for a meeting . . . late in the afternoon he went to Doubleday's where he bought two more copies of his book . . . subject ended up at the Harvard Club for dinner with [names blacked out].)"

Looking back on it, I'm sure Daddy didn't want us to live in fear, and that's why, when he was with us, he would poke fun at his surveillance and at the Red-baiting, and at the untrue label that he was a "powerful Jewish lawyer."

For a while, at least, the climate of fear—of suspicion, of terror—didn't touch us, even though we were bombarded with anti-Soviet slogans on everything from bubble gum to comic books. "Better dead than Red"—we'd recite it like a litany until Daddy told us to stop. We didn't understand what it meant. We didn't know that ultimately the Cold War with Russia would be justification for identifying as "subversive" any social challenge, from racial discrimination to economic opposition.

The year 1947 marked the start of a gigantic anti-Communist purge in America, in the course of which thousands of decent citizens like my father would ultimately be victimized simply for their beliefs and for their associations.

The alliance with the Soviet Union during World War II was long gone; now Russia was seen as the enemy—"the Red Menace" —and American Communism was transformed, in part by J. Edgar Hoover, from a matter of political opinion to a matter of national security.

Hoover saw Communism as a threat to the very survival of America, to the American way of life.

So he put into action a highly publicized and well-organized plan to destroy the Party in this country; this plan was aided and abetted by President Truman.

On March 25, 1947, Truman inaugurated his Employee Loyalty Program. Along with it came the attorney general's List of Subversive Organizations. The starting point: immediate finger-printing and processing of loyalty questionnaires from more than two million federal employees. Helped by the FBI and the House Un-American Activities Committee (HUAC), the object of this search was "derogatory information," which dealt with the question of "reasonable doubt" as to loyalty. All affiliations with "suspect" organizations—any reports of opinions that might indicate some degree of sympathy with Communism—were extracted. There were criminal prosecutions aimed at individual Communists.

"The loyalty programs made the American public think that political dissidents were criminals," my father used to say.

At the start of the Cold War loyalty cases consumed him. He would work pro bono, charging only for expenses. In contrast, his corporate clients would be billed up to sixty-five dollars an hour for his time, a substantial amount in 1947.

Daddy used to get the accused to write his or her affidavit so it would sound more personal; then he would add lawyerly, cautionary language to protect the client from making rash statements. He also encouraged his clients to take the offensive, to sound "hostile" to Communism.

He advocated the use of influential witnesses and drew from his own network to help. He knew what the impact was of having a Mayor Lapham or a Helen Gahagan Douglas as a reference—

they could make a difference. He also didn't hesitate to call on Earl Warren or Senator Bill Knowland if he had to.

He was aware of publicity, so he actively used the press—sometimes the only means to counterattack was to make facts known to the public through the media.

He was unfailingly polite; unlike his radical lawyer colleagues, Daddy always worked within the system and treated his clients and their prosecutors with equal courtesy.

No one would know how many American lives were ruined by the loyalty programs—how many jobs lost; how many suicides. Especially damning in my father's eyes was the Taft-Hartley Act, which required union officials to disclose their political affiliations.

By March 1947 President Truman created the Truman Doctrine, his aggressive plan to save Turkey and Greece from Soviet expansion. It would be the foundation of our foreign policy for the next three decades.

Also in March, Secretary of Labor Schwellenbach proposed outlawing the Communist Party in America. On behalf of the Lawyers Guild, my father immediately declared in print that the proposal was not only "unconstitutional, but utterly stupid." "There is nothing intrinsically illegal about what Communists *do*," he added.

He went out of his way to suggest that American Communists prove their loyalty to the United States by denying they were controlled by the Soviet Union.

That comment was duly recorded in his FBI files along with a note: "(subject) is most certainly a Communist or a hidden Communist"; and then "(subject) always refers to himself as a Catholic or Republican; obviously a double alibi . . ."

Now his overnight trips to Hollywood were surveilled, and undercover agents mingled in the audiences that heard him speak before the Joint Anti-Fascist Committee.

Because of his participation in the Lawyers Guild and the Progressive Citizens of America (PCA), which was openly fighting the purge, Daddy's name was on the first attorney general's List of Subversive Organizations published.

He would refuse to resign from any of the organizations on

the list, even the Joint Anti-Fascist Refugee Committee (JAFRC), which was considered a leading "front group" for Communists and fellow travelers and which was having its records subpoenaed by HUAC. Two of its board members, Howard Fast and Dashiell Hammett, would be cited for contempt for refusing to give up the records and would go to jail.

Daddy (who had never been a Communist) was often described as a fellow traveler or bleeding-heart liberal because he lent his name to so many left-wing groups. For years he was teased by friends for being "used" by the Communist Party, for being a "dupe." For years he laughed off those labels; eventually he stopped laughing, but by then it was too late.

As the personal attacks on him grew throughout the spring of 1947, Daddy continued to live his life as he always had: he helped lead the Lawyers Guild in various actions against the FBI, and he joined the California Committee for Radio Freedom, formed to protest the discharge of six news analysts and commentators from a Los Angeles radio station because they were supposedly spreading "Red slander and propaganda."

And he and Mama would continue to entertain every liberal and left-winger in the Bay Area, from Haakon Chevalier (at one point Daddy's client) and the noted physicist J. Robert Oppenheimer, who would be pilloried for his friendship with Chevalier, to the passionate California liberal Helen Gahagan Douglas (her congressional career would soon be brutally destroyed by Richard Nixon).

Meanwhile, for my thirteenth birthday I got a telephone. It behaved the way the other phones in the house did, buzzing or going dead, and sometimes I would even hear Daddy on another phone, talking very fast to somebody. The reason I remember this is because he told me he was helping to organize some massive Hollywood rally PCA was sponsoring for Henry Wallace in support of his 1948 presidential candidacy.

I would wait for a while, and then the conversations would fade and I'd finally make my own phone call to a girlfriend, usually to talk about my latest crush—like Bradley, a sullen, lanky boy I'd picked up in a coffee shop.

Bradley was a high school dropout who at all times wore an

oversized leather air force jacket. We would drive up to Twin Peaks in the evening and neck for hours, while the city of San Francisco sparkled below us.

Mama did not approve of Bradley when she met him. Where does he come from? she wanted to know. He seemed to live in his car.

Daddy asked no questions. He would always defend my preference for scruffy loner types, for misfits, for men with unsavory reputations.

By April, Brad had given me his ID bracelet, so heavy I could barely lift my skinny wrist. We were not "going steady," but Mama insisted I take another date to the elegant little debutante dances at the Fairmont Hotel. So I did, but I wrote Bradley romantic notes and signed them with my new name: "Patricia Bosworth."

It was Daddy's idea. He thought that when I became an actress—and he was sure I would become an actress and "a great star"—I *might* get bad reviews and critics could write, "Crummy performance by Patricia Crum."

"Use Mama's maiden name," he advised. So from then on I became Patricia Bosworth. I started writing my name over and over and saying it to myself; it sounded nice.

And I wrote it all over my history books and my binder.

My brother was still at Town School, but I'd left Miss Burke's and was now attending the Convent of the Sacred Heart. Mama had wanted me to continue at a secular school, but she gave in to Daddy's wishes. He decided that at least for a while I should be given a Catholic education.

There were endless lectures on Church history at the convent and much emphasis on suffering, penance, and the doctrine of hell.

I learned about the rigors of confession from Mother Mardel, a sweet-faced nun who later was jailed for picketing with Cesar Chavez and his lettuce workers.

Ticking off my sins, of which I was sure I had many, developed in me the funny habit of believing I might be to blame in most predicaments I got myself into (whether or not I was to blame).

For a while I did attempt to be a good Catholic, because being a good Catholic might bring me closer to Daddy—his brand of Catholicism seemed to have a special connection to good intentions and to goodness itself.

But no matter how hard I tried, I was always getting into trouble. For talking in study hall. For sneaking a cigarette at basketball practice. I played a wooden soldier in the school operetta about a toy shop, and after my solo received a standing ovation (led by my father, I might add); I basked in the applause. Reverend Mother scolded me severely "for having the sin of pride." You must be humble, she told me.

I couldn't seem to be, so I rarely won the pink ribbon at assembly, given out for "good conduct."

Oddly enough, my closest friends at the convent always won the pink ribbon. They were Dianne Goldman, a slender, immaculate brunette who went on, as Dianne Feinstein, to be mayor of San Francisco and then a California senator. And Terry Ashe, my principal confidante. She's an actress in New York now and the mother of three sons.

Terry was on scholarship at Sacred Heart; she was the best student in our seventh-grade class. She also rode horses like a cowboy. I admired everything about her, especially her diligent nature and her wry sense of humor.

Some afternoons after class we'd run off together into the dreamy, ageless silence of Golden Gate Park, and we'd exercise polo ponies at the stables there. Other times we'd go back to my bedroom at the Green Street house and pore over my vast collection of movie magazines. We'd fantasize about being actresses or spies, or we'd go and see—for the umpteenth time—our favorite movie, *Duel in the Sun,* a violent western starring Gregory Peck as the sadistic cowboy Lewt, who lusts after the wild half-breed Pearl Chavez, played by a panting, sensual Jennifer Jones. We played the musical soundtrack of that movie over and over again. Movies like *Duel in the Sun* dramatized our secrets and our contradictions.

Most afternoons I'd come home alone to Green Street. During the day our house was as silent as a graveyard. I'd run aimlessly through the rooms—those beautiful, immaculate unused rooms—past the polished antiques, the big grand piano, the voluptuous couches piled with pillows. There were fresh flowers everywhere; the air smelled sweet.

Every so often I'd catch a glimpse of my worried freckled

face in the rococo gilt mirror in the entrance hall. We were more comfortable than ever, but I felt less comfortable; I felt uneasy and I didn't know why.

Occasionally, if I knew I was really alone in the house, I would tiptoe up to Daddy's study. I knew I was trespassing—I shouldn't be there; it was his private place, with a locked file cabinet, diaries and notepads, yellow legal pads scrawled with his writing—of speeches to be completed, letters to be sent.

But I'd slip into the room anyway and sit down in his "judge's wicker chair," and I would tip back in it and study the images on the walls: the awards from B'nai B'rith, from the Chinese American Association, from the Benjamin Cardozo foundation "for Bartley C. Crum's outstanding contribution to the preservation of the American way of life."

I would rummage through the drawers hoping to find something—anything—personal, some item that might reveal my father to me. There were old keys and a gold money clip; there were books of matches from restaurants and hotels in St. Louis, New Orleans, Miami, Chicago, Minneapolis, Dallas, London, Jerusalem.

And a letter from his mother, Mo, in Sacramento: "Dearest Bartley. I mailed you a new shirt and received no reply. Did you get it? Drop me a line. I never hear from you. Your devoted Mother."

I would end up fixing Daddy's scrapbook. I loved touching it, staring at the jumble of clips that documented his public life. I'd study his face in the news photographs, but, even using a magnifying glass, the images were invariably blurred. He usually appeared to be saying something, so his mouth might be slightly twisted, his expression clownish. What was he thinking? He always withheld something of himself no matter how gracious he was —no matter how affectionate.

Oh, I was obsessed with him, trying to figure him out.

I wondered how many people hated my father. He had been receiving ugly letters and threatening phone calls ever since he started defending Harry Bridges. Once a woman had rushed into his office yelling that she wanted to kill him for supporting the antifascists in Spain. He managed to calm her down and didn't press charges when the police arrived to take her away. He seemed fearless to me and impervious to any attack, including the psychological attacks administered by my mother.

Whenever he would return from a trip, I noticed he kissed me first and then hugged my brother. He had stopped embracing Mama because when he tried, she would move away. I was too young to understand the complications between my parents. All I knew was that she still seemed angry with my father most of the time.

Meanwhile, I remained the adoring, unquestioning daughter. I made it clear to him that everything he did thrilled me: the radio talks; the articles he ground out for the *Christian Science Monitor;* the committees he lent his name to, like the Spanish Refugee Appeal (whose honorary chair was Pablo Picasso).

Then there was the vast assortment of people he brought home in Aptos and in San Francisco, sometimes on the spur of the moment: priests, labor leaders, department-store presidents, bankers, journalists, movie stars, spies—the mix of their opinions energized me.

I could sit for hours listening to their arguments and stories and wondered why Mama didn't always seem to enjoy the experience as much as I did.

I always excused his absences, too (something Mama rarely did), because he had taught me that he was fighting for important issues when he was away from us.

I'd become accustomed to him being away; it made it easier for me to obsess on him. I kept track of everything he did—or tried to—by memorizing his schedule; then I would rerun the events he had described, over and over again in my mind. The latest concerned a confrontation he'd had with secretary of the interior Harold Ickes over California water rights.

At this point I accepted Daddy the way he was; he had been traveling all over the place ever since we were small, so my brother and I considered it a given.

I excused his drinking, his evasions; I had never known any other kind of father. He charmed and seduced me with his endless compliments, funny anecdotes, extravagant presents—the latest of which was an expensive Cartier watch, solid gold, with a woven gold band.

Dextra McGonogle, his client, had sent it to him for his birthday, but he couldn't wear it; watches stopped automatically when he put them on.

I remember after he gave me that watch he took my hand in his and read my fortune, tracing his finger down the lifeline in the center of my palm. His finger tickled. "Jesus, baby," he said, "you're gonna live to be a hundred. And you're gonna be married three times and have one kid."

He was right, almost.

In the meantime I tried to be as much like my father as possible. I tried to copy the way he behaved; tried to be charming and funny and polite. I flattered everybody: friends, servants, even our dentist. I ingratiated myself with the world. It was a big effort, but it seemed to work—at least at first. People seemed to like me; I was trusted. I would spend hours listening to the problems of my classmates; I offered no solutions—that wasn't my role—I just listened.

Even Mama was beginning to confide in me—to admit to me how lonely she was. Late that spring she handed me a short story she had written entitled "The Woman and Her Poodle." It was inspired by Chekhov's masterpiece "The Lady with the Dog," she said.

As soon as I read it I recognized Mama as "the woman"—a woman who walks up and down Aptos beach with her poodle, Bonbon, and at some point runs into a seductive bearded philanderer. I recognized him as Dr. Saul.

Saul was a psychiatrist. Mama had met him at an experimental clinic in San Francisco; the clinic specialized in dealing with addictions. She had gone there because she wanted to write a research paper on alcoholism, which was slowly beginning to be accepted not only as an addiction but as an illness, a disease.

Saul was the authority; Mama sought him out. He began "advising" her, giving her books to read, medical journals to cull from.

She was very open with my brother and me about Saul dropping by. She would call us in to say hello. I have memories of us straggling into the living room (in San Francisco and Aptos) and observing a big, shambling man with a thick brown beard and quizzical eyes. He never said a word to us. He just nodded, and then, as I remember, he turned away and acted busy with papers and books they were "studying."

I'm not sure now if Mama swore my brother and me to secrecy —she trusted us, so undoubtedly she didn't, but I felt as if she had. Keeping this latest secret took a lot out of me. I was exhausted holding it in; I felt as if I were an accomplice in what I saw as another betrayal of my father, so I was angry at Mama, but I still loved her. It was very confusing.

Once when Daddy was in the Middle East, Mama documented one of her trysts with Saul:

> June 17, 1947: S. arrived from the city; it was raining. Almost black outside. I closed the shutters and lit a fire and set a decanter of sherry that looked like a big amber bubble on the black papier mache table with the two little malachite green glasses set on it . . . but I forgot those details as soon as I saw him.
>
> The fire was crackling. I didn't notice. I didn't notice the smell of the lemon leaves exuding their oily fragrance . . . the music on the phonograph beat against the green walls . . . the yellow shutters . . . Charles Trenet singing "Douce France" and "La Mer" on my little Victrola . . . Patti and young Bart came in to say goodnight. After they left S. kissed me on the mouth over and over again through the music. . . .
>
> I love to remember what he said. Tonight everything was "adorable." It's a word I never heard him say before. He's so big and strong it doesn't fit him, that word.
>
> "This is an adorable house," he said as we climbed the stairs to my bedroom. "Haven't those curtains been put in since I was here last? Chalais . . . aren't they adorable?"
>
> Then he pronounced me quite solemnly a "magnificent person, a magnificent woman." He usually doesn't go in for superlatives. In the past he'd described me as—regal, stylish, irritating, impossible. But last night I was magnificent. . . .
>
> Dialogue before love-making:
>
> "Do you want to go to bed now?" he asked.
>
> "I always want to go to bed with you," I said.
>
> Saul: "Are you usually this starved?"
>
> Me: "I'm never like this. I usually get bored."
>
> Afterward I kept insisting I wasn't insatiable. Why do I lie and pretend to be so helpless? I kept hoping he'd agree. I

asked again; *am* I insatiable? He put a pillow under my cheek.

"I adore you," he said.

It has taken me so long to grow up. I have always been treated like a little girl. Even Patti calls me "little Mama" and Bart has always called me his child bride.

As the affair with Saul progressed, Mama became more self-absorbed, especially about her body. She began practicing yoga; she drank beakers of hot water and lemon juice ("to move my bowels"). She took long walks on the beach, striding purposefully through the sand, tanned legs moving very fast, Bonbon straining on the leash ahead of her.

She would have a massage once a week as well as facials and pedicures; she developed a mania for health foods; she read Adelle Davis's *Let's Eat Right to Keep Fit;* she weighed herself every day; she never went above 101 pounds.

She also read and reread Karen Horney's *The Neurotic Personality of Our Time* and underlined all the passages about female sexuality.

Midway through the affair she began spending money recklessly, redecorating her entire bedroom at Aptos. She bought an expensive desk topped with a slab of green marble; new rugs were rolled into the house; more prints hung on the walls—antique engravings of fruit in mirrored frames.

Her need to possess seemed to commingle with her passion for Saul.

She took a special painting class that summer, too—a workshop in trompe l'oeil—and enrolled my brother and me in it. We had extra tennis lessons as well; we played in a funny grass court deep in the woods in Rio Del Mar.

"Channel your energies," she would tell me. "I am still trying to channel mine."

That summer she tried to contain hers in the kitchen by putting up preserves. I remember dozens of glass jars on the kitchen table, filled with apple butter and apricot jam, pickled tomatoes, pears and peaches in brandy stuck with cloves. The kitchen was fragrant with smells of melting sugar and boiling fruit.

Years afterward she told me that in the summer of 1947 she

had fallen in love again, which was the reason for all the frantic activity. "I felt as if I was an exposed nerve," she said.

Ultimately the affair with Saul was a disappointment. "I start out with high expectations before we meet," she wrote, "but my hopes are always dashed."

He could never see her as often as she wanted, and he had no intention of ending his marriage. He had other women, too. That was upsetting.

"I like to believe I am the one woman you care for," she wrote him. "Now I am not only disillusioned by marriage, but I am disillusioned by adultery. It is not all it is cracked up to be."

She did not mail this letter to Saul, nor any of the others she wrote him. Instead she saved them and they are included in the bundle of writing she left to me along with her unpublished novels and journals—and a devastating questionnaire she directed at herself about Daddy in July 1947:

> Q: Why isn't my marriage working?
> A: Because you don't feel married. I have never felt married to Bart. I have never felt I was his wife.
> Q: Should I get a divorce?
> A: I'm afraid. Afraid I can't support myself. I enjoy living well. And the children wouldn't want it. Once when Bart and I were having a quarrel, little Patti started sobbing "please don't break up."

We spent the summer at Aptos. If Daddy was with us he stayed up late scribbling briefs or working on fund-raising speeches he was giving around the country for United Jewish Appeal.

There were fewer parties.

But once, unexpectedly, Saul appeared at Aptos for a luncheon, and he joined my father on the porch for a drink, towering above him in his expensive cable-stitched sweater.

In comparison Daddy seemed almost frail, dressed in the patched coveralls he insisted on wearing whenever he was in the country.

I passed them hors d'oeuvres and they seemed determinedly cordial with one another, and then Mama circled around, behaving affectionately to first one, then the other man. I experienced a sizzle and a tension between them. It was a weird charade.

(By this time, I guess my parents had come to some sort of an unspoken agreement; if Mama had lovers, Daddy ignored them, and everybody acted very civilized about the whole thing.)

Strangely enough, my brother and I ended up being grateful to Saul that afternoon because after the other guests had gone home, Daddy suddenly collapsed and couldn't be roused.

Moments passed. Then I dimly remember Bart and me hovering outside the half-open door to the living room and watching Saul fling rainbow-colored velvet pillows onto the floor before he cradled my father in his arms, placed him on the couch, and gave him an injection.

Days later Mama explained to us that Daddy had swallowed —"by mistake"—a lethal combination of barbiturates and Scotch. He had not meant to. He was horribly embarrassed by his reaction and promised Mama it would never happen again.

He always insisted he could stop taking pills immediately if he wanted to. "I am not hooked," he would say.

He confided that many of his friends in Hollywood took pills —David O. Selznick, Judy Garland; taking pills didn't bother *them*. Besides, he swore he took only prescription drugs.

Years later we would discover he had obtained his pills on the black market, mainly through a doctor at Madison Square Garden. Whenever he made a speech at the Garden, he would buy a new stash.

For a long time I was fooled by Daddy's ability to keep up such a gorgeous façade. We were accustomed to his heavy drinking, yet he never looked drunk or drugged—not for years. He could "hold" his liquor—I never noticed that he drank to excess.

But, then, most of our parents' friends drank. The parties we witnessed in our house sometimes disintegrated into rowdy, noisy, drunken brawls. I remember one college fraternity brother of my father's falling off our porch and breaking his leg. I remember a woman friend of Mama's peeing tipsily in the ivy bed. "Cannot help it," she giggled, and then she passed out.

If Daddy loved to drink "it's because he is Irish," Mama excused in her unpublished report on the alcoholic personality, and "besides, he is not yet dysfunctional . . . he had never allowed drink to interfere in his work . . . or with the family, but he does deny categorically there is a problem and *that* is a problem."

But then we didn't know that a combination of drugs and alcohol could be very dangerous—we didn't worry about it, didn't give it a thought.

We didn't know that a regular ingestion of barbiturates and Scotch could become a habit. We didn't realize in 1947 that Daddy was slowly on his way to becoming a drug addict and that he was already very much an alcoholic.

CHAPTER

19

HE was starting to keep a frantic pace; the pills and liquor fueled him. He was in and out of Hollywood a lot; he had attracted some new clients in Los Angeles, so he rented a small office near the Brown Derby. He told us he might have a movie deal for his book *Behind the Silken Curtain*—Edward G. Robinson might option the property and Dore Schary might produce it at RKO. But nothing ever materialized. In the meantime, he and Robert Kenny recruited new members for the Progressive Citizens of America (PCA) and sponsored a series of seminars to air opposition to Truman's loyalty programs. They were alarmed at the outcome of the closed hearings HUAC had organized at the Biltmore Hotel in May to investigate charges that Communists were infiltrating Hollywood.

Committee chair J. Parnell Thomas and committee member Richard Nixon had secretly been interviewing "friendly witnesses," like Screen Actors Guild president Ronald Reagan and Ginger Rogers's mother, Lela, who had objected to her daughter having to say the line, "share and share alike, that's democracy," in a movie called *Tender Comrade* by screenwriter Dalton Trumbo. And not only that, the FBI fed them raw file data on various "politically subversive" actors and writers. As a result, Reagan and Rogers could denounce dozens of their colleagues, calling them "un-American."

Their testimony was leaked to the press along with the committee's allegation that "flagrant Communist propaganda films had been produced during the war at the request of President Roosevelt."

Some people thought the secret hearings were merely a ploy to grab headlines and get publicity for HUAC. The very name "Hollywood" conjured up images of loose living and wild politics.

But there was a growing fear among liberals like my father and Kenny that HUAC's aim was ever more sinister, that their "nosing around," as Daddy put it, could be the beginning of both thought control and censorship.

One of the names that kept surfacing as an "unfriendly witness" was that of the controversial German playwright Bertolt Brecht, author of *The Threepenny Opera*. He was in Hollywood at the time of the hearings, rehearsing his production of *Galileo*, starring Charles Laughton. The play was about the dropping of the atomic bomb on Japan and man's responsibility to man; it was also about political intimidation.

Daddy got it into his head that my brother and I had to see this play; it was so important. He brought us down one weekend —Mama stayed behind in San Francisco.

I remember nothing about the production except that the theater, which was in Santa Monica, was as hot as an oven. Los Angeles was experiencing a deadly heat wave, so Bart and I were bathed in sweat as we watched Charles Laughton as the great scientist Galileo, confronted by a grand inquisition and then conceding to the powers that be in order to save his skin. Many in the audience, including my father, thought the play was a mirror image of the Hollywood hearings.

We went backstage after the performance to meet the pudgy slacklipper Laughton; on the way we were introduced to Brecht— he was unshaven and had a scarred left cheek. My father tried to converse with him in his schoolboy German, and he obligingly puffed on one of Brecht's cheap cigars.

On September 19, HUAC subpoenaed forty-five people to appear at a public hearing in Washington and testify as to their political beliefs.

The first group—made up of friendly witnesses, among them Ronald Reagan and cartoonist Walt Disney—was more than willing to repeat what they had said to the committee in May.

The second group was a loose coalition of liberals and leftist screenwriters, directors, and producers, later dubbed "the Un-friendly Nineteen." They included Dalton Trumbo, Ring Lardner Jr., Gordon Kahn, actor Larry Parks, and playwright Bertolt Brecht. Most of them were or had been members of the Communist Party, as HUAC well knew, since the Hollywood secretary of the party was an FBI informer. With the exception of Brecht they all denounced the subpoenas and vowed they would never cooperate with Thomas's "inquisition."

My father saw the fight to resist HUAC as a chance to test the Constitution, and the idea excited him. When two of the Nineteen—director Eddie Dmytryk and producer Adrian Scott—asked him to be their personal attorney, he agreed immediately. They told him right off that they had been Communists but were no longer. He answered, So what? It's not against the law in America to be a Communist, but it is against the Constitution to ask citizens to reveal their political affiliations.

Dmytryk and Scott happened to be the creators of the recent movie *Crossfire,* one of the first American movies about anti-Semitism. It tells the story of a deranged GI, played by Robert Ryan, who senselessly murders a Jew (Sam Levene) after having a casual drink with him in a bar. On its release, *Crossfire* was instantly labeled subversive by HUAC on the grounds that the American soldier was the villain. In fact, Dmytryk and Scott had been subpoenaed to appear before the committee not because they were so important in the Communist Party but because, as my father observed sarcastically at the time, "HUAC thinks only a Communist could make a movie about an anti-Semitic murderer who also happened to be a crazed American GI."

Dmytryk and Scott talked only briefly with my father; at that point theirs was just one of many different kinds of cases he was handling. He had no idea what was in store for him; in fact, he was much more involved in mediating with PCA and thinking about the future of the Holy Land.

There was a plan afoot at the United Nations to create a partition in Palestine dividing the country into independent Jewish and Arab states, and Daddy was making a great many speeches on the subject. He was so busy with other matters, he didn't even attend all the meetings for the Nineteen that were being held in Los Angeles during the month of September. But he did attend the one at director Lewis Milestone's house to discuss strategy with the other lawyers: Charlie Katz, Martin Popper, and Ben Margolis —all militant members of the Lawyers Guild—as well as Robert Kenny, who was then the guild's president and the former attorney general of California.

Daddy had worked with Popper and Margolis over the years on various guild projects, including appeals for Harry Bridges and the formation of an international lawyers' brigade.

He had differed with them in the past, often over questions of courtroom style. (He had once chastised Martin Popper in a letter for what he felt was an unauthorized statement during a Smith Act trial.)

He assumed Popper and Margolis were Communists, but, like most rank-and-file members of the Party, they hid their affiliation. My father felt uncomfortable with the Party's secrecy; he had a different way of dealing with issues. Unlike most Party lawyers, he had a sense of humor. He would joke and flatter to make a point, tactics the Communists didn't appreciate at all.

"He had the classic liberal mentality," Nineteen screenwriter Waldo Salt told me years afterward. "Bart Crum had no axes to grind, and he was open and flexible, something the other lawyers —with the exception of Robert Kenny—were not."

The atmosphere at the meetings my father attended was intense. Everybody was on good behavior; they all agreed to work together and share all costs. They thought they would win eventually; they might lose in front of the committee and even at the trials and in the lower appellate court, but not in front of the Supreme Court. It had remained a liberal bastion with judges like Hugo Black and Felix Frankfurter. They would support the Hollywood Nineteen; they would uphold the First Amendment.

Choosing a legal strategy was crucial. What were their priorities? Job security? Avoiding prison? They all wanted to denounce the committee—deny its right to existence by attacking it constitutionally. They could do that by refusing to answer questions.

But this would prevent them from presenting their case to the public. Equally extreme would be an acknowledgment that they had been Communists, and in many cases still were (although those who were remained reluctant to discuss any Party affiliation). The Smith Act of 1940 made it possible to prosecute Communists on the charge that they advocated the overthrow of the government.

In the midst of one discussion, my father suggested everybody simply tell the truth. His point: if you're completely open about your beliefs and your political past, there's less chance you'll ever be accused of either conspiracy or subversion.

He added that such a strategy promised to raise genuine political and moral issues.

Screenwriter Alvah Bessie supported this tactic. He had served in the Spanish Civil War, supporting the Loyalists; he was a Communist and proud of it. Robert Rossen, who would later direct *All the King's Men* and *The Hustler*, also wanted to go along with my father's idea. He later told his wife, "I just want to say I'm a member of the Communist Party and fuck you!"

Daddy and the two defendants were argued down by the other lawyers, led by Ben Margolis, who saw himself as an "adversary of political repression," and by Ring Lardner Jr. and Dalton Trumbo, who maintained that to answer questions about political and union affiliations would acknowledge the committee's right to ask them. They thought the wisest decision would be to invoke the First Amendment, which guaranteed freedom of speech and belief as a right that was being violated by HUAC.

They ultimately agreed to challenge the committee's rights. Congress had no right to investigate movies, because it was protected by extension of the freedom of the press clause in the First Amendment. If it had no right to legislate in that area, then it had no right to investigate it, or, by extension, the political beliefs of the Hollywood Nineteen.

The First Amendment also provided a great deal of judicious interpretation that would benefit the Nineteen. The right to free speech could suggest freedom of association, as well as freedom to remain silent. As stated in the amicus curiae brief filed by my father and the National Lawyers Guild on behalf of John Howard Lawson, "Without the right of association and assembly, freedom of speech could result only in useless and chaotic verbalism and the desirable democratic objectives sought to be gained by freedom of speech and assembly would be lost."

By challenging HUAC's right to ask questions about political affiliations, they expected to draw contempt citations, but they planned to fight them in the courts as a constitutional issue.

After they had decided to rely solely on the First Amendment for their defense, actor Larry Parks earnestly requested that all decisions be made unanimously among them and that they all adopt a policy of declining to answer the question "Have you ever been a member of the Communist Party?" but answering indirectly —as they saw fit. The group voted yes to Parks's request.

But not everybody was pleased. Robert Rossen remarked bitterly to his wife, "We apparently can't tell the truth." He was sure the lawyers were protecting the Party.

Months later, Philip Dunne would tell my father he had heard that the CP lawyers had secretly caucused about tactics and were getting their orders on how to proceed from Moscow, and that at the meeting at Lewis Milestone's house, Dalton Trumbo had spoken privately with Larry Parks (who worshiped him) and had persuaded the actor to make the request for group unity, and because Parks was so likable and unthreatening, the Nineteen went along with him.

Later my father would write that "it was decided in retrospect erroneously that the screenwriters, directors and producers act as a unit. I say erroneously because I learned in those sessions that it was not possible for a non-Communist, like myself, to work with Communists."

Privately he worried that the Nineteen's tactics might backfire. He thought they should respect the power of the subpoena and the rights of the committee to investigate. He thought the other lawyers, with the exception of Robert Kenny, were, to put it mildly, too doctrinaire.

He would learn that the unanimity rule was a major tactical weapon for Communists, as was the parliamentary procedure to disrupt and exhaust any prolonged discussion.

What really bothered him was that most of the Nineteen seemed willing to surrender their individuality, but he would not be aware of the full consequences until much later.

He had gone to the meetings unprepared for the need the Communists had to recast every subject, no matter how complex or ambiguous, into simplistic Party ideology.

He had assumed that the Nineteen were close and trusting friends, but he soon discovered that even Eddie Dmytryk and Adrian Scott hadn't so much as shared a meal together, although they had collaborated on two movies.

The Nineteen were, in fact, a disparate bunch, ranging from the bombastic John Howard Lawson, head of the Hollywood branch of the Communist Party, to mild-mannered non-Communist screenwriter Howard Koch, who had been subpoenaed to appear in front of HUAC because his movie *Mission to Moscow* was considered "Red propaganda."

Koch refused to go along with the majority of the Nineteen (he took ads in *Variety* outlining his position as a non-Communist liberal).

As for Bertolt Brecht, who never attended any of the meetings, he maintained that the group's strategy was wrong and he did not accept it. He argued privately with my father and Ben Margolis that the Nineteen should tell the truth about their Party affiliations. He considered martyrdom to be folly in a political struggle.

Throughout September and into October my father and the other lawyers involved themselves in the legal aspect of the Nineteen's case, including the motion to quash the subpoena on the grounds that the committee's investigation lay "wholly within the domain of thought, speech, and opinion safeguarded by the First Amendment."

The lawyers knew they needed public support, so they all joined screenwriter Philip Dunne and actor Alexander Knox in their efforts to found the Committee for the First Amendment, organized to oppose HUAC and its inquisition.

"We wanted to mount as broad a defense as possible," Dunne said, "to enlist moderates and conservatives who would not only support these men and their positions but support their constitutional rights. A constitutional defense was the only total defense; it appealed equally to all who were being slandered, Communists or not."

The first meeting of this committee, at Ira Gershwin's home, attracted Hollywood's biggest celebrities, from Frank Sinatra to Judy Garland. Everyone showed up, irrespective of their beliefs; it was a fight for the Constitution. According to Jules Buck, John Huston's assistant, my father made a big impact the moment he

entered the room. "Bart Crum was considered an important liberal
—a Willkie man. He was accompanied by Katharine Hepburn."

More names followed him to a boisterous rally at the Shrine
Auditorium in Los Angeles, staged by Joseph Losey. Five thousand
people jammed together to cheer the Unfriendly Nineteen and
their attorneys, and money was raised for their defense.

"We were all so optimistic," Ring Lardner Jr. recalled decades later. "We didn't dream our careers were about to be
ruined."

Movie star Gene Kelly, who was master of ceremonies at the
event, hobbled out on the stage on crutches, joking that he broke
his ankle rehearsing a dance routine; he did not do this for dramatic effect. He then introduced my father, who was suffering from
a bad case of laryngitis, so he spoke hoarsely: "In the words of the
Supreme Court, if there is any fixed star in the constitutional
constellation, it is that no official can prescribe or force citizens to
confess what is orthodox in politics or religion . . . it is indeed an
honor to serve these men in defense of Americanism."

He and Robert Kenny had been chosen to act as spokesmen
for the other lawyers; Daddy was excited about being involved in
what promised to be another historical crusade. It didn't bother
him either that he and the other lawyers were splitting approxi-
mately twenty thousand dollars six ways. After that they worked
pro bono.

Years later Ben Margolis told an interviewer that "Crum and
Kenny had been hired for public appearance purposes as well
as legal expertise . . . they were acceptable public figures . . . they
would make a wonderful voice for the press—and because they
were liberals not Communists and had charming personalities . . .
very beneficial when addressing the media."

One week before the hearings the Unfriendly Nineteen
boarded a train bound for Washington and with their attorneys
began to prepare for their defense and counterattack on J. Parnell
Thomas.

On the five-day train ride across the United States, Ben Margolis, with the help of my father and Kenny, conducted mock
examinations and cross-examinations to prepare for a counterattack on HUAC, and after each session the lawyers went over the
written statements each of the Nineteen had prepared. They drilled

up to twelve hours a day "to numb the surprise factor," Daddy said.

At the stopover in Chicago, my father made speeches, more personal appearances. At another stopover in New York the Lawyers Guild had organized a Keep America Free rally at the St. Nicholas Arena (tickets were sixty cents). I pasted an ad for it into Daddy's scrapbook: "Hear those Liberals Bartley Crum and Robert Kenny, attorneys for the 19, talk about HUAC's abuses; the threat of a blacklist; the threat of censorship; the reasons why official inquiry under threat of contempt into citizens' legal political beliefs and affiliations is unconstitutional."

Then the caravan went by train to Washington. There were more rehearsals.

My father urged the Nineteen to be dignified; Ben Margolis exhorted the men "to stick it to 'em!"

"You gotta remember," says Eddie Dmytryk, "our goal was to destroy those sons of bitches!"

HORDES of journalists streamed into the capital from all over the country. Gordon Kahn wrote, "The city of Washington wore a tense air . . . as if on the eve of a coronation or a hanging."

My father had been warned that he would be spied on by the FBI and that he would probably be followed; indeed, odd characters pressed close to him in the elevators of the Shoreham Hotel, where the Nineteen were all staying, and watched him from behind newspapers in the lobby.

Meetings began in a spirit of camaraderie, with the Nineteen and the lawyers in a big suite at the Shoreham. "Great food, expensive booze, delivered on the hour every hour," Daddy said, "rolled in on silver carts."

Everybody was sure the suite was bugged, so as they argued and discussed strategy they kept snapping their fingers so that the FBI devices couldn't pick up what they were saying.

Once the actress Uta Hagen dropped by the suite to say hello to my father and wish the Nineteen good luck, and she found "Larry Parks, Jack Lawson, and Howard Koch snapping their fingers like lunatics. It was the strangest sight imaginable. They looked as if they'd been taken over by some affliction."

Apparently the finger snapping worked, because although the

Nineteen did find bugs in the suite, the FBI was unable to document their strategizing.

The evening my father arrived in Washington he joined Robert Kenny, Charlie Katz, and Ben Margolis for a special meeting with Eric Johnston of the Motion Picture Association and their attorneys, Paul V. McNutt and Maurice Benjamin.

"Bob Kenny was chief counsel," Daddy wrote later. "He set the tone of the meeting—he explained our views. That for the good of the country as well as the industry they must resist the pressure to start a blacklist."

"We had to have that reassurance," he went on. "If the Nineteen were blacklisted hundreds of other writers and directors would be intimidated. The result would be censorship of an entire mass medium without any piece of legislation to back it up."

Daddy believed, with the other lawyers, that they could win the constitutional question before the Supreme Court, but that it might take years; they wanted to make sure that the Nineteen weren't going to be kicked out of the industry before the case was appealed.

"That's why Bob was so brilliant at that meeting," my father concluded. "He kept pointing out that the Hearst papers were calling for censorship and that HUAC was trying to get it without legislative action."

At the close Kenny referred to a press release from HUAC that Thomas had handed out to reporters which claimed that Johnston had already agreed to a cleaning of Hollywood's own house— with a self-imposed purge.

"The report is nonsense," Johnston insisted angrily. "As long as I live I will never be party to anything as un-American as a blacklist."

At this point my father supposedly jumped to his feet and wrung Johnston's hand. "Eric, I knew you were being misquoted," he exclaimed. "I never believed you could go along with anything as vicious as a blacklist."

Charlie Katz added dryly, "The witnesses we represent will be more than delighted to have that assurance from you."

Indeed, when the news was brought to the Nineteen's hotel suite there were shouts of "Hooray! Hooray!" which drowned out, momentarily, the snapping of fingers.

■

"THE Nineteen were relieved but not completely convinced," screenwriter Waldo Salt told me years later. "We weren't that naïve. There had been blacklists before, but we did think the producers were behind us—that they would have to support us and fight against suppression."

Unfortunately there was good reason to be skeptical. It was discovered later that Johnston had secretly proposed a blacklist which the Producers Association had turned down on the advice of other lawyers, who told him it would be tantamount to conspiracy and would be illegal—until and unless Congress outlawed the Communist Party.

CHAPTER
20

ON October 20, 1947, the House Un-American Activities Committee hearings on Hollywood began. More than a thousand women pushed and shoved, trying to see movie star Robert Taylor. Hundreds more lined the halls outside, standing three deep against the wall.

A sixty-five-year-old grandmother, scrambling on top of a radiator for a better look, fell and struck her head. The clothing of many was torn in the mad scramble when the door to the committee room opened.

Inside, the Senate caucus room was unnaturally bright; extra-strong bulbs had replaced the dim ones in the huge chandelier that hung from the ceiling, blazing down on the nine whirring newsreel cameras, the ninety-four members of the press. There were also four major radio networks present, as well as twenty-five news photographers facing the witness table; flashes from cameras went off intermittently. The illumination was blinding—like a hospital operating room, someone said. All who had been subpoenaed or had volunteered to testify occupied choice seats at the center of the action—right behind the witness table.

Minutes before 10:00 A.M., committee chair J. Parnell Thomas, so small he was perched on a District of Columbia telephone book and a red pillow, gaveled the meeting to order. Three committee members had already taken their seats, including Richard Vail from Illinois and Richard M. Nixon, the freshman congressman from California. Their chief investigator was Robert E. Stripling.

Before the witnesses came on, my father and Robert Kenny addressed Thomas, informing him that they were prepared to argue a motion to quash the subpoenas issued to the Hollywood Nineteen on the grounds that the committee and the investigation were unconstitutional and illegal.

With that, Thomas silenced both lawyers with repeated bangs of his gavel, but not before my father had remarked sarcastically, "This is certainly an un-American procedure."

"This committee is without constitutional authority to . . ." Kenny began.

Thomas interrupted him. "What is your name, please?"

After Kenny identified himself, Thomas told him his clients would not be questioned until the following week; he could submit his petition then.

My father stepped forward. "May I ask—do we have the right to cross-examine the 'friendly witnesses'?"

Thomas glared at him: "You may not ask one more thing. Please be seated."

After some prompting from Robert Stripling, counsel for HUAC, the proceedings began with Jack L. Warner, the oily, powerful cohead of Warner Brothers Studio. He proceeded to name nineteen people with "un-American leanings"—among them screenwriter Clifford Odets and novelist Irwin Shaw.

All were members of the Screen Writers Guild (the clear implication was that this officially nonpolitical union was somehow connected to the Communist Party). Warner admitted that what he said was based on hearsay, that he had gotten most of his information out of the *Hollywood Reporter.* Nevertheless, he was permitted to bumble on until 12:30.

After lunch he was followed by director Sam Wood, former president of the Motion Picture Alliance for the Preservation of American Ideals. There was a growing impression that "the industry was made up entirely of Communists, radicals, and crackpots," he said.

As soon as Russian-born novelist Ayn Rand (author of *The Fountainhead*) was sworn in, she testified that showing her countrymen smiling in Hollywood films such as *Song of Russia* was "clearly propaganda." So grim was their lot, she maintained, "that Russians only smiled privately and accidentally."

Most of the friendly witnesses felt confident about labeling various writers as Communists even though they had no proof —merely vague suspicions. When asked if Lester Cole was a Communist, Morris Ryskind answered, "If he isn't a Communist then Mahatma Gandhi isn't an Indian." Other "friendlies" moved on and off the stand, including movie stars George Murphy, Gary Cooper, Adolphe Menjou, Robert Taylor. Each was permitted to read statements, refer to notes, and hurl accusations into the record without any documentation.

Then came Ronald Reagan, president of the Screen Actors Guild. He gave HUAC all sorts of examples of how he had fought off Commie infiltration in his union. He confirmed what had been known for years—that Communists had indeed participated in numerous uprisings within the various craft unions. What Reagan did not say was that Robert Stripling had rehearsed him the night before right down to giving him the Jefferson quote he was about to use. Reagan had been an FBI informant since 1942, but this wouldn't be revealed until after he became president of the United States.

So when he completed his testimony he quoted Thomas Jefferson, something to the effect that Jefferson believed that "if the American people know the facts, they won't make a mistake," which was Chairman Thomas's cue to declare, "That's why this Committee was created, to give Americans the facts, so we can help keep America pure."

"It was enough to make you puke," Waldo Salt recalled years later, after he'd won an Academy Award for his screenplay of *Midnight Cowboy.*

AWAY from the hearings everybody got on the bugged phones to Hollywood, trying to persuade as many movie stars as possible to come to Washington and give the Nineteen moral support.

In the evenings Daddy would spend hours helping Dmytryk and Scott refine the personal statements they would read in front of the committee, explaining why they were refusing to cooperate with HUAC. Then the Party lawyers went over everybody's statements, along with my father and Kenny. The wording was discussed very carefully; it was hoped that possibly some kind of joint position paper could emerge. Because there was always the danger of indictment for conspiracy—much more serious than the misdemeanor of contempt—Daddy believed the legal position on the matter of conspiracy was weak. He still thought that if the Nineteen told the truth about their political beliefs, the conspiracy idea would melt away. He assumed HUAC's counsel would institute a charge. When that didn't happen he decided the committee was out to expose a movement rather than destroy a group of individuals—and this was illegal, immoral, and un-American.

It was important, therefore, to get Congress involved, so Daddy spent much of his free time that first week in Washington lobbying support from senators and congressmen. He was surprised to find it was a losing battle—most of the politicians were afraid to come forward.

Only Emanuel Celler, the powerful chair of the House Judiciary Committee, listened with sympathy and some sadness when Daddy spoke to him. He told him he agreed that what was going on was a witch hunt, that much of what HUAC was doing was both illegal and unjustified, but there was nothing he could do. It was strictly a political matter and he "wouldn't touch it with a ten-foot pole." (Later, during the House debate on whether to uphold the contempt charges, Celler fought long and hard against it, but he was one of the few.)

My father felt deflated after his meeting with Celler. He had been positive that if Congress wouldn't support them, the Supreme Court would, but clearly Celler's implication was that this might not be the case.

That wasn't the only thing that disturbed him. Ben Margolis had started to call meetings in the evenings after the hearings, and my father wasn't invited to some of them, nor were Dmytryk and Scott.

The meetings were for Communists only; there had been one crucial meeting with Howard Koch, which Daddy learned about after the fact. Apparently, Koch had suddenly decided—as a non-Communist—that he no longer wanted to risk his career for the Nineteen's defense. He had decided to testify openly in front of HUAC.

His decision was of great concern to the Communist lawyers,

who wanted unity above all; they were afraid that if Koch broke ranks, Scott and Dmytryk might be swayed.

Arguments went on for hours. Koch wouldn't budge until his wife or girlfriend (no one is sure which) convinced him that he must remain loyal to the Nineteen or she would leave him. Koch kept quiet and was subsequently blacklisted for the next seven years.

Now Dmytryk and Scott discussed the possibility that they should testify as to their past membership in the Party while making it clear that they were no longer Communists. Daddy was enthusiastic; he agreed to discuss it with the other lawyers. The answer came back: an emphatic *no*. Eddie and Adrian were asked to adhere to their pledge of unanimity, which they reluctantly agreed to do.

Two more Party lawyers had arrived from New York to join the Nineteen's defense team; by then my father was completely outnumbered when it came to any future decisions on strategy, and Robert Kenny, the other non-Communist liberal lawyer, always chose to go along with the majority.

According to Dmytryk, my father became concerned; he was outnumbered, outvoted, and without any backup from his clients to speak out; he felt helpless. He could not bring himself to urge them to break their pledge, but he never stopped believing that if there's nothing to hide, why hide it?

Dmytryk and Scott were no longer Communists, but because they kept silent, they were automatically lumped in the public's mind with those who were.

The first days of testimony ended with Walt Disney maintaining that the Communist rebellion in Hollywood made his "happy cartoonists very unhappy."

So far, though, HUAC had not been able to prove that Hollywood was infiltrated with dangerous subversives.

Back in San Francisco, I pasted a *Variety* quote describing the committee's carryings-on as a "Commie carnival" in Daddy's scrapbook. And then an editorial from *The New York Times:* "The Committee is not conducting a fair investigation." Next to it I pasted Quentin Reynolds's assessment from a column in *PM:* "No legal safeguards are being granted," he wrote. "The accusers function as judge, jury, executors . . . this is something new to attorneys

Bart Crum and Robert Kenny . . . they are completely bewildered by it . . . it shakes them to their legal souls."

On October 27 Mama showed up in Washington to join my father. Her journal notes:

> Arrived here almost simultaneously with the Committee of the First Amendment: Danny Kaye, Richard Conte, Paul Henreid, John Huston, Evelyn Keyes, June Havoc . . . all outraged by what is going on. Lucille Ball says she'll read the Bill of Rights on the radio. . . . Philip Dunne has a brain storm. Get the 19 to call a press conference and let reporters ask them all questions including the biggie "are you now etc." This would emphasize that an *official* inquiry into political beliefs is unconstitutional. Felix Frankfurter would make everybody swear they were telling the truth beforehand. Bart thinks it's a terrific idea but probably too late . . . since strategy has already been set. Nixon fled to California before Dunne and Huston could meet him . . . cocktails with Betty Bacall and Humphrey Bogart, who's awfully grumpy . . . later Bart and I had dinner with Adrian Scott at a place called Harvey's in downtown Washington. The restaurant is famous for its steamed clams. J. Edgar Hoover was there. We both noticed him because he has that familiar pugdog face, wary eyes and squashed-in nose we've seen so often in the newsreels. His look of supreme confidence—can confidence be evil?—was absolutely frightening. Oh, and he stank of perfume!

AT the start of the second week of testimony my brother and I hid out in the newsreel theater on Market Street watching Daddy being gaveled down time and time again as he requested the right to cross-examine "friendly" witnesses who had testified the previous week.

> MR. CRUM: May I request the right of cross-examination? I ask you to permit us to cross-examine the witnesses, Adolphe Menjou, Fred Niblo . . . Sam Wood, Ayn Rand . . .
> THE CHAIRMAN: The request . . .
> MR. CRUM: Howard Rushmore—[*chairman pounds gavel*]

THE CHAIRMAN: The request is denied.

MR. CRUM: Morris Ryskind, Oliver Carlson—[*gavel pounding continues*]

THE CHAIRMAN: The request is denied.

MR. CRUM: In order to show these witnesses lied.

THE CHAIRMAN: That request is denied.

At another point Daddy was almost ejected from the hearing room for shouting, "We demand the same rights as Howard Hughes!" (Months earlier millionaire producer Hughes had been allowed to ramble on for hours when he'd been called to testify in front of a Senate investigating committee.) After his outburst *The Washington Post* interviewed my father, and he said that HUAC was a congressional hearing, not a judicial trial; court procedure did not apply. "My clients are being slandered," he said. "They are being denied their rights to cross-examine their slanderers."

Later we would watch more newsreels featuring grainy close-ups of our father smoking, frowning. He would take off his glasses; he would put them back on; he would light another cigarette. His expression was implacable, especially during John Howard Lawson's angry shouting match with J. Parnell Thomas. He was the first of the "unfriendly witnesses," and he was dragged off the stand by police when he wouldn't answer any questions as to his political beliefs.

"You are using scare tactics that were employed in Hitler's Germany!" he screamed. He was cited for contempt of Congress. If convicted, he would face a fine of one thousand dollars and a jail sentence of a year—or both.

Like Lawson, Dalton Trumbo tried to read his prepared statement to the committee comparing Washington to Berlin before the Reichstag fire. When Stripling insisted that he confine his answers to a simple yes or no and then asked, "Have you ever been a Communist?" Trumbo replied, "I shall answer in my own words. Very many questions can be answered yes or no only by a moron or a slave."

As he was dragged from the hearings, he cried out, "This is the beginning of an American concentration camp!" And Thomas yelled back, "Typical Communist tactic!"

Applause and boos from the audience.

During a break the Committee for the First Amendment met with fifty reporters in a suite at the Statler Hotel. It was a tense scene: Danny Kaye chomped on his nails; Humphrey Bogart glowered and chain smoked. John Howard Lawson's behavior had been a PR disaster, but they weren't going to say that. They weren't going to admit that artists often make lousy politicians, although Bogart said that later; instead all the stars took turns at the microphone and talked about HUAC and censorship and Lawson being denied the right of free speech. Dunne recalled, "We were not going to back down. We stuck to our principles."

So the hearings continued for four more raucous days. The Nineteen continued to insult and equivocate, their voices swelling and distorted by the bad PA system and mixed in with hisses and boos from onlookers. Occasionally there would be a spatter of applause.

Later my father would tell me that he "could literally feel the people in the hearing room lose sympathy with each shout from our group. Thomas had made a ludicrous showing by yelling and pounding on his gavel, but the rest of the Nineteen matched him shout for shout and insult for insult. If only they had been more dignified they would have been much more effective."

Only Albert Maltz was allowed to deliver his entire statement (in which he accused the committee of supporting the Ku Klux Klan). Alvah Bessie managed to get four paragraphs out of his statement in which he charged that HUAC was going to abolish every democratic element in American society. Herbert Biberman and Samuel Ornitz were denied permission to read their personal statements or to introduce scripts from their films as evidence that their work was not subversive. All four men were cited for contempt for refusing to answer the now all-too-familiar question: "Are you now or have you ever been a member of the Communist Party?"

After each witness left the stand Louis Russell, an FBI agent now working for HUAC, would read into the record a list of the various Communist organizations attached to the previous speaker.

Mama attended some of the sessions and noted in her journal: "You have to see this spectacle in the flesh—hundreds of spectators, a great many tourists, some foreigners. There is a continuous movement in and out of the chamber, no guides but police wearing guns who drag the various 'unfriendlies' out of the corridor and deposit them there. The public seems respectful. Intent and quite grave. When Bart and I went out for a hamburger a perfect stranger ran over and grabbed his hand. 'I admire your courage,' he said."

During one break, my father hurried into the Nineteen's suite to announce that Truman was so outraged at the committee's behavior that he was going to get the president's Commission on Civil Rights out as soon as possible, and he was also—as a gesture of good faith—going to invite the entire "unfriendly nineteen" to lunch at the White House along with the Committee for the First Amendment.

The Civil Rights report was released early, but the luncheon invitation never materialized.

At another break, Brecht appeared in the suite. He'd asked to see the entire group and their lawyers. He wanted to explain why he was going to cooperate with the committee. He had no record, he was not a Communist, but he wanted to go home to East Germany and he couldn't do that with a contempt charge hanging over his head. He knew all decisions of the Nineteen had to be agreed on unanimously; he wanted to make sure it was okay to tell the truth. And then he launched into a melodramatic story of his flight from the Nazis after Hitler labeled his writings "treasonable." He was on the run for years, hiding out in Denmark, Sweden, traveling by train through Russia, Siberia, finally hopping a boat in Manila. He was never apprehended, and then, upon landing in the United States: *"Here I was caught."*

"Even the most hardened Party liners choked up," Daddy recalled later. The Nineteen unanimously agreed to allow Brecht to testify in front of HUAC as he saw fit.

The playwright seemed relieved. He gave a little sigh, telling everybody he'd been elated at John Howard Lawson's behavior in front of the committee; he congratulated him on his fierce opposition. "Nothing like that could happen in Germany; if it could, fascism wouldn't have occurred." He was impressed with the way most Americans were reacting to HUAC; they seemed appalled by the tactics. He was impressed with the way the newspapers were handling the story, too. "You have free speech and a free press," he finished. "You are freer than you think."

■

AFTERWARD Waldo Salt would recall that "the playwright Bertolt Brecht was the consummate political game player of all time. He was also one hell of an actor. I think underneath he was scared he wouldn't get out of the States. But he never let on. Except while he was talking to us he streamed sweat."

JUST before Eddie Dmytryk took the stand, he and Adrian Scott met hastily with my father. "It had gotten so crazy by then," Dmytryk remembered. "It was out of control—the hearings, the Committee. . . . I was disillusioned. I couldn't support it. I told Bart, 'I just want to stand up there and tell the truth and so does Adrian.' And Bart said, 'That is wonderful!' He met with the other lawyers once more and he argued passionately about how our silence was going to prolong the anguish. He tried to convince Margolis and the others that we be allowed to break rank, but he was argued down again. He was absolutely alone in his conviction that they be allowed to speak freely. Even Robert Kenny said nothing. Howard Koch was furious."

When Dmytryk tried to testify, he attempted to explain the constitutional issues involved that kept him from answering questions about his politics. He, too, was cited for contempt, as was Adrian Scott—they were on and off the stand in a matter of minutes.

Then came Emmet Lavery, president of the Screen Writers Guild, who actually volunteered information about how the guild operated, as well as how small Communist infiltration was; he also volunteered the fact that he had already appeared at a secret meeting with the FBI.

Dalton Trumbo was outraged and Ring Lardner Jr. was angry, too.

Lardner, by the way, was the only one of his colleagues who injected elegant humor into the proceedings. When asked about his Communist affiliations he quipped, "I could answer that question, but I'd hate myself in the morning."

Ultimately cited for contempt, he was half dragged, half carried out of the hearings, murmuring, "I think I am being made to leave by force."

■

By then, "everything was backfiring," my father said. "By baiting Thomas and Stripling the Nineteen descended to the Committee's level," Philip Dunne said years later. "They had lost the chance to defend a very important principle."

Dunne and the other members of the Committee for the First Amendment (Lauren Bacall, Humphrey Bogart, John Huston, John Garfield, Danny Kaye, Lucille Ball) left the caucus room en masse after Lardner was carried from the hearing and went back to Hollywood on their chartered plane.

So they weren't present to witness the performance of Bertolt Brecht.

He was the last witness to testify in front of HUAC, and the day before he took the stand, my father, alternating with Ben Margolis, coached the playwright. (Not that he needed it; he had already rehearsed his testimony with a friend back in New York. He had also chosen his outfit—conservative suit and tie—and decided he would wear glasses and smoke a cigar since J. Parnell Thomas smoked cigars and it might make him appear more sympathetic.)

To ensure privacy from bugging in the Shoreham Hotel suite, the lawyers took Brecht out to Rock Creek Park and walked him round and round, talking and arguing until it got dark.

Margolis almost broke a leg tripping over an FBI agent who had been hiding in the bushes spying on them. Daddy spent most of his time trying to convince Brecht that he was protected by the First Amendment and the Constitution even though he was an alien. Brecht could not be convinced. At some point he got into a rambling harangue about politics. My father left some notes:

> Bertolt Brecht does not approve of the crazy makeup of the American left. He sees nothing but factionalism here, thinks there is something nutty about so much of non-party alignment. "What do you really believe in?" he asked me, and before I could answer, he demanded "Have you ever risked your *neck* to survive?"
>
> "I'm afraid I haven't," I answered.
>
> "Well," Brecht went on in a harsh voice, "where I come from, in order to survive you have to agree to some ugly collaborations, and I'm not so sure you even understand what I am talking about."

I assured him I did and then Brecht ended with a total non-sequitur: "Didn't the capitalists drown thousands of pigs to keep pork prices up?"

Daddy ends the notes with, "Brecht is committed to Lenin's principles . . . he admires Lenin's cunning when dealing with his enemies. . . . 'You have no cunning in your face, Bartley Crum,' he told me!"

Brecht, of course, knew a great deal about cunning. His testimony before the committee the following morning was once described as "a polite exercise in slyness and duplicity." Determined to say nothing that would ruin his chances of leaving the country safely, he followed his carefully planned scenario to the letter, which included smoking cigars throughout. He asked for an interpreter in order to play the dumb foreigner bit, but the interpreter's thickly accented English was harder to understand than Brecht's.

Once on the stand he bewildered everybody. He lied, equivocated, and even confused the plots of two of his plays, *The Measures Taken* and *He Who Says Yes,* so HUAC wouldn't catch the Marxist dogma in both works. And yet he gave the impression that he was answering all questions completely.

He was asked three times if he had been or was now a member of the Communist Party, and each time he answered, "No, no, no, no, no, never. I have heard my colleagues when they considered this question as not proper, but I am a guest in this country and do not want to enter into any legal arguments, so I will answer your question as fully and as well as I can. I was not a member or am not a member of the Communist Party."

Chairman Thomas seemed entranced and asked him to step down. "Thank you very much, Mr. Brecht. You are a good example to the witnesses of Mr. Kenny and Mr. Crum."

Immediately afterward, Brecht, sweaty and white-faced, escaped into a cab with screenwriter Lester Cole. "He became very emotional," Cole recalled. "He wondered if any of us could understand what he'd done and forgive him." He knew he had lied and been a coward like so many of the characters in his plays, but he couldn't help himself. He was alone in a foreign country, and he felt threatened. He had to get out. Indeed he already had passport and plane tickets in his pocket, and he left for Paris the following evening. Later, from the safety of East Berlin, he wrote that the American investigators were better than the Nazis because at least they'd allowed him to smoke.

THE HUAC hearing ended abruptly after Brecht's testimony. Only ten out of the Nineteen had testified. (Although Brecht was number eleven, he apparently didn't count.) Those ten Americans who had testified were immediately cited for contempt by the House of Representatives for their refusal to answer the committee's questions. This led to their indictment and arraignment.

Meanwhile, right after the hearings my father went on radio —the only lawyer to do so for the men who would now be known as the Hollywood Ten.

He was alone with Ed Hart of CBS and he made the following comments, prompted by Hart's questions, beginning with "Mr. Crum, what was HUAC's purpose?"

My father answered, "To frighten the movie industry into surrendering free expression . . . to submit show business to reactionary political censorship. . . . If that happens, the art and craft of producing movies would be subject to political screenings of a Congressional House Committee. . . . If this happened—and it won't—it would begin to condition Americans to the loss of their political rights."

"That's a pretty severe indictment, Mr. Crum."

"Yeah—maybe it is, but I think most lawyers in America would agree with my assessment."

"What is the end result of this investigation?"

"A lot of confusion. More intolerance. More disrespect for each other. Chaos and confusion, that's what HUAC wants. HUAC means to frighten the public with the lie that Communism is infiltrating every facet of American life."

I found this partial transcript balled up in the pocket of his overcoat and pasted it into the scrapbook anyway.

Days afterward in San Francisco, Mama would bug him about that broadcast—some of his friends had heard it, she said, and disapproved.

"Why didn't anyone else go with you to the radio station to support you that day?" I heard her ask him.

"How the hell do I know, Cutsie? Jesus. It's okay. I can handle it."

And handle it he did, in his own way; when archconservative Jack Tenney of the California branch of HUAC called him "a practicing Communist for all practical purposes," Daddy answered him in the *San Francisco Chronicle,* "If Senator Tenney will be brave enough to take off the mantle of privilege and repeat these charges to me, I would be delighted to sue him for libel and prove him a liar."

I pasted the full account into his scrapbook along with remarks from a speech he'd given called by the Progressive Citizens of America at the Washington Press Club, in which he condemned the committee hearings as a "kangaroo court in which 19 men's reputations are being destroyed." He ridiculed the phrase "Communist menace" and said the word had lost its original meaning and become a word of reproach or rebuke; the committee has never attempted to define what it means to be a Communist or a so-called un-American, he said.

He was concerned with the committee's violations of the First Amendment to the Constitution. He challenged the right of J. Parnell Thomas to act as czar to our thoughts.

DADDY was rarely sick, but he seemed to collapse that week after he returned to San Francisco. The doctors ordered "an enforced rest." He slept for hours, and when he was awake he coughed and coughed.

Bart and I hovered around his study/bedroom, plumping up pillows—trying to make him feel comfortable. I remember that everything smelled strongly of Vicks.

When he felt better, I showed him his scrapbook, but he soon lost interest and began making a round of phone calls. (An old phone log from November 1947 shows several calls from Washington columnist Drew Pearson, who had been testifying as a character witness for six members of the Joint Anti-Fascist Committee that HUAC was investigating.)

ON November 24, 1947, the House of Representatives voted contempt indictments for each of the Ten. It was a great victory for HUAC.

That same day, Eric Johnston organized a meeting at the Waldorf-Astoria of all the major studio heads—Louis B. Mayer; Joe and Nick Schenck; Paramount president Barney Balaban; Harry Cohn, head of Columbia; Sam Goldwyn—along with their East Coast financiers. They met in closed conference.

At first everyone seemed outraged by HUAC's tactics, but by the end of the meeting there was a complete about-face and it was decided that the only way to prevent HUAC's encroaching even more in Hollywood was to sacrifice the Ten. The studios decreed that five of them, who had been working under contract in the studios, were to be discharged "without compensation"; none of them would be allowed to work again, unless and until they purged themselves of contempt and swore under oath that they were not Communists.

The blacklist began.

Dalton Trumbo was suspended from MGM and the studio refused to pay him the sixty thousand dollars they owed him. Ring Lardner Jr. was let go from Twentieth Century-Fox. (Eventually both men sued and the two studios had to settle.)

Dmytryk and Scott were fired from RKO. Before it happened, Dore Schary had urged them to recant and purge themselves, but they wouldn't. After the firing, they took the train to San Francisco to see my father, who agreed to continue representing them. They were going to sue, of course.

They went to the Bohemian Club for drinks. When they walked into the bar, nobody would speak to my father; it was as if he were a pariah. Some men even turned their backs. At dinner he tried to make light of it. "It can't be because I'm your lawyer, can it?" he asked. Dmytryk told him maybe it was and he was sorry he had gotten him into this mess, but my father would have none of it. "Forget it, Eddie," he said. "It'll be okay—it'll be okay."

But it wasn't okay—not for him or for Eddie Dmytryk or for Adrian Scott.

The producers' breaking of the Hollywood Ten contracts precipitated seven years of civil litigation, which accompanied the trials of the Ten and the appeals in the hopes of a Supreme Court reversal of the contempt citations. The process was long and financially exhausting, to say nothing of the wear and tear on the emotions—and the souls—of those involved.

Daddy continued to denounce HUAC. During one speech, flanked by Party lawyers he not only lambasted the committee but also the FBI, shouting, "If there are any agents in the audience they can all go to hell!"

A friend who had been at the rally said, "You are being used by those Communists—they just stand there while you go out on a limb. Don't you care?"

And my father snapped, no, he didn't *care;* it had nothing to do with him personally. He said he cared about free speech, about the government's efforts at repressing dissent; he cared about *exposing* this kangaroo court! It had nothing to do with him personally, he repeated.

He began receiving obscene phone calls in the night and hate mail. Mama divided it into two categories: "Jew lover" mail and "Commie lover" mail.

In her journal she noted:

> A sorry time—a dark time. Little Bart snubbed at the Town School by some of his classmates. Many of Patti's friends, except for Terry Ashe, refusing to come over for her birthday party!! . . . The other evening, Bart and I stepped into an elevator with a couple we've known for years—they wouldn't speak to us! And they aren't the only ones—there are others —at least a dozen—maybe more—friends we used to lunch or dine with once a month or spend weekends at their country places in Los Gatos or Marin. They are cutting us dead. And all because Bart is supposedly a "dangerous radical"—"a Commie lover"—"a pinko". . .
>
> Speaking of Bart, we had quite a talk the other night. He's been home most of the month nursing a terrible cold— still can't shake it—so we sat in front of the fire and drank brandy and got pretty mellow. We really let our hair down. I felt in him a great weariness and disappointment.
>
> He is very worried about the witch hunting. He said the Attorney General's lists were getting longer. Anybody the least bit liberal is called "subversive"—every Roosevelt associated, progressive organization is labeled a "Commie front." It is a Republican device, he said, for vote catching in the 1948 elections. New Deal politics are being destroyed . . . there's a real power shift in the making with conservative Republicans emerging as a force. Richard Nixon is going to

come to power he predicted; so are George Murphy and maybe even Ronald Reagan. . . . Bart said he has not accomplished what he set out to do in the last five years—since Willkie's death—and that is to help revitalize the liberal wing of the Republican Party.

I told him that is a pretty big order and he admitted it was, and then he added, as for solving the problems in Palestine (which I don't begin to understand and really don't want to) the problems have got worse, and will continue to get worse. He has made himself persona non grata at the State Department so he thinks he no longer has a role to play in the Middle East, if he ever did. Maybe he was kidding himself, he said. I told him "you want to be all things to all men—why don't you just stick with being a husband and a father and a lawyer?" and he smiled and said, "That wouldn't be enough and you know it." But he can find no place for himself anywhere—he has no power base—no affiliation anywhere. He is one lone voice crying out in the wilderness. He can find no place for himself anywhere in the political spectrum, including the Lawyers Guild, and that is terribly frustrating for him. He is such a political animal. But there is no leader for him to follow, since Willkie. I have always felt he had to have a leader. He is basically a follower. I did not tell him that. . . . But he is uneasy and unsettled by a number of things— not the least is the worry that he has not adequately met the responsibility—financial—emotional—of his family. To Patti, to little Bart and me—the provisions every man feels he should make to his wife and children should he be taken from us suddenly.

He feels he doesn't begin to know his son . . . blames himself for that. They still have a difficult time communicating. He has no trouble with Patti.

Nothing resolved—no conclusions drawn—no plans made, but I felt closer to him than I have in ages. I found myself mouthing clichés. . . . I would go anywhere with him, do anything to make him happy. . . . I told him I still thought he had a great future ahead of him—some people used to think he could run for President . . . he is just forty-eight years old. . . . He put his arms around me—how long has it been since he's done *that?* He put his arms around me and I didn't draw away this time. Of course nothing happened—no fireworks went off. . . .

"You are always full of hope, Gert," he told me (he hasn't called me *that* in years). "You give me great courage . . ."

If that is true, why do I now feel so utterly despairing?

IN December 1947, my father abruptly resigned from the Progressive Citizens of America, an act of protest against PCA's drive to forge a third party for the 1948 presidential campaign of Henry Wallace.

He didn't make any public statement, but he would subsequently write the Justice Department (when they were investigating him), "I resigned from PCA when it became apparent to me that the organization was being dominated by what I regard as Communist thinking."

CHAPTER

21

A T the start of 1948 Daddy told us he was being followed by FBI agents every time he took a trip. He tried to make a joke out of it, but there was an edge to his voice. Early in February FBI agents tailed him on a train from San Francisco to Chicago to New York. He finally lost them, he said, when he ran into St. Patrick's to light a candle. Then he went on to Washington to help in the appeal of John Howard Lawson in federal district court.

He and the other lawyers were gathering evidence to establish that the purpose of HUAC was not to investigate un-American activities but to penalize the likes of Dalton Trumbo and Lawson, who committee members such as Richard Nixon thought were "political criminals."

Daddy was surprised when the court turned down the Ten's request for a collective trial; after Lawson and Trumbo were convicted, the prosecution and the defense agreed to the following: that the others would not be tried by the lower courts, but would accept the final verdict (following the appeals process) rendered to Lawson and Trumbo. Separate trials would be too costly.

Many lawyers Daddy knew were refusing to take on any more loyalty cases; they were considered too dangerous. He did take on one more—the case of a teacher he'd known since college, an instructor at the California Labor School, which was on the attorney general's "subversive" list.

The teacher was an "innocent," a non-Communist, a victim

of the loyalty purge. He was teaching at the school without pay because he believed in adult education.

At one of his loyalty hearings, Daddy was questioned about his own involvement with the school: as it happened it was major. He was on the board; he taught history of American labor to army veterans and longshoremen. He did not add that he had recently convinced his friend Louise Bransten to invest money in the school.

But he was indignant at having been asked any questions at all. The idea of employing both public and secret criteria at such a hearing was outrageous and confusing and he said so.

The hearing dragged on; the teacher was ultimately fired from his paying job at an Oakland high school, where he taught English lit. My father stood by him and never charged him a fee, and for a short while after that he would give advice to other teachers under investigation—meeting them in bars, usually at night. It was a time of intimidation and fear. Soon he stopped handling loyalty cases entirely. His more conservative clients disapproved of his continued defense of subversives.

He was networking all over California seeking out new business. He still had the Palmolive account and Dolly Thackery's radio station, but his partner Philip Ehrlich had written him a letter telling him he must stop his incessant speechmaking. They had been associates for eight years; until recently it had been an association that was beneficial to both of them, but unless he started to practice law full-time again, Ehrlich would not advance him more funds.

Early in 1948, my father began borrowing periodically from his mother. Whether he paid her back I'm not sure. "Mo had scrimped and saved all her life," my cousin Jim said. "She had a nice little bundle from real estate she'd bought before World War I—and from pinching pennies. She always gave Bart money when he needed it, but sometimes she complained."

AND then in March, Marshall Field's attorney Louis Weiss phoned to see if my father would be interested in becoming publisher of the liberal tabloid *PM*. Daddy said he would be very interested and flew to New York for a meeting. (He was a candidate because he met Field's criteria: "Bart Crum was a champion of lost causes and he was left of center, but not very left of center," Samuel J. Silverman, Weiss's colleague, told me.)

Running a newspaper could be a solution, a way out of his untenable financial position in San Francisco. Plus he had always dreamed of running a newspaper—ever since he worked for Hearst. And *PM* was especially appealing—it was considered "a true journal of outrage"; he'd been reading *PM* since Ralph Ingersoll created it in 1940.

PM was often called "a cross between *The New Yorker* and *The Daily Worker*." Its contributors included Lillian Hellman, Dashiell Hammett, and Dr. Benjamin Spock. News features were often accompanied by Weegee photographs. Its idealistic credo was *"PM* is for people who don't push other people around." Until recently it had survived without advertising; even now big advertisers shunned the paper.

But everything hinged on whether my father could raise the cash necessary to keep *PM* afloat. Field, one of the original owners, was now sole owner; he had sunk $5 million into the project and still the paper was losing money at a fantastic rate. In fact, it never made a profit; it never achieved the 225,000 daily circulation it needed to break even.

As soon as he returned to San Francisco, Daddy phoned around and got immediate assurances that, yes, he could "come up with the dough." He sent Field an exuberant telegram stating just that.

"Bart Crum's telegram was like a bolt from the blue," recalls Judge Silverman. "Bart Crum was gonna save *PM*—he was gonna be our knight in shining armor."

The usually reticent Field fired back a wire that said, in effect, he would sell majority interest in the paper to Daddy and to Joseph Barnes, the gifted, imaginative foreign editor of the *Herald Tribune;* he had agreed to be editor of *PM*.

Field's telegram was delivered in the middle of a dinner party at our Green Street house and Daddy read the contents aloud to the assembled guests, who included Barney Dreyfus, secretary of the Lawyers Guild, and Steve Fisher, a close associate of Henry Wallace.

Fisher remembers the last line of the telegram going something like, "I'm selling you my newspaper and throwing in close to a million bucks to help run it."

Everybody at the table was flabbergasted; the deal had happened so fast. Too fast—as did many things in my father's life.

The next morning he flew to New York again, this time to meet with Barnes. They were already acquainted; they had worked together on Willkie's 1940 and 1944 presidential campaigns.

Barnes was as eager as my father to run a newspaper. For the next weeks, the two men were locked in discussions with Field's lawyers. The idea was that they would, individually, put up as much money as they could, and Daddy would also raise funds from outside sources.

For the interim period that would be required, Weiss gave them a vague verbal inexact promise of continued financial support from Field himself until the two men could actually take over *PM*.

As soon as the news leaked out about Bart Crum buying *PM*, Paul Smith, editor of the *Chronicle*, begged him to reconsider. *PM* was too risky a venture to take over in the Cold War climate: "You could be destroyed," Paul said.

Friends of Barnes told him virtually the same thing, but at the time neither man listened—they were supremely confident they could turn *PM* into a newspaper that would make a difference in the politically fractured climate of 1948. It would also serve as a platform for their energies, their enthusiasms, their concerns. "They honestly believed all these things," Joe Barnes's widow, Betty, recalls.

In reality, they were both "hopelessly ignorant," Barnes said later. In fact, in his oral history, he describes the move he and my father made as "sheer folly." They had no idea of the problems involved, and there wasn't time to take them into consideration: the money problems, union problems, personnel problems, organization problems, and the political divisions within the newspaper itself.

But the challenges outweighed the difficulties. Barnes said: "We simply could not turn this opportunity down."

One problem they were aware of and thought they could change was the Red taint of the paper. In some circles *PM* was called "Stalinoid—a Communist front," which was an exaggeration.

At first the battles in the *PM* newsroom had been between the Stalinists and the crypto-Stalinists, but by 1948 the feuding had settled into an all-out war between the Communists and the anti-Communists.

Although there were Communists on the staff and left-wingers, like I. F. Stone, Daddy and Barnes believed they could achieve more balanced editorials while still telling the truth within a left liberal context—that was their goal. Even with the Cold War and loyalty purges raging around them, they intended that to be their policy.

On May 1, Marshall Field sold majority interest in *PM* to my father and Joe Barnes, although Daddy made no secret of the fact that he had no ready cash available (but he kept saying he would have it, in a matter of days). However, Field would continue to loan money to *PM* until finances were raised. In fact, the paper already had funds to operate as a result of a $500,000 loan from Field, secured in March by a chattel mortgage on the paper's equipment and another mortgage on the newspaper's Duane Street building. The money was put aside in anticipation of severance pay required by the various unions, primarily the Newspaper Guild.

As soon as Daddy and Barnes took over *PM*, the guild agreed to the following terms: that the paper's 162 editorial and clerical workers be fired and paid severance pay and all who wished would be hired back immediately, during which time management could hire and fire as it pleased; otherwise, severance pay would be given to employees who quit. Daddy and Barnes would live up to Field's contract with the guild.

PM sports columnist Heywood Broun recalls: "To cut costs, Barnes and Crum began firing right away—so there was a threat of a strike."

The strike was quickly quashed by Barnes, who hastily called a meeting of the staff and explained that if *PM* was struck now it would be the death of the paper.

Only two guild members voted to strike—Broun among them. "Barnes never spoke to me after that," he said.

On May 2, exhausted but elated, Daddy flew back to San Francisco.

I remember him arriving home full of plans. He had so much to say to the three of us as he paced around our living room—mixing himself a drink, puffing on cigarettes, then stubbing them out. He'd always wanted to run a newspaper, ever since he worked for Hearst, and before that the *Oakland Trib*. Journalism was a grand adventure, and owning *PM* would be a grand adventure, too, he promised.

One of the first things he wanted to do was to start an investigation in print about the circumstances surrounding the mysterious death in Prague of his friend, Czech foreign minister Jan Masaryk shortly after the Communists seized control of Czechoslovakia. Indeed the first gesture he made as *PM*'s publisher was getting an editorial written describing more of the facts behind what he believed was Masaryk's murder.

May 2 happened to be our servants' day off (now we had a butler and a new cook; Toy had quit after an argument with my mother), so Daddy announced he would prepare our dinner. I followed him into the kitchen, watching as he began to fix his favorite meal: corned beef hash and coddled eggs. When my brother appeared, he poured us root beer in wine goblets, and as we toasted the buying of the newspaper, Daddy very casually mentioned that we would be moving to New York in June.

Mama hadn't uttered a word. She was setting the kitchen table, a tight little smile on her lips. "I just hope you're not burning all your bridges, Bart," she said.

He told her he would retain his law practice with Phil Ehrlich.

"That's sensible since you have no experience as a newspaper publisher."

He admitted that was true.

"Oh, for God's sake, Bart," Mama cried. "Then, why are you doing this to us?"

My father took a big swig of his drink. Then he placed the glass back on the sink next to his pack of Pall Malls and his gold cigarette lighter.

"Well, Cutsie," he answered, enunciating very carefully. I could tell he was slightly drunk and a little angry, too. "Well, Cutsie, I thought you'd enjoy the idea of us owning a newspaper—you started off as a crime reporter for the *Call Bulletin*."

"*Us?*" Mama's voice trembled. "You never once asked my opinion of what I thought about you buying *PM*. You just told me —after the fact."

There was a long silence broken when my brother demanded, "Will I be able to go to the Philharmonic—Carnegie Hall?"

"Every night of the week if you want to," Daddy assured him grandly. And then he began spooning the yellow batter he'd made for the cornmeal muffins into muffin molds.

Mama rolled her eyes to the ceiling. "Now *I* need a drink. A big one," she said.

DURING the next week, Daddy put our Green Street house on the market and sold it almost immediately for twenty-five thousand dollars.

After hearing the news, Mama locked herself in her bedroom. Daddy had to kneel on the floor, rattling the knob and imploring her to "open up" and "understand"—he'd had to sell in order to pay for our move across the continent, for our new home in New York, for tuition in our private schools.

"We have no savings, Cutsie."

Later she would write despairingly in her journal: "I cannot believe what is happening. Everything I care about—thrown away —destroyed. My beautiful house, my gardens. As usual I feel completely shut out of Bart's life."

And yet within hours she had pulled herself together and joined Daddy in the living room, where he served drinks to Washington columnist Joseph Alsop. I passed around the usual spiced nuts just as Alsop bet my father five hundred dollars that *PM* would close by the end of the year, because such a newspaper could not survive in the Cold War climate.

"You're on, Joe," Daddy told him.

I glanced at Mama; she was sitting ramrod straight, a double strand of pearls at her throat, her honey-blond hair swept back from a perfectly made up face. As usual, façade took precedence over her tumultuous feelings; that evening, as always, she kept up a front of brittle chitchat.

Part of her did admire Daddy for his gallantry and courage—his need to risk his entire life for yet another "lost cause."

Basically, she suffered in silence and hid from the outside world any sign of conflict or unhappiness with my father.

"She submerged herself in him," Marian Javits said. "I remember Cutsie as infinitely sad. She always looked beautifully turned out—but I got the feeling Bart never even noticed what she had on."

Like most women of her generation, Mama practiced the art of deception. Life with Daddy was wonderful—glamorous, grand; it was easier to deceive, to hide the unpleasant things, the darkness. Besides, *her* father had trained her to be emotionally private.

But she wasn't afraid to speak her mind. She told Daddy he "sounded like an idiot" after he gave an interview to *The New Yorker* for "Talk of the Town" in which he explained how it felt to buy *PM* and what he thought was the principal job of a newspaper publisher. "Protecting my editor," he declared. In this case, Joseph Barnes. Protecting him from interference. He went on to say that while he was working for Hearst he watched John Neylan publish the *San Francisco Call Bulletin*, and he realized how easy it was to be a publisher. "If you have the right people to run the paper a publisher is like a vermiform appendix—unnecessary."

Daddy said that his remarks in *The New Yorker* had been taken out of context; he said the same thing when John Neylan phoned very irate to demand, "What in God's name are you talking about? I worked my tail off!"

Throughout May Daddy remained in New York. Everything that happened after he left is a blur in my mind. I remember faintly hysterical dinners with Uncle Carl, Aunt Lib, and Cousin Elena in our pale-blue dining room at Aptos—candles flickering, casting shadows on the candy-striped banquettes. I remember Daddy sending us expensive new suitcases we didn't need. I remember Grandmother Julie giving me and my brother an ornate copy of *The Arabian Nights* to read on the train.

Mostly, I remember driving back and forth from San Francisco to Aptos to San Francisco again—to pack and pack and pack. I remember watching Bernice (our cook) and Robert (our butler/chauffeur) stuffing barrels full of china and kitchen equipment at the Green Street house while movers carried all the furniture into storage vans. My brother and I wandered around the empty rooms, feeling very lost.

We felt the same way at Aptos even though Daddy swore he would never sell the place—even though Mama insisted she was taking only essentials, such as monogrammed towels and linens, the silver candelabra, the antique vases, as well as a few books. She acted very businesslike, trotting around with a clipboard, keeping a detailed inventory, making endless notes.

And then, on that last weekend at Aptos, she suddenly dumped my entire collection of movie magazines and scrapbooks into the fireplace and set a match to them before I could stop her. Images of Ingrid Bergman and Gregory Peck exploded like hot bright bombs before floating up the chimney. Flames crackled merrily around a sullen portrait of Humphrey Bogart.

I did nothing. I felt very still and empty inside and the feeling stayed with me and increased as I climbed the hill and began rocking back and forth on the swing the drifter had constructed for us.

In the distance I could hear the ocean rolling and beating against the sand as I sailed over the myrtle bed so I could view the property I loved so much: the vivid, sweet-smelling gardens, the apple orchards flanking the small white clapboard house with its green roof and red chimneys. Behind the house the two tall redwoods seemed to be guarding everything. I kept rocking back and forth until I felt dizzy, and then I let myself slide off the swing and drop to the myrtle bed; the myrtle was so thick it pillowed my fall.

Just before we left Aptos, one of our cockers, Frisky Senior, was run over on the highway above our house. It was a terrible shock. My brother and I scraped up the dog's bloody remains off the road and then we buried his crushed body next to our hideout.

We tried to accept the fact that everything must die, but death so far had been an abstraction to us. Frisky had been a part of our lives since 1942, when we first moved to Aptos for the summer and he had been a wriggling, adorable little puppy.

By the time we left California, I was in a daze. Mama and my brother were in a daze, too, but none of us ever communicated our hurt, our immense sense of loss.

We behaved with one another as we always had—politely,

almost gingerly. We were so accustomed to hiding our anger, we barely knew we were angry. So we simply didn't think about this brutal tearing away from everybody and everything we loved; we made no effort to subject our pain to any process of understanding. How successfully we disguised our feelings!

WE traveled across the continent by train. I remember Bart and I sitting up in our berths half the night following our journey by flashlight on a big map. We checked off the states as we crossed them—Utah, Illinois, Maryland—and then we were in New York, gliding up Park Avenue in a hired limousine. The streets were very hot. It was the beginning of June. The granite canyons were bathed in rosy light.

CHAPTER

22

WE stayed for a short time in a borrowed penthouse on East Seventy-second Street off Second Avenue. The ceilings were low; there was too much heavy furniture; plants crowded the dining area. I kept hearing the little radio Bart was always turning on because Daddy wanted to listen to the news about Berlin being blockaded by the Russians. Every day the United States was airlifting tons of food into the western part of the city.

I had no interest in the news. I would stare bleakly out the window at the tenements and the skyscrapers of Manhattan and try to conjure up my view of San Francisco Bay. I longed to go back to the beautiful spaciousness of our Green Street house.

For the first couple of days we felt terribly disoriented. My brother and I did touristy things like visiting Rockefeller Center and the Empire State Building. The weather was sultry and strange to me. Every time I walked into the street, I'd get some grit in my eye.

Once I remember we wandered around Central Park, all safe then, silent and clean. I remember soft green meadows and a lake.

Another time Bart and I took a subway to Times Square. I wasn't prepared for the mobs of people, the honking traffic, the blinking signs. The Astor Hotel loomed above us. Police on horseback trotted about near the Paramount Building.

We drank thick chocolate milkshakes at Howard Johnson's and then we strolled down the "Rialto" reading the theater marquees: *Mister Roberts,* starring Henry Fonda; *A Streetcar Named*

Desire with Marlon Brando; *All My Sons* by Arthur Miller; the musical *Brigadoon* . . .

It was my first look at the Broadway of my fantasies and it seemed as glamorous and exciting on that humid afternoon as it would when I worked there years later.

All that month—the month of June—my father and Barnes labored to change the image of the paper. They renamed *PM* the *New York Star*, and they turned it into a morning paper (although New York sadly needed a good afternoon daily). Now the *Star* would be in competition with the *Daily News* and the *Mirror*, past master of the rough-and-tumble newsstand methods.

The front page would no longer be poster-size; the *Star* would also attempt to have full coverage of the news (something *PM* did not have). There would be complete reports on the upcoming presidential campaigns, and local news would be covered, too— like the rise of New York's subway fare to ten cents. And other news—very depressing, Daddy said—like a feature about a special grand jury in Manhattan, which had just indicted twelve American Communists on charges of conspiracy to overthrow the United States government.

IN the confusion and uprooting that had accompanied our move, Mama had given away our remaining cocker spaniel—explaining that we could not have too many dogs in New York—but she had brought her poodle, Bonbon, to the Seventy-second Street penthouse. We were so hurt and angry over the loss of our pet, we refused to walk the poodle, and Daddy took our side and refused to walk her, too.

Mama reacted in stony silence because Bonbon was pregnant (in February she had run off into the Aptos woods with a mongrel dog). At the time there had been mention of an abortion, but Daddy hadn't allowed it. However, when the puppies were born in New York in late June, Mama took an instant dislike to them. They were ugly, hairy little things, she told us irritably—they had no pedigrees, they were bastards.

One morning, very early, around 4:00 A.M., I remember hearing water running. Mama often took baths at ungodly hours. She still suffered from insomnia, and she still believed a hot perfumed bath would relax her—make her feel drowsy.

Anyhow, later that same morning, around 7:30, we straggled out into the kitchen—my brother and me—still in bathrobes, Daddy already dressed to go to the newspaper, and we confronted Mama wrapping the poor dead wet puppies in paper toweling.

She obviously had drowned them in the bathtub.

"Jesus God, Cutsie," my father murmured. "Jesus God."

Mama just went on rolling up the little animals in the paper toweling, lining them up across the kitchen table as if they were Christmas gifts.

For a long moment Daddy stared at the puppies and at Mama, and then, grabbing up his briefcase and his homburg hat, he exited.

None of us mentioned this ugly incident. There were no re-criminations, no outbursts of any kind, but the image stays in my memory to this day: those dead puppies wrapped in paper toweling, and the expression on my father's face as he unsuccessfully tried to wipe it clean of all emotion. I remember his mouth trembled imperceptibly, his eyes grew so big I thought they might pop out of their sockets.

THERE were a great many problems facing the *New York Star*. One of them was Cardinal Spellman, then possibly the most powerful Catholic prelate in America. The *Star* was critical of Spellman's censorship activities and his support of Franco, and the cardinal retaliated by delivering a series of angry sermons against the paper from the pulpit of St. Patrick's; on one occasion he even kept the *Star* from being delivered the day it ran a proabortion editorial. On another occasion he kept certain Catholic department-store presidents from advertising in the *Star*.

Finally Daddy met briefly with Spellman and obtained a promise from him not to attack the paper from St. Patrick's again, and he hired a public-relations expert—an Irishman named Flynn—for the express purpose of soft-soaping the cardinal and put him in an office next to his, but the cardinal went on bad-mouthing the paper anyway.

There were other problems, too, like the cost of distribution. *PM* had always had its own drivers and trucks, and the *Star* inherited that costly situation. When Daddy and Barnes took over the paper, the Metropolitan News Distributing Company approached them and said they would be willing to distribute the *Star*. If that had happened, the savings would have run into thousands of dollars a week. And the paper would have reached twice the fifty-five hundred outlets the *Star* drivers could manage to hit each night. With their own drivers, the cost of picking up the "returns" was becoming prohibitive.

Leaders of the Newspaper and Mail Deliverers Union had agreed to the new plan, but the rank and file vetoed it, so Daddy and Barnes met with as many union members as they could, and they talked and they pleaded and they bargained, and Barnes worked out a plan whereby not a single *Star* driver would lose his job. But the union rank and file stood pat.

Their feeling: the *Star* was a small paper, but using Metropolitan Distribution could set a dangerous precedent. (If the *Daily News*, for instance, decided to use Metropolitan, it would have thrown many news drivers out of work.) In any event, the cost of the union's decision could not be calculated.

Then there was the fantastic expense of the UP Services (for delivering syndicated news). In 1940, Ingersoll had signed a ten-year contract on a sliding scale, which had two more years to go. (By the end of 1948, the UP would be receiving fifteen hundred dollars a week from the *Star*. "It was a bleeding sore on the economics and financing of this venture," Barnes would later write.)

And speaking of finances, Daddy had not been able to raise a dime to complete the purchase of the *Star*. Everybody was getting pretty edgy about it since he had promised that a contingent of American Zionists who'd supported his courageous stand promoting Israel was going to give him the money. It was turning out not to be the case. The *Star* didn't seem like a good business prospect. Luckily, Marshall Field (behind the scenes) was still very much in the financial picture; in fact, he loaned the *Star* all the money on which it operated; nobody knew this except Barnes, my father, and Leon Shimkin, Field's coldly calculating financial adviser who had just been appointed business manager for the *Star*, which made for a very tense situation.

In public, my father kept up his usual confident front. At a luncheon with *Time* magazine editors on June 28, he predicted that he and Joe Barnes would, in the next two weeks, "select from offers of three million dollars in working capital—we have already halved the *Star*'s staggering $15,000 weekly deficit."

During the luncheon he laid out some of the other plans they were putting into operation: a new Sunday magazine called *Pleasure*, edited by Dick Lauterbach; regular columns by liberal Max Lerner and left-winger I. F. Stone. George Welles, lately of *Newsweek*, would run the editorial page. Signed editorials were out. From now on the paper would speak for itself.

Daddy was particularly pleased about signing up cartoonists Bill Mauldin and Edmund Duffy, the three-time Pulitzer Prize winner who'd just left the *Baltimore Sun*. And Al Capp of "Li'l Abner" would be a consultant.

Once that summer my brother and I visited the *Star*'s offices, which were located in a dilapidated old building on Duane Street near the Hudson River. We were given a short tour around a huge, noisy city room, past reporters with green eye shades batting out stories on their typewriters or yelling into their phones. The floor was littered with what seemed like a million cigarette butts.

Before we left, Daddy ran out of a meeting to say hello. He seemed tired and preoccupied, but he still took us to meet Walt Kelly, the talented former Disney draftsman who was the *Star*'s new art director and would soon create "Pogo." We were shown some of his latest cartoons.

Daddy loved his work; he often would bring a discarded doodle home. One of them turned into a Kelly masterpiece—Tom Dewey, the Republican presidential candidate, as a mechanized man with a torso that could be either a cash register or a slot machine.

The presidential election was about to turn into the biggest news story of 1948. No other presidential election in this century has matched it for drama, suspense, and the effect of its improbable climax.

Republican Governor Thomas Dewey was riding the crest of huge popularity. President Harry S. Truman, a Democrat, was the wildly unpopular incumbent—all the polls said he would lose. And then there was Henry Wallace ("the Iowa yogi," Dashiell Hammett called him). Wallace would be running as the first candidate of the newly formed Progressive Party.

All the political conventions were held in Philadelphia in

July. It was the first time they had been covered by television. We didn't own a set, so Daddy took my brother and me to a bar (was it P. J. Clarke's?) around 11:00 A.M. to watch some of the proceedings of the Republican convention.

We couldn't see much—just some flickering images and a disembodied voice describing what was going on in Philadelphia's Municipal Auditorium. There were modest cheers at some point; apparently Dewey had a lead in pledged delegates.

Later I think we watched Clare Boothe Luce telling a cheering crowd that Harry Truman was a "gone goose."

"What baloney!" a voice shouted from somewhere in the depths of the tavern.

Behind the scenes there had been floor infighting; Dewey won the nomination by a landslide. Earl Warren would be his running mate. *Time* magazine commented, "The Dewey-Warren ticket cannot fail to sweep the Republicans back into power."

Daddy attended the Democratic convention on July 9, joining a large press contingent. He must have been in his element; he moved everywhere. As a publisher of the *New York Star* he even got in to talk to the president; otherwise he hung out with Dave Niles, still one of Truman's most trusted aides, who was lobbying delegates.

Subsequently, in a letter he wrote:

> Dear Cutsie—It is hot in Philly—everybody sweating like pigs. There is a floor fight going on led by a young mayor from Minneapolis. A guy named Hubert Humphrey—he just asked the platform to tick off what the Democratic Party stands for—civil rights—national health insurance—public housing . . . Speeches dragged on for hours. . . . Dixiecrats tried to get Sen. Richard Russell of Georgia nominated . . . midnight came and went . . . and at close to 2 A.M., Harry S. Truman (in a crisp white suit!) was finally nominated along with Alben Barkley for V.P.
>
> He started off by declaring "Senator Barkley and I will win this election and make the Republicans like it!" He sounded like a winner although everyone is predicting he will be beaten badly. What gets me is that in spite of this, there is admiration for this man, this underdog. He virtually trans-

formed this convention from what had seemed like a wake into a political rally. The crowd kept roaring . . . he spoke of the poor man, the farmer, he lambasted the Republicans for their representatives in Congress . . . then he did something unprecedented. He said, "We will call July 26th Turnip Day . . . because on that day, I'm gonna call Congress back into session and demand they pass some laws" . . . the Republicans are hopping mad about this. They say it is an abuse of presidential power. I think it is a challenge . . . I think it is great.

Daddy did not attend the Progressive Party convention, but as soon as he won the nomination, Henry Wallace invited my father to come up to his farm in South Salem, New York, for dinner and talk, and he tried to persuade him to get the *New York Star* to endorse him.

Steve Fisher, Wallace's aide, was at the meeting and recalls no mention of the Communist Party, but obviously the overriding issue was not Wallace's criticism of American foreign policy but the claim that the Progressive Party was dominated by Communists. Later Henry Wallace kept saying it wasn't true, although it *was* true, and my father was disgusted because he wouldn't admit it. He stood firm: the *Star* would not support Wallace.

After the dinner, both Paul Robeson and Jo Davidson came by the Seventy-second Street apartment trying to argue Daddy into changing his mind.

Late in the evening, Lillian Hellman appeared. She was heading the Women for Wallace Committee and she was furious at my father for not supporting Wallace. She admitted he didn't have a chance, but she thought the Progressive Party had a chance. "You change your spots too often, Bart," she told him and stormed out. Subsequently Daddy and Joe Barnes had a drink and they decided the *Star* would definitely come out for Truman.

For Cold War liberals, a vote for Truman over Wallace felt just right. Truman was tough on Russia and slightly liberal, but to the Progressives the endorsement was a terrible mistake—practically the entire left-wing readership of the *Star* left in droves. The mail protest was huge because the Progressives were sure that a vote for Truman was a vote for the Cold War.

The decision also caused an uproar in the *Star*'s city room, an uproar that never subsided—most of the reporters were pro Wallace.

Even so, the *Star*'s circulation increased slightly. Some readers seemed to enjoy the wildly different opinions that peppered the pages, from the likes of I. F. Stone and Max Lerner to Albert Deutsch and Alex Uhl.

For the *Star*, the worst result of the Truman endorsement was the loss of a big money source—the private fortune of Anita McCormick Blaine (heiress to the International Harvester fortune). Months later she would donate around $1 million to fund a newspaper called *The Compass*, which did support Wallace and the Progressive Party.

There were other sources Daddy wouldn't name at the time who refused to "come through with the dough." "The only guys who want to fund the *Star* are Communists," he said to me. He turned those offers down.

By mid-July, Marshall Field was furious because it was obvious Daddy had no money contacts, period.

Mama drew up a list of wealthy people they knew in San Francisco: the banker G. P. Giannini, Louise Bransten, the Zellerbachs. Daddy flew out to see them, but the response was negative. He also called Barney Balaban, head of Paramount, who'd donated so much money to UJA, but Balaban said no.

Back in New York there were meetings with Albert Lasker, William Benton, Henry Luce, and the Cowles brothers. No luck there, and when contacted, publisher Dolly Thackery Schiff said she already owned the *New York Post*. "Bart simply could not convince me the *Star* was a good investment," she told me.

What was hardest for my father to bear was that the money men he went to were so negative about the project. They would ask him, what reason does the *Star* have to exist? And—who cares about a left-wing tabloid that's never made a dime?

As for his friends, they didn't support him emotionally. He wasn't used to being called a "fool" or "naïve," but after taking on *PM*, he was called both almost every day by people he cared about. That was hard to take.

He tried to relax. He and Mama would weekend at Herbert Bayard Swope's estate on Long Island, or they would drive to

Broadway costume designer Ailine Bernstein's place in upstate New York.

Edla Cusick (Bernstein's daughter) recalls Daddy "being the center of attention at all of Mother's parties. Everybody asking him the same question about how could he possibly save the paper given the shameful political repressiveness of the times?

"And he would usually come up with some optimistic explanation. But he'd get agitated, he'd drink too much, he'd strain to be funny. Once he couldn't stand the questions and he excused himself in the middle of dinner—said he had to get back to New York."

Edla remembers watching him rush out the door. One of his shoes came off, "and I thought it was a sad looking shoe—it was all scuffed and down at the heel, laces broken . . . he didn't pick it up, but Cutsie did—very grandly. Then in total silence she marched out after him into the night."

CHAPTER
23

SOMETIME in July, my brother was shipped off to friends at Lake Tahoe and I was sent up to the Berkshire Playhouse. My father thought it would be nice if I had some "hands on" experience in the theater, so he arranged, with the help of his friend playwright Marc Connelly, to have me apprentice backstage.

For the next six weeks I lived in an old rooming house on Main Street in Stockbridge, Massachusetts, along with three other apprentices—two strapping ex-GIs and a willowy redhead named Phoebe. She wore gypsy clothes and was terribly affected; later in the summer, when she knew us better, she became frightfully bossy.

I had never been away from home before so I felt quite anxious. I tried very hard not to think about how much I missed my family or how worried I was about Daddy and the fate of the *New York Star.*

Nobody paid much attention to me at first. I was fifteen years old and the youngest apprentice at the theater—skinny, nails bitten to the quick, freckles dotting my face.

I'd chain-smoke and drink cups of strong black coffee to prove how grown up I was. Eventually, Phoebe and I struck up a kind of friendship; occasionally I'd be invited to beer parties she and the ex-GIs threw in the rooming-house living room some evenings. But mostly I was alone.

During the day, we all helped build scenery and hunted for props for the various shows, or we would run errands for Leo

Lavandero, the volatile director of the Berkshire Playhouse. He was from San Juan, Puerto Rico, and his accent was so thick sometimes I could hardly understand what he was saying, but his enthusiasm about theater was catching.

At night, I was given the task of running around knocking on dressing-room doors and calling out, "Places!" Then I'd stand in the wings and watch the actors make their entrances. A few of them seemed actually transformed as soon as they walked out onstage. Two hours later I'd see these same actors taking their bows, sweating, relieved to return to their paler (truer?) selves.

Daddy kept telling me my destiny was in the theater. But was that what I really wanted to do? My heart was in my throat when I performed.

I actually preferred being by myself, scribbling in a notebook. Even in my pretend dressing room at Aptos, I would spend most of my time reading and dreaming. I was not a born performer, although I wouldn't know that until I actually began to act. I really didn't enjoy being stared at—it made me uncomfortable.

Every so often, standing in the wings, I would suddenly think of my father, crusading for Willkie or writing a book or defending the Hollywood Ten, making speeches, and now running a newspaper. Was he performing? Was he playing roles, too? Was he trying on different masks to see which one fit best? And did any of them bring him closer to his sense of self?

I didn't know.

Near the end of summer, I acted in a curtain raiser.

I don't remember the play, but when I walked out onstage for the first time of my life, it was as if I were in a dream. The lights blinded me. I felt almost giddy with nerves. I could see a blur of pink faces gazing up at me. My throat got very sore.

I had, at the most, three lines. I said them, although I couldn't hear what I said.

When the curtain came down and I went back to my dressing room, the stage manager scolded me for not picking up my cues.

The phone was ringing in the downstairs hall of the boarding-house when I got in. It was my father calling from the newspaper, asking how my performance had gone. "It's your opening night," he said.

I tried to tell him it was okay—I couldn't tell him how depressed I was. He kept saying, "This is the beginning for you, my darling!"

What I really wanted to talk about was him and Mama and what they were doing; I wanted to talk about missing California, missing our garden, and ask him, would we ever go back to Aptos?

But I just listened as he assured me that "all is well," and oh, did I know that Bart had caught a fish at Lake Tahoe?

He added that he was having a late-night discussion in his office "with Leon Shimkin, so say a prayer for me, baby," and then he added, "I gotta hang up," and he did, and I burst into tears.

Mama had already written me about Leon Shimkin (or "Shit-kin," as Daddy and others on the newspaper called him behind his back). Shimkin was Daddy's "bête noire," Mama kept saying, whatever that meant, but it didn't sound good. Daddy always acted nervous when he mentioned him.

Leon Shimkin was the *Star*'s business manager, but nobody liked him. Everybody was afraid of him because he was smart— "mind like a steel trap"; he was a step ahead of everybody, financially speaking. He always had an answer.

Shimkin was considered the genius behind Simon and Schuster and Pocket Books (his creation). He had a background in accounting ("he could make figures dance and multiply," someone said). Indeed, he had started as a bookkeeper at Simon and Schuster. He had been hired by Marshall Field and was one of his closest financial advisers—in fact, he had advised Field to buy Simon and Schuster—but he had never believed in *PM*.

"No profit, all loss," he said.

He had absolutely no sympathy with the difficulties my father was having raising money. And he showed it (according to my mother), treating him with a mixture of condescension and contempt (which Daddy tried to ignore). Shimkin had no patience either with his naïveté or his idealism.

"Bart should never have promised Marshall Field he could come up with the financial backing for the *Star* if he couldn't. *I* ran the paper on a day-to-day basis," Shimkin told me bluntly years afterward. "Your father was never around."

Originally Marshall Field had envisioned Shimkin as a sort of superadviser to Barnes and my father, but since Daddy was so frequently away trying to raise money, Shimkin quickly took over the management of the paper—hiring and firing, cutting salaries. He delegated responsibilities to young reporters who had no experience with the business problems of the paper.

As a result, he and my father had a tense relationship. They would run into each other in the city room periodically and Shimkin would buttonhole him. "So, where's the money, Bart?" he would ask, and Daddy would answer quietly, *"Pace, pace,* Leon —I'm really trying," and Shimkin would mutter something like, "Excuses, excuses . . ."

Years later, Shimkin would tell me, "Your father knew nothing about the business end of running a newspaper—production problems, circulation problems."

Actually, Shimkin didn't know anything about running a newspaper either, or its frantic tempo, which differed radically from the leisurely pace of a publishing house. But he *did* understand money—and budgets, and Wall Street strategies, and loans, and stockholders, and stockholding. Daddy was hopeless in that area—he always had been.

IN September, after four months of Daddy's failure at fund-raising, it became clear that something drastic had to be done or the paper would fold immediately. Staff morale was sinking; the politics and union problems were equally difficult. "It was like a three-ring circus," my father's secretary, Pauline Leet, recalled. "We existed day-to-day—there were problems everywhere."

Joe Barnes, the brilliant and highly regarded editor who had imagined his job to be that of revising and improving the *Star*'s contents, now began to take on a more active role in management.

In September the *Star* began putting out a bulldog edition, in an effort to tap into the huge premidnight sales market. It was a move made more out of desperation than calculation, and was based on the fact that the *News* and the *Mirror* each sold one hundred thousand copies between 8:00 P.M. and midnight.

But the *Star*'s bulldog edition never sold more than ten thousand copies. Since there was virtually no promotion in back of it, it had no chance to affect the *Star*'s sales. But production and circulation costs rose.

Barnes and Daddy kept pushing to switch to indirect distribution through Metropolitan News, which handled the *Times* and the

Tribune. It became a major factor in the last months, when it turned into a cornerstone of the final money-raising efforts. All sorts of extravagant claims were made for the beneficial effects the move would produce, ranging from huge cost savings to a large increase in sales as a result of reaching more outlets.

At this point the *Star* was sold at only forty-five hundred newsstands; the news-company distribution might have placed it at an additional twenty-five hundred. In any case, the clause in an old *PM* contract with the deliverers' union barred a change in the methods of distribution.

At the same time Daddy came up with a variety of editorial ideas designed to beef up circulation and uphold the *Star*'s (aka *PM*'s) tradition of different, biased voices.

He got Lillian Hellman to write a series of reports on Eastern Europe, describing her talk with Tito of Yugoslavia. She had been in Belgrade, where *The Little Foxes* had been performed.

And Daddy flew to Israel with Gerold Frank and wrote a week of bylined accounts of what was happening in Jerusalem and Tel Aviv; he spoke to Chaim Weizmann and David Ben-Gurion. He was the last person to interview Count Folke Bernadotte, who mediated truce negotiations in the Arab-Israeli War.

The *Star*'s circulation shot up briefly the day Bernadotte was assassinated by a right-wing Jewish terrorist group since Daddy had spoken to him only hours before.

But even news breaks like that didn't help the *Star* much.

MY return home coincided with an impromptu meeting Daddy was having in our borrowed apartment on East Seventy-second Street with Alger Hiss. I remember opening the door and seeing the tall, austere former State Department official sitting tensely in an armchair. I recognized him from newspaper photographs; he was all over the headlines as a Communist spy.

Daddy introduced me as "his darling daughter just back from summer stock." Hiss did not respond. I excused myself and dragged my suitcases back to my room.

Afterward I learned that Daddy and Joe Barnes, who subsequently dropped by, were trying to persuade Hiss to give his story exclusively to the *New York Star*. He was reluctant; he didn't want to become "the *Star*'s Scottsboro Boy," he said. If he gave the story to anyone, he would give it to *The New York Times*.

Ultimately, for the American public, the great terminating event of the 1940s would be the Hiss-Chambers case. Whittaker Chambers, a former *Time* magazine editor, who was an overweight depressive with appallingly bad teeth, had confessed to spying for Russia, and he'd accused Alger Hiss of being a Communist and sneaking government documents to the Soviets. Hiss, a former Roosevelt aide at Yalta and an architect of the United Nations, denied both charges and sued Chambers for libel.

A sensational investigation followed; the case would eventually be transformed from a matter of Communist infiltration to one caught up in the dreary world of espionage.

Daddy wished that the *Star* could cover the story properly (as a tabloid there simply wasn't the space). He kept notes on it in his unpublished autobiography. He was always worried that if Hiss was convicted (which he was), this would establish the "Communist conspiracy" theory that lurked behind the New Deal era.

BY the fall, the *Star*'s editorial expenses rose sharply as efforts were made to improve the quality of the paper; that coupled with a guild increase sent the deficits up to almost $230,000 a week.

By mid-October, Shimkin concocted his grandest scheme of all—the launching of a huge book-promotion drive. After a long meeting with my father, Barnes, and the board of directors, he entered into negotiations with Unicorn Press for an encyclopedia deal; it was an extremely complicated arrangement in which both the *Star* and Unicorn would take a gamble on the increased circulation that could result from the promotion of the encyclopedias (this included seventy-five thousand dollars for advertising the sale of the books).

Some ninety thousand people clipped the first coupon (including my brother and me). We were then entitled to the first ten volumes. (I remember when we received them Mama's first words were "Oh, God, how tacky they look—we can't put them with the other books in our library!")

Largely as a result of the encyclopedia deal, the *Star*'s circulation rose to 132,000 in the final quarter of 1948.

And of course Daddy was still trying to raise money and still having no luck. Throughout the month of October he traveled to Washington, Chicago, Boston, New Orleans—with no positive results. The main problem was that he had no access to major American fortunes, nor did he have the clout he thought he had with Jewish groups, Seventh Avenue, and the movie business.

The most intriguing idea to save the *Star* was to turn it over to the CIO. This had been discussed in the mid-1940s when Ralph Ingersoll was publisher and he had approached labor leaders like Walter Reuther. It would have involved doubling the paper's circulation through a CIO subscription drive and it had projected a rosy future through advertising; it could have made the paper self-sustaining.

Daddy met with David Dubinsky and Jack Petrosky and asked them to help organize the *Star*—turn the *Star* into a labor newspaper. They said no and so did Harry Bridges when Daddy tried to open discussions with him and other labor leaders in California.

On the rare occasions he was home, Daddy seemed drained and preoccupied. He had so much to do (he was still handing some law cases), he didn't even have time to go to the barber. I remember one night very late I saw him slumped in Mama's dressing room while she trimmed his hair. He was staring blindly at his reflection in the mirror; he looked old and ill.

But he seemed to rally. He would give a speech for Israel at Madison Square Garden and he would tell Mama that being in front of an audience was "better than having an orgasm." He was writing a lot, too—book reviews and essays for *The Nation* and *The New Republic*.

Reporter Gerold Frank would drop by the apartment to help edit. Once I came upon them in the living room, and he was saying something like, "I'll get the rest of the stuff to you by tomorrow morning," and Daddy, nodding, replied, "Gee, thanks—it would be impossible without you."

It dawned on me that Gerold might actually be writing Daddy's articles and reviews. Had he also ghosted Daddy's book? I felt a stab of disappointment and confusion over the deception; the byline was always "Bartley Crum." Why would he want to fool anybody?

Actually, he always acknowledged Gerold's help; he would tell me, "My darling, I simply don't have the time. We do the interviewing together, we discuss what will be in the piece, then he whips it into shape. Does that upset you?"

I assured him that I understood perfectly. But the idea that my father couldn't do *everything* was unsettling to me. It was just another tiny incident that served to chip cracks in the shining armor of his superhuman image.

IN the midst of all this, we moved. Shortly before election day, we went from our borrowed apartment into an elegant town house on East Fifty-first Street off Second Avenue.

I connect part of my adolescence with that house—I remember dancing by myself in the living room to *Kiss Me, Kate* show tunes. I remember necking passionately on the rug with a boy named Johnny Hutton. I remember the garden in the back, so beautifully manicured. I remember Mama referring to the house always as "the Brian Aherne house," because the actor Brian Aherne indeed owned it.

From the outside it was—still is—a rather undistinguished-looking building, four stories, although it appeared deceptively small, the façade thickly covered with ivy. While we were living there, movie companies were constantly asking us if they could use the place for filming, perhaps because the rooms were so grand and there were mirrors everywhere—antique mirrors covering the foyer and the walls and ceiling of the dining room, so I could see my face from any angle.

I. M. Pei had remodeled the second floor's interior, opening up the two front parlors and turning it into one enormous forty-foot room lit by a sparkling crystal chandelier.

It was such a beautiful house, and yet in retrospect I associate it with near death and persecution. During the first weeks we lived there we discovered our phones were being tapped by the FBI. Hate mail started being delivered again; this time the letters accused Bartley Crum of being part of the great Communist conspiracy.

Anyhow, we moved. "What a production!" Daddy would exclaim, although he wasn't around for most of it. He remained at the newspaper and we were in school, but we reached our home in time late that afternoon to see most of our worldly goods—shipped from California at enormous expense—being heaved through the front windows: couches, pillows, etchings, paintings, candelabra, the spinet piano. There was a lot of groaning and cursing from the movers.

Obviously there was too much furniture—too many "things" (some of which had to be relegated to a back hall). The Renaissance desk and a profusion of brass-based lamps, chests of drawers, and a mammoth coffee table made it to the living room. But Mama's specially made silk bed had to be taken apart and carried piece by piece to the third floor.

It took my brother and me several days to put all the books —close to two thousand of them—onto the shelves on either side of the living room. It took us even longer to unwrap the china and glassware, the pitchers of all sizes, the dozens of tiny espresso cups, the bowls, the trays, the big wooden carving board Grandpa had used to display his roast geese, his wild rabbit.

Meanwhile, painters were slapping lemon-yellow paint on the walls of the kitchen and pantry and servants' quarters. (Our chauffeur, Robert, and his wife, our cook, Bernice, would be arriving from San Francisco soon; they were driving our station wagon across the country laden down with more possessions from the Green Street house.)

On election day Mama and Daddy rose at dawn and voted, he for Truman, she for Dewey. We stayed home from school to complete the unpacking. By dinnertime we'd placed the last of the gold-flecked crystal ashtrays on various side tables while the radio blared out the first scattered returns.

Around 10:00 P.M. H. V. Kaltenborn announced that Truman was ahead by twelve hundred votes. Now Daddy was home; he started coughing. He plopped down on the couch, reminding us that two nights before he'd visited the presidential suite at the Biltmore Hotel and found Truman standing in the shower insisting he was going to sweep the country. A few minutes later Daddy left the suite, roaring with laughter, and he ran into A. J. Liebling in the lobby. "The old boy is crazy," he said. "He thinks he's going to win!"

Liebling laughed along with my father and then wrote later in *The New Yorker,* "If, guided by some mystic light, Bart Crum had

believed and ordered the *Star* to headline that flat unique predic-
tion that the President would win, he would have sold more rather
than less papers during the days remaining before the election,
and after the election the *Star* would have been famous from coast
to coast. . . . Crum was rooting for Truman, but he didn't believe
that feedbox tip."

Of course, Truman *did* win the election; it was the upset
victory to end all victories, and when we found out in the early
morning, Daddy raced down to the *Star.*

In the days that followed, he had the paper play up the fact
that the *Star* had supported the winner. He sent at least five telegrams to the White House pleading for some acknowledgment.

On November 6, Truman sent the following note, which ran
on the front page of the *Star:*

> My dear Bartley—
>
> I am deeply indebted to you personally and to the *New
> York Star* for its support of me in the campaign; all the more
> so because of the opposition of such a large part of the Ameri-
> can press. Your championship of the causes we jointly believe
> in was heartening to me throughout the campaign.
>
> Very sincerely yours,
HARRY TRUMAN

Daddy arranged to have the letter blown up to poster size and
plastered it on every *Star* delivery truck. But even then the letter
didn't do much good for the paper.

IN late November twenty-five-year-old Harvard graduate Blair
Clark, who had worked briefly for the *St. Louis Post-Dispatch*,
replaced Leon Shimkin as business manager. Clark recalled: "It
happened very fast. After I left the *Post-Dispatch* Ben Bradlee and
I started a little Sunday newspaper in New Hampshire that was
quite successful. Dick Lauterbach read a couple of issues and
showed them to Marshall Field; we had a meeting and Field asked
me to replace Shimkin and write an assessment of why the *Star*
was failing and what could be done to save it. Suddenly there I
was at a big New York daily. I was excited about being part of what
I assumed was a really professional operation. I had a lot of ideas.

But as soon as I started researching the problems I could see it was too late to do anything. The *Star* was a mess. Morale was down to zero. There was no money and no prospects for money. Poor Bart Crum had run himself ragged trying to raise capital for eight months. He had been completely unsuccessful."

Clark said he liked my father, but found he was "sort of out of his depth. He'd been a big lawyer in California; he knew everybody there, but in New York, he was just another little fish swimming in a shark-infested pond. He had absolutely no support anywhere—from the Wall Street community, from the business or advertising communities; he had no old-boy network to call on. It was an impossible battle.

"He'd exaggerated the support he thought he would get from the Jewish community. Being pro-Israel was fine, but the *Star* was not a viable commercial venture. It was a money-losing left-wing paper—who needed that? The men he spoke to were looking to profits."

Mama noted in her journal: "Bart is beside himself. Marshall will not return his calls. Ruthie Field [Marshall Field's wife] does speak to him periodically, but that is not the same thing. Bart keeps saying 'I must have called Marshall a hundred times by now . . .' That bothers him enormously . . . it is such a rejection . . . he told me 'if only I could speak to him, I know I could convince him to give us more dough.'"

Daddy kept hoping that Field Enterprises, started in 1944 for the avowed purpose of generating enough profits to keep afloat both the *Star* and other pioneering ventures, would infuse the paper with more capital. Finally, Daddy asked Louis Weiss, Field's attorney, if Field Enterprises could help. He said no.

Field was a businessman more than he was a philanthropist. He felt that his liberalism had been sorely tried. "Anyone can back a liberal project if he has enough money," he wrote, "but to survive the project must prove itself to be independent financially."

As it was, Field lent the *Star* all its operating capital, $672,190. Shimkin had invested $150,000, and my father and Joe Barnes $10,000 apiece.

The only money Daddy raised was inadvertent. At some point

a junk dealer from Maryland appeared in his office and plunked down a check for $20,000. He disappeared before anyone could thank him.

On Christmas Eve we received a brace of pheasant from Caumsett, Marshall Field's seventeen-hundred-acre estate on Long Island, with a card wishing us happy holidays. But Daddy could still not get him on the phone.

A final effort to save the paper was made throughout the month of January. A banker named Paul Buckley said he'd try to raise funds from friends, but that failed.

Daddy even asked Glenn McCarthy, the oil tycoon from Dallas, to reconsider (McCarthy had been briefly interested the past summer). He took McCarthy on a tour of the paper. Blair Clark met him, so did Joe Barnes, but the tycoon had no interest in investing in a liberal newspaper; he wanted a newspaper that would express his ideas and beliefs, which were, to put it mildly, conservative.

On January 27, 1949, the *Star*'s 408 employees—100 of them editorial workers—crowded into the city room for a hastily called meeting. My father came out of his office and hoisted himself on top of a desk. "I'm sorry to have something to say I regret very much saying—tonight's issue will be our last. We made every effort to raise capital and get this paper refinanced but it is just not possible." When he jumped down from the desk, Joe Barnes, flushed and close to tears, thanked his staff of reporters.

Everyone went through the motions of getting out the two final editions. In the composing room printers set up the front-page box bearing a curt farewell. As had happened too often, readers had to turn to other papers to get the complete story. The *Star* did not carry the full account of its own death.

When Daddy returned from the newspaper that evening he seemed flustered and exhausted. We were waiting for him in the living room, expecting him to tell us what had happened. But he said nothing; he ran upstairs to Mama's bedroom and shut the door.

The phone was ringing a lot: Paul Smith and John Neylan calling from San Francisco; Dolly Thackery and A. J. Liebling from New York. I said Daddy would get back to them. But he didn't; he stayed closeted with Mama half the night rehashing the past nine months. My brother and I heard them walking around her bedroom; occasionally voices were raised, then silence.

From Mama's journal: "Bart has never experienced such a personal public failure and it is eating him up. He feels humiliated, he feels defeated by it. He blames himself for everything that resulted in the *Star*'s folding. The bad management; inability to raise money. He feels particularly responsible for the hundreds of reporters and editors who are now out of work. He repeated over and over again 'What did I do wrong? What did I do wrong?' Then around 4 A.M. he stopped pacing and began to sob. 'I want my mother,' he cried. 'I want my mother.' " But the following morning he appeared to have recovered. He prepared breakfast for my brother and me and he started phoning some of his friends to joke about his "lousy luck." He made some lunch dates, scheduled cocktail meetings.

His mood darkened when Joe Alsop called to gloat. "I told you the *Star* couldn't last. You owe me five hundred bucks."

Daddy refused to pay him and Alsop never spoke to him again.

That afternoon Daddy flew to Chicago to speak to the Independent Voters of Illinois. Serrill Hillman of *Time* caught up with him at the Ambassador East, where he was staying, and interviewed him about the closing of the *Star.*

The newspaper had been doomed, my father admitted.

Why had he risked his career? For what reason?

" 'Because like every guy I know, I wanted to run a newspaper. I actually thought I could put out the ideal newspaper and given enough time maybe I could.' "

He went on to say the real reason the *Star* folded was everybody believed it was a "Red" paper, a Communist paper, " 'which was not true but we could not wipe out that taint. That in the end killed us. That and the vicious smears by guys like Westbrook Pegler. And the trades treated us savagely too. There was a very hostile attitude about *PM*—from the news dealers—the other newspapers even—nobody wanted us to succeed, that's for sure. We were too opposite, too quirky.' "

He felt they had " 'blundered into the tough morning field and the presses were limited in capacity. We could only print forty-four pages and three hundred thousand copies a day without getting into trouble. Suppose we had fifty pages of ads—we couldn't have got an inch of news into the *Star*. Another limitation. The limitation that the tabloid makes—which we recognized after we got into it. We could give the impression of truth, but we could never give you the entire story—we did not have the space. And yet, within those limitations, we were beginning to do a fairly effective job.' " He admitted being " 'pretty cut up about the *Star's* death.' "

What were his plans? He expected he would open up his own law firm in New York but nothing had been decided yet. He would take his time.

Would he see Marshall Field before he left Chicago?

" 'What in hell would I see him for?' " my father snapped. " 'Joe Barnes and I own the paper, Field had twenty-five percent of the stock.' "

Did he feel optimistic about his future?

" 'I'm Irish. The goddamn Irish are so optimistic always, aren't they?' "

Sometime in early February my father attempted suicide for the first time.

PART FIVE

CHAPTER

24

I THINK it was around 3:00 A.M. on February 9, 1949, when I was awakened by a thud that seemed to have come from the kitchen four flights below in our brownstone. This was followed by a scuffling of feet, voices raised, a phone ringing.

My brother and I had adjoining rooms; we ran out into the hall at the same time, and clutched each other. After whispering nervously we decided to investigate. We moved slowly, however; we were both extremely scared. Yanking on our robes we crept down the stairs barefoot in time to see Daddy being carried out the front door, strapped and inert on a stretcher. Mama followed, wrapped in her mink coat. She was smearing lipstick across her mouth.

We remained huddled in the back of the downstairs hall; a blast of icy wind enveloped us. There was a smell of snow in the air. Daddy was pushed into the back of a waiting ambulance. We couldn't tell whether he was dead or alive.

Mama climbed in after him. I noticed she was wearing her pink satin mules.

After the ambulance drove away, sirens wailing, our servants —Bernice and her husband, Robert—closed the front door and guided us into the warmth of the kitchen.

There was broken glass on the floor, so Bernice began sweeping it up. "Your dad was drinking some milk," she started to explain. "Then he fell down . . . passed out . . . I dunno." Her beautiful dusky face was impassive. "You children better go to bed now."

Bart and I refused to move.

"Well . . ." Bernice glanced at Robert, who finally explained, "Your father, he took a lot of pills . . . an overdose."

"Will he be all right?"

No answer. They seemed to have nothing more to say, so we straggled out of the kitchen and up into our huge, shadowy living room on the second floor.

Dawn was breaking. I could make out familiar objects: the globe of the world we had traced Daddy's many adventures on; the polished chess table where he occasionally played games with my brother. I breathed in a scent of flowers—crushed, dying petals, overripe. Mama had given a dinner party the night before and she had placed crystal vases of roses and daisies all over the room.

Slumping down on one of the big white couches, we fell into a brooding silence. We could not—would not—voice the obvious. Was it possible that our father would die? And worse, did he want to die?

We knew he had been extremely depressed since the *Star* folded, even though he tried to joke about it—his "disaster," his "monumental failure." He kept assuring us he enjoyed being "at liberty," as he put it, and as if to prove it he had taken us on what he called "theater binges." In the last week we must have seen every hit show on Broadway: *The Member of the Wedding, Gentlemen Prefer Blondes, Regina*—Marc Blitzstein's opera of Lillian Hellman's classic *The Little Foxes.*

I remember how determined Daddy was for us to have a good time. Only when the show was over and we walked out into the street to watch him hail a cab did I sense he was in some kind of terrible manic despair, because he would rush out into the traffic, literally risking his life—waving his arms, whistling, calling out, "Taxi, taxi," trying to make sure we could escape into a cab immediately.

AT first we weren't told much; we had to glean information from the servants. Eventually we learned that Daddy was at Memorial Hospital being treated by Dr. Frederic Wertham, who was trying to wean him off both liquor and pills.

We kept asking to see him. Mama kept telling us he couldn't have visitors. She was trying to protect us from observing anything unpleasant. Only she would witness him sobbing on the toilet in acute anxiety as he went into withdrawal.

Meanwhile, between ourselves, my brother and I tried to figure out whether or not our father *wanted* to take his own life. I argued that the Church made it very clear that suicide was a mortal sin. In fact, it could be the shortest route to hell. Daddy was risking eternal damnation.

So, I concluded, he really did *make a mistake.* He had taken those pills by mistake. I was sure of it.

But Bart didn't quite agree with me. Suicide would be a solution, he said, and he quoted from the Greeks—from Plato, who was a favorite of Daddy's—something about the idea that suicide could be justified when and if the circumstances could not be tolerated.

After he had been suffering through withdrawal for about a week, Daddy turned paranoid and banned Mama from the hospital, but he did keep in touch by phone. She tried to convince him he should meet with Dr. Gregory Zilboorg, an expert on suicide, who had helped Lillian Hellman cut down on her heavy drinking.

Daddy refused, but he did speak with Dr. Robert Lindner (the much-publicized author of *The Fifty-Minute Hour*) since Lindner wasn't interested in his addictions but in his "risk-taking character."

However, their conversation went nowhere; Daddy had little use for psychiatry: "Reminds me of confession without the transcendence," he used to say.

He kept insisting he could fight the pills alone. He was going "cold turkey"—he would be off Seconals forever, he would vow to Mama when she called.

But one afternoon while she was at a luncheon on Long Island, Daddy phoned our servant Robert at the brownstone and asked him to bring him some "vitamins" he had stashed in the kitchen skylight.

Robert did so without looking at the label on the bottle, and Daddy gulped down the entire contents before it was discovered that the "vitamins" were actually Nembutals.

His stomach was pumped out just in time.

In the next weeks, we could hear Mama banging away at her typewriter at all hours of the day and night. We couldn't help laughing when Bernice explained that it was good for Mama to hit the machine like that "cuz she is knockin' the worry right out of her."

Otherwise, she behaved as if she didn't have a care in the world. She held to her usual routine of exercise classes and weekly hair appointments. Our meals were served by candlelight, and she kept up a steady stream of conversation—what was going on at the ballet; the grave diggers' strike; the fact that the United Nations building being built near us by the East River would be constructed entirely of glass.

Every so often the phone would ring for Daddy and she would answer it and lie, "Oh, he has the most terrible flu—and on top of that his back is out—but I'll tell him you called."

Listening to her I'd think, what an example of poise and reticence and gallantry. She never breathed a word to anyone about Daddy's ordeal—not even to his mother, Mo, in Sacramento.

On weekends she would take us to movies or to the theater, and she even allowed me to organize a "make-out" party for my schoolmates so we could lie in the darkness of the living room and neck with our various crushes while songs like "Some Enchanted Evening" streamed through the air.

Somehow we managed to go on with our lives.

My brother, Bart, was relatively happy at Collegiate and was doing well. I was at Chapin and feeling quite lost in spite of my ability to have more dates (I thought) than anyone else in my class. I suffered from feelings of inferiority because as soon as I had arrived at the school, I'd been tested and put in the "C" sections of my grade, except for English comp. C was for those who scored lowest scholastically.

Of course, Daddy's suicide attempt threw me into a panic. When he was at home, he would drop everything to hear me out, and he would shower me with extravagant compliments about my looks and my talent.

This attention would usually buoy me up, but it would make me anxious, too—I was always afraid I'd never live up to his grandiose expectations.

I had torturous dreams of running down the stairs to hug him when he came home from the hospital and cling to his leg only to find that the leg was nonexistent, that, indeed, the figure in the pin-striped suit had neither flesh nor bone.

Waking up I would convince myself all over again that the overdoses were a mistake, and that he would survive—and that to believe less in what I thought was his superhuman strength would diminish *me*.

My father was part of my emerging identity, and the way I idealized and romanticized him was part of what I was becoming, too.

I told only my brother of my terrible dreams, and he assured me Daddy would live. "He has too much he wants to do," he said matter-of-factly. But then he added, "At least I *think* he does."

Daddy returned home sometime in March. He did not mention he had ever been in the hospital, and we didn't ask questions. We were just glad he was alive.

He did seem a little knocked out. When he thought we weren't paying attention his face would go utterly slack and I got a terrible premonition of what he might look like when he died.

For the rest of that spring he remained mostly in the brownstone. He would rise very early to study for his New York bar exams. We would pass him at work in the living room, and as soon as he saw us he would run downstairs and prepare breakfast for us before we went off to school.

Sometimes our servants stayed in their little room off the kitchen; they knew Daddy liked to cook. Sometimes they would join us at the table and Daddy would pour them coffee. He treated them like members of the family.

We found ourselves watching him carefully for any sign that might indicate he was back on pills. His deeply scarred hands were a good barometer. In the past when he had fallen asleep drugged, he'd invariably be holding a cigarette between his fingers. The cigarette often burned down to the tip, but he would be so out of it he would not feel the pain. Since his return from the hospital there were no fresh burn welts or scars.

So we would breathe more easily, and eat the scrambled eggs and bacon he had prepared for us, and the biscuits he had baked.

While we were eating, we'd attempt to discuss the news events of the day. The *Times,* the *News,* the *Mirror, The Wall*

Street Journal, were already strewn about. Daddy was a newspaper junkie—underlining columns, tearing out stories. He would compose letters to the editor at the slightest provocation.

He was following the espionage trial of Judith Coplon, a ditzy Justice Department employee who had passed information about FBI political intelligence to a friend in the Soviet embassy. The Lawyers Guild was investigating the FBI's role in the case. Government evidence included twenty-eight FBI reports.

The Coplon arrest in March coincided with both the Smith Act trial of the eleven American Communist leaders and the Alger Hiss perjury trial.

For a while, cartoonist Abner Dean—whose drawings were filled with naked, anxious people, and who lived down the block —would come by in the mornings to argue about Hiss. The idea that Hiss could have passed classified State Department documents to Whittaker Chambers, a confessed Soviet courier, seemed wildly implausible to my father. But Abner thought Hiss was guilty, and he usually ended up accusing Daddy of being a former Popular Fronter who should confront his own delusions.

The only thing they both agreed on was Alistair Cooke's assessment of the case in *The New Republic.* Cooke wrote that Hiss and Chambers were both idealistic at a time when the nature of loyalty was changing profoundly—loyalty to one's friends, one's family, one's country. As a result, an entire generation was on trial, and the political beliefs of the last twenty years were going to have to be reinterpreted.

And all the while Daddy would be fixing Mama's breakfast tray, carefully arranging the grapefruit—halved, in a bed of ice— along with unbuttered whole wheat toast and café au lait. He'd carry the tray upstairs, leaving Abner Dean to call after him: "Hiding behind Cutsie's apron strings, huh?"

And then he would glance at my brother and me; we'd been sitting at the kitchen table, listening to the argument. He would grin and light a cigarette. "We're just playing," he'd say lazily.

Abner and his wife, Eleanor, were my parents' closest friends in New York. They used to come by and have dinner at least once a week. They all laughed a lot together and that seemed important.

Eleanor was a vice president of the David Ogilvy advertising agency—she had something to do with the Schwepps account. "Very powerful lady," Daddy said.

I couldn't quite believe it because she seemed so soft and blond and feminine. "She is *tough*," Abner would insist. "Almost as tough as your mother." He was often antagonistic about women, but Mama and Eleanor were able to handle him. I had never seen behavior quite like that because Daddy was usually genial and polite; Abner wasn't.

"Take that cigar out of your mouth, darling," he would tell his wife when she'd run on about something. And she would stop. But a few years later they split in a bitter divorce because Eleanor fell in love with another man. Mama said she wasn't the least bit surprised.

TOWARD the end of May, Daddy found a place for himself at the firm of Poletti, Diamond and Roosevelt, which had corporate offices on Madison Avenue and in Geneva, Switzerland. They wanted somebody "glamorous and famous who could bring in rich Jewish clients." Daddy seemed ideal because of his ties to Israel.

He was intrigued by his new partners. Charlie Poletti had been lieutenant governor of New York under Herbert Lehman; during the war he'd had a big post in Italy and as a result he had connections in Europe. As for FDR junior, he had just won the election as a congressman in New York's Twentieth Congressional District. So joining the firm could be a way of Daddy moving into New York politics.

He began networking for clients and also went back to work on the Hollywood Ten appeals; at the same time he attempted to coauthor a book called *Government by Suspicion* with his old law-school professor Max Radin. They hoped to show how the FBI and the Communist Party—both secret organizations—were trying to destroy democracy by democratic means.

As far as I know they completed only one chapter because later that year Max was fired from his job at the University of California at Berkeley for refusing to sign the loyalty oath. Afterward he was afraid to continue with the book.

Daddy didn't tell us that the FBI had increased its surveillance on him. Recently the *Herald Tribune* had published the 1949 report on the House Un-American Activities Committee, which

listed hundreds of people as Communist appeasers or fellow travelers—Daddy's name was among them.

We were having trouble with our phones again, too. We were
never sure it was because of Daddy's continued involvement with
the Lawyers Guild (which was about to prepare a report on the
FBI's illegal use of wiretapping) or because he was still helping to
defend the Hollywood Ten.

Maybe because of this he had little patience with my behavior
at Chapin. I kept breaking the rules. I could not seem to complete
a sentence, let alone my homework.

My brother blamed what he called my "idiotic state" on
Montgomery Clift. I was madly in love with Clift, then the hottest
young actor in America. His brooding handsome face was on the
cover of *Life* magazine; I papered my bedroom walls with that
image and I would cut classes to sit through his two latest movies
over and over again: the western *Red River*—in which he played
cowboy Matt Garth, who believes in justice, not violence, and who
gets beaten to a bloody pulp by John Wayne as a result—and Fred
Zinnemann's *The Search*. In the latter picture, Monty's performance as the laconic gum-chewing soldier who rehabilitates a lost
refugee child had just won him an Oscar nomination.

His appeal was such that when the camera zeroed in on him,
something intangible happened—what appeared on the screen
was not just a splendid watchful face or style but a complex,
mysterious presence, full of depth, indisputably alive. And he had
a sense of sexual ambiguity in his expression that was almost
palpable.

Then one afternoon I came home from school to find Montgomery Clift sprawled on the living room floor, talking nonstop to
my father. I could not believe it. I felt as if I were riding in a
too-fast elevator.

We were introduced. Monty jumped to his feet and stared at
me with a mixture of sympathy and curiosity. His eyes glittered
under thick black brows.

I was so flustered, I bobbed a curtsy. Hooting with laughter,
Montgomery Clift bobbed a curtsy back.

Then he went back to his conversation with my father.

I had never met a man who asked so many questions or
smoked so many cigarettes—even more than Daddy. When he left,

the ashtrays were overflowing. I filched one of Monty's butts—I have it still in an old diary of mine.

I saw Montgomery Clift quite often after that. He lived near us in the East Fifties, and he would usually drop by around cocktail time, always clad in rumpled chinos and a not-too-clean white shirt. There was often a stubble of beard on his chin.

Once we had dinner with him at Mario's, an Italian restaurant on East Fifty-second. David O. Selznick and Jennifer Jones joined us.

I remember during the meal Monty began stuffing food into his mouth with his hands. It was disgusting, but nobody said anything and then he stopped.

And then he disappeared to California to make *A Place in the Sun* with Elizabeth Taylor. Daddy arranged with the warden of San Quentin for Monty to spend several days in the death house of the prison as part of his preparation for the role of the killer he was to play in the movie.

A few weeks later he sent me a funny little note: "Hello. How are you? Love, Monty."

I was so excited about hearing from him that I ripped the letter in half and then ran all over the house shouting at the top of my lungs: "Monty wrote me! Monty wrote me!" And I kept waving the torn sheets of paper as evidence.

"So what?" my brother demanded. "He's just being polite. Didn't you write him first?"

I admitted I had.

"Then, it's no big deal."

I was still very pleased and I Scotch-taped the letter together so I could read it again and again and again.

We flew to Aptos for part of June and July. The place was more beautiful than ever—it seemed almost unreal. The gardens were awash with color and fragrance; fruit hung heavy on the trees in the orchards.

Daddy kept assuring us he would always hold on to the property.

That summer Mama announced she would no longer write fiction. Her explanation: "Can't take any more rejections." Doubleday, Viking, Simon and Schuster—all had turned down her novel on the drifter. She had written eight drafts.

When I read the manuscript years later, I realized the best thing about the book was the description of the garden; but she had left out the lurid intensity—the pain of her relationship with Happy, the betrayals, the heartbreak. She had made the heroine, based on herself, controlled and genteel, a "lady" who kissed the drifter only once, quite chastely on the lips. And there is none of the self-examination that she ruthlessly applied to herself in her journal. The tone of the narrator in her novel is oddly girlish.

But the decision to stop writing fiction really upset her— she'd had an image of herself as a novelist for a long time. She would continue to write after that, but only unpublished essays and notes: "Diary of My Facelift"; "My Trip to the South of France."

In her journal, dated July 1949, she wrote: "I will sublimate my energies in cooking. I will rhapsodize about food. Tomato and dill soup topped with curried mayonnaise; calves' liver sautéed in wine; glazed ham steaks; baked bananas in lemon juice and molasses; orange and grapefruit slices with crystallized sugar. Ginger cookies. Toasted angel cake dripping with caramel sauce. My mouth waters at the thought, but then when I eat I feel nauseous. Sometimes after a big meal I'll tiptoe to my bathroom and retch."

In July, Daddy flew to Aptos, but he was so busy he joined us for only a few days.

Mama gave him an elaborate dinner party and the evening manifested in a kind of chemical frenzy given the elements thrown together: Paul Smith of the *Chronicle*, Dore Schary up from Hollywood with Helen Gahagan Douglas and Mel; Carey McWilliams and Judge Mary Kohler holding forth about the UN and the horrors of the Korean War.

Daddy appeared genial and relaxed, but I had the feeling it was agony for him to face his friends. He kept making light of the *New York Star* disaster, but then he would break into a terrible coughing fit and Mama would get a stricken look on her face.

JUST before he left for New York, we wandered down to the stream that cut through our property. Long ago, Happy had dammed it up, so the stream formed a deep, glistening brown pool of satiny, lukewarm water. We often sat in it up to our waists and read comic books.

But that afternoon Daddy and my brother played chess on a

floating chessboard—all in silence, very serious, very intent. The water lapped around their soft pale arms and chests. Mama and I sat on the bank and watched, and I wondered why this sweet, sad image conjured up such a feeling of estrangement.

AFTER that summer we broke apart as a family. Bart went off to Deerfield Academy. He'd been enrolled there for ages; it was part of Mama's plan for him and he was pleased; he couldn't wait to be on his own.

I felt differently. I begged to stay in New York. But I'd done so badly at Chapin, Mama felt I needed a "change." She wanted me to learn French and get acquainted with Europe, so I was sent to École Internationale ("Ecolint"), a coeducational boarding school in Geneva, Switzerland.

The first weeks there I felt increasing anxiety, and then I began to cry and couldn't stop. I developed a high fever and nausea, too, and landed in the infirmary. Nobody diagnosed my illness as a form of acute homesickness.

When I recovered I spent every moment between classes at Charlie Poletti's villa overlooking Lake Geneva. Charlie was Daddy's partner, so there was a tie line to their New York law office. But the circuits were often busy, so until they were free I would wait in the garden.

Sometimes Jean Poletti, Charlie's wife, would bring me a cup of tea; she was often quite drunk and the tea would spill on the grass and she would weave back into the house and I'd just sit there until dusk. By then the city of Geneva would be spread out in the distance beyond the lake, resplendent with red and blue lights, and above the city and above the lake the snowy majesty of Mont Blanc and the Alps glittered in the background.

Finally, the phone would be free and I'd reach my father and threaten to run away.

He'd pretend not to hear me—he would ask, "Aren't you having any fun?"

I'd tell him of course not since all the conversation was supposed to be in French at the school and I couldn't speak the language that well, so I felt cut off from everybody and abandoned.

"Then, you must learn French, my darling."

So I did, at least well enough to get by, and over Christmas I seemed to have adjusted—I didn't feel so disoriented. I began making and breaking alliances with the wildest bunch of students at Ecolint—South American millionaires' sons, French diplomats' daughters, American army brats. I was now hiding my emotions behind a world-weary air. I had my picture taken skiing at Gstaad: I looked vapid and stern, a Gauloise cigarette drooping from my lips.

I sent the snapshot to my brother in a box of chocolates. He wrote back, "Have you forgotten? I hate chocolates." It was the only time he ever wrote me.

I kept hearing about various upheavals at home via letters from Mama. The worst: Daddy selling Aptos—although he'd promised he never would—presumably to pay for our tuitions and other mounting expenses.

It was hard to respond to any news that seemed so far away, particularly since I was so deeply engrossed in myself and the agonies of my adolescence.

I remember rolling around in the grass with an Arab student as he tried unsuccessfully to teach me "the spoon position" fully clothed. I don't think I even knew that the Supreme Court had turned down the Hollywood Ten appeals, which meant the Ten would all go to jail.

After New Year's I grew more reckless. At night I'd sneak into the boys' dorm to neck, and whenever possible I'd escape from school in an attempt to experience myself as a free creature —which of course I was not. But I thought I was as I prowled around the dim, smoky boîtes in Geneva's old city. Once a couple of my friends and I biked around the lake at dawn yelling at the top of our lungs. Another time the Polettis allowed me to give a party for my class at their villa, and the evening ended in a noisy brawl with broken furniture and broken glasses and students vomiting on the lawn.

And that wasn't all. Over Easter, I began to conduct a romance with the school dishwasher, a curly-haired boy from the Italian Alps. Soon the entire student body was whispering about it; I wasn't supposed to be "consorting with the help"—he wasn't of my "class." But I didn't care.

After a teacher caught us necking behind a sack of rotting

potatoes in the kitchen storeroom I was promptly expelled and sent home. I had just celebrated my sixteenth birthday.

My brother was sent home, too, at almost the same time. He had formed a passionate attachment to another student in his class at Deerfield. Then this boy hanged himself from a tree, and Bart was put onto a train only hours after his friend's body had been discovered.

So, by the summer of 1950 we found ourselves back in New York again experiencing various forms of trauma and disgrace, and ensconced in an even bigger, grander brownstone on East Sixty-eighth Street, which Mama was decorating to a fare-thee-well.

I never understood why Daddy allowed her to move. There was no need to, especially since my brother and I would no longer be living at home, except on vacations. I think Mama imagined she could somehow keep us together as a family by creating yet another refined, tasteful home.

And there was something soothing about always living surrounded by familiar arrangements of overstuffed furniture and cozy settees. No matter how many times we moved, the same lovely watercolors and Audubon prints would be hung in symmetrical groups across off-white walls.

When I arrived from the airport, I found workmen polishing the ground floor of our new, unfamiliar home, and Mama had to sidestep a painter on a ladder in order to hug me. Looming behind her, looking skinnier and taller than I remembered him, was my brother, Bart. He just stared at me vacantly.

We ate supper in the kitchen because a huge mirror was being glued to the dining room door. We felt shy with each other and a bit uncomfortable. Nine months had passed since we had been together as a family. How could we possibly catch up? Were our phones still tapped? Was Daddy again on pills?

I glanced at my father. His face appeared more haggard than usual; there was a stubble of beard on his chin. But he was talking animatedly and smoking cigarette after cigarette. He did not touch his food, and we avoided speaking about what had happened to us. We did not seem to know how to explain ourselves. At the end of the meal, Mama referred almost gingerly to the subject of my expulsion from school, but none of us mentioned Bart's friend's violent death.

Daddy had already phoned Deerfield demanding to know why his son had been sent back on the train without even informing his parents so they could have at least met him at the station. And why had he been sent home in the first place when he had nothing to do with his friend's death; it was as if he had been personally blamed for the suicide.

The school could give no satisfactory explanation, so Daddy went up to Deerfield to speak to its headmaster, Frank Boynton, personally.

The autocratic, crotchety Boynton had been headmaster of Deerfield since 1902; he ran the school with an iron fist in a velvet glove. He was tight-lipped with my father. All Daddy could get from him was that there had been an emotional involvement between the two boys. "Emotional" was emphasized in an ominous way, Daddy told us when he returned. Otherwise he had found that teachers and students alike had seemed to agree to pretend that the incident hadn't happened. They refused to speak about it.

(Indeed, when in 1993 I tried to find out about my brother at Deerfield, I received a letter stating there was "no record of Bart Crum Jr. ever attending Deerfield." I sent a photocopied page of his yearbook where his name had appeared; another note came back—something about "we guess our records must be incomplete." Obviously they wanted to bury the incident.)

I would not find out for decades that Bart's friend had been plump and jolly and exceedingly bright, and that for eight months he and my brother had been inseparable, and then one afternoon they had been discovered in the gym, arms about each other, and everybody went into a panic. They were both fourteen years old at the time.

Was my brother a homosexual?

"Bart didn't know what he was then," Mama would say later, and Daddy refused even to discuss the possibility.

Back then the subject of homosexuality wasn't in our frame of reference. I, for one, didn't know anything about the details of a homosexual act and I'm not sure my brother did either. Yes, I'd met homosexuals, and Mama had read the Kinsey report and talked about it one morning at breakfast, announcing that something like 10 percent of American men were homosexual—but we didn't know what that meant either.

One of Mama's closest friends was a homosexual, an effete interior decorator who used to be her "date" when Daddy was away. And then there was another family friend—Fred Tillman, our neighbor across the stream at Aptos—but he didn't "look" like a homosexual; he was big and burly, he lifted weights.

Just before we'd left California in 1948, Fred had been murdered by a sailor he had picked up in a bar and brought home.

I remember Bart and I were horrified. It was Mama who explained that men and women can be passionate with one another and violent, too, and that men can be passionate with men and that could turn violent as well. She added that some men prefer being with their own sex. "They're homosexuals," she said.

"Fred was a pansy—Fred was a queer," Daddy interjected.

"Is that bad?" my brother wanted to know.

"The Catholic Church believes that homosexuality is not natural, that homosexuality is an illness," Daddy answered somberly.

"Oh, for God's sake!" Mama had exclaimed.

"Well, it's true, Cutsie."

"Not necessarily."

Back then, in the 1950s, being gay was thought to be disgusting; being gay was being "sick," taboo. I'm afraid Daddy thought that in his heart of hearts. Mama was more tolerant. She always said no simple code of morality could apply when it came to the intricacies of sex.

Throughout that hot, sultry summer Bart remained bewildered and increasingly remote. He didn't want to see anybody, but there was one friend from Collegiate—I forget his name—who used to drop by the brownstone and play algebraic analysis with him, differentiating and integrating equations. Oh, they enjoyed testing each other.

Otherwise, he remained in his room listening to music. Music would be on full blast—something like Mahler's bombastic Eighth Symphony, the sound turned so loud the floor would literally vibrate; the bare empty spaces would resound with choral pronouncements of revelation and redemption, while trumpets and trombones blared.

Bart would be lying facedown on his bed. I would tiptoe in

and sit next to him for what seemed like hours. I secretly hoped I could comfort him.

It was obvious he was still grieving, still caught up in the nightmare of what had happened at Deerfield. I imagined he would finally rage and cry in my arms and explain why his friend had hanged himself. But my brother never moved. Finally, he would say, his voice muffled by pillows, "If you care about me at all, you'll leave me alone. Go away, *please.*"

I think he would have been content to stay forever in his room enveloped by music, but Daddy insisted he leave the house and "get some air." He took us both down to Penn Station the day the Hollywood Ten were sent to prison. "You should see this—it's historical," he said.

I have a vague memory of joining a jostling, respectful crowd of more than a thousand people, some holding signs proclaiming the Ten's innocence. A few people recognized my father and ran over to shake his hand.

When we returned home there was a sedan parked outside our brownstone with FBI agents in it; Daddy rushed us inside the house and bolted the door. We peered out the window a few minutes later and the sedan was gone.

It was obvious we were continuing to be harassed. I remember Mama running around and closing the shutters and then the curtains; there was no air-conditioning, so it grew very hot, but for at least a day we remained inside the house in stifling darkness. And then Daddy told us the attorney general was suggesting that lawyers who defended Communists should be disbarred. Not long after that Ethel and Julius Rosenberg were arrested as spies and charged with masterminding a plot to steal atomic bomb secrets.

By the end of the summer, it suddenly dawned on my brother and me that Daddy was spending a lot of time at home. Then Mama explained that when we were away in school, he had been asked to leave the Roosevelt firm—he supposedly hadn't brought in enough "rich Jewish clients." He'd had an argument over that with Roosevelt, who told him, "Look, I don't need you anymore. I can get my own Jews." Daddy didn't say a word; he just walked out of the office and that night took another overdose.

But it hadn't been fatal. He'd had his stomach pumped out,

and a few days later he was back networking for new clients and scheduling speeches for Israel.

This last suicide attempt didn't seem to affect him; on the contrary, he was almost in radiant spirits; he taught me how to make a lemon pie, a sure sign he was in a good mood. He didn't even seem to mind having to make calls from a pay phone on Third Avenue (he was sure we were still bugged). Sometimes when he didn't have enough change I'd accompany him and stand there feeding him nickels from my piggy bank while he had long conversations with friends in Washington and sometimes Jerusalem.

Years later I would conclude that the pressures he created for himself—the speeches around the country; the radio talks; the meetings in bars, always in hopes of striking a new deal, or of enticing a new client to help support his lavish lifestyle—all these pressures produced in him, depending on the situation, either extreme highs or extreme lows.

He still missed California, he missed his old San Francisco friends and he hated practicing law in New York. So life must have been close to unbearable for him until he decided that no matter what the disappointments or rejections, he could function quite happily as long as he knew he had a means of escape—in the form of those pills.

Meanwhile, in September 1950, in an effort to appear "less subversive," he resigned from the Lawyers Guild (which had just been labeled "a bulwark of the Communist Party" by HUAC) and all the other left-wing organizations he belonged to. He told us that from now on he was going to practice only corporate law. But he did advise Eddie Dmytryk when he broke with the Ten and decided to name names in order to start directing movies in Hollywood again.

Eddie was the only one of the Ten to inform; he was called a traitor by his colleagues, and Daddy was called a traitor for representing Eddie. None of his fellow lawyers ever spoke to him again.

Robert Kenny was especially bitter; he had believed it was crucial for all of them to be unified, no matter what the cost.

"Bart Crum rolled over," he would say later. "Bart was with us all the way through the appeals up to the Supreme Court. Now he has no friends on either side."

My father would not dignify that statement with a response. But he didn't enjoy being thought of as a traitor simply because he'd stood by a client who changed his mind. All he'd ever wanted was for Eddie to feel free to tell the truth.

Nothing had worked out as he imagined it would, yet he was sure most Americans either didn't think Communists should be punished for their beliefs or at least were unsure on this point. But the fact remained that during this period the Soviet Union's actions were threatening and the public was justifiably anxious and eager for American Communists and ex-Communists to explain just where their loyalties lay.

Then there was Senator Joseph McCarthy, an overnight sensation playing to the newsreel cameras—swinging treason charges like a sledgehammer, hitting out in all directions, as the Democrats and the State Department parried defensively but the administration remained silent. Daddy and Carey McWilliams, now editor of *The Nation,* had lunch and confided to each other that they were afraid that if they wrote anything or spoke out they might be subject to a sustained attack.

That fall, my brother and I were sent away again—this time to the same boarding school, called Stockbridge. It was coeducational and progressive; the setting was beautiful, a rambling estate on nine hundred acres of rolling Berkshire hills.

Headmaster Hans Maeder, a German exile, envisioned Stockbridge as a laboratory for democracy. I saw it more as a depository for strays and misfits. The student body was an odd lot. From Chicago, Siam, Los Angeles, and the Bronx. We all seemed to be there for the same reason, some terrible family breakdown; it could be divorce or illness or bad politics. Several of my classmates had relatives who had been labeled "subversive." But we never talked politics among ourselves; nobody even mentioned the blacklist or the growing menace that was Joseph McCarthy. It was funny because several members of the faculty had been fired from other schools for being Communists.

Instead there were frequent discussions in the huge, drafty main living room that focused on subjects like religion or leadership. Once Fred Friendly came up to talk about the future of television, and once Daddy appeared and proceeded to give us a lecture on the challenges of living in an Israeli kibbutz.

We all had projects to complete by the end of the year—communal projects, like building rooms or painting johns—and we all had personal essays to write. I chose Abraham Lincoln (he was a big hero in my family, so there were all sorts of books in our library that I could crib from).

I became obsessed with studying for my college boards. My parents expected me to go on to college and I wanted to please them. All that year I lived alone in a tiny room at the school and flung myself into my classwork, and for the first time in my life I began to learn something and got decent grades.

But I was miserable at Stockbridge, partly because I had no boyfriend, and partly because my brother seemed to be avoiding me. Sometimes he would help me with my math homework (he was easily the best student in the school), but he had become totally involved with a group of grungy misfit boys, and I didn't like them. They were troublesome—spiteful, picking verbal fights, disrupting meetings. Hans paid no attention to them. He treated them with genial indifference, but I thought they were creeps and I told my brother so.

He just laughed. "Well, I *like* them," he said. He seemed to get a huge kick out of their self-mocking attitudes, their open distrust of the world.

We went home periodically for weekends.

Mama had given us the entire top floor of the brownstone, but she hadn't gotten around to decorating it yet, so the only furniture we had were our beds and a couple of standing lamps.

I remember I used to pass Bart in the hall and he'd seem in a trance. He would ignore me and glide into the bathroom, but he'd leave the door open and I could see him standing by the mirror squeezing his breakouts until they bled. Then he stopped. He didn't believe in mutilation or self-mortification, he said.

As I recall, that was one of the few remarks he made to me or anyone all that year—that and the one to Daddy when he informed him that he was no longer a Catholic, and that he no longer believed in God.

In the late spring of 1951, I found out I had passed my college boards and been accepted at Sarah Lawrence.

Daddy had good news, too: he had become a full partner in a

Wall Street firm—Hays, Podell, Algase and Crum, as it would now be called. And that wasn't all. He had become Rita Hayworth's lawyer, he said, and the first thing he was going to negotiate was her divorce from Prince Aly Khan.

CHAPTER

25

For a while, being Rita Hayworth's lawyer revitalized my father's career. It made him feel successful again and got him onto the front page of the *Daily News* almost every day.

As for me, I'd always been one of her adoring fans. I'd seen every one of her movies, from *Blood and Sand* to *Cover Girl* and *Gilda,* her most popular movie. Her performance as the alluring, wanton, unredeemable Gilda had elevated her beyond her genuine triumph as Fred Astaire's dancing partner and turned her into an international phenomenon.

I could quote from *Photoplay* magazine about her, chapter and verse. I knew, for example, that her photograph was the top pinup of World War II, that it had been glued onto the first atomic bomb detonated at Bikini Atoll, and that the bomb had been named "Gilda" (which had upset Rita a lot).

I knew one of her eyes was smaller than the other; I knew she'd gotten pregnant by Howard Hughes and he made her have an abortion.

I knew that during her affair with Prince Aly Khan she had traveled from Paris to Dublin to Gstaad with sixty suitcases— helicopters buzzing, crowds swarming after her, screaming as she left for Havana in his private plane to escape hordes of photographers. Their romance had caused a scandal since both were married to other people.

When Rita, age thirty-three, came into our lives in the spring of 1951, she had just left the prince after less than two years of marriage. She had been in the midst of an African safari when she escaped back to New York. She was penniless.

The first thing my father did as her attorney was to arrange for her agent at William Morris to loan her twenty-five thousand dollars so she could pay her bills at the Plaza Hotel and hire a nanny to take care of her two daughters, Rebecca Welles and little Princess Yasmin Khan.

I happened to be home from boarding school the first time Rita slipped into our brownstone to discuss her move to Nevada, so she could begin divorce proceedings. She had already told my father why she had to divorce Aly: he never stopped being unfaithful to her—"It was humiliating; sometimes up to four new girls a day."

She had arrived that evening by chauffeured limousine. I answered the door and was disappointed in the way she looked—not at all like her glamorous on-screen image: no makeup; hair brown, not dyed red; dressed in a man's baggy shirt, slacks, and bobby socks.

We shook hands without speaking. She seemed melancholy and reserved.

Then Daddy appeared; there were brief hellos and then he and Rita disappeared into the back study on the second floor.

My brother and I grew used to Rita Hayworth slipping into the brownstone at odd hours. She was always alone, always a little out of it. She'd make a beeline to the bar in the back study where she'd sit with my father, sometimes for hours. When I was there he did all the talking. She hardly ever reacted. I got the feeling she had no real way of expressing how she felt deep inside herself except through her moodiness and her drinking.

But then, at some point, she'd toss her thick mane of hair—sometimes dyed a brilliant shade of russet—and gaze at my father with such a look of wide-eyed wonder and drugged sexiness, he couldn't do enough for her. Mama didn't mind. She'd feel protective. "Rita is the most baffled, defenseless creature I've ever known," she'd say.

Once, when she was quite drunk, she began reminiscing about her second husband, Orson Welles, and how he had taught her magic tricks and made her laugh. She said that just before she had married Prince Aly she impulsively phoned Welles and asked him to come back to her.

She had been apprehensive about her future life with Aly. He already had been unfaithful, and she disliked his entourage of "freeloaders"—they traveled with him, they were rude and indifferent to her, and they played bridge obsessively from dawn to dusk.

Anyhow, she and Welles rendezvoused in a hotel at Antibes, but it hadn't worked out; he had rejected her.

Soon after she returned to the prince's sumptuous villa on the Riviera—Château L'Horizon—feeling very depressed. It was the eve of her wedding; servants were dumping gallons of perfume in the swimming pool "so it would smell nice."

A rehearsal had been called for the bridal party. People, mostly strangers, were milling about on the vast lawn, which rolled down almost to the Mediterranean, and suddenly she saw that a drowned man had been washed up on the rocks. A body, grotesquely twisted and silent, lay there, and nobody had noticed. Her voice thickened as she remembered the image. She began shaking her brown hair over her face so we couldn't see her expression. "Lousy omen," she muttered. "Gave me the willies."

Soon Daddy was off to Paris on "Rita business" so often he'd joke, "I feel as if I'm flying the transatlantic mail route."

There were endless hassles over child support and visitation rights for the tiny two-year-old Princess Yasmin. She used to appear at the brownstone, too. I have a vivid memory of her cavorting around the living room in a funny comic dance. It was one of the few times I ever saw Rita smile.

Since she refused to give interviews, Daddy began serving as her press secretary, telling her side of the story over and over again to reporters who followed him out of airports and into hotel lobbies from Hollywood to Reno to Paris and New York.

He was asking for a million-dollar settlement, which at the time was unheard of. But she doesn't want the money for herself, he'd explain; all Rita wants is financial security for Princess Yasmin. And then he would add how, on the eve of their wedding, Rita had signed a prenuptial agreement which stated that if her marriage failed she would ask Aly for nothing. The prince had been so impressed, he had given Rita a "diamond as big as a belt buckle."

He would leave out the sordid details—that before, during, and after their marriage Aly hung out at his favorite brothel (even as he was attempting a reconciliation with Rita). As for Rita, she was juggling several new lovers, among them a makeup man and producer Charlie Feldman, who had just presented her with a monogrammed Cadillac, which she'd turned down.

Occasionally Daddy would get so wound up after a press conference that when he returned home, he would repeat what he'd said until Mama begged him to stop.

She didn't approve of all the tabloid publicity he was getting; she thought it might diminish his real achievements—as author of *Behind the Silk Curtain*, as a former adviser to President Truman and to Wendell Willkie.

But although Daddy was caught up in Rita Hayworth's divorce, he managed to spend time with my brother, who was suffering through another depression. Daddy and Mama accompanied Bart to see the first of several psychiatrists, and then they drove me up to Sarah Lawrence College; our car was laden down with my suitcases, topped by my Raggedy Ann doll.

I'd been assigned to Westlands, a large Tudor-type building complete with stained-glass windows, which housed the administrative staff and some boarders. It stood at the top of the tree-studded green hills that were part of the campus grounds rising above Bronxville.

I was going to share a room with two other freshmen—Joyce Rudenko and Harriet Green. They were already unpacking when I arrived with my parents. We introduced ourselves and then Mama and Daddy kissed me good-bye and left, saying they'd see me soon in New York.

I remember experiencing a momentary feeling of panic at being abandoned—the same feeling I'd experienced back in Switzerland—but then it passed and Joyce and Harriet made it easy for me; they were decent, well-meaning young women. For a while they indulged me, but they ended up being pretty exasperated because I could not finish unpacking.

For the next three months, my suitcases lay open on the floor, most of my possessions scattered about: movie magazines, my baby pillow, a quilt. As soon as I took off an item of clothing, I'd drop it onto the floor, and often I'd just push junk under my bed—old newspapers, candy wrappers, an umbrella. I even left half-drunk cartons of milk on the windowsill to sour. I was very spoiled; a maid had always picked up for me.

But my excuse was I had no time to clean up my portion of the room. The first weeks in college I was running around trying to absorb everything. I can still see myself clad in black leotard and green jersey bounding up and down the campus hills, dropping notepads and books in my eagerness to get to a lecture on time, or to explore the new dance studio, or to audition for the drama department's first play of the season (I wasn't cast).

I was intoxicated by the creative ferment at Sarah Lawrence. All around me something was happening. There were jazz concerts in the student lounge and Norman Dello Joio was rehearsing his opera *St. Joan*, which had a cast of 120. Joseph Campbell was lecturing on heroes and myths and Horace Gregory taught poetry; Merce Cunningham taught modern dance.

At the same time the college was being attacked by the West-chester branch of the American Legion, and later HUAC, for "harboring Communists." There had already been one outrageous incident: a student named Lovey had been kept from returning to college from her home in Toronto because the immigration authorities said she was a member of the Communist Party in Canada.

There were emotionally charged meetings with the student body resulting in a resolution sent to the board of trustees asking for intervention and for lawyers to get Lovey back. And college president Harold Taylor led the crusade, "defying the bullying outside meddlers in education."

Handsome, life-loving Harold was quite a phenomenon. At thirty-two, he was the youngest college president in America. He played tennis like a pro, he loved jazz; his friends included Alger Hiss and Duke Ellington. A former philosophy professor from the University of Wisconsin, he never stopped fighting for academic freedoms during his fifteen years as president of Sarah Lawrence.

But at one point he fired a teacher at Sarah Lawrence—not because he was a Communist (he was), but because he had lied to the students, the faculty, and the board about his affiliation. "Probably he was under Party orders to do so, but that didn't make it any better," Harold used to say.

I admired Harold. He reminded me of my father; they were both liberals—both idealists. As a matter of fact, they served on many panels together, speaking out against the loyalty oaths for teachers.

Harold became my friend during my tumultuous first months at college. I was studying hard but I was playing hard, too—going out almost every night. If I didn't have a date with someone from Yale or Harvard, I'd wander down to the local greasy spoon—a little bar near the Bronxville train station, which was the favorite student hangout. It was smoky, noisy, jammed with kids, the juke-box blared with Rosemary Clooney singing "Come-On-A-My House."

I was seeing several different young men, but I longed to be swept off my feet. So far the only boy who'd ever done that was scruffy Bradley back in San Francisco. I still had his ID bracelet in my little black velvet jewelry bag.

Then, over Thanksgiving, I met a twenty-one-year-old student from Columbia University who claimed to be an artist. He seemed all nerves and pain and sensitivity. I noticed he needed both a haircut and a shave. I was violently attracted to him. We began an affair almost immediately. My roommates were impressed. I did not inform them beforehand when we eloped to Mt. Vernon over New Year's. I was afraid I might be talked out of it.

At our wedding ceremony, which was performed by a very bored Mt. Vernon judge, I wore my favorite fuzzy purple angora sweater and a dress embroidered with silken butterflies. That night in the motel my husband pretended the butterflies were real and made me stand in front of him while he pulled them off one by one and crushed them in his hand.

My parents wanted the marriage annulled. I turned to Harold Taylor for help. In a matter of hours he'd called an impromptu meeting in his office allowing Mama to sound off about ruining my life and then Daddy, between coughing fits, to plead with me not to get married in the church.

Harold declared that I had made a choice—a decision—to be married, and he was going to respect that. I was over eighteen so he would honor that decision. He hoped my parents would, too.

To my surprise they agreed, and the next thing I knew they had sent out engraved cards from Tiffany's. "Mr. and Mrs. Bartley Crum announce the marriage of their daughter, Patricia, January 2, 1952," and they added "at home at 236 East 68th Street," which made no sense since my husband and I never set foot in that brownstone as man and wife.

In fact, as I recall, my parents spoke to my husband only on two rather uncomfortable occasions, and they never even bothered to meet my in-laws, although we were already living with them temporarily in their Bronxville apartment.

We shared a narrow room off a rather grubby kitchen. The place smelled of Lifebuoy soap and turpentine. The main light came from two leaky fishtanks. The single decoration on the wall was an oil painting of one breast. I never found out whose. Throughout our marriage it hung above our bed; it was the only painting my husband ever completed.

It goes without saying the marriage was a terrible mistake. What began as a mad love affair would end in disenchantment and not a little violence.

College saved me. I began studying until I dropped. Sometimes I'd read so late my brain would fairly ring with fatigue. But it didn't matter; I became totally caught up in my Ten Books course with Alistair Reid. I escaped into the novels of James Joyce and Virginia Woolf and F. Scott Fitzgerald—these were just a few of the writers I was discovering. I escaped into their imaginations, their stories.

And I danced. I'd enrolled in a choreography workshop taught by my don Bessie Schonberg, a powerful outspoken woman whose kinky hair was yanked into a topknot. She'd been a member of Martha Graham's original company and she had Graham's faith in the integrity of work—the *process* of work.

I began creating dances for her, among them a duet with my own reflection in the rehearsal-hall mirror. I felt pagan and free as I danced, and I seemed to grow larger and more important to myself.

DADDY was paying for my tuition, nothing more, so I started working part-time as a model. In between classes, I'd go to New York and hunt out jobs.

I earned my first paycheck modeling in an automobile show inside a vast exhibition hall on Lexington Avenue. I made $250 a day smiling at crowds, standing in a shiny open convertible as it revolved around and around a turntable. I remember I wore a blue strapless dress; my hair was coifed in a French twist. Daddy and Bart dropped by to see how I was doing.

Mama did not. She'd sent a message that she was still so "undone" by my marriage, she couldn't bear to look at me.

I'd had one very tense meeting with her right after the meeting in Harold Taylor's office. She asked me if I knew about birth control. I said yes, but I was lying. Mama never told me what to do, but she warned me, "If you get pregnant, I swear I'll take you to the nearest abortionist myself."

I eventually learned the so-called facts of life from my sister-in-law.

A year passed.

By then we had moved to an attic apartment in Fleetwood. My husband was working during the day, sorting mail at the post office. He painted most nights in our living room, by the light of a gooseneck lamp.

I would either be studying or trying to sleep in our alcove bedroom down the hall, but I could still breathe in the fumes of turpentine and hear the slap of brushes against canvas. The windows would all be open; we were directly over a parking lot, so there was the frequent sound of car doors slamming shut and of tires churning in the thick, soft gravel far below.

It was an unsettling time for me. By choosing a man my parents disapproved of I found myself released from all traditional expectations, which made me feel deliciously independent in spite of my unhappiness. Most mornings I'd rush off at dawn—for an early class or to make the 7:40 train to Grand Central if I had a modeling assignment.

I was earning money and that made me feel strong, and I was so busy I didn't dwell on the drabness of my surroundings or the fact that my marriage had turned into an arrangement for two roommates who barely spoke to each other and only occasionally had sex.

I longed to tell my mother what was happening inside my

head, but we remained estranged. She did write me letters and I wrote her back. She'd order me "to keep a journal so you'll know what you think." And she frequently commented on my modeling pictures, deploring my Camay Beauty Bride campaign. She even tore out one of the ads from the *Ladies' Home Journal*, scrawling "You look miserable" across the woebegone closeup of me as a "happily young married."

Mama and I reconciled in early 1953, but she never forgave me for marrying someone she didn't approve of. I don't know whether my brother approved either.

I had lost track of him during most of my marriage. He never wrote or called. I'd heard from Daddy that he'd graduated from Stockbridge and gone on to MIT. Then one afternoon in the early spring of 1953 he showed up unannounced at my apartment looking scrawny and depressed. I happened to be alone, but he refused to come in; I suggested we get something to eat.

We wandered across the parking lot and over to a hamburger place and ordered melted cheese sandwiches and lemon Cokes.

I tried to draw him out; I told him about my latest job—a live TV commercial for Prell shampoo. He didn't seem to be listening. I noticed he had pimples dotting his cheeks. "Mama wants me to get them burned off," he said, smiling crookedly. "She hates looking at me."

"What's the matter?" I asked him in our private language.

He didn't answer right away, but gradually it came out.

All his life he had aimed for MIT—his grades were tops —and when he was accepted at age sixteen, and the letters of congratulations poured in from faculty and student clubs, it was quite natural for him to take the leap, even though Mama and Daddy had suggested he take a fifth year at Andover and then go to college. But he didn't want to wait.

The months in Cambridge were a nightmare for him. He made no friends. He wasn't asked to join any of the fraternities he had visited.

As usual, his grades were straight A's, but he couldn't connect. It had been so hard to go to Mama and Daddy and tell them he had to leave MIT; he gave an excuse: he said he didn't want to stay there because he was no longer interested in science.

Now he didn't know what to do. He was living at home, which he didn't like. "Mama pays too much attention to me—Daddy pays no attention at all."

He was working as a copyboy at the *Daily News*. "Keeps me out of trouble," he joked. And then he withdrew into himself and I couldn't get him to say another word.

"I wish I could do something to help," I said.

"How?" he mumbled, and then he retreated again into the isolated little world I was no part of. And I saw him as I guess he was: a miserable eighteen-year-old boy, saddled with brains and bitterness.

I knew he had always absolved me of any responsibility for his troubles, but I could not absolve myself.

He hadn't eaten his sandwich. "Aren't you hungry?" I asked. He shook his head.

The walk back to the train took a while. It was close to a mile. There was a wind blowing. He wore no coat, but he didn't seem to mind.

We had to climb a long flight of steep metal stairs to reach the train station. Underneath us cars and trucks whizzed up and down the Bronx River Parkway. For some reason my heart began to race. My brother pushed past me and ran ahead to the train platform, then he turned back. "Was it worth it?" he demanded, his voice full of scorn. "Is sex that great?"

I didn't know what to say.

I didn't know what to say to my father either.

He would phone me regularly to ask how my marriage was going, and I couldn't answer directly. Instead I'd tell him the three things I was learning at college: how to use a library, how to memorize, and how to fall asleep practically anywhere.

"I wish you could teach me that," he would kid.

We tried to meet when our schedules permitted. His routine was virtually the same: speeches for Israel; trips back and forth to Hollywood and Paris for Rita Hayworth. United Jewish Appeal and Rita were his priorities. He had a few other clients and cases he attended to, but he never talked about them.

He ate lunch almost every day at the 21 Club. Pete Kriendler, the raspy-voiced owner, liked Daddy and let him run up big tabs and take forever paying them.

His table near Mrs. Douglas MacArthur's was upstairs in the paneled dining room known as the "A" section of the restaurant. The table always overflowed with Washington lobbyists; real estate brokers from Tel Aviv; gossip columnists like Earl Wilson or Leonard Lyons, waiting to grab a juicy quote about Rita.

There were also the "regulars"—the hangers-on—like out-of-work character actor Bill Hanley, slope-shouldered, slope-nosed, full of anecdotes about Hollywood and Broadway. Perennially good-natured, Bill was a fixture in our home as well, attending Christmas and Easter dinners, coaching me with all my auditions.

And there was Dave, a freelance press agent who had a tough-guy manner and wore a bad toupee. Dave ran errands for Daddy. Once he traveled halfway round the world to deliver a biography of the eccentric modern dancer Isadora Duncan to Rita Hayworth. Daddy thought Rita should play Duncan in the movies.

Dave never stopped complaining about delivering that book, but it was the biggest thing that ever happened to him.

These "regulars" were joined occasionally by two women: Helen Strauss, the powerful William Morris agent; and Judge Mary Kohler (now working in children's court on Centre Street).

The lunches would drag on until after three. I was always struck by the efforts Daddy exerted to make everybody happy. He would go to tremendous lengths—promising to do extravagant favors; flattering; using his gift for gossip and gab—anything to keep the table harmonious. Usually his efforts worked. When they did not, he was upset. He felt he'd failed.

Sometimes during a lull in the conversation he would ask for a phone and call his mother in Sacramento.

"Hello, Mo? Guess where I am? At Twenty-one, having scrambled eggs with Lennie Lyons and . . ." He'd ask about his sister and the aunts, but he didn't talk very long. Mo didn't want him to spend too much money on long-distance.

Finally, lunch would be over; the table would empty, Daddy would sign for the check, and then he would sometimes look at me and say, "You wanna see *Gilda?*" He often screened that movie just for himself. The Columbia Pictures Building was three blocks from 21; it was very convenient.

There was something almost illicit about sitting alone in the darkened, luxurious screening room with my father, watching the mythic power of Rita Hayworth radiate from the screen.

He would be lounging next to me, smoking greedily, his eyelids blinking very fast, the way they did when he was excited about something. Was he imagining what it would be like to unzip the zipper of Gilda's glittery white gown? In the movie she keeps having trouble with zippers. At the start she lies on a big bed waiting for her dress to be unzipped by a man she hates (George Macready), who happens to be her husband. Later she has more trouble with her zipper, just before she goes into her striptease dance and sings "Put the Blame on Mame," and Glenn Ford (her ex-lover in the film, who loves her but acts as if he despises her) slaps her silly. The whole thing is barbaric—but deeply pleasurable.

I'd heard rumors that my father was having an affair with Rita. ("Men go to bed with Gilda and they wake up with me," Rita was quoted as saying.)

He had followed her to Key West when she was taking time off incognito. He said he'd flown down to get her to sign some important papers, but they were photographed going into a nightclub together.

Whatever their relationship was, it seemed to be evolving into something rather special. He teasingly called her "the Sphinx." Director Bob Parrish, who worked with her in *Fire Down Below*, told me, "The only letters Rita would read on the set were letters Bart Crum sent to her—she threw all her other mail away."

He had begun to involve himself in all aspects of her career. By 1952, he was reading scripts for her, suggesting roles. He wanted her to play Salome and the Egyptian queen Nefertiti. "Nerfer-whoo?" Rita asked.

And he had to deal with the FBI for her, too, which seemed ironic since the FBI was still harassing *him*. While Rita was married to Orson Welles, she had lent her name to all the left-wing causes he was involved in. As a result, Hoover had a big, fat file on her marked "X" (which meant political activity of a suspect nature).

Eventually, Daddy got Martin Gang, a liberal attorney who handled a lot of celebrity informers, to compose a written statement for Rita about her loyalty to America, so she wouldn't have to make a public statement.

But the FBI continued to be involved with Rita. There were death threats on Princess Yasmin's life, and Daddy demanded a full-scale investigation from J. Edgar Hoover, complete with FBI lab reports dealing with the death-threat letters—the kind of note paper used (it was discovered that the paper had been bought in New Rochelle); the fingerprints, if any, that might be in the Bureau's files. He kept phoning the FBI agents to get the results of the investigation, even as he knew the FBI was dogging him. "Sometimes I want to say, hey, you guys, lay off me, will you?"

Once I remember we sat in the darkened screening room after *Gilda* was over and he began telling me very quietly, very intently, that the persecution was starting to drive him a little crazy.

He was a rational guy, he said—he could not understand why he was under such scrutiny. "I have done nothing wrong!" he exclaimed. He then peppered his sentences with words like *justice, loyalty, fairness,* and *trust,* and they all sounded like clichés; understatement became overstatement.

I think he exaggerated his position of importance with the FBI, but he underestimated the toll it would take on him.

He'd talk about what the FBI and HUAC had done to his personal friends, like John Garfield, the actor who died not long after he was humiliated in front of the committee. Garfield insisted he couldn't name any Communists because he didn't know any; he was accused of perjuring himself.

He had visited our house. Daddy had spoken to him, but didn't know how to comfort him. The strain was such that Garfield had a heart attack six months later.

Daddy empathized: he really couldn't name any Communists either.

Now he seemed to be expecting the worst. The phone taps were still on; he was being followed. Only doom and despair seemed to be in his future.

I would sit and listen to him. I guess he thought he was teaching me something. All I knew was that I loved him helplessly, although not everything he said made sense to me. Or maybe it did and I was just too young and callow to absorb what he was trying to tell me.

∎

AT the start of 1953, he hired a detective to find the wiretaps on the phones in our brownstone.

The detective's name was Guy. A former FBI agent, he ran a small agency out of the Empire State Building. He maintained he'd done everything in his time: he had made illegal break-ins; he'd tailed Lee Mortimer of *Confidential* magazine, "What a sleazebag!" He'd also, he said, been in the CIA as a Secret Service agent during World War II for "Wild Bill" Donovan. "Bill and J. Edgar despised each other," he said.

Mama thought Guy was a pathological liar. She begged Daddy not to "consort" with him. But my father was desperate. He got it into his head that Guy could fix our phones.

I met Guy at the Drake Hotel restaurant. Daddy went there occasionally because he enjoyed the steaks—they were char-broiled and basted in Worcestershire sauce and garlic. The after-noon I arrived, Guy was already seated with my father near the bar. He was a slight, balding man with a three-day growth of beard to cover his bad complexion.

Throughout the lunch Guy drank double tequilas and gos-siped about Hoover, Roy Cohn, and Joe McCarthy. They were all high-level fags, he said—a top-secret faggot group—and they often went to the Stork Club. Cardinal Spellman was part of this group, too, but he didn't go to the Stork Club.

Daddy listened to Guy babble on and then he interrupted, "I don't care whether the cardinal screws goats. I want you to fix our phones!"

Guy assured him he would.

They had several other lunches. Daddy said he asked Guy if the FBI had any solid proof that he was a member of the Commu-nist Party, and Guy answered that they didn't have proof he was *not* a member—get it? "If any informer does not change his mind, you'll be on the FBI's shit list till hell freezes over," he told him. He added that there were close to a million people under surveillance in the United States.

Mama finally let Guy into the brownstone so he could check our phones there. He took them apart, but he couldn't find the wiretapping devices, and then he couldn't reassemble the phones.

In early April, the State Department made noises and advised my father that his passport might not be renewed because "It has been alleged that Crum is a Communist . . . in the opinion of the Department there is evidence that indicates that there has been a consistent and prolonged adherence to the Communist Party line on a variety of issues."

Daddy began to pull together a sheaf of very impressive references from the likes of Earl Warren, Richard Nixon, Bill Knowland, and his old law partner John Neylan—all in an effort to prove that he was a loyal American.

He also phoned Lewis Nichols, one of Hoover's intimates and head of public relations at the FBI. Nichols tried to have him at least taken off the Security Index (which meant that in the event of an emergency, my father would be put into a concentration camp). My father stayed on the index and the surveillance continued.

Around this time, Mama invited me home for Easter lunch.

Nothing went right. It rained buckets. As soon as I entered the brownstone, Mama informed me that the cook had fallen ill and Daddy was late coming home from Las Vegas. We met him at the Sutton Theater, and then we all sat through a long feature of W. Somerset Maugham short stories. Afterward we went to P. J. Clarke's for hamburgers.

It was exceedingly uncomfortable. We hadn't all been together for months. We'd lost touch with each other; we had nothing to say, although there was plenty to say—if we'd been able to—particularly to my brother, Bart.

"He couldn't adjust," Mama whispered to me. "Adjust to *what?*" I whispered back. Meanwhile, Bart sat there tearing paper napkins into bits, and Daddy said nothing, but he looked absolutely exhausted.

He had returned from Nevada, having filed a petition to get Aly to pay forty-eight thousand dollars for child support, but he couldn't enforce it because neither the prince nor his lawyers showed up.

In the middle of our lunch he was called away. He came back trembling. "Jesus H. Christ," he muttered. "That was J. Edgar Hoover on the pay phone. He said my passport will be taken away unless I go down to Washington and answer some questions—then I'll get it back."

We spent the next half hour trying to figure out if it really was Hoover on the phone—Daddy said he recognized his voice—and if so, how had Hoover known his exact whereabouts? Obviously, we had been followed to P. J. Clarke's. And maybe someone had sat behind us in the darkness of the Sutton Theater. It all felt very creepy.

We rode back to the brownstone in a cab. It was still raining. I remember Daddy running into the house and turning on all the lights. And then he built a fire and we huddled around it. Mama served us hot tea; then inexplicably we began to recite limericks.

It had been a family ritual dating back to Aptos. Whenever it rained, we would sit around a blazing fire, reciting limericks. It served in lieu of conversation—it was a way of avoiding things— but in the past it had always been fun.

At one point that rainy night Daddy recited:

> *His sister, called Lucy O'Finner*
> *Grows constantly thinner and thinner*
> *The reason was plain*
> *She slept out in the rain*
> *And was never allowed any dinner.*

In the past whenever one of us would finish a limerick we'd roar with laughter, Daddy hardest of all. But this night, he tried to laugh, but the laughter turned into a coughing fit, which turned into a near choking convulsion. We watched while his cheeks blew up like balloons—he wheezed and gagged.

Mama ordered gently, "No more limericks," and she put her arms around him and he sort of sagged against her breast. His expression turned stricken, ashy white. I glanced at my brother. His eyes were glaring at I knew not what.

On April 21, 1953, Daddy gave oral testimony at the State Department in private session.

There was so much at stake, he said he thought he might pee in his pants. He was afraid that no matter how persuasively he answered, they might not believe him.

He was questioned for hours on every aspect of his long legal career both in San Francisco and in New York—clients, trips, meetings in Europe and the Middle East—and about references in the endless taped conversations they had listened to on our phones.

The government officials (Daddy did not name them) were especially interested in his meetings during 1943 with Bill Schneidermann, the then president of the American Communist Party. There was mention that my father had been Schneidermann's lawyer. He corrected them; Carol King had been Schneidermann's lawyer. Daddy had been advising Wendell Willkie, who, along with King, defended Schneidermann when he was threatened with deportation. They took the case all the way up to the Supreme Court and won.

Later he wrote, "Everyone wants to be honest about their beliefs and their associations. But when HUAC, in clear violation of the First Amendment, compels you to say what you believe in —that's different."

He followed up his oral interrogation with a written testimony, ending with:

> My general political conviction can be summed up by saying I am one who hopes to be worthy of freedom. I embrace a belief in the human personality—the conviction that progress lies in the free exercise of individual energy. I believe in the ultimate freedom of all individuals and groups from totalitarian oppression. I believe in the power of government —that it should be used for the purpose of maintaining the condition within which individual enterprises can thrive (example—the Sherman Antitrust act—preventing abuses of power—example—First Amendment rights).
>
> I believe that our citizens should have the means to acquire mastery over their talents (example—the public school system).
>
> I believe in establishing equal opportunity for all . . .
>
> I am a practicing Catholic. My religious and political views are not and have never been compatible with Communism or Socialism, which banish free initiative and responsibility from the economic sphere—we have seen the results of this in Communist countries—namely the destruction of political freedom and the growth of police states.

My father thought the interrogation had gone fairly well. He was certain he would get his passport back, and he did—temporarily. He was pleased enough to phone me with the news at the John Robert Powers Model Agency, where I was busy collecting my booking slips.

CHAPTER
26

B Y the summer of 1953 I had left my husband. My brother picked me up in the family car. He didn't ask questions; he just packed the trunk with my stuff and we drove in silence through the damp heat into Manhattan.

A couple of days later, Daddy sent me to Reno for my divorce.

I lived alone there in a boardinghouse on the banks of the Truckee River. Occasionally I explored the town with a colleague of my father's, an elderly judge; we'd walk up and down the main street, lined with neon-spangled gambling casinos. There were slot machines everywhere—in delis and drugstores and gas stations.

Daddy showed up one weekend. Something about financial complications with Rita Hayworth's divorce. After he had done his business in the courts, he drove me to visit Henry Kaiser, the millionaire building tycoon, who had a big estate on Lake Tahoe. The afternoon I met him he took us for a ride in one of his speedboats. He said he was testing a new engine.

Otherwise, during my six weeks in Reno I learned to type and mastered beginning Spanish at the University of Nevada. At the end of my stay, there was a little party for some of the summer students—many of them teenagers from all over the United States. It turned out most of them were getting divorces, too, but we were all too ashamed to admit it.

As soon as I got my divorce, I flew to Sacramento to visit my relatives there, the Cavanaughs and the Crums. I hadn't seen them for years. We sat out in the big backyard, a communal backyard because Aunt Sally's garden adjoined Mo's. It was blazing hot. I could see the Sierra Nevada range in the distance and I vaguely remembered gazing at those same mountains when I was very little. I seemed to be repeating the experience—drinking iced tea from heavy green glass tumblers while my relatives fussed over me and Mo asked questions about Daddy's health.

Late in the afternoon I slipped into Mo's house. It was actually cooler inside. I noticed a little shrine had been set up on the fireplace mantel, honoring my father's achievements. There were photographs of him with President Truman and Governor Earl Warren; a copy of his book *Behind the Silken Curtain;* and the last yellowing edition of the *New York Star,* dated January 27, 1949.

The afternoon after I returned to New York, my brother and I drove up to the new weekend home Daddy had bought for us in Garrison. The place was set on a wooded hill overlooking the Hudson. It had sweeping views of the river, the Palisades, and West Point. I remember we took a stroll around our new property while Daddy described his plans for a garden and Bart strode ahead, sullen and preoccupied, until Mama called after him, "What's the matter, Boofie?" "Boofie" (short for beautiful) was her nickname for him. "Nothing is the matter, *Mother,*" he answered in the weary, ironic tone he had suddenly affected.

I found out later that Daddy had announced he couldn't go off to some music camp in the Caribbean because the tuition was "exorbitant." But the real reason was that he and Mama had heard that the music camp was run "by fairies"; the composer Marc Blitzstein was attached to it, and he was a "fairy," Daddy said.

Bart was furious. He spent the rest of the weekend by himself, away from the house, shooting at tin cans with his .22-caliber rifle.

He forbade me to accompany him. "It would break my concentration," he said.

I'd hear the crack of gunshots as I lay on my bed trying to read a magazine. The sound gave me an unsettling feeling.

In August, Bart was sent to a Quaker work camp somewhere in Missouri.

I SPENT August at Garrison with Mama. She and Daddy were renovating the house and it became a kind of battleground of competing designers and workmen. Fixing up a home seemed the only way my parents could communicate.

Soon the place had sliding glass doors and a big deck and a garden overlooking the Hudson, and the rest of our furniture and books were taken out of California storage and sent to Garrison, including the big white altar.

Since Mama didn't know where it should go, Daddy placed it in the little courtyard behind the kitchen. He liked to sit there by himself with a cocktail in the evening, gazing at the statue of the Mother of God.

In spite of all the work she was doing on the house, Mama was restless. To calm herself she practiced yoga, and she had a masseuse drive over from Peekskill once a week "to keep my muscles from getting atrophied."

She worried about getting old and threatened to have a face-lift, but Daddy refused to give her the money, so she sulked. Once in a while she would appear in my bedroom stark naked and demand, "Don't you think I have the body of a young girl?"

She had just turned fifty-three, but her thighs and stomach were as flat as a teenager's, her arms almost sinewy from tennis and golf. She topped the scales at ninety-eight pounds, and she was a glossy nut brown from hours under her sunlamp.

"Yes, Mama," I'd say. "You have the body of a young girl," and I'd mean it.

She seemed to want my company. She'd linger by the door, then wrap a towel around herself and join me on the bed.

"Saul phoned me today," she announced suddenly one evening just before the sun set. "Do you remember Saul?"

Yes, I did. Anger welled up. I didn't want to hear any more.

She continued: "I wanted to drive to New York to see him, but I decided against it." She stopped, and I realized she was almost in tears.

"I miss Saul," she said. "It's been over five years. When we moved from San Francisco we decided it would be better if we didn't see each other . . . we wrote for a while—I wrote him a great many letters I'm glad I didn't mail."

"Did you love him, Mama?" I found myself asking.

"Very much. I felt I would die when we stopped seeing each

other. It was agony. It's a different kind of love than the love I feel for your father. You won't understand what I mean. You won't understand what I mean now, but you will someday."

She was right. I did.

I can still hear her light, youthful voice telling me, "Oh, I wish I could learn to live without love. I wish I didn't depend so on love! Saul made it possible for me to continue as your father's wife. You won't understand that either yet, but someday you will."

As I do now, decades later—remembering my own infidelities, my betrayals and secret longings I had for various men other than my first husband.

But back in Garrison in 1953, at the beginning of those sleepy Eisenhower years, I was like most of my generation—self-involved, apathetic, drifting. I didn't feel very strongly about anything; so I'd get bored listening to Mama's ramblings. She frequently returned to the same subject—Daddy and his pill problem.

Did I think it had gotten any better? No, I would answer. And then Mama would say, well, she didn't think it had gotten any worse.

Although he had not kicked the habit—he still swallowed a variety of anti-depressants and sleeping pills every day—he seemed to have no intention of stopping, and it seemed under control. Somehow he was managing to have a career and a sort-of life—in spite of the addiction.

On a trip to Paris he had been introduced to the philosopher Jean-Paul Sartre, who "ate pills and drank and seems no worse for it." (In truth, Sartre was a very sick little man.)

Unless we had a guest at Garrison, Daddy would retire immediately after dinner. He and Mama had bedrooms on opposite ends of the house on the second floor, so he could perform his little ritual—knocking himself out with pills—alone. He would always say he was watching TV and we were welcome to join him, but we didn't.

However, it was my responsibility, or my brother's, to make sure he hadn't fallen asleep with a lighted cigarette in his hand. Bart refused the task. When I'd plead with him—"You do it this time"—he'd make a face and say, "You do it—you're the oldest," and he would run off to his room before I could stop him.

So I would wait until close to midnight, and then I would cross through the living room and kitchen and up to my father's cozy little room under the eaves. I would find him there, amid a welter of books and newspapers, snoring thickly on his pillows, a shine of saliva on his chin. I would turn off the TV and the lamp and tiptoe out, feeling unbelievably sad.

As I walked back through the kitchen and into the living room again, Mama would call out, "Is everything all right?"

"Yes," I would answer.

That fall, my brother obtained a passport although he had no travel plans. Then he sent me and Mama copies of his ID photo without any note, just the image of him staring out at the camera with his riveting, mournful gaze.

After that he was off to Reed, a small progressive college in Portland, Oregon. He'd enrolled because a close friend from the Stockbridge school was already attending classes there and really liked it.

I don't believe we said good-bye.

CHAPTER

27

LATE fall, 1953. Very cold suddenly. Weather chilly, bleak. The trees covering the Yonkers hills were only briefly gold. Every time I'd take a walk from the Sarah Lawrence campus into Bronxville, I'd pass leafless elms, and the stream that ran through the town was already frozen. The buildings on Main Street nudged a low-lying sky, pale gray and inert.

Daddy had started to host a local TV talk show, sponsored, I think, by United Jewish Appeal. When Israelis devastated a Jordanian village sometime in October, he brought on United Nations officials to condemn the attack and to talk about what to do about the ongoing terrorism.

Then he flew to California for a round of speeches and business meetings.

Mama was busy creating a gourmet shop in the basement of Bloomingdale's department store. Our house was filled with all manner of exotic goodies—fine French wines, cheese, truffles, pickled frogs' legs, jams, rich cookies, and cakes.

I was caught up, not only in my writing classes at Sarah Lawrence, but I'd also started to audition for Off Broadway shows and live TV commercials, and I was dancing a lot and trying to choreograph dances, too. My entire life seemed to revolve around performing and creating. I felt keyed up and very much alive.

In fact, on the afternoon of December 12, 1953, I was rehearsing in Reisinger Auditorium for a dance concert when I was called to the phone.

I had to run down to the basement to answer it. The floor was freezing-cold cement, I remember; I started shivering, because I was barefoot and wearing only a leotard. I thought the call was from one of my boyfriends, but instead I heard my father's voice on the line from San Francisco, talking very fast.

"Your brother has killed himself," he said. "At Reed College. Shot himself in the head with the twenty-two Granddad gave him."

I felt my body tense up. As yet I did not—could not—grasp the unbelievable loss of my sweet, gentle, melancholy brother. Then the wall came down, and I wondered inside myself, why did you and Mama permit Bart to take his gun to college with him? But I didn't say that; instead I kept my voice calm. "Have you told Mama?"

"No!" my father cried. "I've been trying to find her. But she's out, the maid says. She's out shopping or at the hairdresser's. God knows."

Then he continued. "I want you to go home right away."

"Of course," I said.

"I can't understand why he did it," my father rambled on. "I saw him two days ago, and he was fine—in good spirits." I heard him swallowing. He sounded close to tears. "I better hang up."

The receiver clicked.

I remained in the basement of the auditorium. My feet seemed glued to the icy cement. Someone ran in and put a coat over my shoulders. People already knew that something awful had happened to my brother. Later I discovered that Daddy had been so frantic to speak to me, he'd blurted out the tragedy to the college phone operator in the hopes that he could find me quicker.

After gathering up my things, I stumbled into the freezing air; it was dusk, and I started across campus to my dorm. A classmate stopped me, and I'll never forget her question: "How does it feel to have your brother kill himself?"

The question stunned me. How does it *feel?* I don't know how it *feels,* except that his death has made me feel guilty all my life for having survived it.

EVENTUALLY my best friend Marcia Haynes drove me home to the East Sixty-eighth Street brownstone and remained there. The Christmas tree was already up, lights twinkling; there were gay, wrapped presents under it, some marked "For Bart, Jr." A fire snapped and crackled in the fireplace. Candles glowed in ornate silver candelabras. Mama had been told, but she gave me no sign that Bart's suicide had in any way affected her. While she prepared drinks for us and passed out the usual delicious hot and cold hors d'oeuvres, she demanded to know how college was going—our classes? And what about the teachers? Her face was bunched up with grief, but she strained to keep calm while I chattered inanities. She began pacing back and forth across the floor. I remember thinking how strong her legs looked as she strode up and down the beautifully decorated room.

"Your father says we shouldn't go to the funeral," she announced suddenly. "He will go alone. Bart will be buried in the family plot in Sacramento."

"Mama, I think we should go to the funeral," I began. "I want to go to the funeral."

My mother glared at me. "Oh, no, you don't," she said emphatically. "Nobody wants to go to a funeral."

So I didn't go to the funeral—something I'll regret till the day I die.

A FEW days later I spoke to my old nurse, dear Nell Brown, on the phone—plump, tender, trusting Nell, who had adored my brother as much as he had her, who had taken care of him all those years in Berkeley when he was little.

"Your father asked my husband, Fred, and me to the funeral at the cathedral. We drove up. First we went to the undertaker's with your father, and I saw little Bart's face shot away and I got hysterical, and your father comforted me. Then we went to the cathedral—to the Mass of the Angels. Everybody in black, in mourning clothes—me, your aunts and cousins, uncles. It was a big deal. Nobody could understand why your mother wasn't there. Your father lied and said she'd been too ill, too upset to make the trip. After the Mass we drove out to the cemetery, and the coffin was put into the earth. Your father wouldn't leave the grave. He stood by it all alone. I felt so sorry for him. 'I'm glad you came, Nell,' he said. 'Thank you.' And I said, 'What are you going to do, Mr. Crum?' 'I don't know, Nell,' he said."

■

THERE seemed no letup to the pain. When he returned to New York, he and Mama had to face Bart's friends.

From Mama's journal, December 20, 1953:

> I am not sure I am capable of absorbing what just occurred tonight. Perhaps if I write it out, the thing will lose its power to surprise or hurt me. . . . I have gone to great lengths to avoid believing that my beautiful son is dead. I would not attend the funeral. I told Bart I want the FBI to investigate the death. I suspect it may be murder. I feel even more so tonight.
>
> Bill dropped by, along with Michael—they were two of Bart's closest friends from Stockbridge school. I thought they had come by to offer condolences, to comfort and grieve with us, but instead Bill let loose with a hideous diatribe against both of us as parents. We stood there like fools and took it! I felt as if I was being flayed by whips. My heart pounded as loudly as it pounded when I heard the ghastly news. I tried to be calm. I even listened to what Bill had to say, and it wasn't pleasant.
>
> That we had not been good parents. That Bart had felt lost and alone and misguided and unloved. He heaped particular insults on Big Bart, calling him "an absent father."
>
> "You killed him, Mr. Crum," he told Bart angrily.
>
> I was absolutely horrified by the cruelty of it—and then he turned to me and said, "You killed him, too."
>
> My Bart stood by the fireplace with bowed head. He didn't move—he didn't speak. I finally got the two boys out of there and we huddled in the living room until the maid called us to dinner—a dinner we could not eat.
>
> That night we clung together in one bed. We haven't slept together in years. We didn't speak. We said nothing— just clung together as if on a life raft. The next morning Bart rose and went out before breakfast. It is so awful.

For the next year, Daddy and I would go over and over the incidents leading up to Bart's death, his last hours on earth: he'd done his laundry, brought it back to his room, and laid his khakis and T-shirts neatly on the bed before he pulled the trigger.

He left no note.

Months after his death, we received Bart's meager possessions in a cardboard box. A book on astronomy, a biography of Albert Einstein. There were no family photographs.

The rifle was there, too, wrapped in a pale-blue blanket, which I recognized as a blanket Bart had used back at Aptos.

Mama kept the rifle in the closet of her apartment until she died. She stubbornly insisted Bart had been murdered, and she forced Daddy to get the FBI to investigate, and agents did come back with the following report: no suspect; no motives; no evidence; no clues—all facts pointed to Bart Crum Junior's death having been a suicide, nothing else.

Years later, whenever she'd get angry with me, Mama would cry out that my marriage had driven Bart to suicide. The idea was so preposterous, I would counter with, "You drove my father to kill himself." Later we would apologize to each other, but I could never shake the feeling that if I hadn't been so caught up in my chaotic life with my husband, I might have paid more attention to my brother.

Eventually I would grope for fragments, for clues, for anything that would soothe me, help me understand. I would always wonder why we had all managed to fail him, in ways we could not comprehend. Those last years must have been so torturous for him, those years of sadness.

I would discover that Bart was so depressed at Reed College, one of his friends went to the college psychiatrist and made an appointment for him, which he refused to keep. He was sleeping most of the day and missing a great many classes.

I was told he seemed bored with everything. He had lost interest in everything.

He was living off campus in a rooming house outside Portland. His landlady would describe him as "lonely and very quiet. He kept to himself; wouldn't discuss his affairs with anybody." He did mention he was starting to have trouble completing his assignments; that made him anxious.

About three weeks before he shot himself, he suddenly began talking to another student about his best friend at Deerfield, who had hanged himself, and this had upset him so much he'd had to leave the school. Then he added, "Today I have realized for the first time that I am fundamentally unstable."

When Daddy came to see him a few days later, Bart asked if

he would buy him a car. It was next to impossible for him to go to and from his classes without the use of a car; he had to hitch rides. Daddy said no.

Finally, I would visit my brother's psychiatrist, who had an office in a brownstone on East Ninety-first Street. He told me right away he would say "very little," since "the patient/analyst relationship is sacred."

I said all I wanted was to understand what happened; anything that he would tell me would help.

He had a fat file on his desk marked "Bart Crum, Jr.," but he refused to share it with me. All he would say was that my brother came to see him in the spring of 1953. "I diagnosed him as a schizophrenic—he lived in a fantasy much of the time. He was isolated, alienated, hostile, remote. He spoke very little, used to fall asleep in session. I think he sensed he was in some kind of deep trouble, but he couldn't articulate what was bothering him. He couldn't seem to make up his mind about anything. He never mentioned having a sister or parents."

I asked him if he had known about the incident at Deerfield when a fellow classmate—a boy he cared about—hanged himself from a tree, and then Bart was thrown out of school and sent home.

The doctor shook his head. No.

Did he think Bart had sought to glorify himself in death?

Absolutely not. He did think that the extent of his misery was both unrecognized and denied by my parents.

He also said a big factor was the availability of that gun— the .22-caliber rifle. That my parents had allowed him to take the gun to college with him was irresponsible. They should have forbidden it, he said. They should have gotten rid of the gun.

"They trusted him," I said.

"They didn't know him," the doctor said.

He added grimly that the disorder in young suicides tends to be familial; father or mother depressed—or alcoholic or suicidal.

I did not tell him that Daddy had attempted suicide twice. I could not bear to hear him say that if a parent tried to kill himself, the child often thinks, "Hey—that's a solution. If Dad can do it, so can I."

The doctor told me he became so concerned for Bart's welfare —he was sure he would eventually take his own life—that he met

with my parents and told them Bart should be institutionalized, sent to the Austin Riggs Center in Stockbridge at once. He
should get proper treatment and care right away before it was too
late.

My father would not hear of it. He denied there was anything
wrong with my brother other than "growing pains." He expressed
doubts about psychiatry. He was not at all sure that it could allevi-
ate suffering, and he added that he thought he was paying too
much for the sessions.

"As a matter of fact, he did not pay me for the last session
[in 1953]," the doctor told me.

I immediately got out my checkbook and told him I would
pay for it now.

"Oh, no—no," the doctor said. "Never mind." He then read
from a ragged clipping he had kept about Bart's suicide and my
father's immediate reaction to it:

> Attorney Bartley Crum learned of his son's death a half
> hour before a scheduled speech in front of the Chanukah
> Banquet of the Jewish National Fund at the Mark Hopkins
> Hotel in San Francisco . . . he delivered his speech as
> planned in a room brightened by the symbolic candles of the
> joyful Jewish Feast of Lights. . . .
>
> Crum had been in Portland visiting his son and found
> him in good health and excellent spirits, he said. But who
> could tell if he was troubled? Parents are the last to know,
> don't you think?
>
> Crum was applauded at the banquet by an audience who
> had no knowledge of the boy's death . . . however, Crum
> ended his speech with "the future of man rests with a little
> segment of the world in Palestine . . . in honor of my son I
> pledge a thousand trees to be planted there."
>
> When Crum left the banquet room, Ben Swig (owner of
> the Mark Hopkins) rose to tell the audience the significance
> of those thousand trees.

The doctor stopped reading and turned to me. "Your father
was capable of the grand gesture, but he had no awareness of any
real problem with your brother. He completely denied the existence of any problems either with your brother or with himself."

He refused my check, again. Nor would he say anything more, other than to mention that Mama had come to see him after Bart's death, to go over what had happened, and to seek help from him about Daddy, who was deeper into the pills.

CHAPTER 28

THE two years I spent in college after my brother died are a blur to me. I lived on campus, but I didn't always stay in my room; instead I'd crash in friends' dorms. I'd sleep on a couch or on the floor. Sometimes I'd wake up and find a student climbing over me on her way to fetch her morning coffee. I liked it that way. I'd remain on the floor listening to the chatter and gossip over silly things. It made me feel better.

But I was always tired. I attended classes but I could never relax. I had to keep busy researching papers, attempting to write a novel about my marriage.

I began auditioning for the Actors Studio. I'd go back and forth to New York on the train, and once there I'd rehearse scenes for my audition with a talented young actor named Rick Morse, whom I briefly fell in love with.

I also tried to get interested in what Daddy was doing. By late spring of 1954 he'd completed the agreement with Prince Aly Khan regarding visitation rights with Princess Yasmin, and then there was the question of her inheritance—the settlement came to three million dollars; there were headlines in the papers about it. Daddy set the whole thing up as a trust fund for the little girl.

The papers were full of the story; it was front-page news. Once again reporters camped outside our doorstep or followed Daddy into 21.

Four years of negotiations had taken place around the world. He was exhausted, but he immediately started coping with Rita's new husband, crooner Dick Haymes. Haymes had all sorts of problems with the immigration department and with Internal Revenue. He owed hundreds of thousands of dollars in back alimony to two ex-wives.

For a while Daddy seemed to involve himself almost pathologically in the chaos of Rita and Dick's marriage—maybe to keep from thinking about my brother or his own despair, I don't know. He'd even ask the couple up to Garrison for the weekend, and then it would get ugly because Dick was a mean drunk and sometimes he'd knock Rita around. He wanted her to get serious as an actress, he wanted her to play Sadie Thompson without make-up or a girdle, and they fought about that, and Daddy had to pull them apart and call their limousine to take them back to New York.

But problems kept arising—back rent had to be paid on a house in Connecticut that Rita had used only once and then left in a mess; then Rita was accused of being an unfit mother by a baby-sitter in White Plains.

Daddy would come home from each new crisis looking drained, and then he would slump down in front of the TV set to catch the Army-McCarthy hearings. The country was obsessed with Communism and witch hunting, and McCarthy had reached his zenith as a Red-baiter, humiliating witnesses.

We watched the hearings at Sarah Lawrence, too—the entire student body of 340 packed into the lounge at Reisinger Auditorium. We all watched as McCarthy was finally destroyed by attorney Joseph Welch; it became apparent during the ninth day of hearings that McCarthy was losing ground when he tried to claim that he had a "carbon copy" of a letter from J. Edgar Hoover to the army warning of thirty-four security risks at Fort Monmouth, New Jersey.

Daddy was so appalled by McCarthy's tactics he said that he was going to write about it in his book *Autobiography of an American Liberal;* Simon and Schuster had given him a contract for his memoirs and he had started to wax nostalgic about the Willkie campaign and the frontier atmosphere of California. But as soon as he saw McCarthy on TV he began to try to interpret his "horrific brand of intimidation," and he referred to Adlai Stevenson's address to southern Democrats, in which he described how "a party divided against itself—half-McCarthy, half-Eisenhower—cannot produce national unity."

In the spring of 1954 Daddy surfaced at Sarah Lawrence when seven teachers from the faculty were subpoenaed to appear in front of the Senate Internal Security Subcommittee, then chaired by William R. Jenner, an archconservative Republican from Indiana, to testify as to their political beliefs. Daddy joined Harold Taylor in a debate with the students about First Amendment rights, the meaning of loyalty, and the importance of academic freedom.

I don't believe I heard that debate.

I GRADUATED in June 1955, but I have no recollection of either the ceremonies or being handed my diploma.

I came home to live with my parents. Home was now two duplexes in a brick house on East Fortieth Street. Mama had convinced us she had to leave the Sixty-eighth Street brownstone; it was haunted by the spirit of my brother, she said—so we moved and I was given the larger of the two duplexes, the one with two bedrooms upstairs and a slanting living room with parquet floor and shuttered windows.

My parents chose the smaller one in the back. It had a huge deck overlooking a garden, but only one bedroom, which meant Daddy would be sleeping on the living room couch again. He insisted he didn't mind, and Mama had a special couch built that pulled out into a double bed. He said he liked sleeping in the living room next to the hall that connected both duplexes so he could call out to me. If I was around I'd come running in to see how he was.

My best friend, Marcia Haynes, a beautiful, taciturn blonde, shared my duplex with me until she got married. Daddy took a special interest in Marcia and in her fiancé, Gene Hill, a husky copywriter from Young and Rubicam. They were an intelligent, graceful pair and became like surrogate children to both my parents.

They were in and out of both duplexes constantly. We would share suppers together. Marcia often cooked spicy meat loaf, which Daddy professed to love, and sometimes Mama would organize a dinner party in my duplex and invite "the San Francisco exiles"

—like the Louis Laphams and Mary Kohler, along with playwright Marc Connolly and cartoonist Abner Dean.

That summer I acted in a new play at Westport called *Blue Denim,* directed by Arthur Penn, and when I came home I began sleeping all day. I'd wake up late in the afternoon and then I'd stagger down to the back deck of my parents' duplex; my father was often sitting there by himself.

He could see I was depressed so he would ask me silly questions like, "Can you make love with a straight face?" Then we'd barbecue a steak and polish off an entire bottle of red wine. Sometimes thunderstorms would break the heat and we'd sit in the darkness watching the rain stream down.

We spent a lot of time on that deck together that summer, Daddy and I. It became our favorite place. It was huge and cool and full of green shadows from overhanging trees and a faded green awning.

"It's like Havana," he once told me, and then he went on to describe a recent trip he'd taken to Cuba to meet some director who wanted to work with Rita.

All that summer Mama was away. After making the disruptive move from Sixty-eighth Street, she disappeared—packed up and spent the next three months traveling to Sweden, Denmark, Turkey, and Israel. We'd read her letters out loud—enthusiastic, bubbling, funny, long letters about recipes she was collecting, sights she'd seen, people she'd met. She would try to phone us, but the connections were usually bad, so we could hardly hear what she was saying. Daddy, though, seemed genuinely pleased she was having such a good time. "She needed to get away," he said.

So we were by ourselves a lot. By August Gene and Marcia were married. We had arranged for a champagne reception before they went off on their honeymoon. Now we were alone. We'd wander around both duplexes feeling lost. "Which living room shall we sit in tonight?" Daddy would tease, and his eyes would twinkle, and his cheerful smile never let up even as anxiety etched new lines near his mouth.

He wanted me to believe that everything was in my reach; now that I'd graduated from college, I should be ready to take on the world.

That summer he introduced me to some of his theater friends, like the stern balding Broadway director Herman Shumlin, who'd directed Lillian Hellman's *The Little Foxes* and was her longtime lover. During the war he and Daddy had worked together on the Joint Anti-Fascist Committee.

As a favor, Shumlin auditioned me for his hit play *Inherit the Wind,* about the Scopes Monkey Trial. I replaced one of the understudies and joined the cast of seventy, which included Paul Muni, who played Clarence Darrow, and Tony Randall as H. L. Mencken. I had no lines, but I was in the crowd scenes and was listed in the *Playbill* as the "town hairdresser."

My big moment came when I carried a placard across the stage right after Muni made his first entrance.

In the fall Daddy began handling *New York Times* editor Turner Catledge's divorce and tried to get back into California politics, first as an adviser to Bill Knowland when he tried to run for governor but failed, then to Goody Knight, who also ran for governor and won. There were meetings with both men and dinners at 21 and more meetings in Sacramento, but nothing ever materialized.

In late September Mama returned from Europe, and then Daddy collapsed again. He couldn't seem to get out of bed. We convinced him that he should be committed to a hospital and he agreed. He went off to Silver Hill in Connecticut, which he described later as "a haven for rich drunks." He was to remain there until close to Thanksgiving. "So I'm not going to see the leaves change at Garrison," he told me over the phone.

Then one night he showed up backstage at *Inherit the Wind* just as the curtain was coming down. After I took my bows I ran to hug him as dozens of costumed actors milled around us. There was no place to talk, so we ended up trying to have a conversation on the darkened set until the stage manager shooed us out into the alley.

Daddy assured me that he had left Silver Hill only temporarily. He was out on "good behavior" and he was definitely going back.

He was getting a terrific rest, he said. And he was collecting some prospective clients, too. "Everybody needs the advice of a lawyer when they're in the loony bin," he said.

"Is it a loony bin?" I asked. "I thought it was a sanitarium."

"That's a polite way of saying it's a loony bin—it's a nut house," he laughed. He had made a few new friends. Although he had just lost one he'd liked a lot, "a funny little redheaded dame." The other afternoon she'd wandered off on the highway and was killed by a truck.

I'M not sure when I decided to move from the Fortieth Street duplex. Maybe it was a couple of months after Daddy came home from Silver Hill for good and I saw him asleep on the couch with a cigarette burning between his fingers, and he didn't wake up even after I pulled the white hot burning stub away from him— even after I bandaged his hand.

Anyhow, I moved, in spite of his pleas—and Mama's—that I stay. Neither one of them would loan me the money when I found an apartment, so I borrowed five hundred dollars from a friend and settled into a little studio on East Sixty-sixth Street. I felt relatively happier by myself.

They visited once—climbed the four flights and had some coffee and Mama gave me a housewarming present, a big wooden salad bowl which she told me must be rubbed with olive oil after each use. Daddy said he loved my apartment because it had a wood-burning fireplace. "Always have a fireplace in your apartment," he told me, and so I did for the next twenty years.

Late in 1955, I left *Inherit the Wind* because I got cast in another Broadway play; I had a nice speaking part, but the show was a flop so I had to take odd jobs to support myself.

For a while I worked at Macy's as a product demonstrator; for a while I worked as a hat-check girl at the Stork Club on the graveyard shift.

The place was the anti-Communists' favorite hangout.

Smarmy-voiced Roy Cohn; the heavy, menacing Joseph Mc-Carthy—they trooped past the noisy picket lines and entered the club at least three times a week.

It didn't matter to them that Stork's owner, Sherman Bil-lingsley, was embroiled in a nasty labor dispute; they sort of en-joyed watching him shoot his gun off at the picketers. Once police had to wrestle the weapon out of his hand.

I could see everything from my vantage point. The coatroom

faced the entrance and foyer, as well as part of the bar area, which for some reason Cohn and McCarthy favored. I used to watch them eat breakfast there at 2:00 A.M.; watched them huddling with J. Edgar Hoover and right-wing columnists Walter Winchell and Westbrook Pegler, who frequented the club for gossip items.

Every one of those men had bad-mouthed my father—had intimidated him, spread lies about his politics, his character. So it was strange taking their coats and sweet-talking them into giving me big tips (the tips were my salary) even as I fantasized hurling insults.

But I'd been ordered to keep quiet no matter what and of course I did; I was my father's daughter, polite and soft-spoken, especially in unpleasant situations.

Billingsley had the Stork Club bugged. He recorded conversations (even in the ladies' room), and then he would play them back in his office. I learned this my first night on the job from one of the other hat-check girls. It was the same night she introduced me to the hat-check girls' "lounge" when we took our 3:00 A.M. break, guiding me up into an airless, smelly little attic directly above the coatroom.

The place was filled with shoes, hundreds of pairs of shoes. We ate our dinner (plates in laps) surrounded by sandals, oxfords, moccasins, dancing slippers, buckled pumps, and a great many galoshes—all abandoned by drunken customers over the years. There were styles of shoes dating back to the 1920s, when the Stork Club opened.

I forgot about the shoes after a while because others joined us in the attic: the Stork's photographer, a statuesque brunette, and a couple of off-duty waiters. They tried to fill me in on what was to be expected of a hat-check girl. Never date a customer, never ask questions about what goes on in the club, and that includes the bugging; apparently the listening equipment and the recording system were hidden in an elaborate bar set up in Billingsley's office. It operated manually, but could supposedly pick up the barest whisper. Nobody knew why Billingsley taped conversations and nobody seemed to want to know.

At one time or another the hat-check girls had all experienced Billingsley's hysterical rages. They warned me not to cross him. Recently he slapped his favorite maître d', Ralph, across the face right in front of the coatroom. "Why'd you do that, boss?" Ralph asked sorrowfully; his cheek was beet red. "Because I *felt* like it," Billingsley snarled.

When I told my father about the recording devices at the Stork, he murmured, "Jesus Christ, what next," but that didn't stop him from dropping by the club to see me "in action on the job."

He brought Mama there for Easter Sunday lunch. It was right after the big parade up Fifth Avenue, so the place was mobbed with ladies in great flowered hats and pastel suits and men in morning coats.

I had Ralph guide my parents to an excellent table near the rumba band, and before their chef salads came they got up and danced.

They looked very stylish together, swaying back and forth to the pulsing beat of the music, and they exuded such a life force and dazzling energy they put me to shame. They were quite amazing.

A few weeks later I was fired from the Stork Club for refusing to go on a date with Billingsley. He didn't ask me himself; Ralph asked for him. I was to come up to his office alone for a "glass of orange juice." Those were the key words—*orange juice* meant "date." Anyhow, I refused and made some sort of snotty remark to one of the hat-check girls. An hour later Ralph was guiding me out the door. I didn't even get paid.

It hadn't occurred to me that the coatroom was bugged, too.

AFTER I was fired from the Stork, Mama began phoning me every day: Where was I headed? What about my future? I was twenty-two. She didn't approve of the life I was leading.

I didn't approve of my life much either. I was starting to sleep until noon again, and when I awoke, the numbness I'd experienced right after my brother's suicide had lessened only to be replaced by a sickening feeling of apprehension, of dread. I was worried, I was on guard, but I did not know why.

In between auditions I'd escape to my cloistered sessions at the Actors Studio. I was a member now so I could hang out all day there and sometimes I did, watching the likes of Estelle Parsons or Anne Bancroft explore their craft. In class I acted in a comedy by Shelley Winters called *Hansel & Gretel in the Oven.* Gene

Wilder and Gene Saks performed brilliant comic turns; Jane Fonda chewed up the proverbial scenery while the implacable master teacher Lee Strasberg presided. His reputation was based on nurturing movie stars like Marilyn Monroe, and he could free talent in miraculous ways, but he was cold. I was more interested in attracting the attention of Elia Kazan, the brooding visionary director who'd founded the Studio and had radically altered the face of modern theater with his productions of *Death of a Salesman* and *Cat on a Hot Tin Roof*. He was currently casting the film *On the Waterfront*. I hoped to win the part of Brando's girlfriend. One morning before class Kazan called out to me. I whirled around, expecting I might be asked to audition, but all he said was, "Kid, you know something? You got strong hands."

Mama wasn't impressed. She wanted me to lead a more conventional life and to think about getting married. The men I was seeing—the actor with the glass eye; the nightclub comic who told dirty jokes—were definitely not "husband material," she said.

She'd assure me Daddy was "fine." He was doing the usual: making speeches for Israel all over the country; attracting new clients, like Judy Garland and TV comic Ernie Kovacs, and keeping the others, like Rita Hayworth and Dextra McGonogle. But she wished he would stop going to 21 so much with the hangers-on—his entourage of "seedy little men" who had been dogging him ever since he became Rita's lawyer.

She wanted him to come home after work so they could do things together, spend time together. Often, as in the past, she was forced to make plans without him—"It's the same old thing," she'd say.

She used to drive up to Garrison by herself for weekends with friends—Daddy often had something else he *had* to do. She entertained a lot when he wasn't around; he'd complain that her friends were too "social."

Years later some people expressed surprise to me that they had remained man and wife after my brother died.

"I thought your parents had divorced," someone commented. "I rarely saw them go anywhere as a couple."

ALMOST every afternoon (except weekends) Daddy drank with Dave, the press agent, or with a lawyer named Kal Nulman. They always went to the King Cole bar at the St. Regis Hotel. Kal was a balding, reclusive man who'd never married. He lived by himself on Park Avenue and practiced law in both New York City and Long Island.

He called himself my father's best friend.

In his office Kal kept a photograph of himself with Daddy taken at a party; they are both wearing funny hats and laughing uproariously. They had met in Washington during World War II. They were in constant touch. Kal was devoted to him.

Daddy phoned Kal the afternoon my brother shot himself.

"I said, 'What do you want me to do, Bart? I'll come out there right away.'

"And he said, 'No, Kal—just talk to me.' He was very broken up—there was nothing I could say—nothing I could ever say."

Kal maintained, "Bart's reach exceeded his grasp of things. He wanted to do so many things he wasn't able to. He was a decent, good man; terrible things happened to him, and they shouldn't have. He was an innocent." Kal said he never saw my father drunk. "Never heard him slur a word. I didn't know anything about the pills." Kal maintained he knew nothing about Daddy's barbiturate addiction or his alcoholism.

Kal visited him at Silver Hill and brought him booze. "He asked me to, so I did."

Once when we were talking, Kal suddenly informed me, "Your mother thought your father and I were lovers. We weren't, but I loved your father more than anybody in my life."

CHAPTER

29

In 1958, Daddy won the Pepsi-Cola account; it would be hugely lucrative for the firm, so his partners were pleased.

Mama decided they should move again. She found another duplex, in a brownstone on East Eightieth Street, that was more spacious than the two duplexes combined; she could take some of her beloved antiques out of storage. "This is the last move, I promise," she said.

Toy returned. He appeared out of the blue one afternoon in Daddy's law office. Something about the Chinese cooks network. Apparently, Nixon's Chinese cook had told Rockefeller's Chinese cook about my brother's death and he had told Toy. Toy was very upset, so he dropped by the office unannounced to tell Daddy how sorry he was and to offer to cook for our family again every once in a while.

It would please him, he said. He was making plenty of money working for some very rich banker—a bachelor who lived on East End Avenue and had no appreciation for his culinary skills. "All he wants is hamburger," he said.

Daddy seemed happy having Toy around. He would come home from his office and putter in the kitchen with him; he started baking biscuits again and Toy taught him how to make ladyfingers covered with powdered sugar.

That same year, Daddy got another client: Godfrey Schmidt, a lawyer who was representing the Teamsters against James Hoffa.

Schmidt, a devout Catholic, taught theology at Fordham. He

was also a rabid anti-Communist and the founder of a shoddy witch-hunting pamphlet called "Aware, Inc." His friends included Joseph McCarthy and Roy Cohn.

Even given Daddy's devotion to the right of counsel, it was difficult to understand why he would represent Schmidt since the man seemed to stand for everything he was against.

But when I brought this up, Daddy actually snapped at me that by defending his right to counsel, "I defend *your* right to counsel. Besides, I need the dough."

Schmidt's firm represented rank-and-file Teamsters who were concerned about the terrible corruption within the union, which had been infiltrated by gangsters lured by the union's $250 million pension fund.

Robert Kennedy, chief investigator of the Senate Rackets Subcommittee, was urging Schmidt to bring suit on behalf of Teamster dissidents who were challenging James Hoffa's 1958 election as president. (Indeed, thousands of anti-Hoffa ballots had been found dumped unceremoniously down a laundry chute.)

Nineteen dissident Teamsters got an injunction against Hoffa and kept him from taking office until Schmidt and Hoffa's lawyer, Edward Bennett Williams, met secretly to settle the suit. As part of the settlement, Schmidt was appointed as one of the three monitors to oversee the union; the goal—to make Hoffa clean up the union and kick out all the gangsters and racketeers.

Hoffa loathed Schmidt and knew he wanted to destroy him. He therefore wanted him off as monitor, so he kept him from being paid.

That's where my father came in; he was hired to collect Schmidt's fees. As of August 1958, Schmidt had been paid for only six months of his services; he claimed he was owed $25,000 for his job during the year, plus $105,000 for representing Teamster dissidents in 1957.

My father's fee was contingent on whether he collected Schmidt's fees.

For the next year Daddy was part of a bizarre series of secret meetings with Hoffa, Robert Kennedy, and Harry Bridges, not to mention the FBI. It was supposed to be hush-hush. Mama and I never quite understood what was going on.

Teamster lawyers would appear at the duplex and at Garrison;

so would various federal investigators and Eddie Cheyfitz, Hoffa's loyal PR man. They would have whispered conversations with my father, and then leave. The phone would ring. One night I picked up the receiver and a guttural, rasping voice demanded, "Is Bart Crum there? Tell him Jimmy Hoffa wants to speak to him."

Daddy would never explain the reason for the phone calls or the mysterious meetings.

Sometimes Godfrey Schmidt would drop by. A pudgy, genial man with small lifeless eyes hidden behind thick glasses, he would tease my father about "still being too soft on Communism," and he'd add that he was going to have to toughen him up, and they would laugh and then Godfrey would ask if there had been any progress made getting him his fee.

He said he was so broke he couldn't pay his light bill; his electricity had been turned off and his wife and six kids were living in darkness. Then he would change the subject. "The world is a dangerous place," he would say. He always carried a gun. Apparently Jimmy Hoffa had threatened his life six times and warned that he was going to burn his house down. All because he was so relentless about exposing the union leader's corruption.

Robert Kennedy was equally relentless about gathering evidence to expose that corruption, too.

By 1959 his staff had grown to more than one hundred lawyers; fifteen hundred witnesses had testified to a pattern of stolen union funds and conflict of interest between employers and union leaders, and one man was blamed: James Hoffa.

My father was discovering the same pattern in his secret talks with Teamster bosses. Hoffa had total disregard for the welfare of the rank and file. Small wonder that whenever Daddy was in Washington Robert Kennedy would grab him for a quick lunch in the Senate cafeteria, and often Senator John Kennedy (who was also a member of the Rackets Committee) would join them, and Daddy would repeat off the record stuff he'd been collecting from pro-Hoffa Teamsters.

In return for such information Robert Kennedy obtained one of Daddy's FBI files and gave it to him. After reading it he was exultant. "They have nothing on me!" he cried. "Nothing!"

He'd come back from a trip to the capital full of praise for the Kennedy brothers. "They are like sticks of dynamite," he'd tell me. He had never met such driven, ambitious young men. All the clichés were true; they were tough, they were ruthless, and they were going to stop at nothing "to get Hoffa." They had amassed thousands of pieces of evidence to trap him. They were using everybody, he said.

He did not add, "And they are using me." If he saw it that way (I certainly do in retrospect) he didn't seem to care. He saw himself as a failure. ("I'm just one big zero," he told me.) Exhausted spiritually, emotionally depleted, in despair, he seemed briefly energized from moving behind the scenes with so many powerful, famous men.

So in July 1959, when Robert Kennedy asked him to testify in front of the committee and describe what was going on behind the scenes vis-à-vis the monitors, my father agreed immediately.

His senior law partner, Mortimer Hays, ordered him not to do it. It wasn't necessary and it could be damaging to the firm. Hays had been warned that if he testified, Hoffa could stop Pepsi-Cola from being delivered around the country. Hays did not want to lose Pepsi as a client.

Mama didn't think my father should testify either. He was in and out of depressions; the pills made him jittery and forgetful. But he wouldn't listen to Mama or his law partner. "This is important," he said. "It's important what I have to say."

I suppose it was.

He went down to Washington on the train by himself and had lunch with Edward Bennett Williams, Hoffa's lawyer. He told me later he wasn't nervous. He would be testifying in the same caucus room in the old Senate office building where he'd defended the Hollywood Nineteen eleven years earlier. This time, instead of newsreels there were television cameras with gum-chewing technicians squatting behind them. And reporters elbow-to-elbow at the four big press tables; a few of them said hello.

Georgetown matrons crowded in the spectators' section; they all wore dark glasses and pale summer frocks. Perle Mesta had a prize seat behind the committee table; she waved at Daddy; he had attended some of her parties. A very pregnant Ethel Kennedy led a crowd of her friends to a key observation post on the side, and Robert Kennedy, freshly crew-cut, walked down front. He never even looked at my father, and attorney Edward Bennett

Williams didn't either; he sat next to his client, Jimmy Hoffa, who was so plump his neck bulged above his collar. He didn't have on his usual white socks, Daddy noted—instead he wore light-blue ones with his polished black shoes.

The hearings began and ground on in routine style, and then, according to Hugh Sidey, who was reporting on the story for *Time*, "Bart Crum, a bespectacled, mild mannered attorney, snapped reporters out of their naps with a tale of an attempt to buy off a witness."

My father began by identifying himself as Godfrey Schmidt's attorney.

He said Hoffa started pressuring him in the summer of 1958, when three lawyers—Sidney Feldshuh, Joseph Louroto, and Bernard Fierson—drove up to Garrison and told him they "spoke for Hoffa."

They said they would arrange to pay $45,000 in monitors' fees and an additional $105,000 (for representing twelve anti-Hoffa truck drivers) to be paid to Schmidt if he quit the monitorship.

My father added that they wanted him as Schmidt's replacement—to be a monitor and to "vote for Hoffa." My father said he thought Hoffa wanted "a stooge—not a monitor," so he rejected the proposal. But he did go on to say he had reported all this to Federal Judge F. Dickinson Letts (who was in charge of the dissident Teamsters' case). He immediately ordered him to inform the FBI of every move the pro-Hoffa Teamsters made to him after that. Which he did.

In the next year he relayed conversations he'd had with Harry Bridges in San Francisco and his number-one aide, Louis Goldblatt, secretary treasurer of the Longshoremen's Union. They urged my father to accept the offer Hoffa's lawyers had presented to him earlier. Bridges then explained—according to my father—that the Longshoremen were completing arrangements for a merger with the Teamsters Union to form a giant transportation union in the United States, Alaska, and Hawaii. Schmidt had opposed such an arrangement, so Bridges wanted to remove him as a monitor. Daddy made it clear that he felt Hoffa was directing this maneuver, although he had never spoken to the Teamster president about it.

At this point Senator John Kennedy interrupted with "This is just another example of the Teamsters Union and Mr. Hoffa attempting to corrupt justice."

My father ended his testimony charging that the day before he'd had lunch with Hoffa's attorney, Edward Bennett Williams, at Duke Zeibert's restaurant in Washington and Williams had offered to pay Schmidt's fee of forty-five thousand dollars the very next day if Daddy agreed not to testify in front of the Senate Rackets Committee.

This remark brought shocked murmurs from the caucus room.

"I thought this was an immoral exercise of power," my father added. "I refused."

Chairman John McClellan cautioned Daddy that he'd made a pretty serious charge and reminded him that he was under oath.

"Well," my father said, "it is the truth."

With that, Williams, who had been sitting with Hoffa in the caucus room, angrily demanded that McClellan let him testify immediately and deny under oath "this false, vicious, contrived smear."

McClellan agreed. Williams was so undone he forgot to put out his cigarette as he held up his hand to be sworn in. He then proceeded to call my father's story "completely, unequivocally, unqualifiedly false." And he denied that he had offered Schmidt any inducement to resign or to keep my father from testifying. He said he had a witness to prove it. (Daddy hadn't mentioned anyone else at the lunch.)

Williams identified the third man as Harold Unger, a Justice Department lawyer. So Unger was sworn in under oath and described the lunch conversation with Bart Crum as "mostly anecdotes." He never heard a word about payment to Schmidt. He added that he had gone to that lunch because he had always wanted to meet Bart Crum.

The hassling continued, with Williams denying, my father reaffirming. Finally Chairman McClellan asked, "Mr. Crum, do you have anything [more] to say?"

"No, sir, except to repeat what I said."

With that the chairman shook his head. "Someone has veered from the truth. This matter should not go unattended."

DADDY'S testimony created a sensation. It was front-page news across the country. Our phones rang and rang. Then, the next day, Hoffa got on the stand and denied being party to a bribe or that there was any plan for a merger with the Longshoremen's Union. He ridiculed my father's story and accused him of associating with Communists.

There were humiliating repercussions: Harry Bridges also maintained that there was no truth to my father's story; *The Washington Post* called him a "slanderer"; and his law partner Mortimer Hays said he should be "institutionalized" for what he'd done, and if he didn't recant he would be asked to leave the firm immediately. "Perjure myself?" I remember Daddy crying out. I can still see him pacing around the living room of our Eightieth Street duplex, his face rigid, drained of color. "Perjure myself? I cannot do that," he kept repeating.

And he didn't. He returned to Washington and met with Supreme Court Judge Felix Frankfurter (whom he'd last met when he and Wendell Willkie were working on the Schneidermann case in front of the Supreme Court).

Together he and Frankfurter and Williams hammered out a statement repudiating any inference that he'd been bribed or that Williams had made unethical demands.

But my father did not change the language of his original statement—he just modified it. He maintained that he had inadvertently put together more than one conversation; there had been so many many meetings over the past year.

He added, "My testimony remains as it was given. However, I am willing to accept Mr. Williams's statement that he did not intend to offer a bribe when he said Mr. Schmidt's fee would be paid."

He returned to New York and sat on the couch hunched over his drink. The phone rang and rang but he refused to take all calls. Every so often he would repeat sadly and quietly, "I told the truth. I told the truth."

YEARS later I would discover that my father was indeed telling the truth. I would learn that Edward Bennett Williams did offer him a bribe, but at lunch in New York at the St. Regis Hotel on a Tuesday, rather than at Duke Zeibert's on Thursday in Washington.

Tragically, the pills and liquor made him suffer not only blackouts but also severe memory loss. He would grow bewildered and forget where he had been twenty-four hours previously; he would make mistakes about dates, places, people he had seen.

His friend, lawyer Kal Nulman, explained the confusion years after the fact, "Because I saw your father for our usual drink the evening of the day he was bribed at the St. Regis."

And Godfrey Schmidt told me the same thing. "Yes, yes," he said. "Your father was telling the truth. Absolutely, he never lied." (Then, why didn't he stand up and vouch for his integrity at the time? He ignored my question.)

Williams would never see me and now, of course, he is dead, too. But there is an intriguing paragraph in Hoover's FBI files on Williams. The file confirms that "Williams offered a lawyer a bribe in New York in July of 1959; the lawyer was to be 'bought off,' " but, the FBI informant states, "Williams was too shrewd and too smart to be involved in a fraud."

A few days after testifying Daddy returned to his law office and tried to get back to work. Joseph Wershba, who later became a producer of *60 Minutes*, interviewed him for the *New York Post*. In a letter to me he remembered my father as "rather shy and sad." He said he simply could not ask him any questions about his testimony; instead he found himself summing up his career. "I had to. This was a man—for better or worse—to whom attention must be paid."

For some people Bartley C. Crum is best remembered as Rita Hayworth's lawyer. They remember his handsome debonair figure moving calmly through those breathless early years of the 1950s when every headline cried havoc about the trials and tribulations of Hollywood's sex goddess and her children and her lost Prince Aly Khan and then her husband Dick Haymes and what of Orson Welles?

For other people Bartley Crum is remembered as the Wendell Willkie campaign manager who came out of the West as a liberal Republican and who wound up publishing the tempestuous ill-fated *PM* and the *New York Star*.

And then there is also Bartley Crum the Roman Catholic who spent his most vigorous years fighting for a Palestine homeland for uprooted European Jews . . . even today his

1947 book *Behind the Silken Curtain* makes for powerful moving documentation for events so shatteringly described in Leon Uris's *Exodus*. . . .

This week long after people had begun to wonder whatever happened to him, Bartley Cavanaugh Crum reappeared on the public scene in Washington. As in days gone by it was something of an explosion.

CHAPTER

30

AFTER the Senate Rackets Committee debacle, Daddy's career fell into a shambles. His law firm kept him on, but they ordered him to bring in more clients or get out. They were tired of his extravagances, his promises. They remained angry at his testimony in front of the committee, refusing to believe he had told the truth. In fact, some of the lawyers in the firm knew he was telling the truth, and Hoffa knew, and so did Ed Williams, but nobody stood up for him publicly—his own client, Godfrey Schmidt, didn't stand up for him—but even so, Daddy decided he would move to Schmidt's firm in January 1960. He didn't tell us of his plan.

Meanwhile, I'd visit him almost every morning at the brownstone. I'd feed him cup after cup of coffee. The sleeping pills hadn't always worn off; he would be groggy, his speech slurred. When it was time to go to his office, he could not walk steadily. It was as if he were drunk.

Mama and I begged him to see a specialist, who urged him to withdraw from all barbiturates; they were poisoning his system. But he refused.

In September he fell out of bed; he'd taken so many pills that when he reached to turn on his lamp he blacked out and tumbled onto the carpet. He lay there unconscious, his nose bleeding. Mama summoned our landlord, Dr. Lutz, who lived in the downstairs apartment. He somehow managed to lift my father back onto the pillows.

■

A WEEK went by. Then on September 15, 1959, a date Mama said she would never forget (she kept notes), Daddy rushed into the brownstone. He'd come back from his office because he had forgotten something—"My raincoat," he called out. He seemed terribly excited—jittery—but he was in and out of the apartment before Mama could run down from the second floor.

She opened the closet. He had not taken the coat, so she reached into the pocket and found a just-opened bottle of Seconals containing two hundred tablets.

That same night, around eleven o'clock, Daddy returned from a business dinner and collapsed right in front of us, onto the living room rug. He fell with a terrible, moaning cry.

While I tried unsuccessfully to lift him onto the couch, Mama rushed to the apartment landing and screamed for our landlord, Dr. Lutz.

I thought Daddy was dying. He lay stiff and white-faced on the rug and appeared not to be breathing. I knelt down beside him and took his hand in mine. It was as cold as ice.

Within moments Lutz ran up from the downstairs duplex. He got there in time to see Daddy begin convulsing. He seemed to be having an epileptic seizure. (Years later I would learn that this kind of seizure happens when one is not only addicted but being poisoned by pills.)

Lutz loosened his collar and belt. When Daddy came to, he did not recognize the doctor. And the next day he had no memory of the doctor having been in our apartment at all.

Mama told me afterward that she had never been able to take the pills away from my father for one reason: "I know he will buy more, and black market pills are so costly—no good doctor would prescribe a bottle of two hundred pills." They would save money if he kept to the supply he had.

She wondered hysterically if she should ask him to choose between her and the pills. She had repeated to him time and again that she could not go on watching him destroy himself, but then she *had* gone on, and he had repeated the same pattern.

In November 1959 he was hospitalized, but still he managed to get pills—Tuinals, Nembutals, Seconals; somehow he managed in spite of the doctors and Mama pleading with him that he must break the habit. He got them on his own—he had pills in his shoes, in the lining of his coat. While he was in the hospital, he was put under twenty-four-hour surveillance with a male nurse; a psychiatrist advised long-term treatment at some drug rehab center. He refused, saying he would fight commitment in every court of the land.

My father was truly addicted. He took quantities of pills for the last ten years of his life. Now everybody knows that Seconal, Tuinal, all barbiturates, are not only addictive, but there are a number of terrifying side effects: disturbing irrationalities, memory loss, blackouts, convulsions, and a frightening loss of judgment, not to mention paranoia.

DECEMBER 8, 1959, Mama decided to give a dinner party. She said it was to celebrate Daddy's birthday, which had occurred two weeks before. Otherwise there was no particular reason. She hadn't entertained much in the last year; most of their friends had been told that my father was "ill"—a discreet way of saying he was still trying to kick the barbiturates habit.

I came to that dinner party dreading the evening and anticipating the worst.

I already knew, for starters, that as soon as I entered the brownstone duplex I would be "on" for fifteen minutes, describing my day. (My "day" at that point revolved around acting on the NBC-TV soap opera entitled *Young Dr. Malone.* For the past six months I'd had a running part playing nurse Fran Merrill, who happened to be engaged to young Dr. Malone's son.)

Daddy had a TV set hooked up in his law office so he could watch my performance. Usually, he would phone me after the show to tell me how I'd done.

He hadn't phoned me today, so sure enough, the minute I appeared at the party he called out, "Hey, baby, give your old man a kiss," and as soon as I did he began plying me with questions about *Young Dr. Malone.*

His voice sounded so eager, so intense, that some of the guests gathered round to listen as I described the crisis, the catastrophe, that had occurred that afternoon. In the middle of the broadcast (the show was broadcast live), I'd carried a patient's breakfast tray into the hospital room set and dropped it in the middle of my big closeup. There was nothing I could do, but I was so thrown that instead of ad-libbing, I'd said my line: "Here's your breakfast."

Everybody in the cast broke up. Even I had a hard time keeping a straight face. "It was like a farce," I told my father. "But I may be fired."

"You'll never be fired. You're too popular."

"Oh, Daddy."

I tried to stop him, but he was warming to his subject. "How many letters do you receive from your fans every week?"

"I don't remember."

"You said at least five hundred letters a week." He turned to some of the guests. "My daughter gets five hundred letters a week —I've never received five hundred letters in my life. How many of you in this room can say . . ."

Luckily this conversation went no further because more guests were drifting in—playwright Marc Connolly, editor Clay Felker, the actress Louisa Horton and her husband, director George Roy Hill, about to direct *Look Homeward, Angel* with Tony Perkins.

The dinner was perfect, like all the dinners Mama planned. That night she served an international meal: Japanese chicken curry with peach chutney; French waffles for dessert.

Conversation was lively. There was no mention of the McClellan Senate Rackets Committee hearings.

What was so extraordinary about that evening is that midway through it Daddy's mood changed totally. When I'd come in I sensed he'd been fighting a depression, which is why he questioned me so maniacally about the show. He had been chainsmoking, drinking a lot. His brown eyes had a strange, faraway look—preoccupied by something very deep and very dark. It was almost as if he were about to take off into another world.

He began to speak to us about mortality, about communicating, getting in touch. "Life is preposterous," he said. "You go through the motions and then you wake up and realize something is missing—something big is missing."

He may have alluded to his son, my brother, Bart, whose suicide had occurred five years ago, because he murmured, "Not a day goes by that I do not think of my boy and mourn him."

He added that he was no longer frightened of death. He even described the kind of wake he would like—a good Irish wake, with great food cooked by Cutsie, and lots of booze and old friends from Sacramento, Berkeley, and San Francisco.

Just mentioning California seemed to put him in a better mood. Suddenly he became my Daddy of the past: teasing, funny, drawing everybody out about themselves, and he flirted with my mother and she flirted back.

Old anecdotes poured out of him, too—memories of the challenges he'd had of writing speeches for Wendell Willkie; the all-night debate he'd had with Bertolt Brecht about American left-wing politics; dancing with Rita Hayworth in Paris: "she made me feel like Fred Astaire"; sharing a Chinese dinner with President Truman in San Francisco: "the Secret Service guys ate all our fried rice"; walking through the desert outside Jerusalem with Chaim Weizmann, discussing the possibility of partitioning Palestine.

These were some of the highlights of his life and he wove them in and out of his conversation like jewels on a necklace—the more memories you have, the more you have lived.

For a few brief moments Daddy started to enjoy himself and everybody noticed; as the party was breaking up some of the guests remarked, "Bart Crum is his old self again." They repeated it as they said their good-byes, before strolling out into the chilly night. Had it started to snow?

I stayed on to gossip with Mama. We talked about clothes and the latest movies and what was the title of that great short story by John Cheever in *The New Yorker?*

Then Mama blurted out, "Your father is not going to take any more pills. He promised me." Her eyes filled with tears. "I have been going through such hell with him lately, I don't know how much longer I can stand it."

"What are you two girls whispering about?"

It was my father calling from his bedroom upstairs.

"Nothing important, Daddy."

"I bet. Hey, come and give me a kiss good night before you go." His voice was just the slightest bit slurred.

Mama and I looked at each other. I embraced her—something I rarely did. I left the brownstone shortly afterward without going up to see him.

The next morning I was wakened by a phone call. Mama spoke very formally: "Your father is dead."

THERE was a funeral mass in New York at St. Ignatius Loyola. Then Daddy's body was shipped out to California for burial. A memorial was held at the cathedral in Sacramento. Neither Mama nor I attended. I cannot offer any logical explanation for my absence.

I was told by my cousin Jim that afterward at the graveyard my grandmother Mo was startled to see twelve rabbis rocking back and forth as the coffin was lowered into the earth; on the way back to her car one of them approached her to say, "Your son was a great man. He did so much for the nation of Israel. We came to pay our respects."

Mo tried to be polite. Later she told my father's sister, "They should not have been there." She believed all of Daddy's troubles began when he took on *"those* people, and they had never helped *him.* He should have stuck to the law and stayed out of foreign affairs."

My father was buried in the family plot, next to his son, my brother, Bartley Crum Jr.

EPILOGUE

AFTER my father died I was very much by myself. I acted on television and in theater, but I had very little social life to speak of, unless you count the on-again, off-again affair I was having with an aspiring playwright named Mel Arrighi. He eventually became my second husband.

For the most part the only other people I saw were admirers of my father's, friends of my father. I actually sought them out. It was something I felt compelled to do.

I saw the lawyer Kal Nulman and Dave, the press agent Daddy enjoyed being with so much, and the Holocaust survivors who came to see me in all the plays I acted in. They called my father a hero—a saint.

They would remind me that he had been important once: during the winter of 1946, when he saw himself called upon to tell the world about the terrible plight of the one hundred thousand displaced persons, rotting away in internment camps all over Eastern Europe.

Sometimes I'd be invited for Passover by Dave, and I'd sit at his long table with the traditional dish of apples, raisins, honey, walnuts, and wine—which I was told symbolized the mortar the Israelites used to bind the bricks for the pharaoh's palaces in ancient Egypt—and I'd be introduced to people as "Bart Crum's daughter" and there would be "oohhing and ahhing," and then they might tell me they had celebrated other Passovers with my father in cities like Cleveland or Dallas after he had made a speech.

Nobody knew he was married or had a family. "Bart Crum was such a mensch," someone said, but he often acted uncomfortable at those seders, as if he didn't belong.

Apparently he would make excuses and leave early, go back alone to his hotel or run to catch a plane. He was always on the move.

I remember, too, hearing that as a result of his devotion to Israel—to Zionism—and his incessant speechifying, often for no pay, streets were being named in his honor throughout the Holy Land, and money was being raised for forests to be planted in the deserts—forests that would be named "Bartley Cavanaugh Crum."

Years later I began searching for those streets. I'd ask Israelis from Tel Aviv or Haifa if they knew of streets in their cities named "Crum." They didn't. Nor were there any forests rising up in my father's memory, or my brother's, for that matter. I asked the library in Jerusalem to please check.

"Sorry," the fax read. "There is no record of any street or any forest in the state of Israel named Bartley Cavanaugh Crum."

And then I realized that Daddy wouldn't have cared one way or the other. He would have been flattered—but he wasn't about memorials.

I did not tell Mama any of this.

IN 1962 I took a job as double understudy to Betsy von Furstenberg and Barbara Bel Geddes in the Broadway comedy *Mary, Mary*, so I had to be on standby at the theater six nights a week.

Mama used to phone me regularly. I'd have to race down the four flights of stairs from my dressing room to the pay phone near the stage door. I'd stand there holding the receiver to my ear, not saying much because the show was still in progress. Jean Kerr's *Mary, Mary* was the biggest comedy hit of the early 1960s. I could hear Bel Geddes and Barry Nelson belting out their lines; the audience kept roaring with laughter—waves of laughter rolled around me.

I tried to listen to what my mother was saying, dimly aware that I kept crossing back and forth from the world of make-believe into the world of my family's tragedies, because whenever Mama phoned I was forced to confront some problem; often it had to do with her isolation or her financial precariousness.

But she would never talk about what was bothering her. Instead she would make excuses. She was worried about *me;* worried I'd never marry; worried I would never be "successful at anything"; worried I was getting old (I was pushing thirty); worried that I had too many lines in my face.

DADDY had died broke—bankrupt, the newspapers said. He had left fourteen thousand dollars in his bank account, but piles of debts.

Mama refused to pay some of the bills, including an enormous one from 21—"Because your father brought them so much business, they should pay *him.*"

There had been a $100,000 insurance policy, but she had gone through that in less than two years. She had been forced to leave the spacious Eightieth Street duplex and she'd moved to a studio apartment off Sutton Place.

To support herself she worked for a while at the Frank Travel Agency and she also did catering for Hanover Trust, organizing lavish breakfasts for "hordes of bankers."

In time she created an ingenious little menu-planning service by mail, and soon she had more than seven thousand subscribers (including Jacqueline Onassis and Mrs. Herbert Hoover). They subscribed to a wide variety of meals, from summer picnics to "notable feasts" at a cost of seventy dollars a year.

Although the service was popular, she always operated at a loss. At one point a San Francisco friend, banker Lewis Lapham Sr., arranged for Heinz Foods to buy the service for a tidy sum, but Mama refused the offer. "I loathe ketchup," she said.

She went on living as she always had—beyond her means. She never had enough money for her extravagant tastes, so she was not above borrowing from friends or from me. Sometimes she'd use the loans to finance lavish dinner parties she'd give, complete with champagne and caviar, in her little one-room apartment.

I would periodically pay her rent (luckily her apartment was rent-controlled), and I indulged her as much as I could. When she wanted more engraved stationery from Tiffany's or a "divine new pair of shoes" she'd spotted at Bergdorf's, I'd give her the money.

Hadn't Daddy ordered me to take care of Mama? He had been saying that to me and my brother ever since we were little.

Whenever he'd go off to Washington or Hollywood, he'd repeat, "Take care of Mama. I'm counting on you." Finally I would totally support her. I would always rationalize that I wouldn't have worked so hard if I hadn't been responsible for Mama.

But over the years her demands sometimes threatened to suffocate me.

And yet she never stopped being surprising and somehow endearing. While I was in *Mary, Mary* she became embroiled in a secret romance with a man young enough to be her son (he was thirty; she was sixty-two). He was married and lived in the sub-urbs. I didn't even know his name. She never let me meet him.

She told me her young lover made her feel like a "complete woman." She had always longed for that feeling. "I wanted to experience it before I died." She was "grateful" to him—she said that word almost humbly, as if she didn't deserve it; she was grateful for having finally experienced those "jolts of feeling, those stabs of feeling—of emotion—like bolts of electricity" from the base of her neck to the center of her groin.

The affair would continue for a decade. Once she phoned to whisper to me, "He just called me a c-u-n-t. Is that good or bad?"

It depends on the situation, I told her.

We didn't usually exchange such intimacies when we saw each other. We usually made small talk, which we were both adept at. I would see her once a week, dreading the occasion because she was not the most soothing companion, but looking forward to our meetings in some perverse way since she was the only member of my immediate family who was still alive.

We would meet around 5:30, right after she came home from work. She lived a few blocks from her office in her studio apart-ment on Sutton Place. It was fixed up with the elegant remnants of our homes in San Francisco and New York. I could stay with her only for about an hour since I had to be backstage promptly at 7:30.

I used to fidget outside in the mirrored hallway of her apart-ment building, certain that when she opened the door she would be immaculately dressed in navy blue cashmere and pearls, her honey-blond hair perfectly coifed ("I'd rather starve than miss my appointment at Kenneth's"). And she would be smiling radiantly even if she felt miserable. She had an overwhelming need to deny and suppress her pain (as did I), so we could never comfort each other.

As soon as I entered the apartment, a ghastly feeling of melancholy would wash over me. Because every piece of furniture, every object, reminded me of my father—especially the ornate silver candelabra that had been an anniversary present and the oil painting of my brother at the age of five, which Daddy had commissioned when we were living in Berkeley.

My mother and I did not embrace. Instead I would sit down on the chartreuse-green silk couch while she walked briskly about fixing us drinks at the beautifully appointed little bar. I always noticed her shapely legs and tight little bottom; she exercised religiously and scolded me because I did not.

Within a couple of minutes we would face each other. Like an automaton I would recount my auditions of the week, reading for Sir Tyrone Guthrie and Richard Burton, getting into the finals for a spark plug commercial.

She thought I was wasting my life as a Broadway understudy. "You behave as if you're all washed up. We gave you every advantage. Where is your backbone? You'll never go on for Bel Geddes. She's healthy as an ox. When will you get a real job to prove what you can do?"

I'd sit silently frowning during these harangues, my fists clenched. I had no answer. I couldn't admit how unhappy I was, how baffled by my misery. I couldn't figure out why I was hiding out in my dressing room (I would stay there more than four years), except in some strange way it seemed not only inevitable but a natural way to grieve. And I was grieving—I realize this now—for so much that I couldn't even think to write about yet.

A part of me actually enjoyed the routine of understudy rehearsals and then wandering around in the squalor and glitz of Times Square before rushing up the stairs again to that bleak little dressing room where my typewriter was and the cot against the wall and the books piling up on the floor.

But I lived in a daze in those years—in a total daze—only vaguely aware of the Vietnam War and the social upheavals of the 1960s.

Finally, Mama would stop talking about me and begin reminiscing about Daddy and the "old days" in California, when everything had been "golden and beautiful." And then she would declare dramatically, "Your father was the only man I ever loved!"

Whenever she said that I tried not to feel emotion, but the anger would rise up in my throat and threaten to choke me, and after a few seconds I could stand it no longer and I would blurt out: "If you loved him so much, why did you have lovers? If you loved him so much, why did you seem angry all the time?"

"I wasn't angry all the time!"

"If you loved him so much, why did you make him feel guilty for every lost cause he embraced, for every new friendship he made?"

"With those seedy little men he drank with every afternoon at the St. Regis? He preferred them to me, and they were beneath him!"

"You were so angry all the time. So angry for as long as I can remember. Sometimes I think you drove him to his death."

And then she would get the look of someone who's walked away from a plane crash and survived: "You don't know what you're talking about," she'd say.

(What I really wanted to say was, Why didn't you love him the way I did, without question and with total abandon?)

We must have repeated that dialogue a hundred times. Or variations of it. We played that scene over and over again, without ever resolving it. Nor did we resolve the question of the suicide note. According to Mama, Daddy had not left one. I couldn't believe he wouldn't jot down something. He had a pad and pencil on his bedside table. I was sure he would have written to me, if not to Mama, unless it was some terrible remark she didn't want me to know about.

Once I even accused her of keeping the note from me.

She got furious. "How *dare* you!" She cried and that prompted her to go over *again* how she found him at seven in the morning, lolling back on the pillows, book in his lap, eyes wide open.

"Have you ever looked into a dead man's *eyes?*"

And the subject was dropped again and we took up the issue of the will.

Daddy had left no will and he was a lawyer, for God's sake. He'd always been so scrupulous with his clients, and an expert in estates.

And then there were his files. I'd tried to retrieve them from his office after he died, but Mama was in litigation with the firm—something about money from fees she felt were owed her. She asked me to wait until she came to terms with them. I was in such an emotional state I agreed. When I finally did receive the files, which were passed on to me unread, the correspondence and notes were in a dozen or so folders, period. But where were the complete files?

His partners maintained, "That's all there is." When I tried to find his secretary, she seemed to have vanished.

The contents of the files were a huge disappointment, a curious hodgepodge: one-liners to Richard Nixon; a series of carbons to Westbrook Pegler in which Daddy seems to be defending his takeover of *PM;* letters to J. Edgar Hoover, to Truman; handwritten notes about a conversation with Bertolt Brecht; and a strange letter to someone I'd never heard of in which Daddy claims his first meeting with Earl Warren took place in a Chinese brothel outside Sacramento!

But there was very little to reflect either his thirty-year law practice in California and New York or his personal life. Was this the way he wanted it? To leave virtually nothing of himself behind?

Mama didn't seem to care if the complete files were lost. Her attitude was the same—indifference—about the two scrapbooks she had burned immediately after the funeral, two scrapbooks full of images of the private moments of her courtship and marriage to my father. She admitted to burning them only after I asked to borrow them.

Later she would say she regretted the burning of those scrapbooks, but at the time something had impelled her to throw them into the fireplace and strike a match. She was sorry. But she had saved his Palestine diary, and his notebooks and the personal letters he'd written to her on the Willkie train, as well as the rough draft of his own memoir. I should be grateful for that.

And then one rainy afternoon in the mid-1960s, she suddenly presented me with *her* papers, her files, her writings, all stuffed into cardboard boxes. She didn't ask me whether I wanted to read them or keep them or throw them away. "Do what you want with them, lambie-pie," she said, but the sound of her voice was contemptuous—despairing—and it made my stomach ache.

Of course the act of giving them to me seemed to dictate: "Please read, my daughter. This is how I coped with my agonies and my joys."

Once I started reading them I couldn't stop. The pieces of writing served as clues in the puzzle that was my father: absent parent; absent husband; contradictory, quixotic, driven man.

Mama's novels had funny titles, like *Emerald Kettles* and *Female Tyrants*. They seemed to be based mostly on what she called "the perverse burdens of love."

And there was correspondence and looseleaf notes labeled "Gardens," "Recipes," "Travels," "Happy Kanta aka the drifter."

Her journals documented her marriage and her love affairs in almost clinical detail.

Here I had almost a double narrative: her exterior life with Daddy (dinner parties, lunches with their friends, mixed in with brief descriptions of flirtations and even weather reports) alongside an interior life filled with fantasy and depression.

"Pain is valid," she wrote in 1937, "because it is a symptom of being alive."

She wrote relatively little about my brother and me when we were small. When she did she painted us romantically but impersonally, too. She rarely mentioned Bart's dark moods or my intense self-absorption. Instead she rhapsodized, "the children grow more beautiful every day. . . . Patti is like a flower . . . Bart Jr. is delectable, solemn, serious and so firm like a baby apple you want to take a bite out of him. Is it unwise to be so fatuous?"

Many of her reflections focused on my father: "I sometimes think Bart has been struggling all his life to come to terms with a desolation inside himself . . . instilled perhaps by his father's sense of failure. It is a desolation that is as hurtful to me as it is to him."

And then, "Bart is a *sociable* person but not intimate; he spends a lot of energy trying on different personas."

In her journal she is constantly writing about doing everything to keep him happy and keep him at home: "I am determined to be the best wife and the best mother and the best cook and bottle washer imaginable. And I'll write novels, too, by God!"

But the truth is he abandoned her very early on, as he abandoned the entire family, and we compensated for it each in our own ways. I put up my cheerful wall, Mama threw tantrums and had affairs. My brother killed himself.

The journals stop abruptly at my brother's death in 1953, but there are ghastly notations about my father's descent into addiction starting in 1955, mostly on handwritten slips of memo paper.

Sifting through those last notes wasn't pleasant. It was obvious from reading them that Mama and I, together, had cleaned up his messes, hidden his liquor; we'd lied and protected and rescued him; we'd told his law partners he was home with a cold when he'd taken another overdose.

We had believed in the power of love to save Daddy. And, oh, how we loved him! But what a perilous love—what an unrequited passion (a daughter's love for her father!). We did not go to AA or Al-Anon—and Children of Alcoholics did not exist then.

After reading these notes, I came to the conclusion that I was an addict, too: I'd been addicted to my father and now I was addicted to preserving his memory.

I also seemed addicted to living in the midst of emotional chaos. I didn't drink, but I gorged on candy and I loved knocking myself out with Seconals.

My personal life was filled with violence. Not long after my father died, I fell in love with an alcoholic guitar player and he was killed in front of my eyes during a barroom brawl. Then, after the show I was in closed, I worked for a half-crazed lawyer, who subsequently blew himself up in a private plane.

It wasn't until I closed myself off, nunlike, in my dressing room at the Helen Hayes Theatre that I began getting slightly more perspective on myself.

But recognizing an addiction and doing something about it are two different things. I seemed to need to go on collecting facts about my father. I must have collected hundreds over the years and I talked to scores of people who purported to know him. Often their memories did not jibe with my fantasy image of Daddy as Superman—Don Quixote—glamorous brilliant lawyer; there were things I started finding out about him that I didn't like. But how was that possible when I still loved him so passionately? He would always remain a puzzle. I would never be able to figure him out. So many mixed signals. But he did have an inexplicable talent for hope.

I had the feeling that Mama probably possessed more "facts" about Daddy than she ever let on. In retrospect, she kept a great deal to herself. Maybe because she didn't want me to be as disappointed in my father as she had been.

To her credit, she was unfailingly loyal to him in spite of all that had happened between them; she never stopped caring for him.

For some reason, Mama never mentioned the FBI or the surveillance in her journals. It was as if the Cold War hadn't existed. The Red-baiting, the persecutions—they didn't seem to have touched her. Even our phone taps aren't mentioned.

By chance, I learned more specifics about the FBI from Dave, the press agent, who had been one of my father's favorite hangers-on.

I continued to see Dave pretty regularly even after I married Mel Arrighi in 1966 and we moved to the Village and I left acting and became a journalist and Mel began getting his plays produced Off Broadway. I always hoped he'd tell me how Daddy spent his time away from us—since once or twice Dave had traveled halfway round the world with him. I imagined he had some glorious anecdotes but the stories he told me were not only boring but usually a little sad.

And then one afternoon in 1977 he phoned and said he had to see me immediately. His voice sounded urgent.

We met as we always did, at Daddy's favorite haunt—the King Cole Bar at the St. Regis Hotel. We both ordered gin and tonic. We both lit cigarettes, and then Dave mopped his brow with a grimy handkerchief. He was sweating profusely.

I assumed he was finally going to admit that, yes, Daddy once had a short affair with a dark, voluptuous Israeli woman named Hava. I'd met her at one of his seders and she'd described driving my father through Jerusalem in 1957 to a meeting with Mayor Teddy Kollek. Something about getting Pepsi-Cola delivered to Israel, and afterward she and Daddy spent the evening drinking at the King David Hotel. The way she referred to his charm and elusiveness and the calls he made to her months later from Paris and San Francisco made me believe they'd been romantically involved.

But Dave didn't mention Hava or drinks at the King David

(although supposedly he had been there, too). Instead he ominously intoned, "You're old enough to take what I'm about to impart to you." And then he launched into a long, convoluted story, which I'll abbreviate here.

According to Dave, my father gave information to the FBI about the Lawyers Guild and two colleagues in the hopes that Hoover would finally leave him alone. "The two guys he informed on were Communists—known Communists—and Bart didn't see anything wrong in naming them; they had been named time and time again. By then it was a matter of playing the game. If you want to look at it this way, your father chose between honor and self-preservation. By then, in 1953, the FBI and HUAC knew everything they wanted to know. They ruined literally thousands of lives."

Dave finished with, "Your father was very matter-of-fact with me about his whole thing with the FBI. He seemed to want to get it off his chest, but he showed no emotion."

And I showed little if any emotion either that evening listening to Dave.

Although I had no idea my father had cooperated with the FBI. Or maybe I had blocked it. Because certainly those few letters I'd read in his files to Hoover implied he had done something along the lines of passing information to the Bureau.

"Did you tell my mother?" I asked Dave.

"Shit, no! Your father hid everything from her."

I let that remark pass.

"Why did he tell you?" I had to ask.

Dave shrugged. He supposed because he happened to be hanging around my father that particular afternoon at the St. Regis bar. "We had a couple of drinks. Bart started talking. Maybe he felt more comfortable telling somebody he wasn't close to." Dave added that he didn't recall many people my father was close to.

I let that remark pass also.

Still, I wondered why my father had confessed this dreary incident to a two-bit press agent Mama refused to allow in our house. Why hadn't he told me? Or told my mother?

But of course he wouldn't want to tell either one of us because he had a heroic image to uphold with both wife and daughter, didn't he? He was a crusading liberal, a champion of the First Amendment.

I wondered whether he behaved differently when he wasn't with us. I became confused.

By the same token, if *I'd* found out he had given information to the FBI, and asked him about it, would he have admitted it to me? Probably not.

Sometimes it seemed to me that my need to know about my father's private life away from us was overwhelmed by his equally strong need to keep us from knowing.

Still I thought it was uncharacteristic of him to betray two colleagues even in order to save himself. The two lawyers he named—Ben Margolis and Martin Popper—were tough old birds, known Communists. They had never had much use for my father even as they used him and he fronted for them during the HUAC hearings. His style, his ebullient manner, clashed with their rude, plodding dogmatism, their habit of secrecy. They knew he distrusted ideology; if he had a political conscience it was an ethical conscience. His was a Utopian spirit, something the hard-boiled Communist lawyers had little patience with. Margolis once stated that Daddy was an "idealist" but that he longed for money and fame, and these longings corrupted him.

But none of this had anything to do with his informing, and yet why had he felt it so essential to inform? To get the FBI off his back? To prove his patriotism? Perhaps it was as simple as that he did not believe it was so terrible to inform and that maybe he thought of it as telling the truth. Because within the world of the First Amendment, which he believed in implicitly, there was room for Communists, John Birchers, Holy Rollers, Democrats, Republicans—for anyone who worshiped strange gods. Stating that someone was a Communist was simply a fact as far as he was concerned —it was not meant as a term of abuse. He supported the *rights* of his Communist colleagues while he in no sense defended their policies, which were completely irrelevant; it was the constitutional issue that mattered to him.

However, for a long time I was ashamed of my father. For a long time I felt what he'd done amounted to a betrayal. It wasn't until recently that I realized I felt betrayed—I'd wanted him to be as publicly brave as Arthur Miller, who refused to name names and risked going to prison and is now an icon. It wasn't until recently that I realized I felt betrayed that he'd betrayed *me* and my impossible fantasies of him.

Still, I mentioned his informing to no one (except my husband). I never even told my mother. I was uncomfortable when I met other children of the blacklist, who'd also been kept in the dark about their parents. Tony Kahn (Gordon's son) said he lived in fear always. Carol Rossen (director Robert Rossen's daughter) was trying to piece together her father's story (he named names—a lot of names). I did not tell Carol my father had informed, too—albeit to a lesser degree.

The one thing we agreed on among ourselves was that we had existed during our childhoods in the middle of a mystery—no one ever told us *anything* about the blacklist, or McCarthyism, or explained why there was such persecution and harassment of innocent people. Our parents kept silent, and their friends kept silent. We grew up behind a curtain of silence.

By the 1990s, the Cold War histories of the period were starting to be published. Writers obtained my father's FBI files—at least some of them.

I discovered to my discomfort that he was in several footnotes (among them a massive Ph.D. thesis on the Lawyers Guild) with, of course, no explanation, just a cold "Bartley Crum informed . . . etc."

In 1992, I wrote a sentimental little piece about the blacklist for *The New York Times.* I said my father had been destroyed by HUAC, but I did not mention his informing. After the piece was published, I received a long, irate letter from a woman whose father's career had also been destroyed by HUAC, but he had not been a "fink," she said.

She accused me of lying—of falsifying the record. Bart Crum was a "stool pigeon," she said. She mailed copies of her letter to the *Times* and to *The Nation* in hopes she would get her letter published.

Victor Navasky, then the editor of *The Nation,* suggested we confront each other in the pages of the magazine. I refused. I said I would answer the accusations in this book.

I remember what Brecht had said: "Sometimes in order to survive, you agree to very ugly collaborations."

Many people believe that those who resisted HUAC were heroes, and that those who informed were to be despised. What happened to my father can't be so easily explained. He was a decent man caught up in a nightmare. Yes, he went along with the stylized ritual of naming names to prove his loyalty. The whole meaning of loyalty changed during the 1950s. "Communists often bring out the worst in people," he once said.

After the HUAC hearings in Washington, he had flown to a meeting of the Committee for the First Amendment in Hollywood. He'd listened to an idea Philip Dunne and director William Wyler had put to the "unfriendlies" on radio—have them take an oath and then testify freely as to their political beliefs. "If any of them were Communists," Dunne said, "the promotion show would back-fire."

Daddy was outraged—most of the Nineteen had sworn to him that they had never been Communists. When he learned he had been lied to by some of them, he asked, "Why did you lie?" The answer: "You were a bleeding-heart liberal, Bartley; we knew you would always be a sucker for a good cause."

He couldn't get over their refusal to speak openly to him about their political convictions. He hated being called "a sucker for a good cause"; he felt very demeaned.

What was terrible about that remark was what it had done to his sense of self, his sense of innocence—he felt defiled.

I took little comfort in Dalton Trumbo's noble statement about informing, in which he'd said, "The blacklist was a time of evil, and . . . no one on either side who survived it came through un-touched . . . each person reacted as his nature, his needs, his par-ticular conviction compelled him to . . . It will do no good to search for villains or heroes or saints . . . because there were none; there were only victims. That is why none of us—right, left, or center—emerged from that long nightmare without sin."

I would never fully know the terrible pressures my father was under, financial and otherwise, that had forced him to inform.

ON that evening with Dave I said nothing. I listened to him talk and wondered how much longer I could stand being with a man whose toupee needed cleaning and whose breath was sour on my face.

Just before we said good-bye he handed me a tattered enve-
lope. I opened it and pulled out a carbon of father's statement to
the Justice Department. I had never seen it before.

"Your dad gave this to me as a souvenir," he said. "I was to
keep it for you."

I didn't believe him.

"I thought maybe you could sell it. We could share in the
profits."

"How much do you think we could get?" My voice rose sarcastically, and I hugged the tattered statement to my breast. "Don't
you realize this belongs to *me?* I'm Bart Crum's daughter."

"I was kidding," Dave assured me weakly. "I just thought it
might be valuable."

"Only to me." I hugged the statement tighter.

"Sure, sure, but I just thought—you mentioned once you
were planning to write a book—I thought we could collaborate."

"Collaborate—why?"

"Because there are certain incidents in your father's life you
might not be aware of."

"And maybe don't want to be." I rose from the table.

Dave followed me out onto the street. "You're not mad at me,
are you?" He tried to kiss my cheek, but I drew away.

After that Dave phoned me several times to see how I was
getting on. He wanted to get together again, but I put him off.
Finally, we lost touch completely.

It took another thirteen years for me to piece together the
extent of my father's private agonies. I learned about some of them
by reading between the lines of his FBI files, which I finally
obtained in 1988. I learned from his files that surveillance continued long after he testified as to his loyalties to the State Department and long after he gave his paltry bits of information to the
FBI. Agents continued to harass him.

Just as he thought he could relax, he would spot an agent
tailing him or he'd hear the phone click. (Once I asked my mother
if she ever suspected the extent of the harassment, and she replied,
"Oh, dear, no. Bart wouldn't tell me anything that unpleasant.")

How he managed to hide it from us I don't know, but he did
—and, then again, he didn't. We knew about Guy and his hopeless
attempts to find the wiretaps; and Daddy once described the FBI

agents visiting him in pairs "like nuns" at his Wall Street office, but he described the experience with genial amusement. I didn't take it as seriously as I should have.

I assumed he had resolved his problems with the FBI, just as I assumed he was able to resolve all unpleasantness and difficulty in his life, but obviously it was a different story.

As soon as he realized the surveillance was continuing, he began to phone J. Edgar Hoover; according to his files, Hoover never returned his calls. Once when he was in Washington, he stopped by the Bureau and asked to see Hoover; he was told "the Chief" wasn't available.

My father waited for a bit—read a magazine, smoked a couple of cigarettes—and then he left.

I learned all this long after his death, after I obtained two thousand pages of his FBI files in 1988. I am still trying to get the remaining five thousand pages, but I've been told they are "top security." After forty years.

My father was kept on the Security Index through 1957. During that time he would periodically send Hoover stuff he'd received in the mails—a radical pamphlet; some morsel of political gossip he had picked up at a party that might be "subversive" —and he'd write Hoover notes that were effusively polite. Hoover would acknowledge these tidbits of nothingness.

Once my father even wrote Lewis Nichols a congratulatory note after reading a speech Hoover had given because he knew Nichols had written the speech, and Nichols wrote back his thanks; he was still trying to get Daddy off the Security Index, and he managed to in 1958, when Daddy started doing undercover work for Robert Kennedy.

As a small gesture of appreciation for what my father was doing, Kennedy gave him one of his FBI files to peruse. An early one—circa 1948.

There wasn't much in it; actually, all the file contained were phone transcripts of idiotic conversations between me and my boyfriends back in San Francisco.

BEFORE my mother died in 1980 she had to sell our weekend place at Garrison.

My husband and I helped her move. We couldn't take much

since we were living in small Manhattan apartments. So friends drove up and chose what they wanted from the vast trove of possessions spread out on the grass.

These were possessions that had seamlessly filled our homes in California and New York since the 1930s: piles and piles of books, pictures, overstuffed couches, antique chairs, side tables, desks—so many desks, pillows, lamps, brass candlesticks, china, lacquered trays, silver pitchers.

Every single object reflected a predictable understated style; comfort was the basis of Mama's taste.

Nobody picking at the stuff in the grass could see those possessions in the context I did—that they were links to another life, another world, a warm, safe world filled with light and ideals and rich cooking and fabrics and love—that they all provided a background for a family that was no more.

Nobody wanted the altar, the white altar that Daddy had loved and prayed at. He used to sit by the statue of the Virgin Mary as he drank his Jack Daniel's and puffed on his cigarettes.

We couldn't even give the altar away, so we left it behind in the tiny court off the main part of the house and drove into the twilight, my husband and I.

Two days later Mama phoned us, distraught.

The house in Garrison had caught fire the previous night and burned down.

"What?" I said.

"The house in Garrison has burned down," she repeated. Nothing was left—nothing.

Apparently, at five in the morning, near dawn, the neighbor below us on the hill had smelled smoke.

He had wandered out onto his deck, which faced the Hudson River, just as ours did, and he was just in time to see our place explode into flames, "like a bomb hit it."

Hot orange flames shot up into the air. It was a terrible conflagration. He phoned the fire department, but it was too late. By the time the engine arrived twenty minutes later from Cold Spring, our property was transformed into a smoky ruin.

Mama drove up the following day to view the wreckage. Blackened, scorched earth surrounded what resembled the bombed-out foundations of our house.

All that remained were a couple of pieces of overturned wrought iron garden furniture; they looked like Giacometti sculptures.

Then there was the altar. It rose miraculously untouched and strangely pristine in the tiny court off the main part of the house.

It stood, with the statue of the Virgin Mary, holding her hands clasped to her breast, her eyes raised to Heaven.

I remembered that the last time Daddy came to Garrison he'd painted the altar "off-white"—painted it over and over, using an entire can of paint, until the altar gleamed.

And then he sat down and looked at the Virgin Mary, Mother of God, until he was called in to supper.

NOTES

BC = Bartley Crum
GBC = Gertrude Bosworth Crum
PB = Patricia Bosworth
WW = Wendell Willkie

PROLOGUE

15 *"Bartley C. Crum, lawyer"*: The New York Times, December 11, 1959.
16 *"a fighter for justice"*: Rafael da Costa, *American Zionist*, January 1960.

PART ONE

CHAPTER 1

27 *"Mr. Justice Edmonds and some recent trends in the law of civil liberties"*: Bartley C. Crum, *California Law Journal*, 1940; Willkie archives, manuscript department, Lilly Library, Indiana University, Bloomington, IN.
29 *In San Francisco the Cavanaughs raised eight kids:* interviews with James Wiard, James Wiard Jr., Bartley Cavanaugh Jr., Maggie Cavanaugh, July 1986.
31 *"I never heard of"*: Jim Wiard interviews with PB, July 26, 1986.
32 *"He had a smile"*: Helen McWilliamson interview with PB, September 14, 1987.
32 *"He was the first person"*: Jim Wiard interview with PB, August 4, 1986.
32 *"You can't pull the"*: Ibid.
33 *"In politics you can have"*: BC letter to GBC, summer 1940.

CHAPTER 2

35   *"bravado—a kind of"*: Portia Hume interview with PB, August 17, 1986.
36   *"You remind me"*: Jim Wiard interview with PB, July 1986.
37   *"Bart tells me"*: GBC journal, March 1925.
37   *"I told him to"*: Ibid.
40   *"Cutsie was madly"*: Lib Logan interview with PB, July 17, 1985.
40   *"You are full of"*: BC letter to GBC, April 14, 1927.

CHAPTER 3

44   *Neylan was a tough Catholic conservative:* Jane Neylan Childs interview with PB, January 22, 1987.
45   *rumors of an impending strike:* Charles P. Larrowe, *Harry Bridges: The Rise and Fall of Radical Labor in the United States* (New York: Lawrence Hill & Co., 1972), 32.
46   *"We ended up"*: Peter Cusick interview with PB, September 10, 1980; information on Hearst and information on the San Francisco dock strike: Paul Smith, *Personal File* (New York: Appleton, Century, 1964), 152–57; W. A. Swanberg, *Citizen Hearst* (New York: Bantam Books, 1971), 530.
46   *"vast tangle of fighting men"*: Larrowe, 32.
46   *"Barricades were erected"*: GBC journal, July 1934.
46   *"Blood in the streets"*: San Francisco Examiner, July 11, 1934.
49   *"It was prickly"*: BC, *Autobiography of an American Liberal*, unpublished.
49   *"Yeah, your father and I"*: Harry Bridges interview with PB, July 1984.
52   *In January 1934, Alex opened:* Cynthia Stokes Brown, *Alexander Meiklejohn, Teacher of Freedom* (Berkeley, Calif.: Meiklejohn Civil Liberties Institute), 36–38.
53   *"Bart Crum is here to learn"*: Myer Cohen interview with PB, February 19, 1987.
56   *great importance in the law firm: Time* interoffice memo, February 1936.
57   *"Bart Crum would be happier"*: Jane Neylan Childs interview with PB, December 8, 1987.
58   *"Dear Chief, I've resolved"*: BC letter to John Neylan, May 13, 1938; manuscript department, Bancroft Library, University of California, Berkeley.

CHAPTER 4

63   *Erikson wanted to see Bart:* Notes of Erik Erikson's observations about Bartley Crum Jr. are contained in Chapter 2, "The Theory of Infantile Sexuality," in Erikson's book *Childhood & Society* (New York: W. W. Norton & Co., 1986), 154–56. The boy in the chapter is given the pseudonym "Peter," but when I checked with Mrs. Erikson in July 1990, she confirmed that the boy named Peter was certainly Bart Crum Jr.; Erikson wrote that my brother's frenetic improvised statements not only revealed his dominant fantasy but showed how completely he surrendered to the secret he so strenuously retained in his bowels.

CHAPTER 5

69   *It's hard to explain the Willkie miracle:* information regarding the 1940 Wendell Willkie presidential campaign drawn from interviews with Marcia Davenport, July 23, 1984; Ruth Bishop, 1986; and Oren Root, July 27, 1987; files and Willkie letters at the Lilly Library at Indiana University, Bloomington, IN.

69   *"He was an old-fashioned":* Marcia Davenport, "Unconquerable," *The New Yorker,* April 22, 1991.

69   *"And he could charm":* Marcia Davenport interview with PB, June 25, 1991.

71   *"he is also Irita Van Doren's lover":* Irita Van Doren, the editor of the *Herald Tribune Book Review,* was a truly radiant personality and one of the most influential literary figures in America at that time. She and Willkie became inseparable; he often called press conferences at her New York apartment. Daddy enjoyed telling the following anecdote: during the 1940 campaign, a group of reporters confronted Willkie and demanded that he explain his "relationship" with Van Doren since he was, after all, married to somebody else. Willkie agreed. "Yes, gentlemen, I am in love with another woman and I don't pretend to apologize or say it isn't so. However, if you print this story my presidential aspirations will be ruined. But that is your decision. I have made mine." The reporters kept quiet. In 1940 it didn't seem necessary to nose around a presidential candidate's private life.

72   *"The Willkies in a daze":* BC letter to GBC, July 20, 1940.

73   *"Bart Crum helped":* Oren Root interview with PB, July 29, 1987.

74   *"Your mother treats":* Terry Ashe-Croft interview with PB, February 2, 1987.

75   *"Total carnival atmosphere":* GBC journal, summer 1940.

77   *"I don't know whether":* Ibid.

78   *"One of the things":* BC letter to WW, 1940.

78   *"Bart had a lot of ideas":* Peter Cusick interview with PB, March 3, 1981.

81   *Willkie was being pressured:* information about the Willkie campaign train: Paul Smith, *Personal File* (New York: Appleton Century, 1964), 253–74; Joseph Fells Barnes, *Willkie* (New York: Simon & Schuster, 1953); Steve Neal, *Dark Horse: A Biography of Wendell Willkie* (New York: Doubleday, 1984), 142–76.

82   *"Willkie spread himself":* Turner Catledge, *My Life and Times* (New York: Harper & Row, 1971), 121.

PART TWO

CHAPTER 6

92   *"He understood all the issues":* David Silver interview with PB, February 9, 1992.

93   *it's no crime:* Nate Cummings interview with PB, August 10, 1979.

95   *"California is unpredictable":* BC unpublished article, 1943.

95   *whenever Bart Crum was:* Ruth Bishop interview with PB, September 21, 1986.

96 *"They can twitch"*: Theodore White, *Breach of Faith* (New York: Atheneum, 1975), 53.

96 *"Clem will try to charge you"*: BC letter to WW, June 23, 1943.

97 *"Fresno looks good"*: BC letter to WW, March 23, 1943.

97 *"The Republican State Committee"*: BC letter to WW, March 24, 1943.

97 *"Earl insists he has"*: BC letter to WW, May 1, 1943.

98 *"Nobody is setting things"*: BC letter to GBC, May 1943.

CHAPTER 7

106 *"What makes him so odd"*: GBC letter to BC, June 1943.

107 *"He is thirty-eight"*: GBC journal, June 24, 1943.

108 *"I asked him"*: GBC journal, June 23, 1943.

CHAPTER 8

116 *William Schneidermann was secretary:* information about the William Schneidermann case and Willkie's defense: Steve Neal, *Dark Horse* (New York: Doubleday, 1984), 266–68.

117 *"Wendell Willkie is the only"*: Neal, *Dark Horse.*

117 *"It was the thing to do"*: WW letter to BC, December 3, 1941, Lilly Library, Indiana University, Bloomington, IN.

117 *"I am itching to do more"*: BC letter to WW, August 1943.

119 *"when Niles approached"*: BC letter to Joe Barnes, February 15, 1952.

119 *"Bart enjoyed being"*: Peter Cusick interview with PB, September 20, 1980.

120 *"concerning you and the Presidency"*: BC letter to WW, April 14, 1943.

CHAPTER 9

128 *"It did a lot of good"*: BC telegram to Robert Kenny, August 1943.

130 *"The Boss"*: BC letter to GBC, March 30, 1944.

CHAPTER 10

135 *"He knows it is OVER"*: GBC journal, May 22, 1944.

141 *"Close call"*: GBC journal, June 1944.

144 *"To whom shall I"*: Arthur Rimbaud, *Season in Hell,* trans. by Delmore Schwartz (New York: New Directions, 1939), 27.

CHAPTER 11

147 *"because if we had a non-partisan"*: Drew Pearson.

148 *"As we drank coffee"*: David Dubinsky and A. H. Raskin, *A Life with Labor* (New York: Simon & Schuster, 1977), 285–87. Other information about FDR's formation of a third party with Willkie: Samuel Rosenman, *Working with Roosevelt* (New York: Harper & Bros., 1952), 463–70.

149 *"Wendell's idea"*: BC notes for a Drew Pearson column, November 1944.

150 *"Willkie just didn't take care"*: Ruth Bishop interview with PB, September 17, 1987.

151   *"to work harder on MY MARRIAGE"*: GBC journal, 1944.
153   *"Why [are] drunks almost always persons"*: Charles Jackson, *The Lost Weekend* (New York: Farrar Rinehart, Inc., 1944), 221.
153   *"He only wanted to be the Artist"*: Jackson, 46.

PART THREE

CHAPTER 12

158   *"I have kept my confidence"*: BC letter to Sam Rosenman, December 13, 1945.
159   *"menace of Soviet expansionism"*: Walter Isaacson and Evan Thomas, *The Wise Men* (New York: Simon & Schuster, 1986), 379.
163   *"Bart Crum was"*: Herb Caen interview with PB, July 22, 1986.
164   *Mama would phone Mary:* Mary Kohler interview with PB, January 5, 1982.
165   *"pick Bart up"*: Jim Wiard interview with PB, July 26, 1986.
165   *"On his"*: Fritz Godwin, *Time* magazine memo, December 1945.
166   *"information in the Bureau's files"*: FBI file—Crum, Bartley, FOIA, 25975581345.
166   *"I think it was somebody"*: Sam Rosenman letter to BC, December 11, 1945.
166   *"If you dish it out"*: BC letter to Sam Rosenman, December 14, 1945.
167   *"The President asked"*: Bartley Crum, *Behind the Silken Curtain* (New York: Simon & Schuster, 1947), 3.
172   *"We went in a body to meet them"*: Crum, *Silken Curtain*, 6.
172   *"I had been wondering"*: Ibid.

CHAPTER 13

174   *"It seems to me"*: BC letter to family, December 1945.
174   *"As for your hero"*: BC letter to BC Jr., December 1945.
175   *"As I listened to him"*: BC diary, December 1945.
175   *"Your father's naïveté was staggering"*: Ladislas Farago interview with PB, June 4, 1984.
176   *"The Committee's discussions grow"*: BC diary, January 1, 1946.
176   *"No, it does not please me"*: BC diary, January 1, 1946.

CHAPTER 14

177   *In London:* Anthony Crossman Howard, *The Pursuit of Power* (London: Jonathan Cape, 1990), 108–26; Leonard Dinnerstein, *America and the Survivors of the Holocaust* (New York: Columbia University Press, 1982), 73–101; Richard Crossman interview with PB, July 20, 1966; and Crossman papers, Mideast Centre, St. Anthony's College, Oxford University.
177   *"I am being tailed"*: BC letter to GBC, January 14, 1946.
177   *"Bart was the only member"*: Gerold Frank interview with PB, June 13, 1985.
177   *"Bart threw himself"*: Ruth Gruber interview with PB, March 11, 1993.
178   *"Yesterday, we were invited"*: BC letter to GBC, January 11, 1946.
178   *"Jan told me"*: BC letter to family, January 14, 1946.

179   *"a long boisterous evening"*: Connie Ernst Bessie interview with PB, October 9, 1987.

180   *"The occupation authorities"*: BC letter to family, January 20, 1946.

180   *"We are questioning"*: BC letter to family, January 1946.

181   *"There are only a few Jewish children"*: BC notebook, January–February 1946.

181   *"It was material that"*: Ibid.

181   *"I sat for an entire afternoon"*: BC letter to family, February 1946.

182   *"I could not believe"*: BC diary, 1946.

182   *"One woman told us"*: Ibid.

182   *"As for the German people"*: BC letter to family, February 16, 1946.

182   *"Sometimes when we finished"*: BC diary, 1946.

183   *"Bart Crum stood"*: Ruth Gruber interview with PB, February 11, 1993.

184   *"It is obvious"*: BC diary, February 19, 1946.

184   *He continued to make waves:* information regarding BC in Vienna from Ruth Gruber interviews with PB, February 11, 1993, and November 15, 1996; Gerold Frank interviews with PB, April 20 and 21, 1987; and Crum, *Silken Curtain,* 120.

184   *"Everything well coordinated"*: BC letter to GBC, February 24, 1946.

185   *"So the DPs know we care"*: BC letter to GBC, February 1946.

185   *Dave Niles sent him a confidential cable:* Truman Library, Independence, MO. Other information regarding the liberation of the death camps and underground immigration to Palestine from Abraham Sachar, *The Redemption of the Unwanted* (New York: St. Martin's Press, 1983), 190.

185   *"Manningham Buller is anti-Semitic"*: BC notebook, February 1946.

185   *"Anti-Semitism is"*: Crum, *Silken Curtain,* 130–31.

186   *"I have been advised"*: BC notebook, February 1946.

CHAPTER 15

189   *"I am here in the shadow"*: BC letter to family, February 1946.

191   *"an armed camp"*: BC diary, February 1946.

191   *"I feel as if"*: Ibid.

191   *"Very impressive as he explained"*: Ibid.

191   *One morning as my father left:* Crum, *Silken Curtain,* 214.

192   *"My British colleagues"*: BC notebook labeled "Jerusalem," 1946.

192   *"It is pretty scary"*: BC letter to GBC, March 1946.

192   *"It has gotten worse"*: BC notebook labeled "Jerusalem," 1946.

193   *"I become more and more convinced"*: Ibid.

193   *"He is a big man"*: BC letter to GBC, March 1946.

CHAPTER 16

195   *Once in Lausanne:* Crum, *Silken Curtain,* 262; Sachar, *The Redemption,* 190.

195   *"We are starting to get"*: BC letter to family, April 1946.

196   *"the Judge and his leadership"*: Crum, *Silken Curtain,* 280–81.

CHAPTER 17

200   *"Zionist leaders like Rabbi Silver"*: Abe Feinberg interview with PB, August 10, 1988.
200   *"Obviously Bart has found"*: GBC journal, April 1946.
201   *"stop tangling with"*: Peter Cusick interview with PB, March 2, 1980.
201   *"Bart Crum tore"*: *PM*, August 22, 1946.
202   *"was crucial"*: Yehuda Hellman interview with PB, March 1986.
202   *"Bart Crum, who called"*: *World-Telegram*, September 14, 1946.
202   *"the beginning of a red-smear"*: *San Francisco Chronicle*, September 16, 1946.
202   *"In the minds of most"*: Yehuda Hellman interview with PB, March 10, 1986.
204   *"We had to stop"*: Philip Dunne interview with PB, January 20, 1990.
205   *"In the best"*: Marquis Childs, *The New York Times Book Review*, April 13, 1947.

PART FOUR

CHAPTER 18

210   *"special agents observed Bartley Crum"*: FBI file—Crum, Bartley, FOIA, NY, 100–68539, April 1947.
221   *"I start out with high"*: unmailed letter to Saul, May 1947.

CHAPTER 19

224   *"flagrant Communist propaganda"*: Walter Goodman, *The Committee* (New York: Farrar, Straus and Giroux, 1968), 203; information regarding HUAC findings from Third Report of Joint Fact Finding Committee on Un-American Activities, Sacramento, California, 1947; information on Hollywood in 1947: Nancy Lynn Schwartz, *The Hollywood Writers' Wars* (New York: Alfred A. Knopf, 1982), 239–89; Otto Friedrich, *City of Nets* (New York: Harper & Row, 1986), 291–337.
226   *But he did attend:* Edward Dmytryk interview with PB, 1986; 1992–93.
227   *"He had the classic"*: Waldo Salt interview with PB, July 7, 1987.
228   *"I just want to say"*: Victor Navasky, *Naming Names* (New York: Viking Press, 1982), 303.
229   *"it was decided"*: affidavit of Bartley C. Crum to the State Department, May 6, 1953; information regarding BC reaction to Communist lawyers: Mary Kohler interview with PB, January 4, 1982.
230   *"We wanted to"*: Philip Dunne interview with PB, January 20, 1990.
231   *"Bart Crum was considered"*: Jules Buck interview with PB, September 11, 1993.
231   *"We were all so optimistic"*: Ring Lardner Jr. interview with PB, September 7, 1989.
231   *"Crum and Kenny had been hired"*: Erica Boise, "Three Brave Men" (senior thesis, Vassar College, 1993).

232   *"The city of Washington"*: Gordon Kahn, *Hollywood on Trial* (New York: Boni & Gaer, 1948), 5.

232   *"Larry Parks, Jack Lawson"*: Uta Hagen interview with PB, September 2, 1980.

233   *"Bob Kenny was chief"*: BC unpublished autobiography.

CHAPTER 20

235   *On October 20, 1947*: information on HUAC hearings from *Hearings Regarding the Communist Infiltration of the Motion Picture Industry,* Eightieth Congress, First Session, October 20–24, 1947, pp. 27–30; Edward Dmytryk interviews with PB, July 22, 1986, and September 20, 1992; Waldo Salt interview with PB, July 10, 1987; David Silver interview with PB, January 20, 1992; Edward Dmytryk, *Odd Man Out: A Memoir of the Hollywood Ten* (Carbondale, Ill.: Southern Illinois University Press, 1996), 37.

239   *"The Committee is not"*: The New York Times, October 26, 1947.

239   *"No legal safeguards"*: PM, October 26, 1947.

240   *"May I request"*: HUAC hearings from session, 1947.

242   *"We were not going to back down"*: Philip Dunne interview with PB, January 20, 1990.

242   *"You have to see"*: GBC journal, October 1947.

244   *"the playwright Bertolt"*: Waldo Salt interview with PB, July 18, 1987.

244   *"It had gotten so crazy"*: Edward Dmytryk interview with PB, April 4, 1992.

245   *"By baiting Thomas and Stripling"*: Philip Dunne interview with PB, January 20, 1990.

245   *"Bertolt Brecht does not"*: BC notebook, October 1947.

246   *"He became very emotional"*: Otto Friedrich, *City of Nets* (New York: Harper & Row, 1986), 331.

247   *"Mr. Crum, what was HUAC's purpose?"*: BC interview with Ed Hart, CBS, October 30, 1947, the Wisconsin Center for Theater Research, Robert Kenny/ Robert Morris Collection, 29AN Box 6.

248   *"If Senator Tenney"*: San Francisco Chronicle, November 11, 1947.

248   *"kangaroo court"*: The New York Times, October 26, 1947.

249   *"It can't be because"*: Edward Dmytryk interview with PB, July 22, 1986.

250   *"You are being used"*: David Silver interview with PB, February 14, 1992.

250   *"A sorry time"*: GBC journal, November 1947.

252   *"I resigned from PCA"*: affidavit of Bartley C. Crum before the State Department, May 6, 1953.

CHAPTER 21

255   *"Bart Crum was a champion"*: Judge Samuel J. Silverman interview with PB, June 10, 1993.

255   *"PM is for people"*: Ron Hooper, "When Ralph Ingersoll Papered Manhattan," *Columbia Journalism Review,* December 1984, p. 25.

255   *"Bart Crum's telegram"*: Judge Samuel J. Silverman interview with PB, June 10, 1993.

256   *"I'm selling you my newspaper"*: Steve Fisher interview with PB, March 20, 1987.

256   *"They honestly believed":* Betty Barnes interview with PB, June 1992.
256   *"hopelessly ignorant":* Joseph Fells Barnes, 1907–1970, *Reminiscences of Joseph F. Barnes,* Oral History Project, Columbia University, 1953, pp. 260–95.
256   *"We simply could not":* Ibid.
257   *"To cut costs":* Heywood Broun interview with PB, June 1992.
257   *"Barnes never spoke to me":* Ibid.
259   *"I cannot believe":* GBC journal, April 1948.
259   *Washington columnist Joseph Alsop:* interview with Jane Neylan Childs, March 8, 1987.
260   *"She submerged herself":* Marian Javits interview with PB, April 11, 1993.
260   *"Protecting my editor":* "Talk of the Town," *The New Yorker,* May 23, 1948.

CHAPTER 22

266   *"It was a bleeding sore":* Barnes, *Reminiscences,* 260–95.
266   *"select from offers":* *Time,* June 28, 1948.
268   *"Dear Cutsie—It is hot":* BC letter to GBC, July 9, 1948.
270   *"Bart simply could not convince me":* Dolly Schiff interview with PB, April 20, 1987.
271   *"being the center":* Edla Cusick interview with PB, August 1983.
271   *"And he would usually":* Edla Cusick interview with PB, March 2, 1980.

CHAPTER 23

274   *Leon Shimkin was the* Star's *business manager:* information on the *New York Star*'s bad management and financial predicament: Leon Shimkin interview with PB, July 11, 1987; Blair Clark interview with PB, June 5, 1992; Barnes, *Reminiscences,* 260–95.
274   *"Bart should never":* Leon Shimkin interview with PB, July 8, 1987.
275   *"It was like":* Pauline Leet interview with PB, March 2, 1987.
277   *By the fall, the* Star's *editorial expenses:* information regarding the *New York Star*'s failure from Blair Clark report to Marshall Field, February 18, 1949.
280   *"The old boy":* A. J. Liebling, *The Press* (New York: Ballantine Books, 1961), 48.
281   *"It happened very fast":* Blair Clark interview with PB, June 8, 1993.
282   *"Bart is beside":* GBC journal, November 1948.
282   *"Anyone can back":* Marshall Field statement quoted by Frederic C. Klein and Harlan Bryan in "The Field Enterprises," *The Wall Street Journal,* August 28, 1972.
283   *"I'm sorry to have":* Herald Tribune, January 27, 1949.
284   *"Bart has never":* GBC journal, January 1949.
284   " *'Because like every guy'* ": Serrill Hillman, *Time,* January 30, 1949.

PART FIVE

CHAPTER 24

301   *My brother was sent home:* Arthur Mejia interview with PB, April 1993; correspondence with David G. Pond, assistant headmaster at Deerfield Academy, September 15, 1993:

> Dear Ms. Bosworth:
> Unfortunately we have no record of Bart Crum Jr. ever attending Deerfield.
>
> Sincerely yours,
> David G. Pond

Note: According to p. 251 of the Deerfield Academy yearbook for 1950, undergraduates included Bartley C. Crum Jr., 326 E. 51st St., New York.

CHAPTER 25

309   *For a while, being Rita Hayworth's lawyer:* BC correspondence; John Kobal, *Rita Hayworth: The Woman* (New York: Ballantine Books, 1982), 190–250; Barbara Leaming, *If This Be Happiness: A Biography of Rita Hayworth* (New York: Viking Press, 1989), 203–302.

313   *I was intoxicated by the creative ferment:* interviews with Harold Taylor, former president of Sarah Lawrence, taped by Carole Nichols, June 1985.

320   *"The only letters Rita would read":* Robert Parrish interview with PB, July 1, 1989.

323   *"It has been alleged that Crum":* BC FBI file, 1951–52.

325   *"Everyone wants to be honest":* BC unpublished autobiography.

325   *"My general political conviction":* affidavit of Bartley C. Crum before the State Department, May 6, 1953.

CHAPTER 27

334   *"Your father asked my husband":* Nell Brown interview with PB, August 14, 1985.

336   *"Today I have realized":* information about Bartley Crum Jr.'s suicide from Portland, Oregon, police department Dead Body Report, December 9, 1953.

337   *"I diagnosed him as a schizophrenic":* Dr. W. interview with PB, August 20, 1986.

338   *"Attorney Bartley Crum learned":* San Francisco Examiner, December 9, 1953.

CHAPTER 28

349   *"I said, 'What do you want me to do' ":* Kal Nulman interview with PB, August 30, 1986.

CHAPTER 29

351 *Schmidt's firm represented:* information on Senate Rackets Committee and attitude toward Bartley Crum's testimony at Hay Podell firm: interviews with lawyers Ben Algase (August 7, 1987), Maury Spanier (September 20, 1986), Kurt Villadsen (March 8, 1987), Mary Kohler (January 5, 1982), and Joan Crawford (October 2, 1967); Robert Kennedy, *The Enemy Within* (New York: Popular Library, 1960), 86; Evan Thomas, *The Man to See: Edward Bennett Williams: Ultimate Insider; Legendary Trial Lawyer* (New York: Simon & Schuster, 1991), 127–28.

354 *"Bart Crum, a bespectacled, mild": Time,* July 13, 1959.

354 *My father began:* transcripts of Congressional Investigation of Improper Activities in the Labor Management Field, July 13, 1959, pp. 19621–55.

355 *"This is just another example":* Ibid.

355 *"Well, it is the truth":* Ibid.

355 *"this false, vicious, contrived smear":* Thomas, *The Man,* 127–28.

356 *"slanderer": The Washington Post,* July 13, 1959.

357 *"Because I saw your father":* Kal Nulman interview, August 30, 1986.

357 *"Williams offered a lawyer":* Thomas, *The Man,* 500.

357 *"rather shy and sad":* Joseph Wershba letter to PB, December 25, 1992.

357 *"For some people": New York Post,* July 17, 1959.

EPILOGUE

375 *"The two guys he informed on":* Dave interview with PB, February 19, 1977.

377 *I discovered to my discomfort:* Percival Roberts Daily, *Progressive Lawyers: A History of the National Lawyers Guild 1936–1958* (Ph.D. dissertation, Rutgers University, 1979), 50–66 (letters from special agent in charge, New York, to director of FBI, October 1 and October 26, 1953); according to these FBI files my father became an informer, furnishing the FBI with information about the San Francisco chapter of the Guild and naming two colleagues as Communists.

377 *In 1992, I wrote:* Patricia Bosworth, "Daughter of a Blacklist That Killed a Father," *The New York Times,* Arts & Leisure section, September 27, 1992.

378 *"The blacklist was a time of evil":* Dalton Trumbo speech at Screen Writers Guild 1970, in *Additional Dialogue: The Letters of Dalton Trumbo, 1942–1962,* edited by Helen Manfull (New York: M. Evans & Co., 1970), 569–70.

BIBLIOGRAPHY

Alpern, Sara. *Freda Kirchwey: A Woman of the Nation.* Cambridge, Mass.: Harvard
   University Press, 1987.
Beck, Carl. *Contempt of Congress: A Study of the Prosecutions Initiated by the
   Committee on Un-American Activities.* New York: Da Capo Press, 1974.
Belfrage, Cedric. *The American Inquisition: 1945–1960.* Indianapolis: Bobbs-
   Merrill, 1973. Reprint. New York: Thunder's Mouth Press, 1989.
Bentley, Eric. *Thirty Years of Treason: Excerpts from Hearings Before the House
   Committee on Un-American Activities, 1938–1968.* New York: Viking Press,
   1971. Reprint. New York: Viking Compass, 1973.
Bessie, Alvah. *Inquisition in Eden.* New York: Macmillan, 1965.
Brown, Cynthia Stokes, and Ann F. Ginger, ed. *Alexander Meiklejohn: Teacher of
   Freedom.* Berkeley: Meiklejohn Civil Liberties Institute, 1981.
Caute, David. *The Great Fear: The Anti-Communist Purge Under Truman and Eisen-
   hower.* New York: Simon & Schuster, 1978.
Ceplair, Larry, and Steven Englund. *The Inquistion in Hollywood: Politics in the
   Film Community, 1930–1960.* Reprint (by arrangement with Anchor Press).
   Berkeley and Los Angeles: University of California Press, 1979.
Clifford, Clark, with Richard Holbrooke. *Counsel to the President: A Memoir.* New
   York: Random House, 1991. Reprint. New York: Anchor Books/Doubleday,
   1992.
Cogley, John. *Report on Blacklisting.* 2 vols. The Fund for the Republic, 1956.
Collier, Peter, and David Horowitz. *The Kennedys: An American Drama.* New York:
   Summit Books, 1984.
Congressional Record—Senate. Debate on Internal Security Act. September 11,
   1950.
Cottrell, Robert C. *Izzy: A Biography of I. F. Stone.* New Brunswick: Rutgers
   University Press, 1992.
Crossman, Richard, ed. *The God That Failed.* New York: Harper & Bros., 1950.
   Reprint. New York: Bantam, 1952.
Crum, Bartley C. *Behind the Silken Curtain: A Personal Account of Anglo-American
   Diplomacy in Palestine and the Middle East.* New York: Simon & Schuster,
   1947.

Crum, Gertrude Bosworth. *Strumpet Wind.* New York: Covici Friede Pubs., 1938.

Dick, Bernard F. *Radical Innocence: A Critical Study of the Hollywood Ten.* Lexington, Kentucky: University Press of Kentucky, 1988.

Dinnerstein, Leonard. *America and the Survivors of the Holocaust.* New York: Columbia University Press, 1982.

Dowdy, Andrew. *The Films of the Fifties: The American State of Mind.* New York: William Morrow & Co., 1973.

Draper, Theodore. *The Roots of American Communism.* New York: Viking Press, 1957.

Duberman, Martin Bauml. *Paul Robeson.* New York: Alfred A. Knopf, 1989.

Duffield, E. S., and Walter Millis, eds. *The Forrestal Diaries.* New York: Viking Press, 1951.

Eisen, Jonathan, and David Fine, eds. *Unknown California.* New York: Collier Books, 1985.

Erikson, Erik H. *Childhood & Society.* New York: W. W. Norton & Co., 1963.

Fast, Howard. *Being Red: A Memoir.* Boston: Houghton Mifflin, 1990. Reprint. New York: Dell, 1991.

Feis, Herbert. *The Birth of Israel: The Tousled Diplomatic Bed.* New York: W. W. Norton & Co., 1969.

Friedrich, Otto. *City of Nets: A Portrait of Hollywood in the 1940s.* New York: Harper & Row, 1986.

Gentry, Curt. *J. Edgar Hoover: The Man and the Secrets.* New York: W. W. Norton & Co., 1991.

Gilliam, Harold. *San Francisco Bay.* Garden City, N.Y.: Doubleday, 1957.

Gunther, John. *Inside U.S.A.* New York: Harper & Bros., 1951.

———. *Roosevelt in Retrospect: A Profile in History.* New York: Harper & Bros., 1950.

Hamby, Alonzo. *Beyond the New Deal: Harry S. Truman and American Liberalism.* New York: Columbia University Press, 1973.

Hoopes, Roy. *Ralph Ingersoll: A Biography.* New York: Atheneum, 1985.

Hoover, J. Edgar. *Masters of Deceit.* New York: Henry Holt, 1958. Reprint. New York: Pocket Books, 1959.

Kahn, Gordon. *Hollywood on Trial: The Story of the Ten Who Were Indicted.* New York: Boni & Gaer, 1948.

Kanfer, Stefan. *A Journal of the Plague Years: A Devastating Chronicle of the Era of the Blacklist.* New York: Atheneum, 1973.

Kempton, Murray. *Part of Our Time: Some Monuments and Ruins of the Thirties.* New York: Simon & Schuster, 1955.

Kennedy, Robert F. *The Enemy Within.* New York: Harper, 1960.

Ketchum, Richard M. *The Borrowed Years, 1938–1941: America on the Way to War.* New York: Random House, 1989.

Kimball, Penn. *The File.* San Diego: Harcourt Brace Jovanovich, 1983.

Kurth, Peter. *American Cassandra: The Life of Dorothy Thompson.* Boston: Little, Brown, 1990.

Larrowe, Charles P. *Harry Bridges: The Rise and Fall of Radical Labor in the U.S.* New York: Lawrence Hill, 1972.

Lattimore, Owen. *Ordeal by Slander.* Boston: Little, Brown, 1950.

Lerner, Max. *Actions and Passions: Notes on the Multiple Revolution of Our Time.* New York: Simon & Schuster, 1949.

Luce, Robert B., ed. *The Faces of Five Decades: Selections from Fifty Years of the New Republic, 1914–1964*. New York: Simon & Schuster, 1964.

MacDougall, Curtis D. *Gideon's Army*. New York: Marzani & Munsell, 1965.

McCullough, David. *Truman*. New York: Simon & Schuster, 1992.

McKelway, St. Clair. "Some Fun with the FBI." *The New Yorker*, October 11, 1941.

Miller, Arthur. "The Year It Came Apart." *New York*, December 30, 1974, and January 6, 1975.

———. *Timebends*. New York: Harper & Row, 1988.

Mitgang, Herbert. *Dangerous Dossiers: Exposing the Secret War Against America's Greatest Authors*. New York: Donald Fine, 1988.

Moldea, Dan E. *Dark Victory: Ronald Reagan, MCA, and the Mob*. New York: Viking Penguin, 1986. Reprint. New York: Penguin, 1987.

Morgan, Ted. *FDR: A Biography*. New York: Simon & Schuster, 1985.

Morris, Roger. *Richard Milhous Nixon: The Rise of an American Politician*. New York: Henry Holt & Co., 1989.

Navasky, Victor S. *Naming Names*. New York: Viking Press, 1980. Reprint. New York: Penguin, 1981.

———. "The Case Not Proved Against Alger Hiss." *Nation*, April 8, 1978.

Neal, Steve. *Dark Horse: A Biography of Wendell Willkie*. New York: Doubleday, 1984.

Nelson, Bruce. *Workers on the Waterfront: Seamen, Longshoremen, and Unionism in the 1930s*. Champaign, Ill.: University of Illinois Press, 1990.

Patner, Andrew. *I. F. Stone: A Portrait*. New York: Pantheon Books, 1988.

Phillips, Cabell. *From the Crash to the Blitz, 1929–1939*. New York: Macmillan, 1969.

———. *The 1940s: Decade of Triumph and Trouble*. New York: Macmillan, 1975.

Powers, Richard G. *Secrecy and Power: The Life of J. Edgar Hoover*. New York: Free Press, 1987.

Ringgold, Gene. *The Films of Rita Hayworth: The Legend and Career of a Love Goddess*. Secaucus, N.J.: Citadel Press, 1974.

Rovere, Richard H. *Senator Joe McCarthy*. New York: Harcourt, Brace, 1959. Reprint. Cleveland: World Publishing, 1960.

Sachar, Abraham L. *The Redemption of the Unwanted: From the Liberation of the Death Camps to the Founding of Israel*. New York: St. Martin's/Marek, 1983.

Schneir, Walter and Miriam. *Invitation to an Inquest*. Garden City, N.Y.: Doubleday, 1965. Reprint. New York: Pantheon, 1983.

Schwartz, Nancy L. *The Hollywood Writers' Wars*. New York: Alfred A. Knopf, 1982.

Sheehy, Gail. *Character: America's Search for Leadership*. New York: William Morrow & Co., 1988.

Sherwood, Robert E. *Roosevelt and Hopkins: An Intimate History*. New York: Harper & Bros., 1950.

Simon, James F. *The Antagonists: Hugo Black, Felix Frankfurter, and Civil Liberties In Modern America*. New York: Simon & Schuster, 1989.

Smith, Paul C. *Personal File*. New York: Appleton-Century, 1964.

Sperber, A. M. *Murrow: His Life and Times*. New York: Freundlich, 1986.

Stone, I. F. *The Haunted Fifties*. New York: Random House, 1963.

Stone, I. F. *The Truman Era*. New York: Random House, 1972.

Terkel, Studs. *"The Good War": An Oral History of World War Two*. New York: Pantheon Books, 1984.

Thomas, Evan. *The Man to See: Edward Bennett Williams: Ultimate Insider; Legendary Trial Lawyer.* New York: Simon & Schuster, 1991.

Truman, Harry S. *Years of Trial and Hope: 1946–1952.* Garden City, N.Y.: Doubleday, 1956.

Trumbo, Dalton. *Additional Dialogue: Letters of Dalton Trumbo, 1942–1962.* Edited by Helen Manfull. New York: M. Evans, 1970.

U.S. Congress. House. Committee on Un-American Activities. *Communist Infiltration of Hollywood Motion-Picture Industry.* Parts 1–7. 82nd Cong., 1st sess., 1951.

U.S. Congress. House. Committee on Un-American Activities. *Guide to Subversive Organizations and Publications.* 82nd Cong., 1st sess., 1951, and 87th Cong., 2nd sess., 1961.

U.S. Congress. House. Committee on Un-American Activities. *Hearings Regarding Communist Infiltration of Radiation Laboratory and Atom Bomb Project at the University of California, Berkeley, Calif.* 3 vols. 81st Cong., 1st sess., 1948 and 1949.

Vaughan, Robert. *Only Victims: A Study of Show Business Blacklisting.* New York: G. P. Putnam's Sons, 1972.

Vidal, Gore. *At Home: Essays 1983–1987.* New York: Random House, 1988.

Watkins, T. H. *Righteous Pilgrim: The Life and Times of Harold L. Ickes 1874–1952.* New York: Henry Holt, 1990.

Wechsler, James A. *The Age of Suspicion.* New York: Random House, 1953.

Willkie, Wendell L. *One World.* New York: Simon & Schuster, 1943.

Wilson, Edmund, and Leon Edel, ed. *The Thirties: From Notebooks and Diaries of the Period.* New York: Farrar, Straus & Giroux, 1980.

Wood, Michael. *America in the Movies.* New York: Basic Books, 1975.

INDEX